the RISING STARS of MANGA™

Vol. 1

TOKYOPOP®

Los Angeles • Tokyo • London

Associate Editor - Bryce P. Coleman
Retouch - Paul Morrissey
Cover Layout - Aaron Suhr
Graphic Designer - Gary Shum

Senior Editor - Mark Paniccia
Managing Editor - Jill Freshney
Production Coordinator - Antonio DePietro
Production Manager - Jennifer Miller
Art Director - Matthew Alford
Editorial Director - Jeremy Ross
VP of Production & Manufacturing - Ron Klamert
President & C.O.O. - John Parker
Publisher & C.E.O. - Stuart Levy

Email: editor@TOKYOPOP.com
Come visit us online at www.TOKYOPOP.com

A TOKYOPOP® Manga
TOKYOPOP® is an imprint of Mixx Entertainment, Inc.
5900 Wilshire Blvd. Suite 2000, Los Angeles, CA 90036

ISBN: 1-59182-224-6

First TOKYOPOP® printing: April 2003

10 9 8 7 6 5 4 3 2 1

Printed in Canada

the RISING STARS of MANGA™

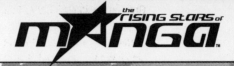

:TABLE OF CONTENTS

INTRODUCTION

::

Manga is an oft-misunderstood concept. Contrary to popular belief, there is no pre-determined "manga look." Manga is a broad Japanese term, literally meaning "entertaining visual." In Japan, people refer to manga the way Americans refer to film. For example, if a friend tells you about something wild that happened to him recently, you might respond "sounds like something out of a manga," which is obviously similar to what we may say here in the States: "sounds like something out of a movie."

We at TOKYOPOP support this true meaning of manga as a broad entertainment concept, not a certain look. These first Rising Stars did not win our contest by redrawing American superheroes with big eyes and round faces—this is not what manga means to us. The key to becoming a Rising Star of Manga is passion—the passion to tell a great story; the passion to bring vision to the written page; the passion to create unforgettable characters; the passion to move a reader.

This is a tremendous challenge. Our first Rising Stars of Manga contest was also the first-ever manga competition in the United States, but by no means will it be the last. The age of manga is beginning to dawn on us here in the States. As more publishers sponsor manga competitions and more manga is published in general, we at TOKYOPOP believe there is an entire generation of U.S. manga stars waiting to shine.

These ten Rising Stars are the trailblazers. After reviewing hundreds and hundreds of entries, our TOKYOPOP editorial team kept narrowing down the field until we came up with these ten unique selections. Each story is different and each Rising Star's approach towards the concept of manga is just as different. We sifted through the work of many talented artists and choosing the ten winners was more difficult than one can imagine.

I encourage all entrants—not just the ten winners—to keep working hard to find your story, your sense, your vision. Don't give up—there will be many opportunities to improve and master your craft. To the ten winners—congratulations! Just remember, this is only the start. If you choose to become a professional manga artist, there are still many bridges, many challenges. All ten of you have room to improve and perfect your work—you were chosen as a Rising Star because of the potential our TOKYOPOP team felt in your abilities, not because we believe your work is perfect. Diligence and dedication is the key to manga success.

Finally, to the reader—thank you for supporting the field of manga and these ten Rising Stars. We at TOKYOPOP would love to hear your feedback—which style was your favorite, which stories you liked and why, which ones stayed with you. Visit www.TOKYOPOP.com and let us know what you think. Enjoy the first ever Rising Stars of Manga™ !!

Stu Levy
Publisher and CEO

06

::

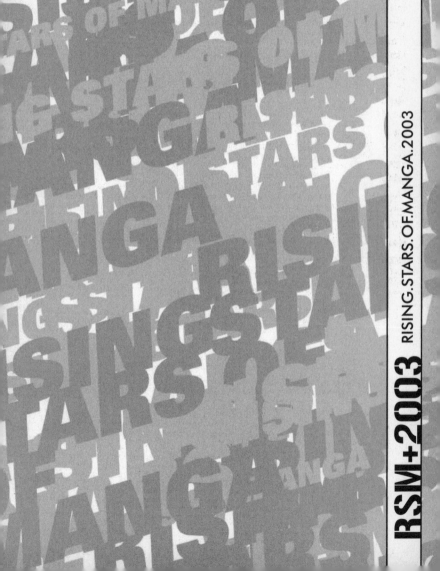

rising st.ars of
m★nga™

RSM+2003 RISING.STARS.OF.MANGA.2003

DEVIL'S CANDY
GRAND PRIZE WINNER
RISING.STARS.OF.MANGA.2003

::

DEVIL'S CANDY :: Grand Prize Winner ::
The creative team of Priscilla Hamby and Clint Bickham

Priscilla Hamby was born in St. Joseph, Missouri, in 1982 and currently resides in Houston, Texas, where she studies art. You can see some of her other work at www.megaten.net/zombie/open.html.

Inspiration for this story:
I wanted to create something that was immediately striking without sacrificing my dark style or alienating readers. I tried to design characters that were likable or funny despite their rather grotesque appearances at times. Character designing was half the work, since there are so many of them and I tried to make them all look unique.

Favorite Manga:
One Piece, Hikaru no go, Tenjou Tenge, Naruto, Shaman King, Berserk, Trigun, Jojo's Bizarre Adventure, Bastard, Yuyu Hakusho, Level E, Eyeshield 21

Favorite Manga Artists:
Eiichiro Oda, Obata Takeshi, Yasuhiro Nightow

Clint Bickham was born in Angleton, Texas, in 1981 and currently resides in Houston, Texas, where he studies art.

Inspiration for this story:
I wanted to make something that felt familiar but had not been done before. I took inspiration from all kinds of manga to create something that was absolutely packed with paradise and gags. The idea was to create a "typical" manga that was still completely original.

Favorite Manga:
One Piece, Naruto, Tenjou Tenge, Berserk, GTO, Trigun Maximum, JoJo's Bizarre, Shaman King, Leviathan

Favorite Manga Artists:
Masashi Kishimoto, Eiichiro Oda, Kentaro Miura

Judge's Comments:
Priscilla Hamby and Clint Bickham's "Devil's Candy" is absolutely bursting with energy. The luscious, high contrast artwork is packed with detail—each time I read their story, I notice something new. The Goth-cute look of the characters is reminiscent of manga-ka Junko Mizuno (*Cinderella*), and Hamby's action scenes play out in perfect manga fashion, but she doesn't just imitate. The way the characters move has so much personality—it's so unique.

"Devil's Candy" shows great confidence in its use of sound effects, both in English and in Japanese. Sugoi! It's also commendable that in a 21 page manga dominated by comedy and action, Bicham and Hamby could also pull off a scene as touching as the Cyclops girl's moment of unrequited love. Oh, and how could a story in which Gym Class is taught by a character named "Skeleton Ninja-sensei" not win the grand prize?
-Jake Forbes

::

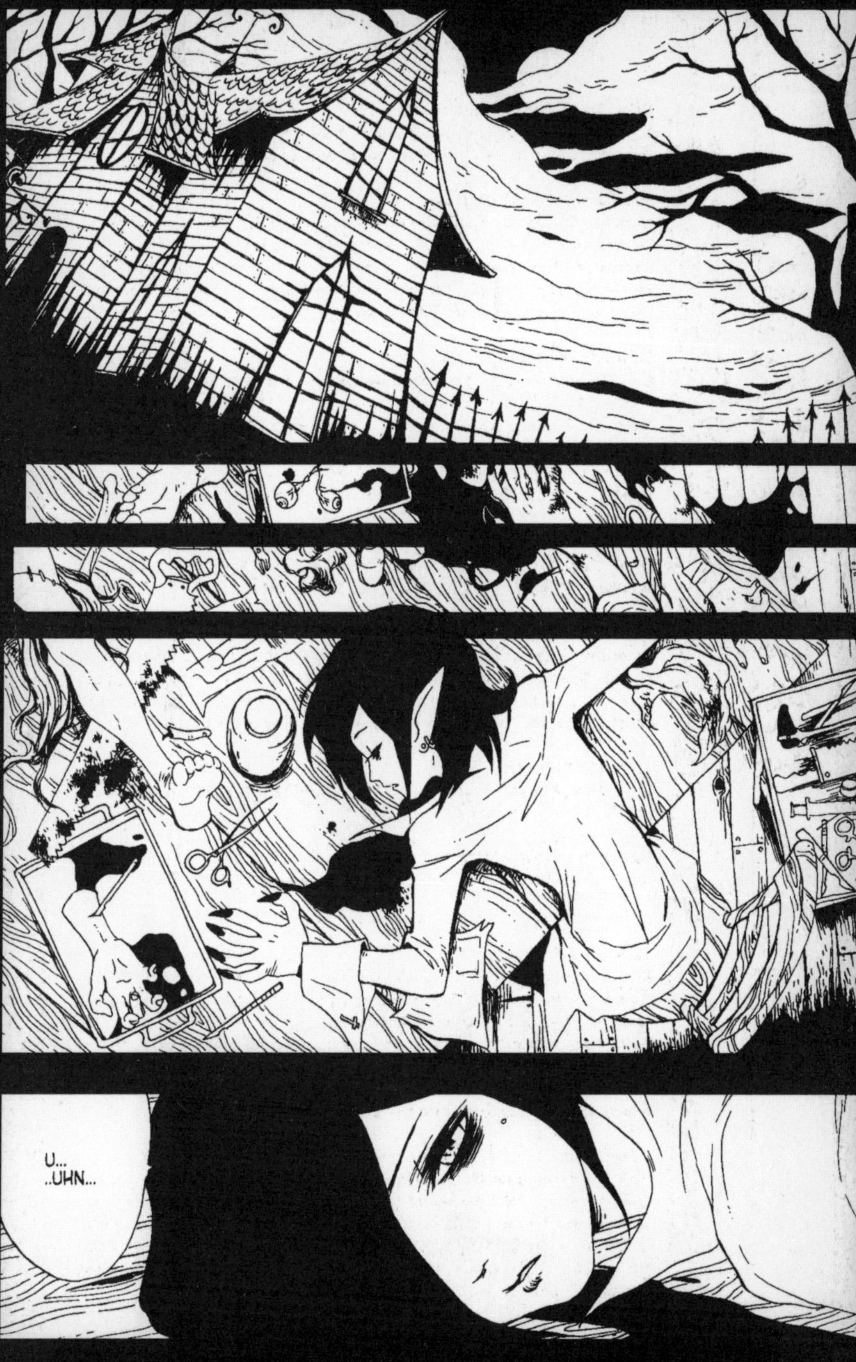
U...
..UHN...

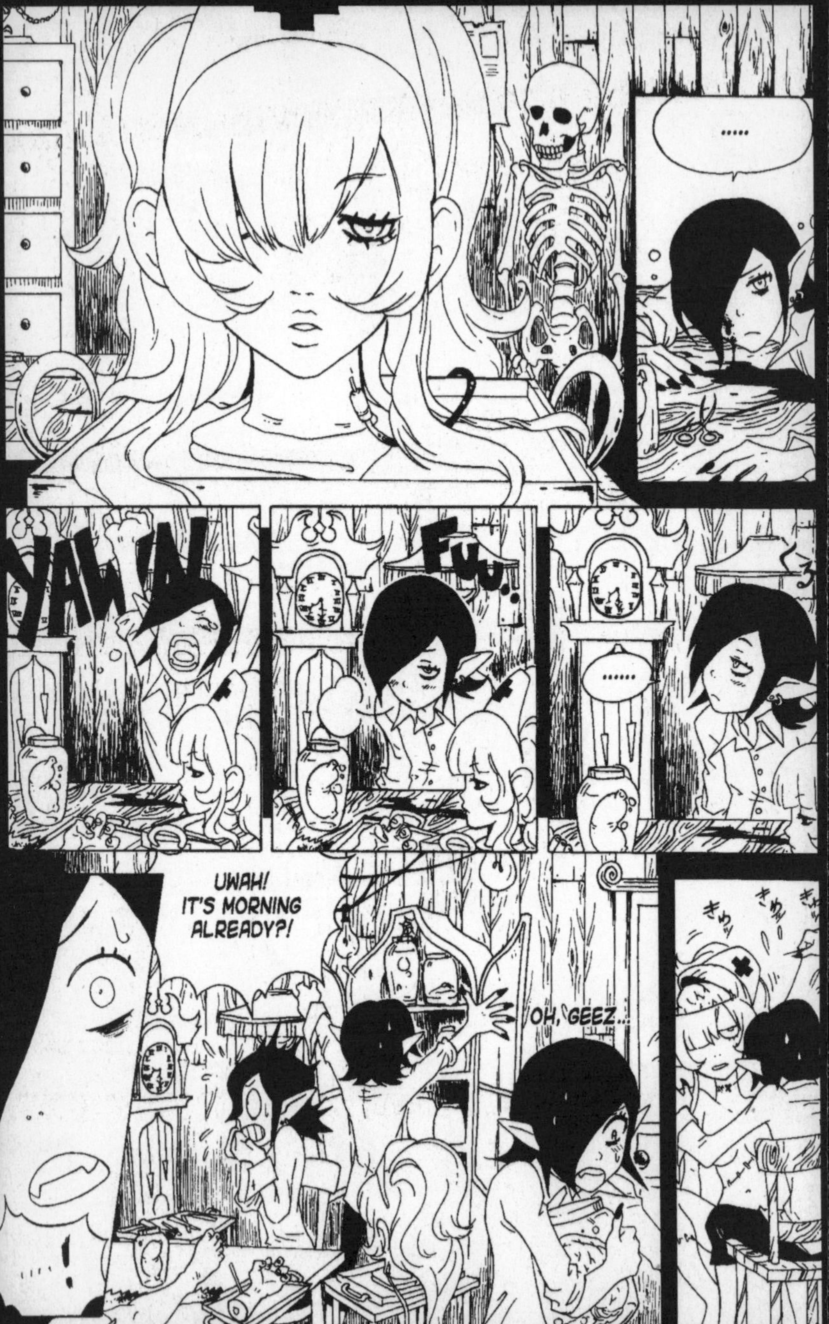
......
YAWN
FUU..!
......
くる
UWAH! IT'S MORNING ALREADY?!
...!
OH, GEEZ...
きゅッ
きゅッ
きゅッ

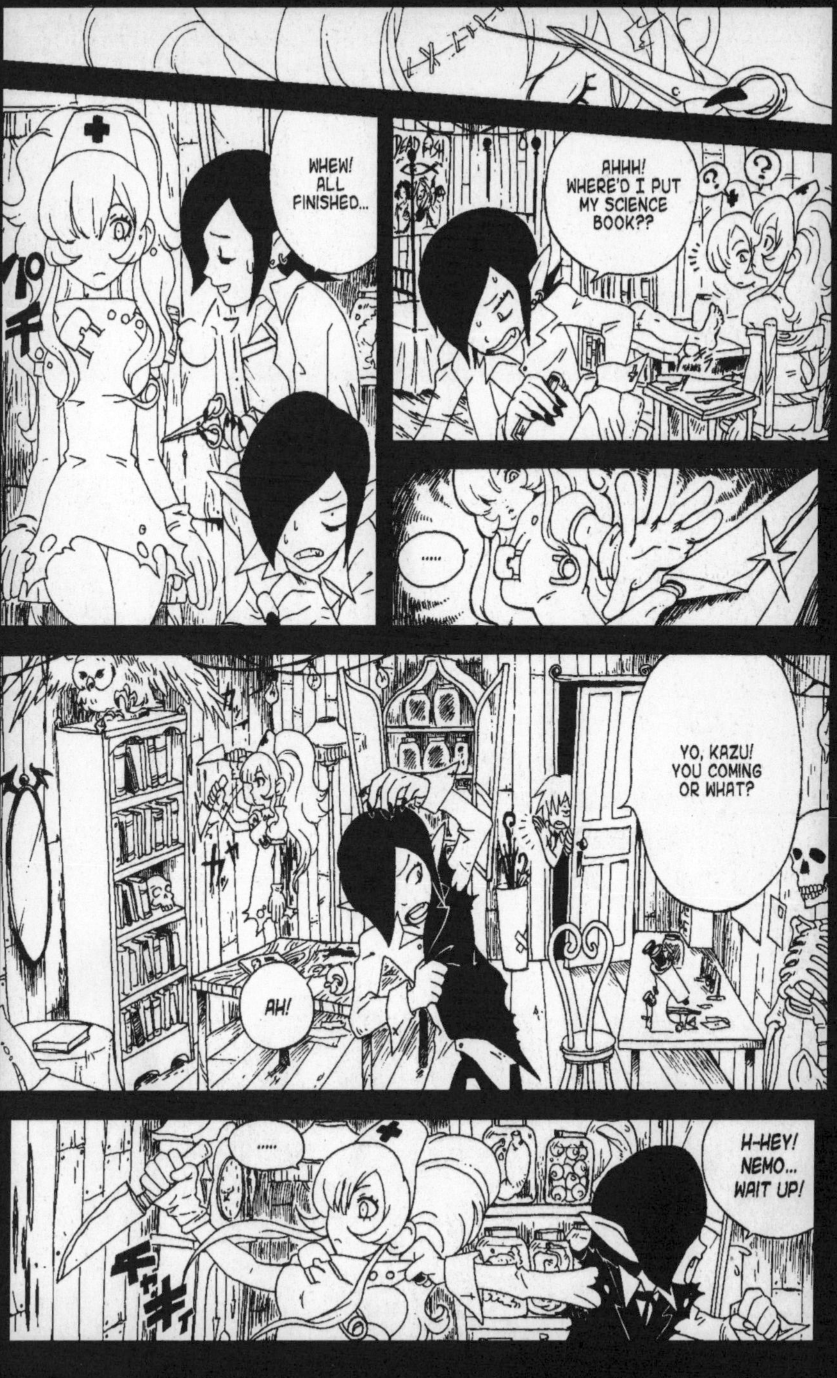
WHEW! ALL FINISHED...
AHHH! WHERE'D I PUT MY SCIENCE BOOK??
.....
YO, KAZU! YOU COMING OR WHAT?
AH!
.....
H-HEY! NEMO... WAIT UP!

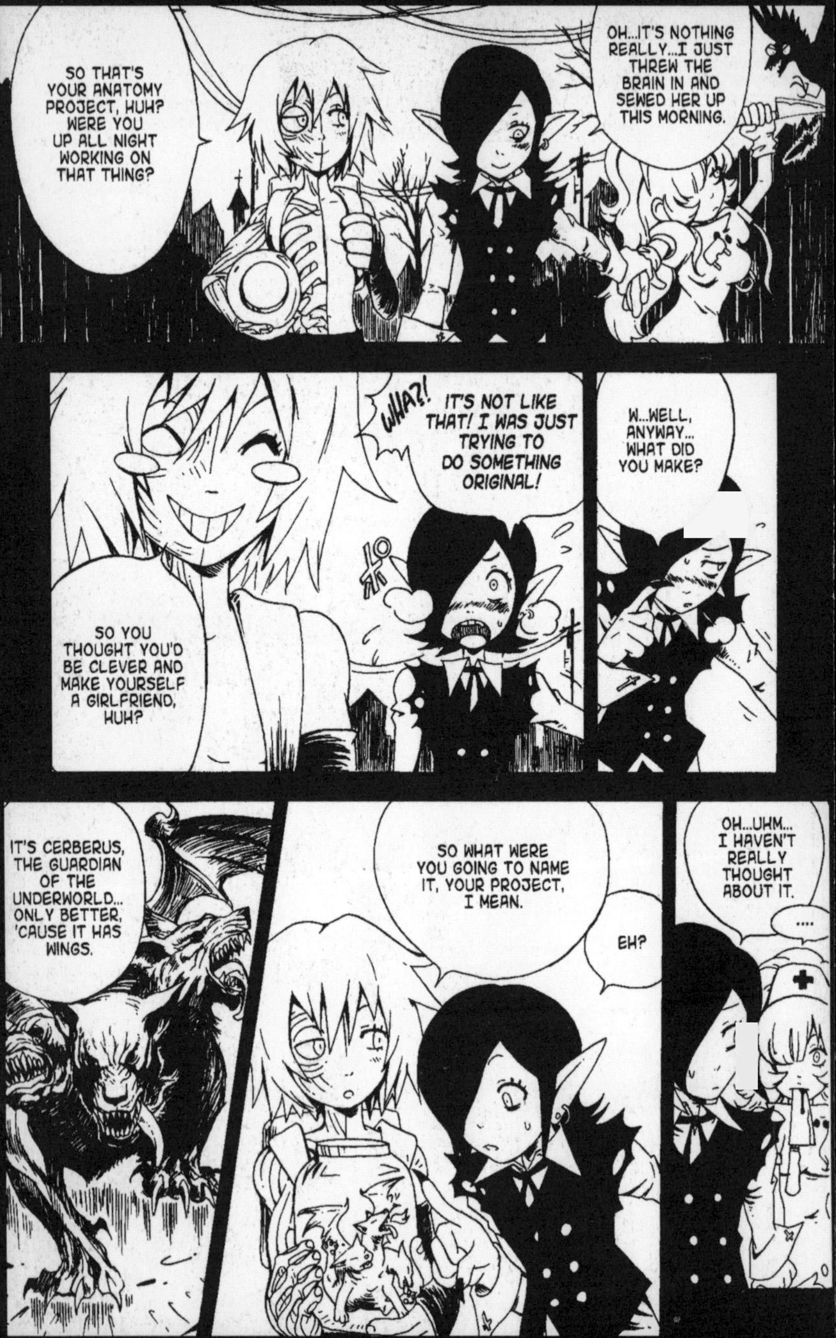
SO THAT'S YOUR ANATOMY PROJECT, HUH? WERE YOU UP ALL NIGHT WORKING ON THAT THING?
OH...IT'S NOTHING REALLY...I JUST THREW THE BRAIN IN AND SEWED HER UP THIS MORNING.
SO YOU THOUGHT YOU'D BE CLEVER AND MAKE YOURSELF A GIRLFRIEND, HUH?
WHA?!
IT'S NOT LIKE THAT! I WAS JUST TRYING TO DO SOMETHING ORIGINAL!
W...WELL, ANYWAY... WHAT DID YOU MAKE?
IT'S CERBERUS, THE GUARDIAN OF THE UNDERWORLD... ONLY BETTER, 'CAUSE IT HAS WINGS.
SO WHAT WERE YOU GOING TO NAME IT, YOUR PROJECT, I MEAN.
EH?
OH...UHM... I HAVEN'T REALLY THOUGHT ABOUT IT.
....

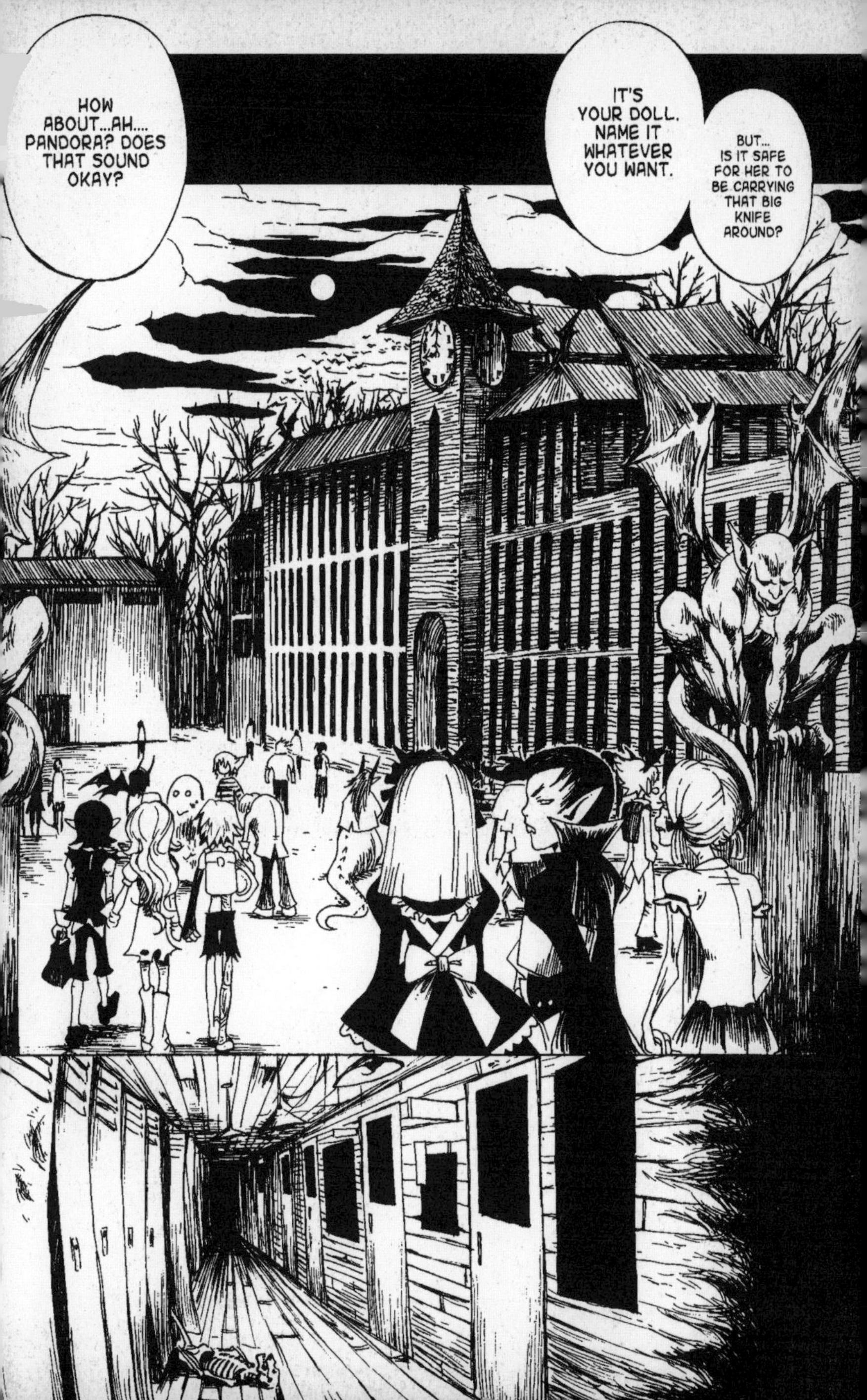
HOW ABOUT...AH.... PANDORA? DOES THAT SOUND OKAY?
IT'S YOUR DOLL. NAME IT WHATEVER YOU WANT.
BUT... IS IT SAFE FOR HER TO BE CARRYING THAT BIG KNIFE AROUND?

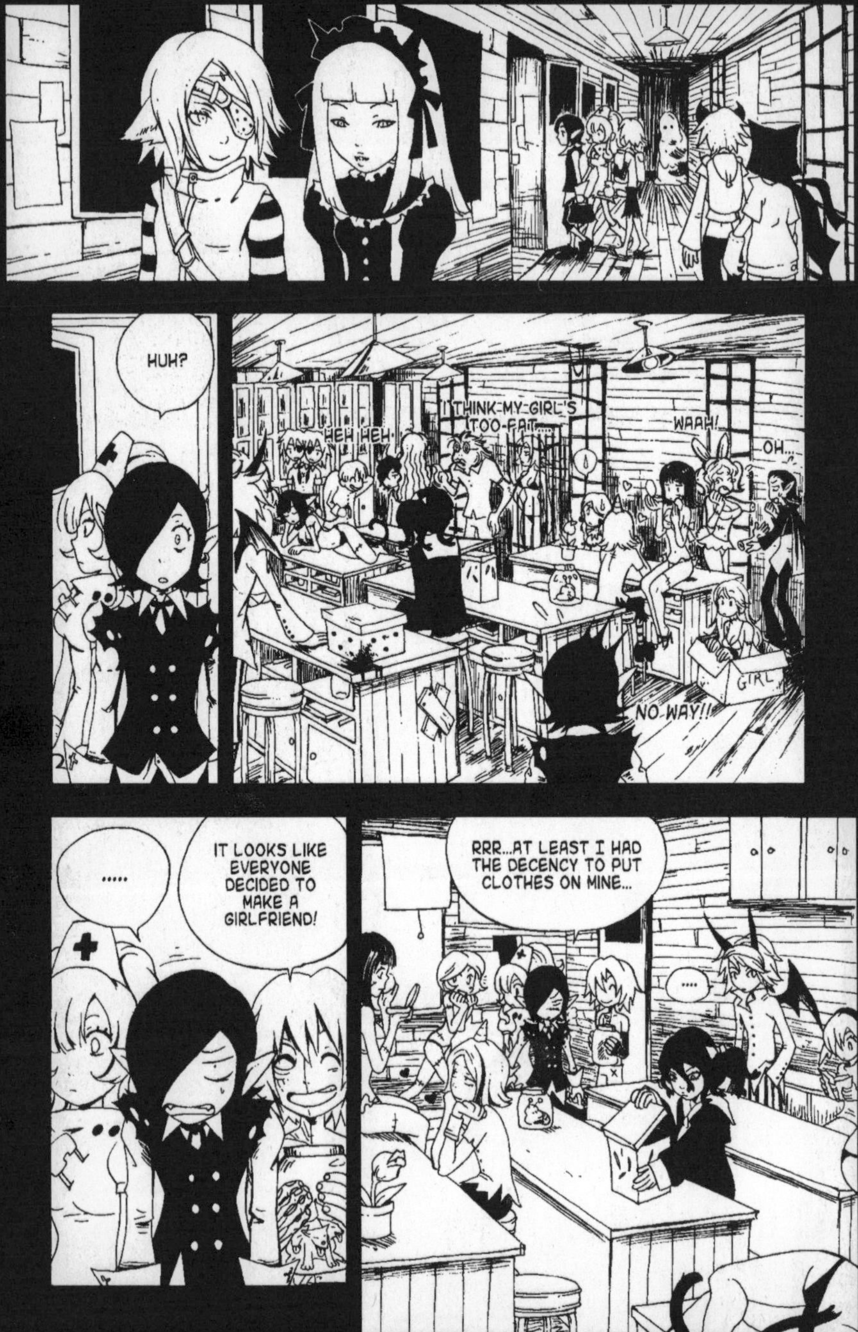
HUH?
I THINK MY GIRL'S TOO FAT...
HEH HEH
WAAH!
OH...
GIRL
NO WAY!!
......
IT LOOKS LIKE EVERYONE DECIDED TO MAKE A GIRLFRIEND!
RRR...AT LEAST I HAD THE DECENCY TO PUT CLOTHES ON MINE...
....

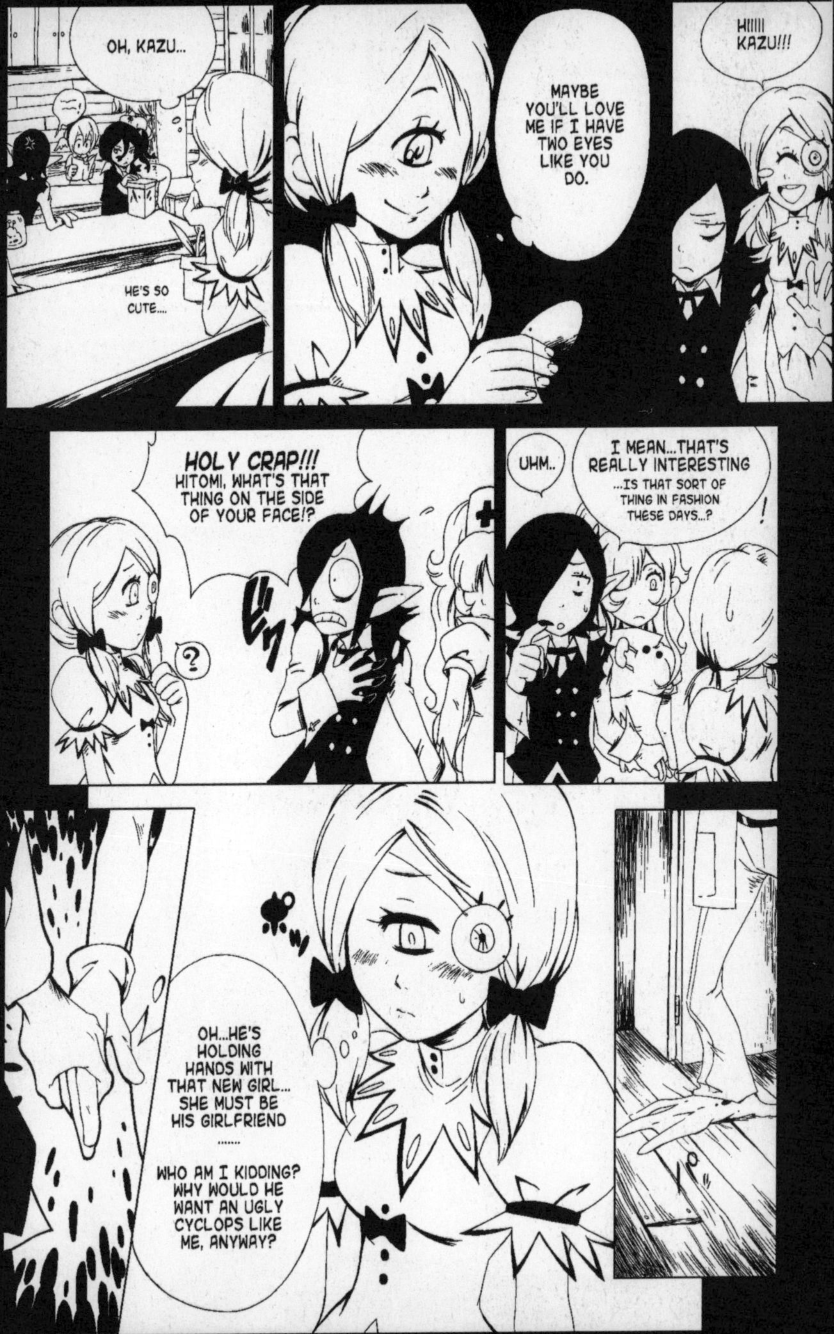
OH, KAZU...
HE'S SO CUTE...
MAYBE YOU'LL LOVE ME IF I HAVE TWO EYES LIKE YOU DO.
HI!!!! KAZU!!!
HOLY CRAP!!! HITOMI, WHAT'S THAT THING ON THE SIDE OF YOUR FACE!?
?
UHM..
I MEAN...THAT'S REALLY INTERESTING ...IS THAT SORT OF THING IN FASHION THESE DAYS...?
!
OH...HE'S HOLDING HANDS WITH THAT NEW GIRL... SHE MUST BE HIS GIRLFRIEND
....
WHO AM I KIDDING? WHY WOULD HE WANT AN UGLY CYCLOPS LIKE ME, ANYWAY?

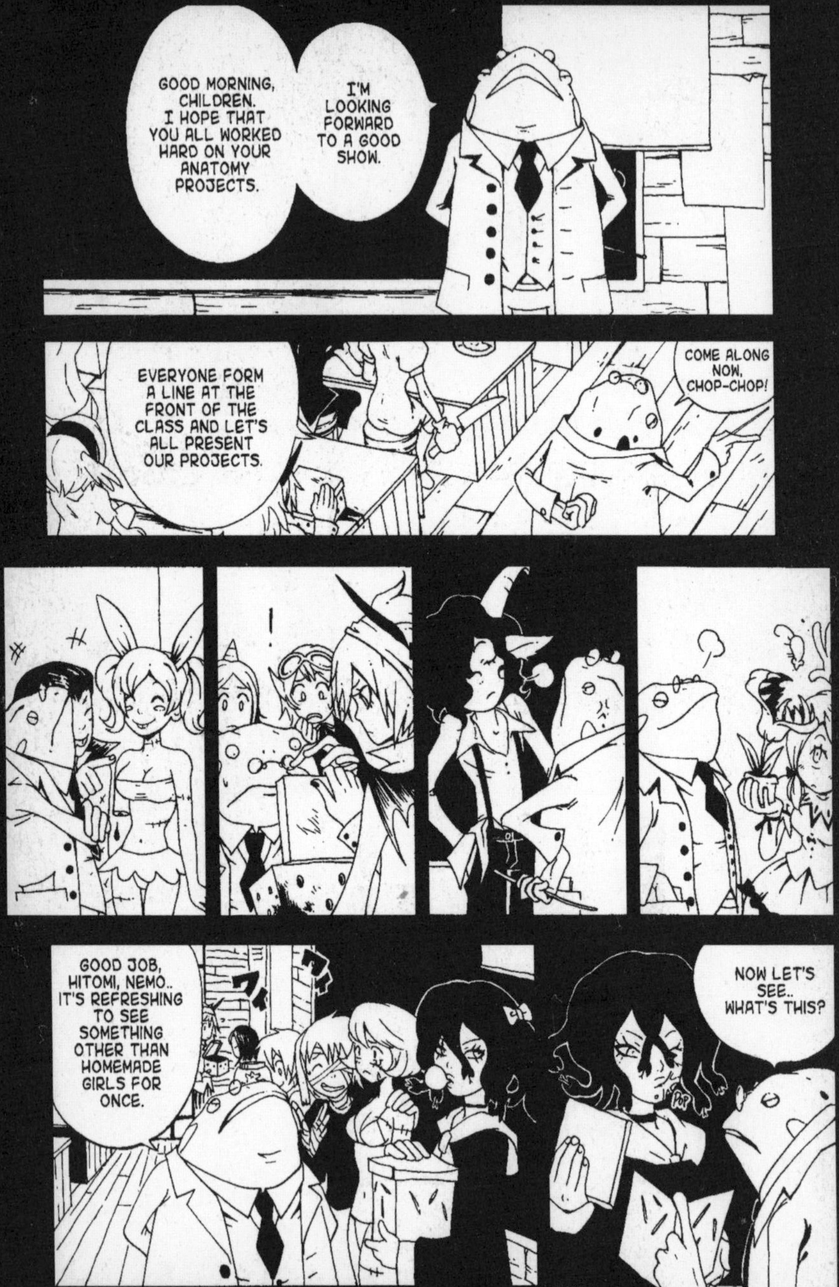
GOOD MORNING, CHILDREN. I HOPE THAT YOU ALL WORKED HARD ON YOUR ANATOMY PROJECTS.
I'M LOOKING FORWARD TO A GOOD SHOW.
EVERYONE FORM A LINE AT THE FRONT OF THE CLASS AND LET'S ALL PRESENT OUR PROJECTS.
COME ALONG NOW, CHOP-CHOP!
!
GOOD JOB, HITOMI, NEMO.. IT'S REFRESHING TO SEE SOMETHING OTHER THAN HOMEMADE GIRLS FOR ONCE.
NOW LET'S SEE.. WHAT'S THIS?

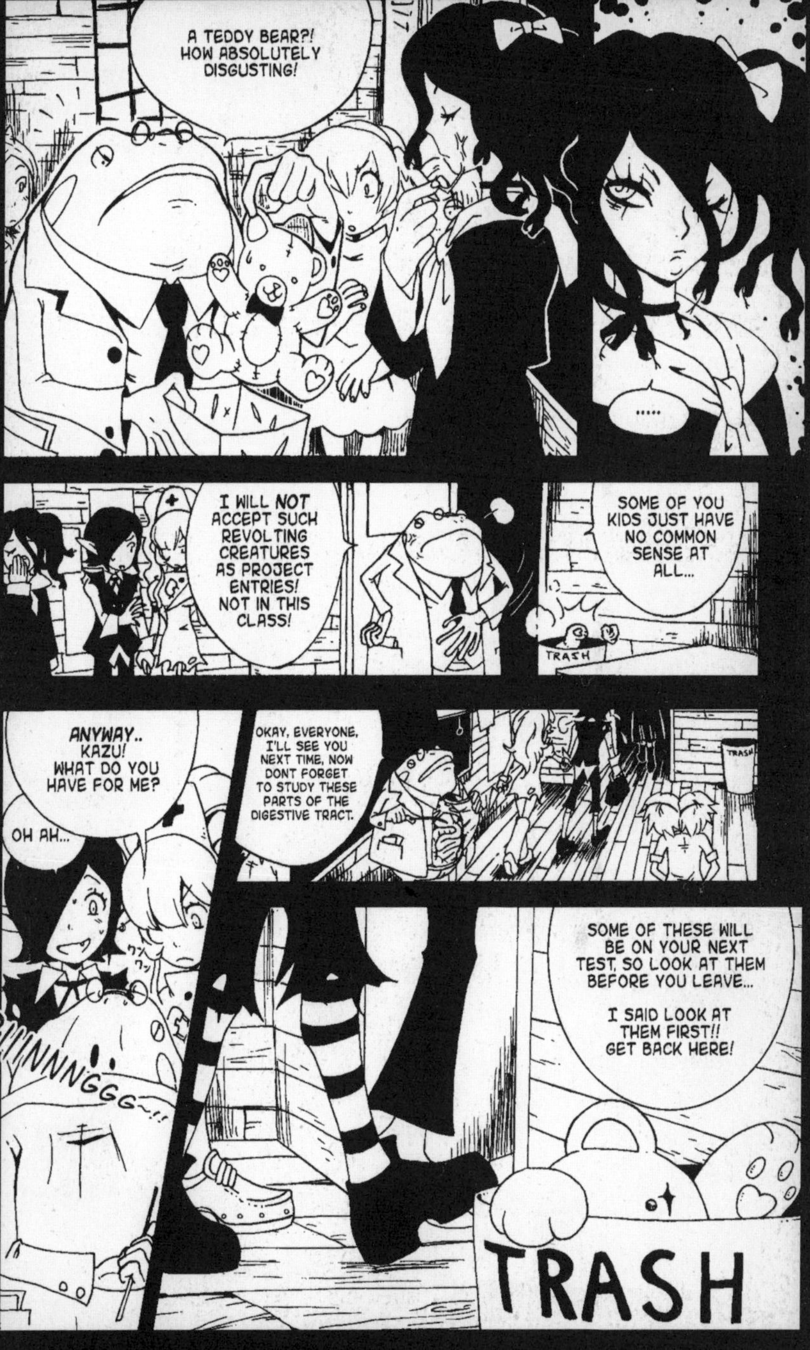

A TEDDY BEAR?! HOW ABSOLUTELY DISGUSTING!
......
I WILL **NOT** ACCEPT SUCH REVOLTING CREATURES AS PROJECT ENTRIES! NOT IN THIS CLASS!
SOME OF YOU KIDS JUST HAVE NO COMMON SENSE AT ALL...
TRASH
ANYWAY.. KAZU! WHAT DO YOU HAVE FOR ME?
OH AH...
RIIINNNNGGG~!!
OKAY, EVERYONE, I'LL SEE YOU NEXT TIME, NOW DONT FORGET TO STUDY THESE PARTS OF THE DIGESTIVE TRACT.
TRASH
SOME OF THESE WILL BE ON YOUR NEXT TEST, SO LOOK AT THEM BEFORE YOU LEAVE...
I SAID LOOK AT THEM FIRST!! GET BACK HERE!
TRASH

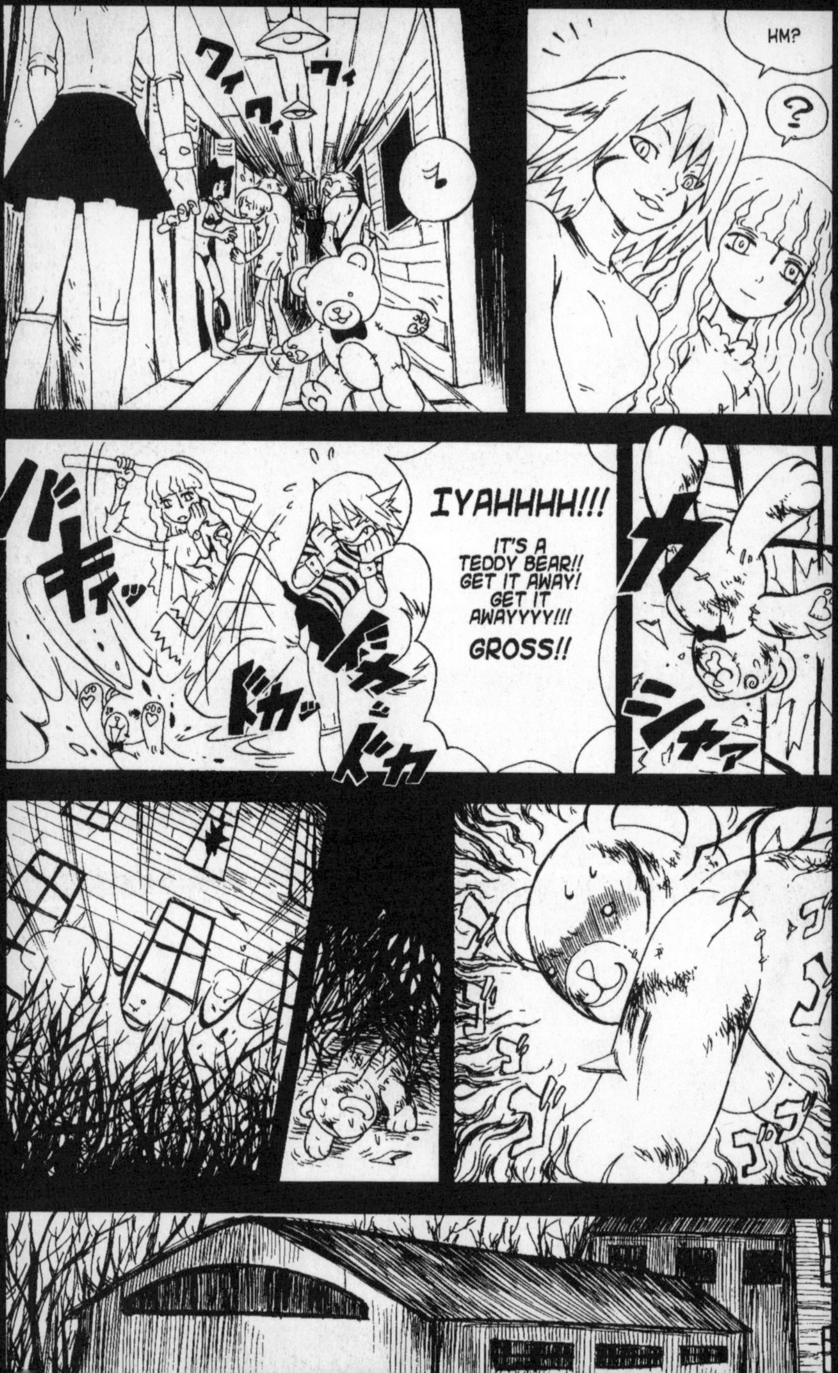
HM?
?
IYAHHHH!!!
IT'S A TEDDY BEAR!! GET IT AWAY! GET IT AWAYYYY!!!
GROSS!!

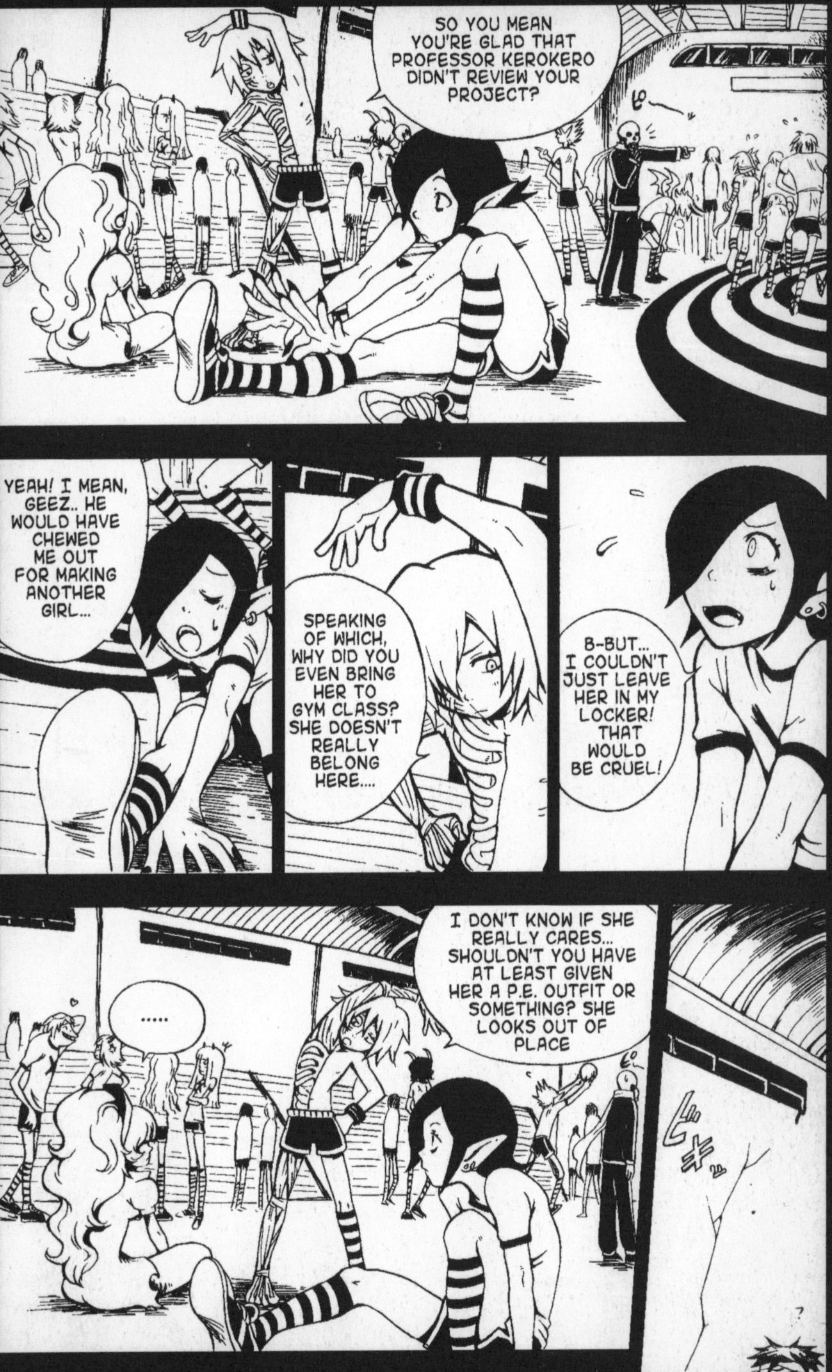
SO YOU MEAN YOU'RE GLAD THAT PROFESSOR KEROKERO DIDN'T REVIEW YOUR PROJECT?
YEAH! I MEAN, GEEZ.. HE WOULD HAVE CHEWED ME OUT FOR MAKING ANOTHER GIRL...
SPEAKING OF WHICH, WHY DID YOU EVEN BRING HER TO GYM CLASS? SHE DOESN'T REALLY BELONG HERE....
B-BUT... I COULDN'T JUST LEAVE HER IN MY LOCKER! THAT WOULD BE CRUEL!
.....
I DON'T KNOW IF SHE REALLY CARES... SHOULDN'T YOU HAVE AT LEAST GIVEN HER A P.E. OUTFIT OR SOMETHING? SHE LOOKS OUT OF PLACE

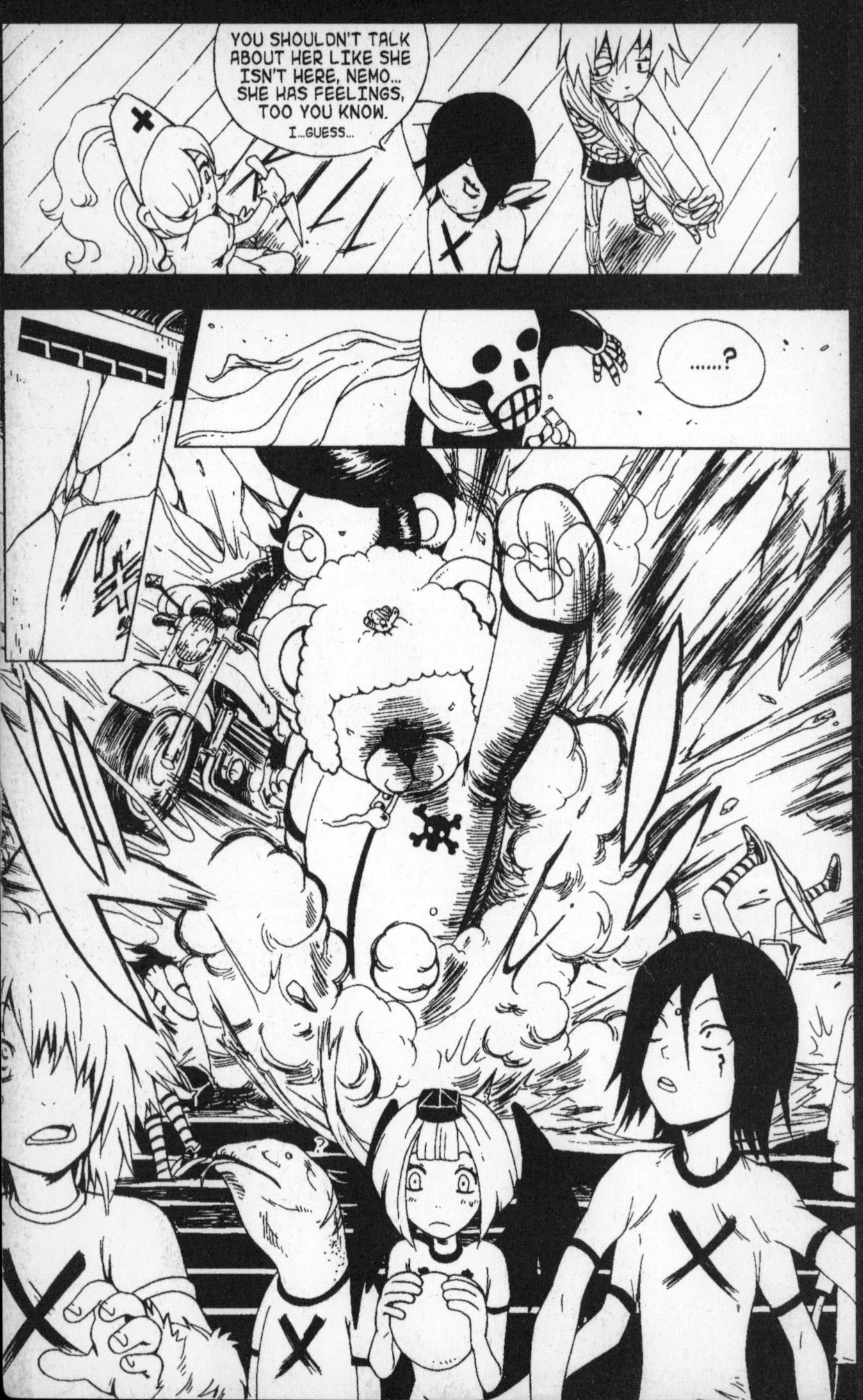
YOU SHOULDN'T TALK ABOUT HER LIKE SHE ISN'T HERE, NEMO... SHE HAS FEELINGS, TOO YOU KNOW.
I...GUESS...
......?

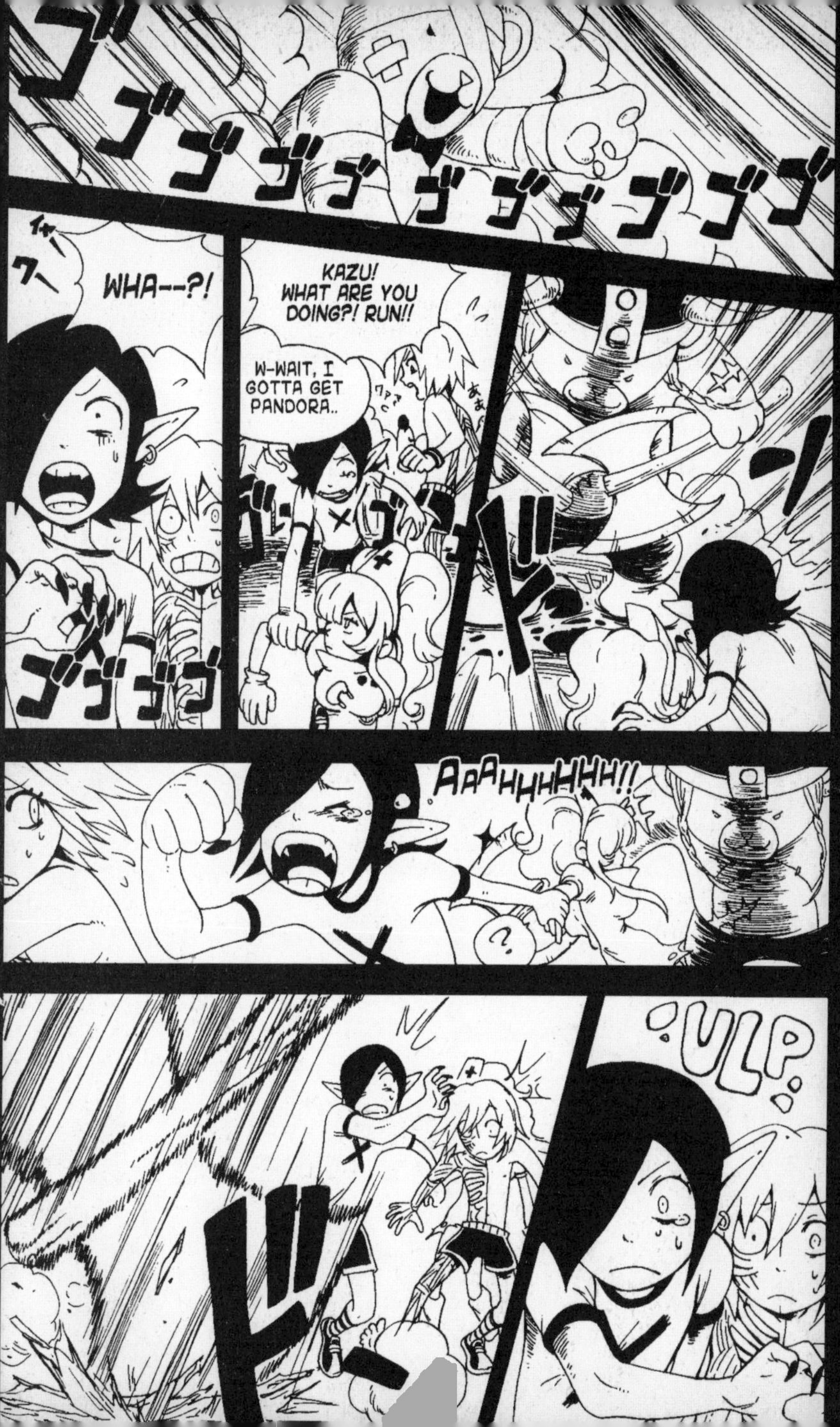
WHA--?!
KAZU! WHAT ARE YOU DOING?! RUN!!
W-WAIT, I GOTTA GET PANDORA..
AAAHHHHHHH!!
ULP

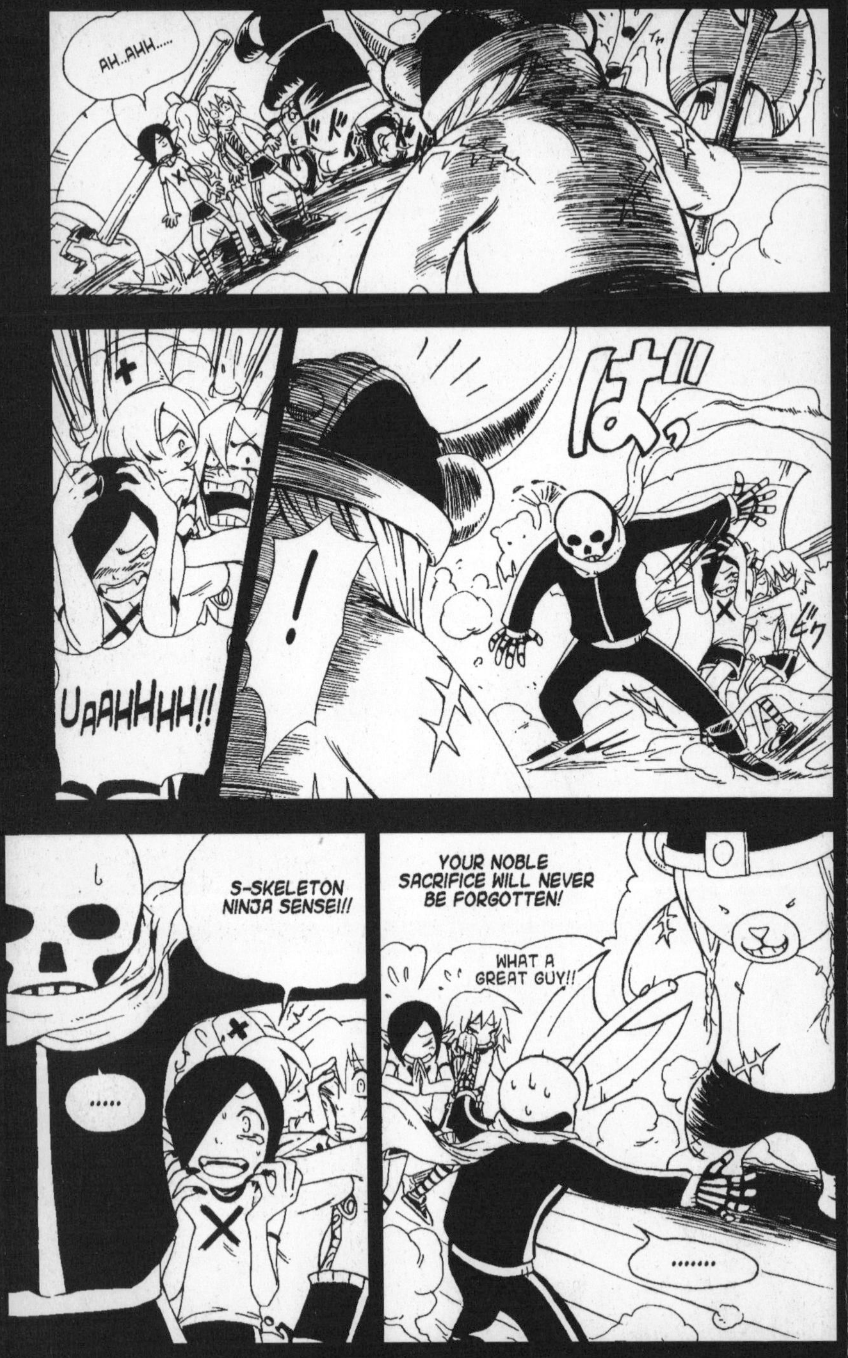
AH..AHH.....
UAAHHHH!!
!
S-SKELETON NINJA SENSEI!!
......
YOUR NOBLE SACRIFICE WILL NEVER BE FORGOTTEN!
WHAT A GREAT GUY!!
....

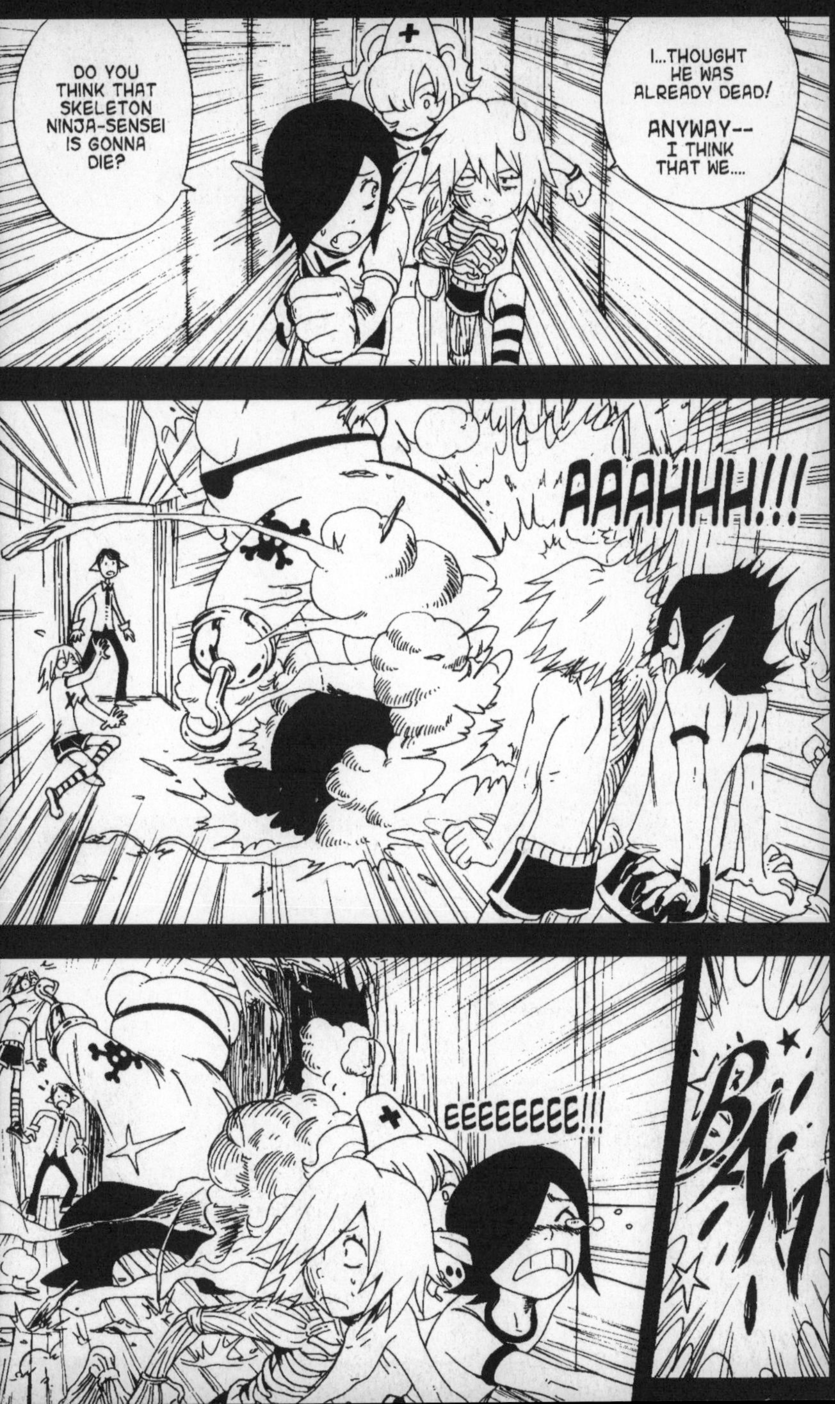
DO YOU THINK THAT SKELETON NINJA-SENSEI IS GONNA DIE?
I...THOUGHT HE WAS ALREADY DEAD!
ANYWAY-- I THINK THAT WE....
AAAHHH!!!
EEEEEEEE!!!
BAM

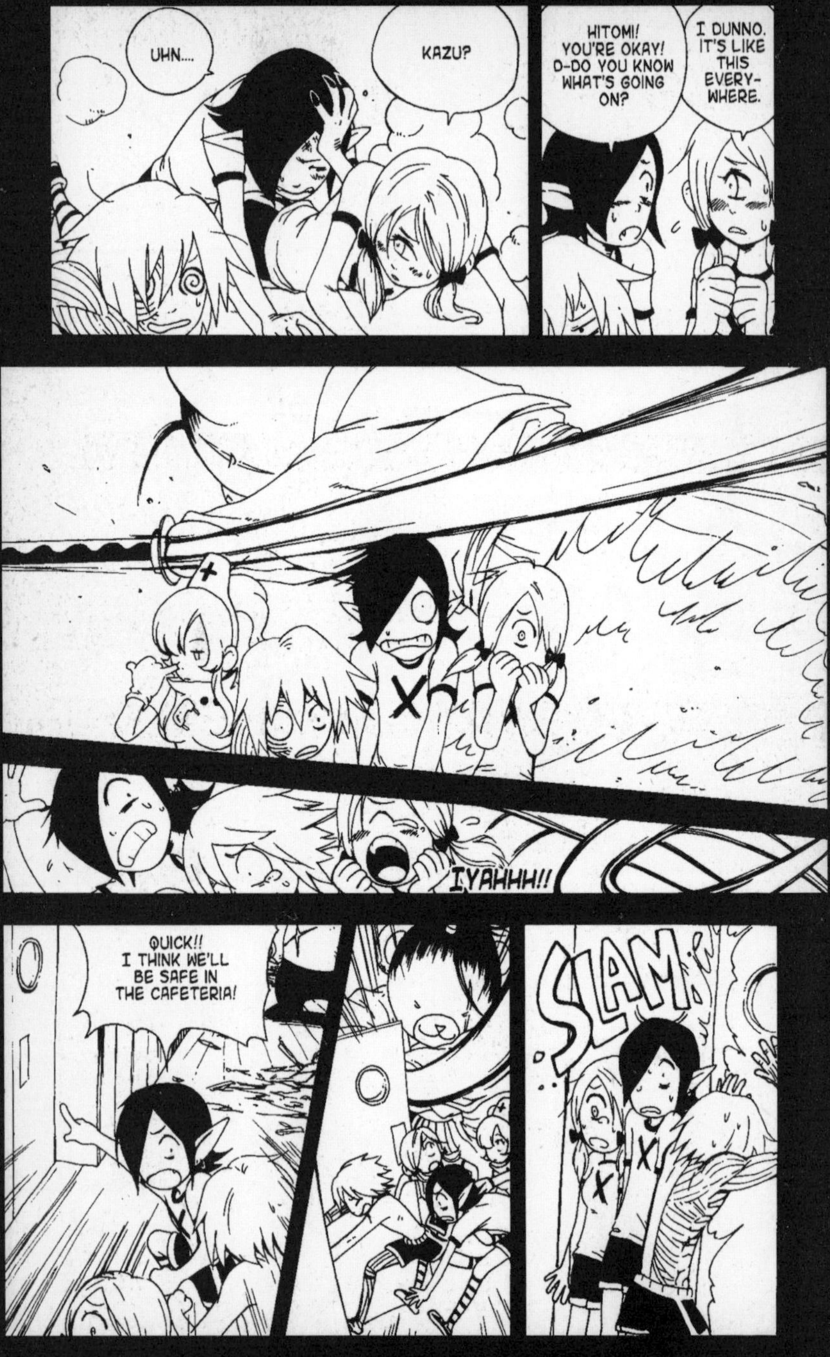
UHN....
KAZU?
HITOMI! YOU'RE OKAY! D-DO YOU KNOW WHAT'S GOING ON?
I DUNNO. IT'S LIKE THIS EVERY-WHERE.
IYAHHH!!
QUICK!! I THINK WE'LL BE SAFE IN THE CAFETERIA!
SLAM!

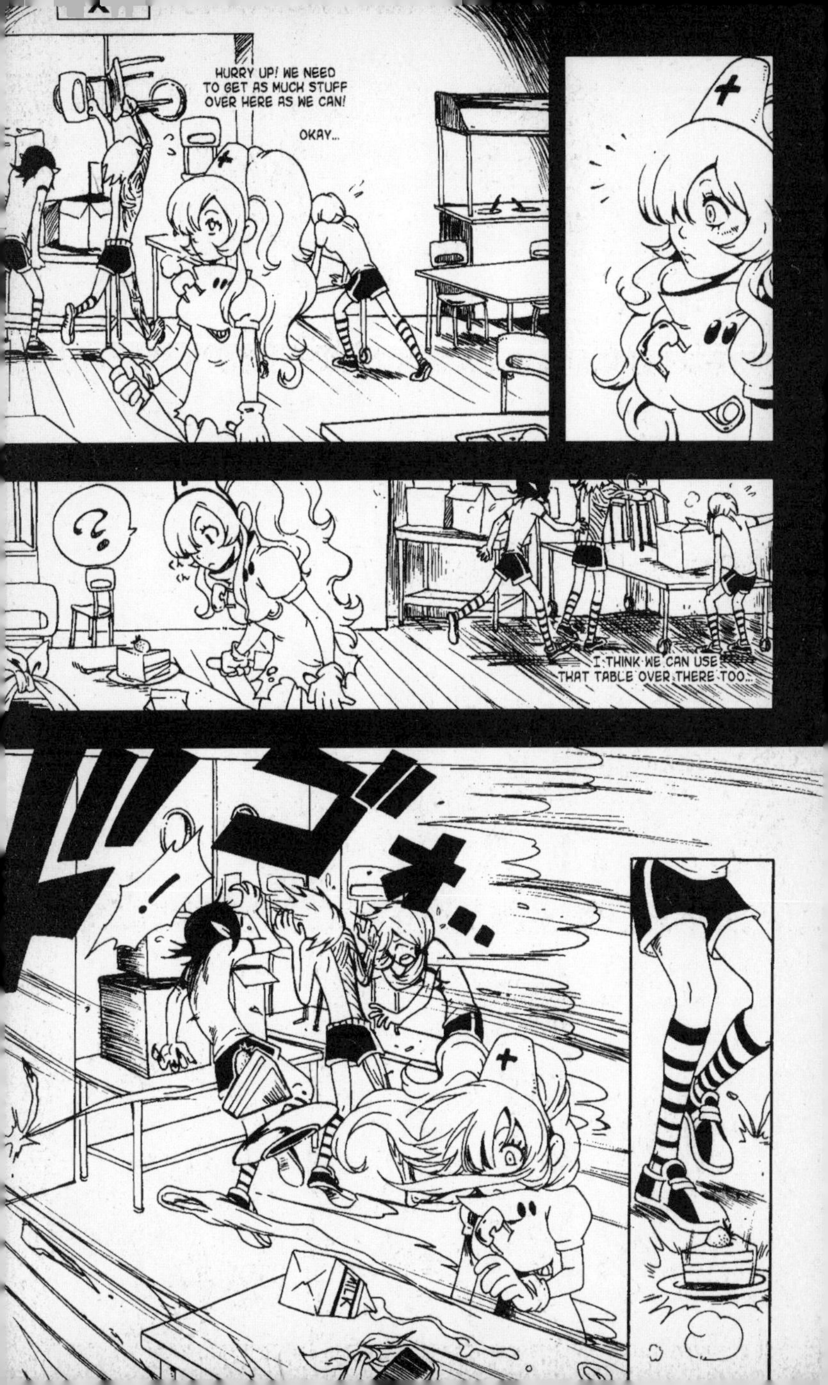
HURRY UP! WE NEED TO GET AS MUCH STUFF OVER HERE AS WE CAN!
OKAY...
?
I THINK WE CAN USE THAT TABLE OVER THERE TOO...
!

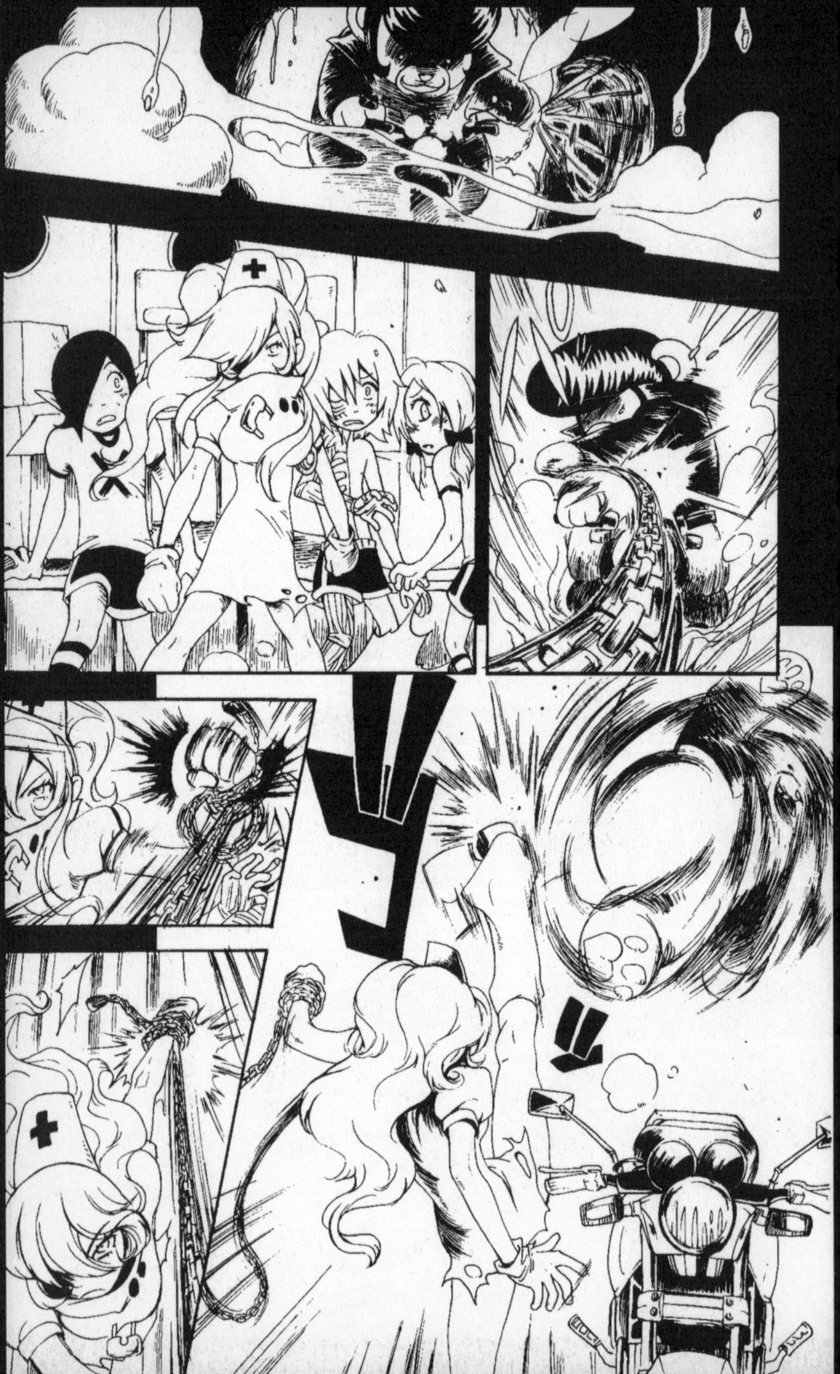

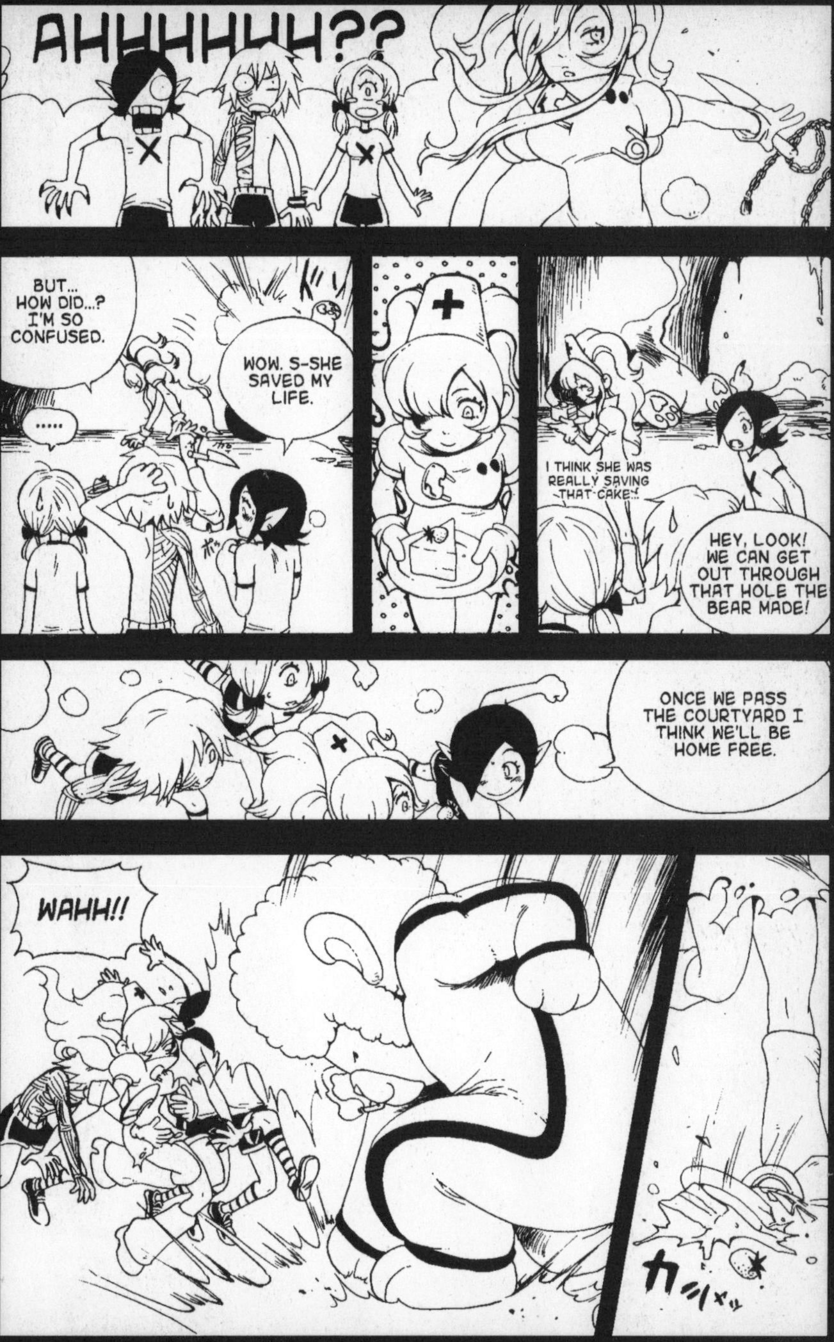
AHHHHHH??
BUT... HOW DID...? I'M SO CONFUSED.
......
WOW. S-SHE SAVED MY LIFE.
I THINK SHE WAS REALLY SAVING THAT CAKE...
HEY, LOOK! WE CAN GET OUT THROUGH THAT HOLE THE BEAR MADE!
ONCE WE PASS THE COURTYARD I THINK WE'LL BE HOME FREE.
WAHH!!
カシャッ

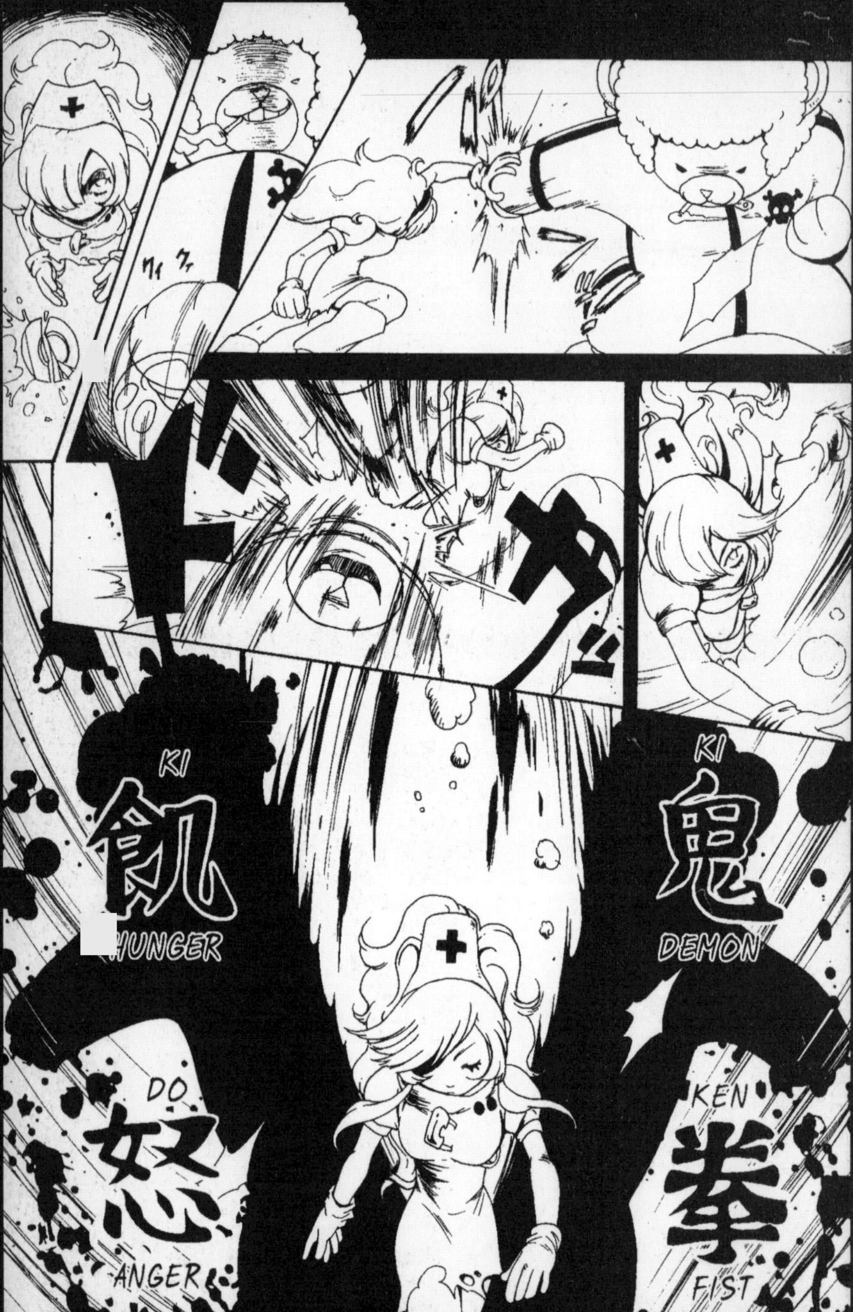
KI
飢
HUNGER
KI
鬼
DEMON
DO
怒
ANGER
KEN
拳
FIST

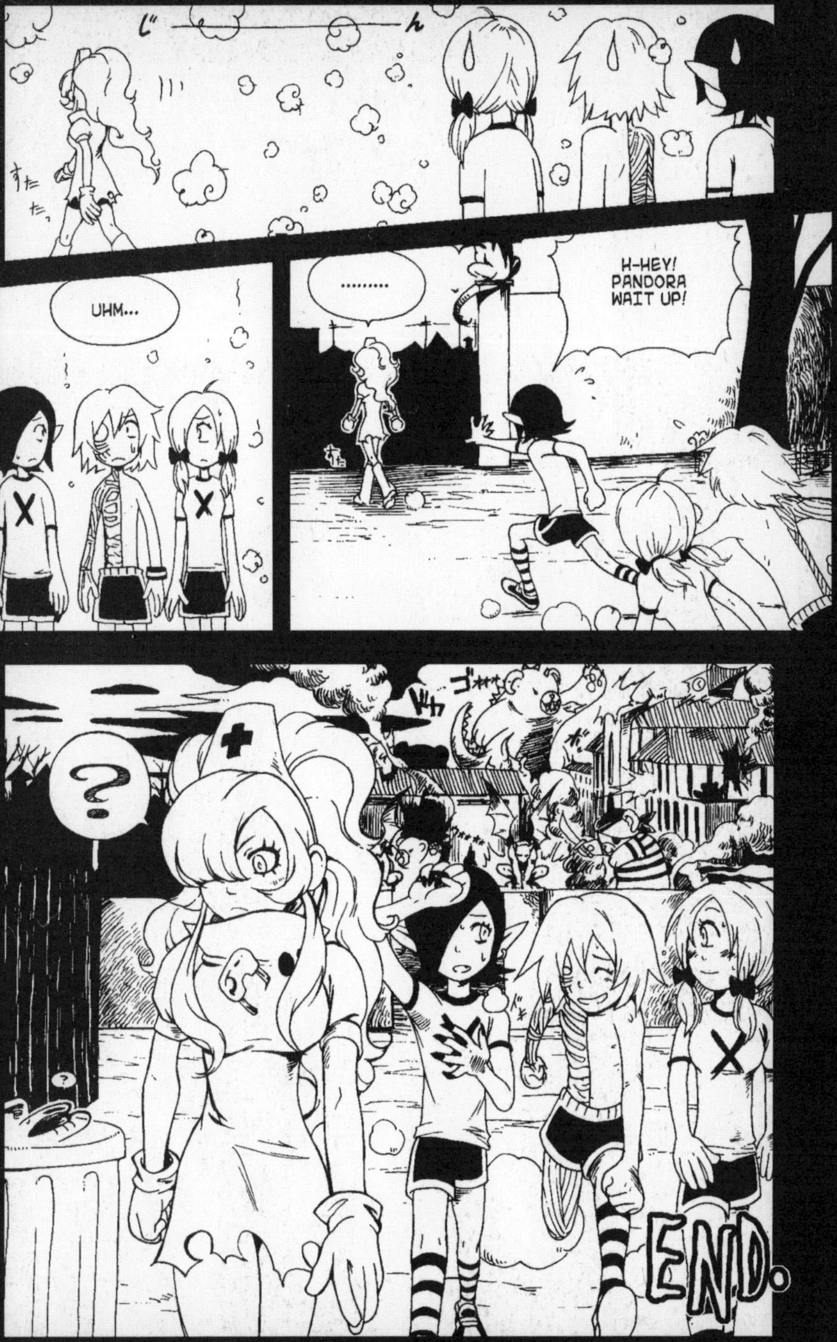
じ―――ん
すたたっ
UHM...
....
H-HEY! PANDORA WAIT UP!
?
END.

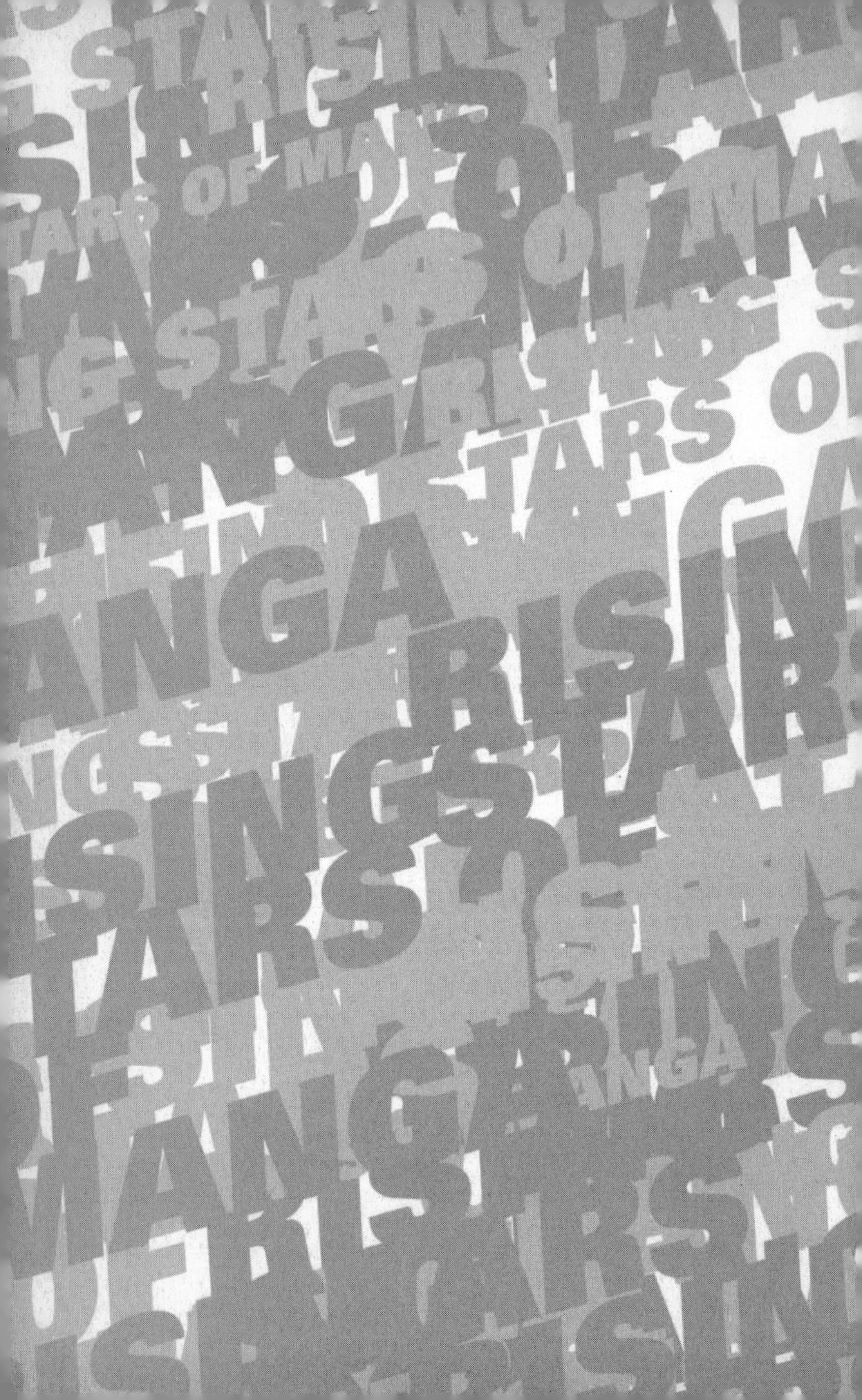

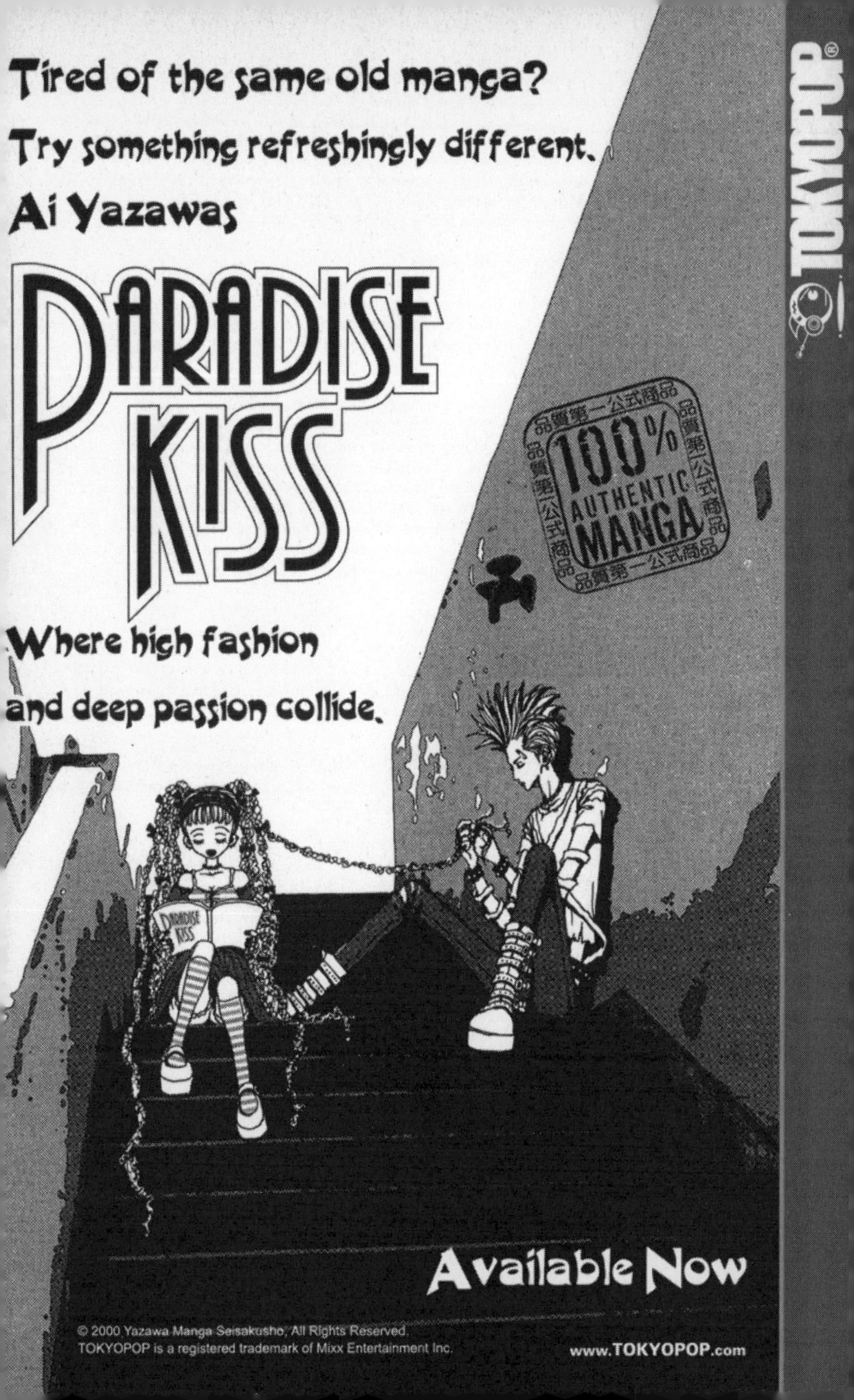
Tired of the same old manga?
Try something refreshingly different.
Ai Yazawas
PARADISE KISS
Where high fashion
and deep passion collide.
100% AUTHENTIC MANGA
Available Now
© 2000 Yazawa Manga Seisakusho, All Rights Reserved.
TOKYOPOP is a registered trademark of Mixx Entertainment Inc.
www.TOKYOPOP.com
TOKYOPOP

VAN VON HUNTER

FIRST PLACE WINNER

VAN VON HUNTER: CIRCLET OF NECROMANCY :: First Place Winner
The creative team of Mike Schwark and Ron Kaulfersch

Mike Schwark was born in 1975 in "excitement-filled Ohio," where he still lives today (in Fairview, to be exact). He's a graphic artist for a sign company by day and an animator/illustrator by night! (Well, mostly weekends, actually.) His artwork was featured in the independently created and released video OAV II: Prologue.

Inspiration for this story:
V.V.H.: Circlet of Necromancy was worked on by both Ron Kaulfersch and myself. I did all of the pencils, the lettering as well as some of the shading work, while Ron handled all of the inking and a lot of the tones. The story and characters were created by the two of us, through various brainstorming sessions.

The concept for Van Von Hunter himself came from a number of different sources, but I think I was most compelled to create the character after listening to some rock versions of *Castlevania* sound tracks. Since coming up with the original idea of V.V.H. the vampire hunter some years ago, Ron and I have recently reinvented him as a more generalized "hunter of evil… stuff." We find a lot of inspiration from watching anime where characters exhibit completely irrational behavior, which led to us giving Von Hunter the special ability to point out his adversaries' logic flaws, thereby defeating them.

Favorite Manga:
Blade of the Immortal, Gunsmith Cats, Battle Angel Alita

Favorite Manga Artists:
Hiroaki Samura, Yukito Kishiro, Kenichi Sonoda, Kosuke Fujishima, Rumiko Takahashi, Yu Watase
....

Ron Kaulfersch was born in 1975 in Italy, Ohio. He now lives in North Royalton, Ohio, where he works as an associate support representative (otherwise known as a "computer techie").

Inspiration for this story: Dumb anime titles.

Favorite Manga: *Love Hina*

Favorite Manga Artist: Yukito Kishiro
....

Judge's Comments:
Mike Schwark's and Ron Kaulfersch's short story about a clueless warrior in a realm of sorcery and magic was a clever and professionally executed parody of the fantasy genre in the vein of Sorcerer Hunters and Slayers.

The art was clean. The artists had a good handle on anatomy, fun body language, humorous expressions, impressive tone work and effects. While most artists either avoid backgrounds altogether or overcrowd them, Mike and Ron showed promise with appropriate rendering and an understanding of perspective.

We enjoyed the well-thought-out story and its send-ups of the many clichés in modern manga. The highly competent art and the wit displayed in the dialogue and plot moved this entry to the top of the pile. Polite zombies, a tipsy young mage and a homophonetically-challenged hero made this our pick for first prize.
-Mark Paniccia

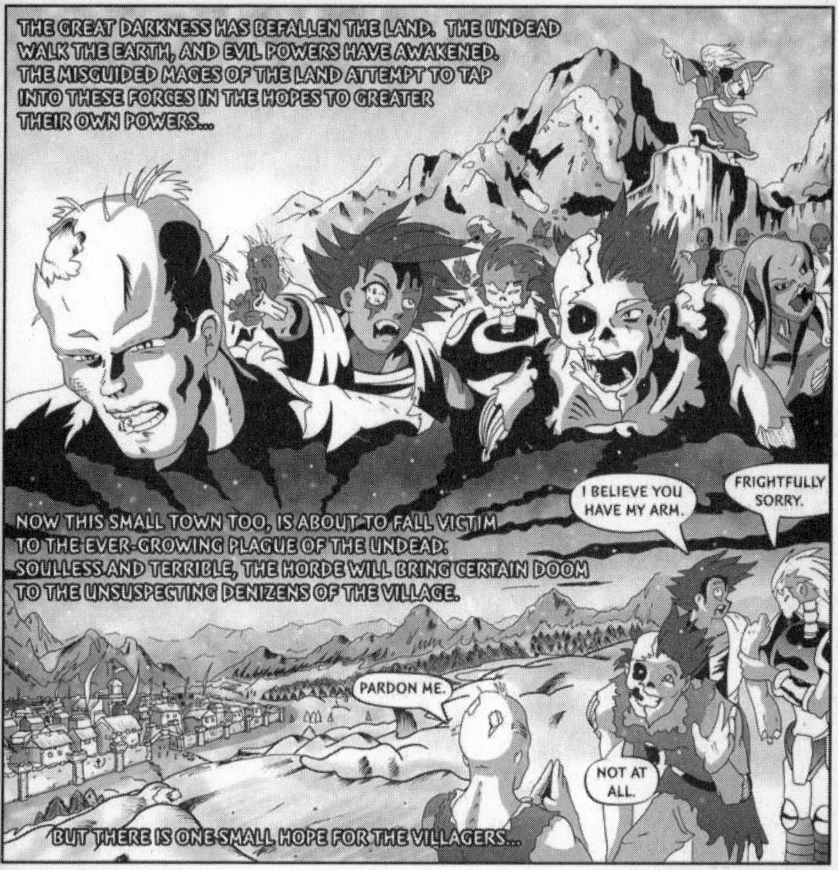
THE GREAT DARKNESS HAS BEFALLEN THE LAND. THE UNDEAD WALK THE EARTH, AND EVIL POWERS HAVE AWAKENED. THE MISGUIDED MAGES OF THE LAND ATTEMPT TO TAP INTO THESE FORCES IN THE HOPES TO GREATER THEIR OWN POWERS...
NOW THIS SMALL TOWN TOO, IS ABOUT TO FALL VICTIM TO THE EVER-GROWING PLAGUE OF THE UNDEAD. SOULLESS AND TERRIBLE, THE HORDE WILL BRING CERTAIN DOOM TO THE UNSUSPECTING DENIZENS OF THE VILLAGE.
I BELIEVE YOU HAVE MY ARM.
FRIGHTFULLY SORRY.
PARDON ME.
NOT AT ALL.
BUT THERE IS ONE SMALL HOPE FOR THE VILLAGERS...
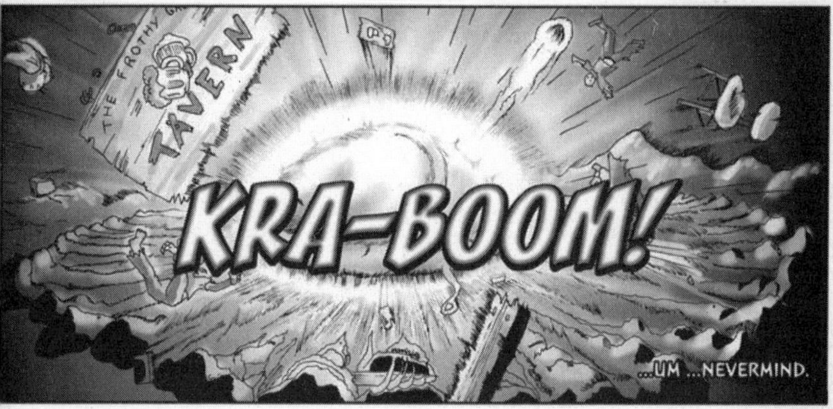
THE FROTHY
TAVERN
KRA-BOOM!
...UM ...NEVERMIND.

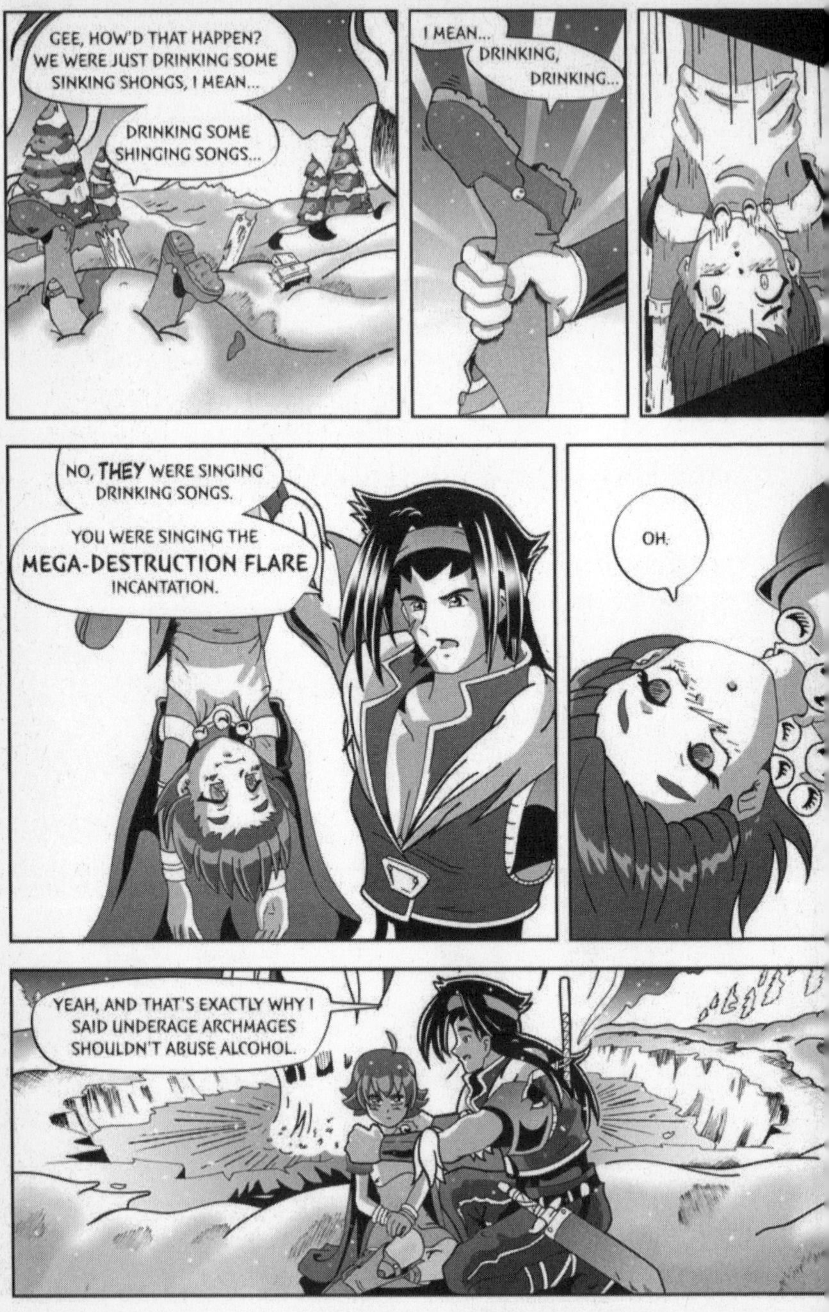
GEE, HOW'D THAT HAPPEN? WE WERE JUST DRINKING SOME SINKING SHONGS, I MEAN...
DRINKING SOME SHINGING SONGS...
I MEAN...
DRINKING,
DRINKING...
NO, **THEY** WERE SINGING DRINKING SONGS.
YOU WERE SINGING THE **MEGA-DESTRUCTION FLARE** INCANTATION.
OH.
YEAH, AND THAT'S EXACTLY WHY I SAID UNDERAGE ARCHMAGES SHOULDN'T ABUSE ALCOHOL.

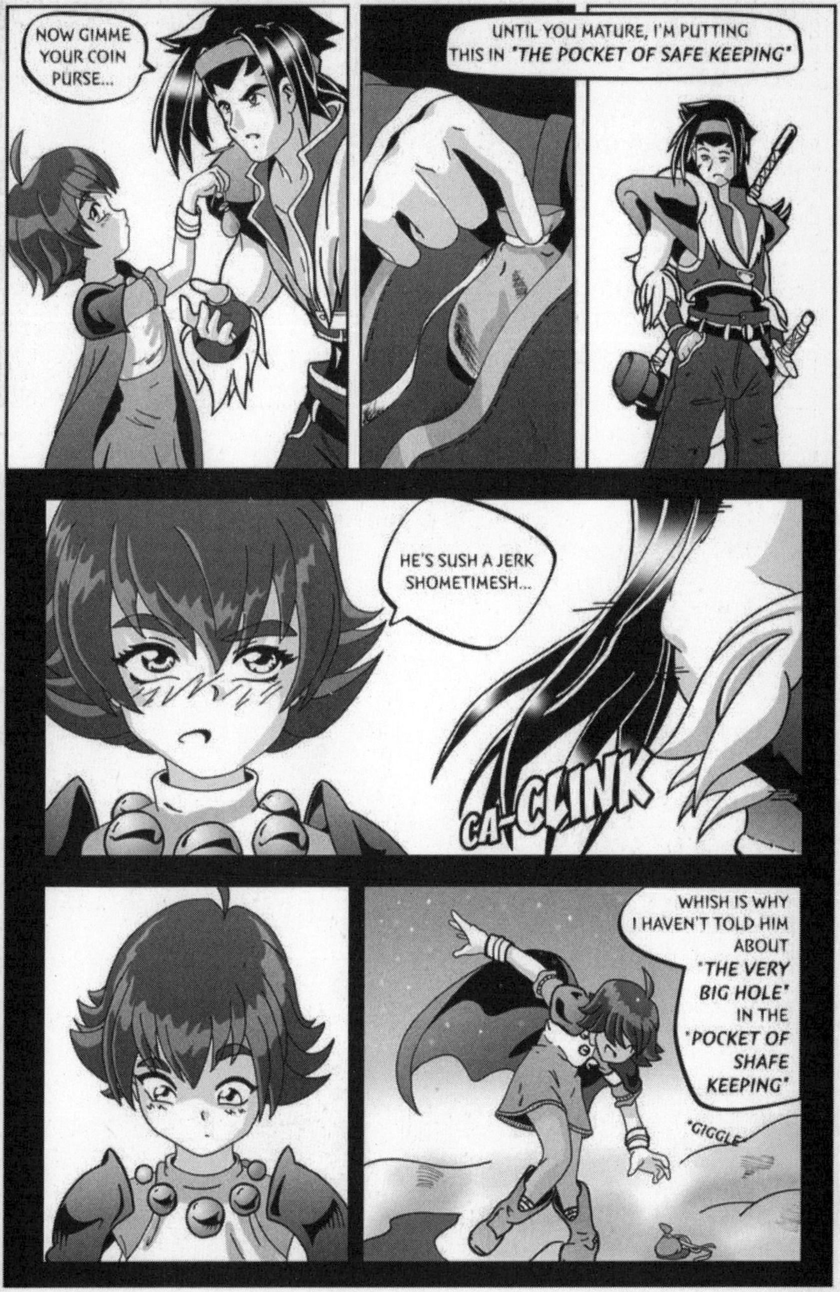
NOW GIMME YOUR COIN PURSE...
UNTIL YOU MATURE, I'M PUTTING THIS IN *"THE POCKET OF SAFE KEEPING"*
HE'S SUSH A JERK SHOMETIMESH...
CA-CLINK
WHISH IS WHY I HAVEN'T TOLD HIM ABOUT *"THE VERY BIG HOLE"* IN THE *"POCKET OF SHAFE KEEPING"*
GIGGLE

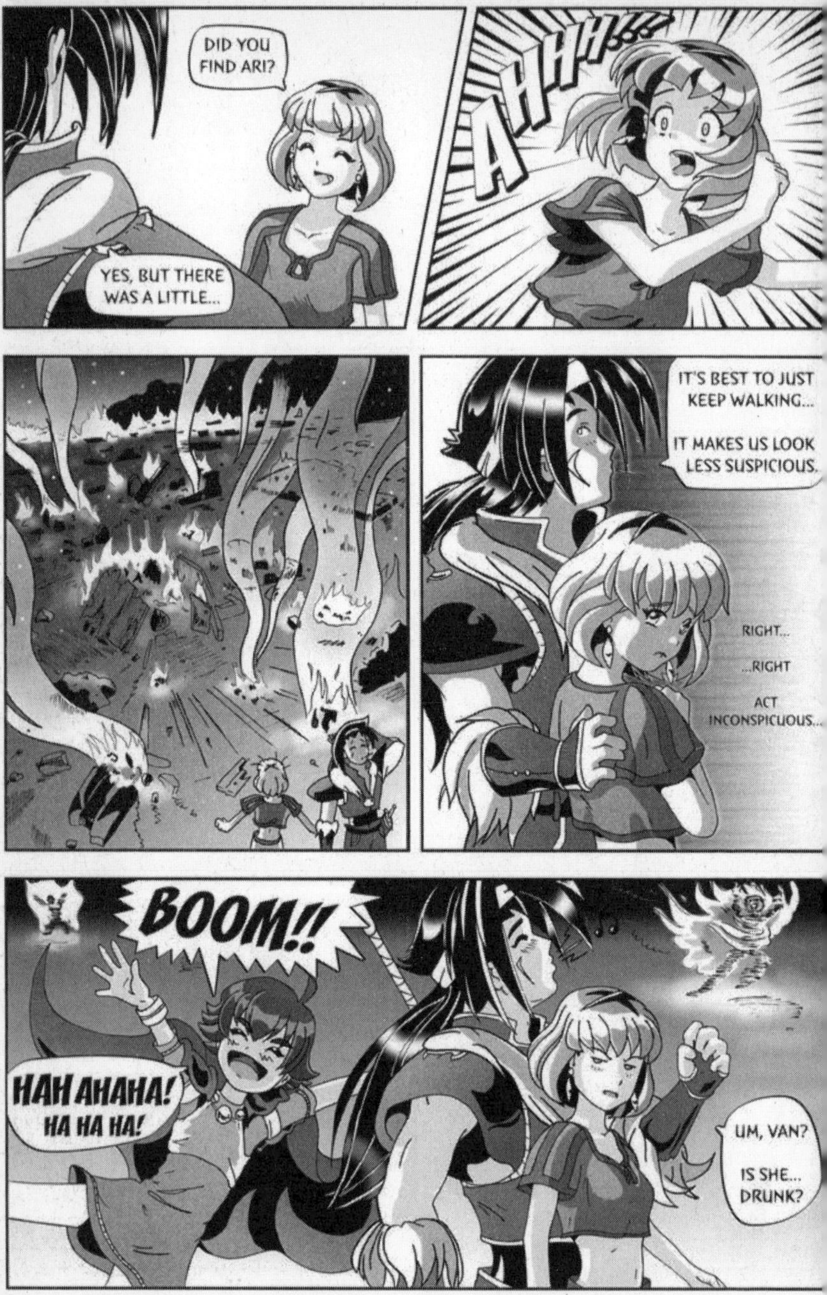
DID YOU FIND ARI?
YES, BUT THERE WAS A LITTLE...
AHHH!!!
IT'S BEST TO JUST KEEP WALKING...
IT MAKES US LOOK LESS SUSPICIOUS.
RIGHT...
...RIGHT
ACT INCONSPICUOUS...
BOOM!!
HAH AHAHA! HA HA HA!
UM, VAN?
IS SHE... DRUNK?

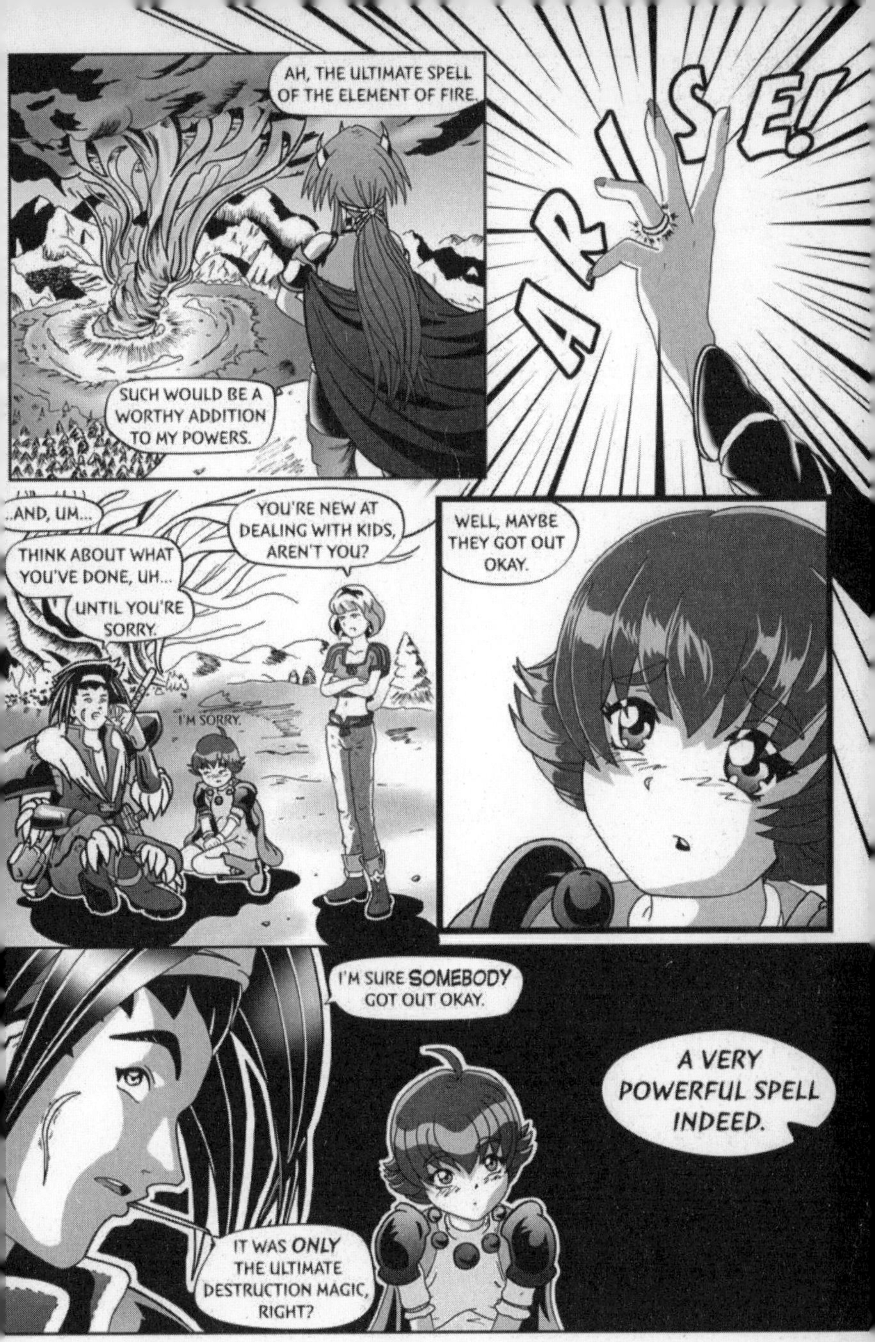
AH, THE ULTIMATE SPELL OF THE ELEMENT OF FIRE.
SUCH WOULD BE A WORTHY ADDITION TO MY POWERS.
ARISE!
..AND, UM...
THINK ABOUT WHAT YOU'VE DONE, UH...
UNTIL YOU'RE SORRY.
YOU'RE NEW AT DEALING WITH KIDS, AREN'T YOU?
I'M SORRY.
WELL, MAYBE THEY GOT OUT OKAY.
I'M SURE SOMEBODY GOT OUT OKAY.
A VERY POWERFUL SPELL INDEED.
IT WAS ONLY THE ULTIMATE DESTRUCTION MAGIC, RIGHT?

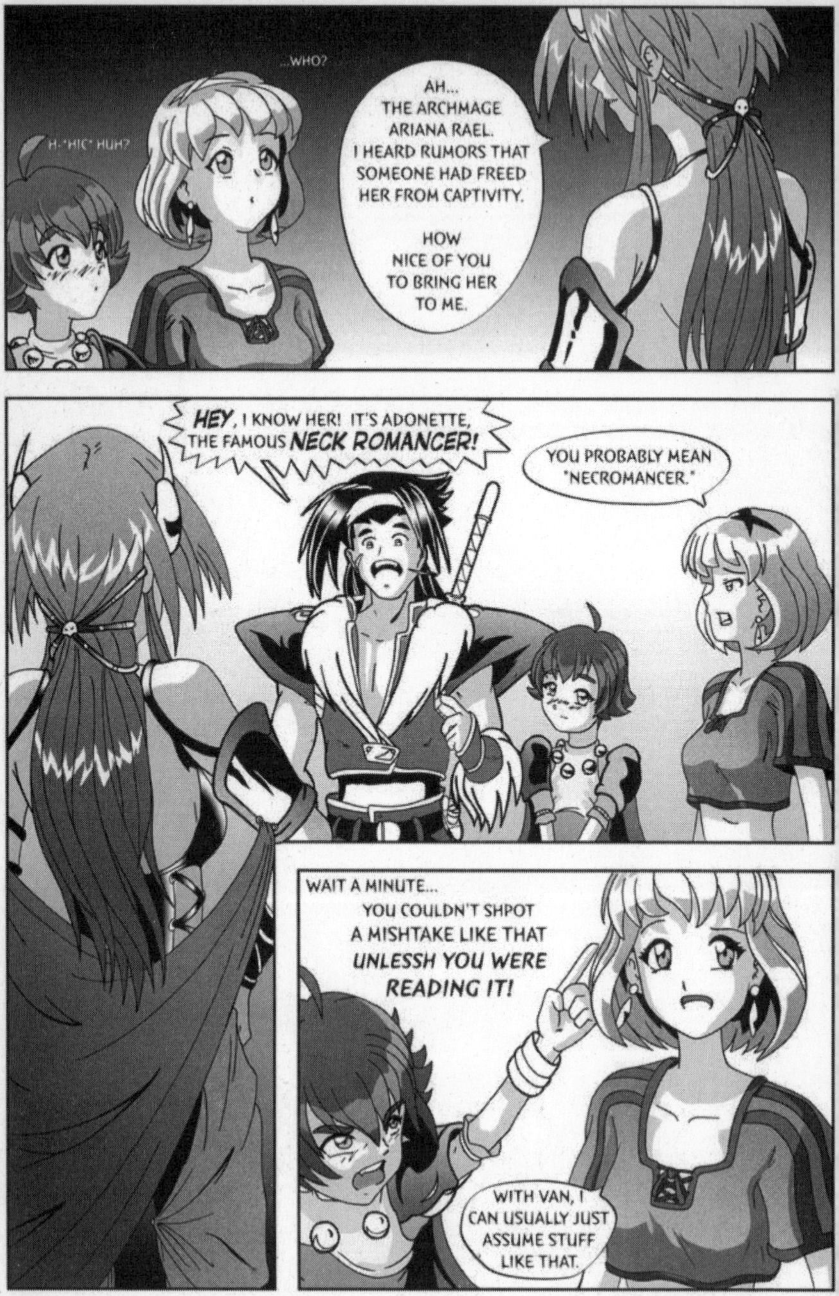
...WHO?
H-*HIC* HUH?
AH... THE ARCHMAGE ARIANA RAEL. I HEARD RUMORS THAT SOMEONE HAD FREED HER FROM CAPTIVITY.
HOW NICE OF YOU TO BRING HER TO ME.
HEY, I KNOW HER! IT'S ADONETTE, THE FAMOUS NECK ROMANCER!
YOU PROBABLY MEAN "NECROMANCER."
WAIT A MINUTE...
YOU COULDN'T SHPOT A MISHTAKE LIKE THAT UNLESSH YOU WERE READING IT!
WITH VAN, I CAN USUALLY JUST ASSUME STUFF LIKE THAT.

WE'RE SAFEGUARDING, TO KEEP HER POWERS OUT OF THE HANDS OF EVIL.

...AT LEAST UNTIL WE CAN FIND A GOOD PLACE TO DITCH HER.

RIGHT!

BESIDES, THE KID ONLY KNOWS ONE SPELL. IT'S A DOOZY, BUT STILL...

WHAT GOOD DOES THAT DO YOU?

OH, ONE SPELL IS ALL SHE'LL NEED.

IT'S PROBABLY ALL SHE'LL REMEMBER ONCE SHE'S A ZOMBIE.

BEHOLD, THE CIRCLET OF NECROMANCY!

ZOMBIE??

WHILE I WEAR IT, THE DEAD MUST OBEY!

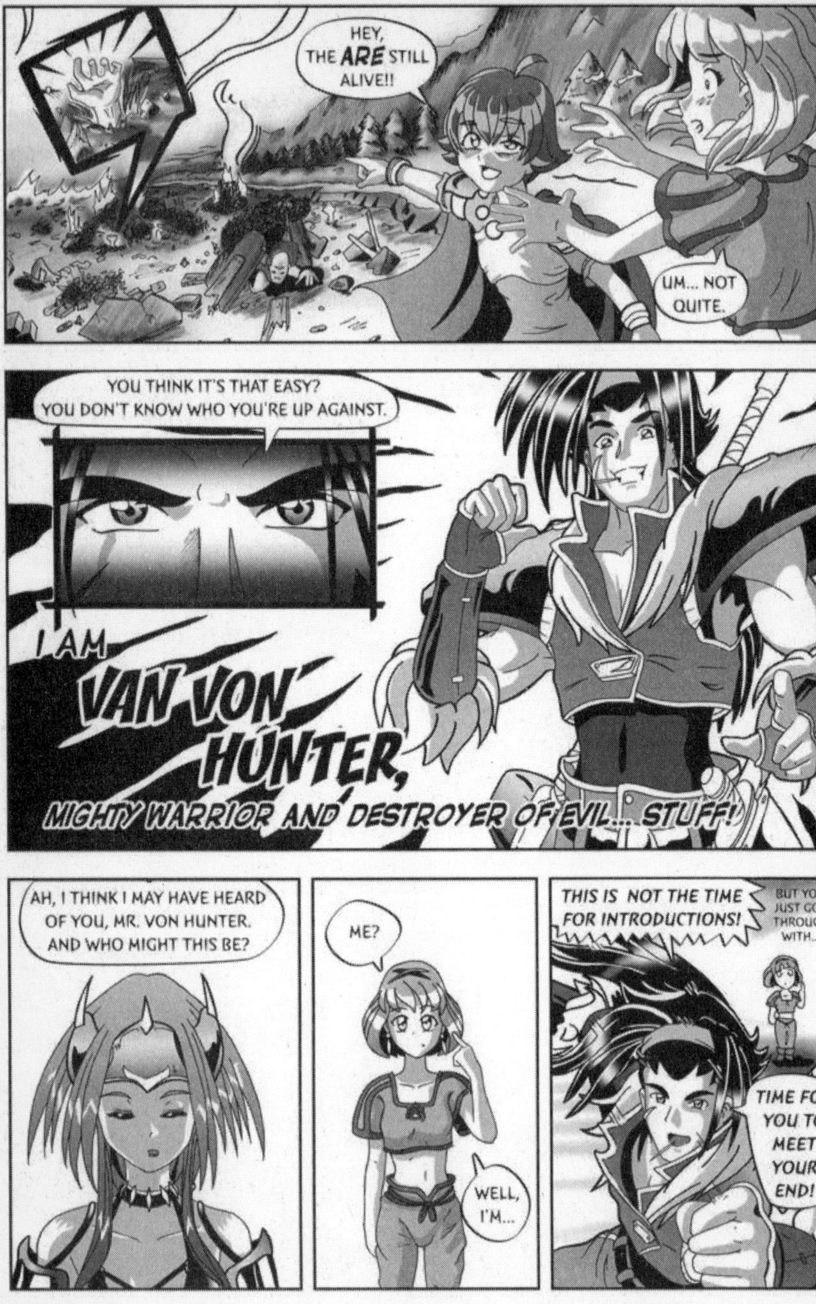
HEY, THE ARE STILL ALIVE!!
UM... NOT QUITE.
YOU THINK IT'S THAT EASY? YOU DON'T KNOW WHO YOU'RE UP AGAINST.
I AM VAN VON HUNTER,
MIGHTY WARRIOR AND DESTROYER OF EVIL... STUFF!
AH, I THINK I MAY HAVE HEARD OF YOU, MR. VON HUNTER. AND WHO MIGHT THIS BE?
ME?
WELL, I'M...
THIS IS NOT THE TIME FOR INTRODUCTIONS!
BUT YOU JUST GOT THROUGH WITH...
TIME FOR YOU TO MEET YOUR END!

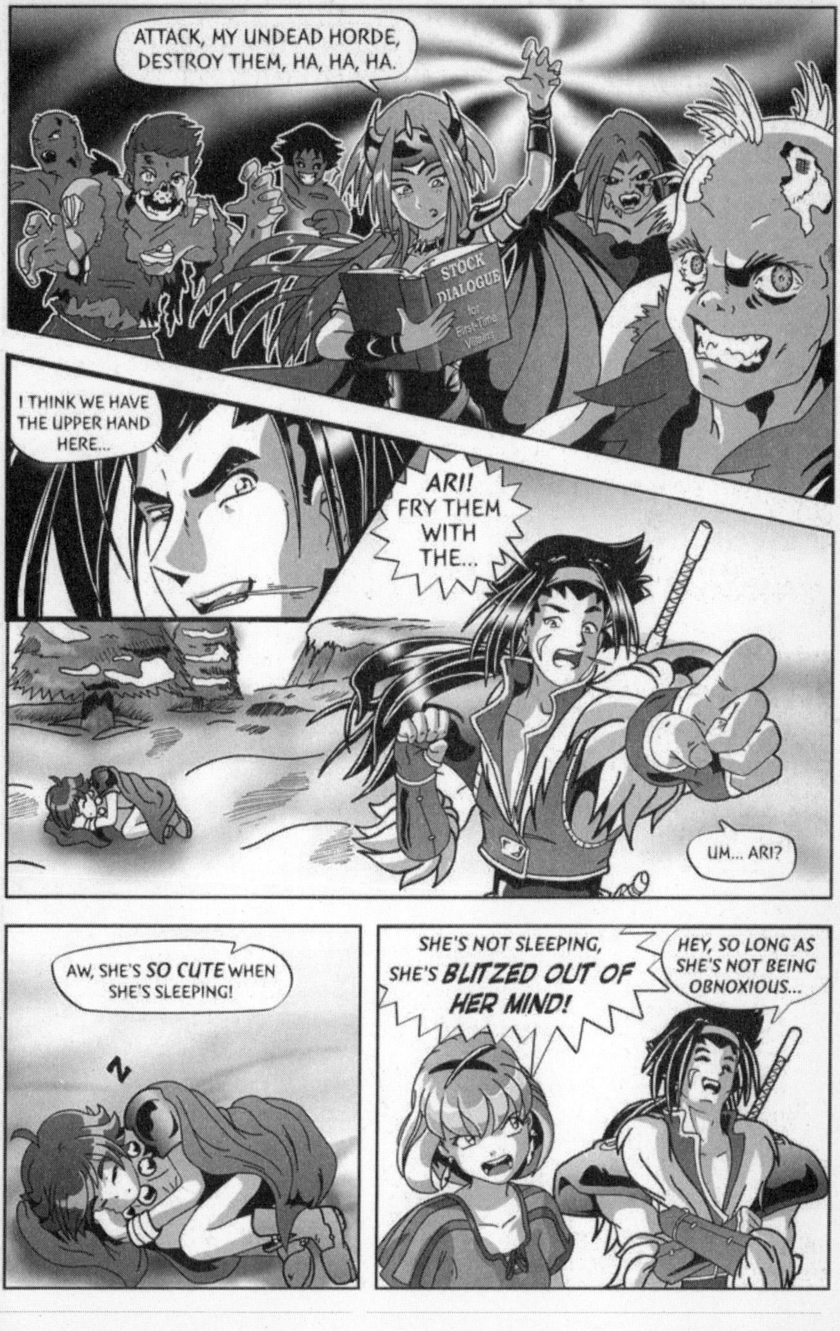
ATTACK, MY UNDEAD HORDE, DESTROY THEM, HA, HA, HA.
STOCK DIALOGUE for First-Time Villains
I THINK WE HAVE THE UPPER HAND HERE...
ARI! FRY THEM WITH THE...
UM... ARI?
AW, SHE'S SO CUTE WHEN SHE'S SLEEPING!
Z
SHE'S NOT SLEEPING, SHE'S BLITZED OUT OF HER MIND!
HEY, SO LONG AS SHE'S NOT BEING OBNOXIOUS...

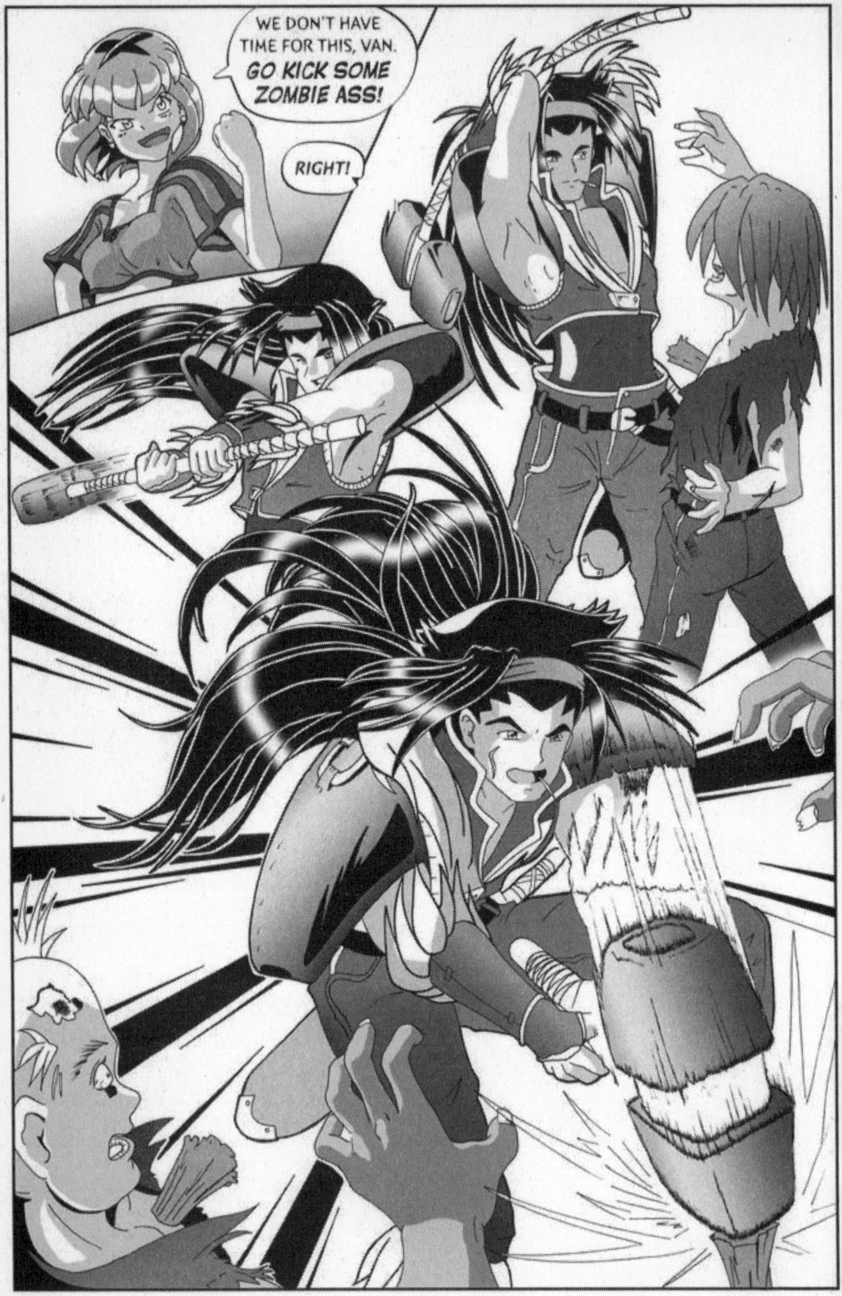
WE DON'T HAVE TIME FOR THIS, VAN. GO KICK SOME ZOMBIE ASS!
RIGHT!

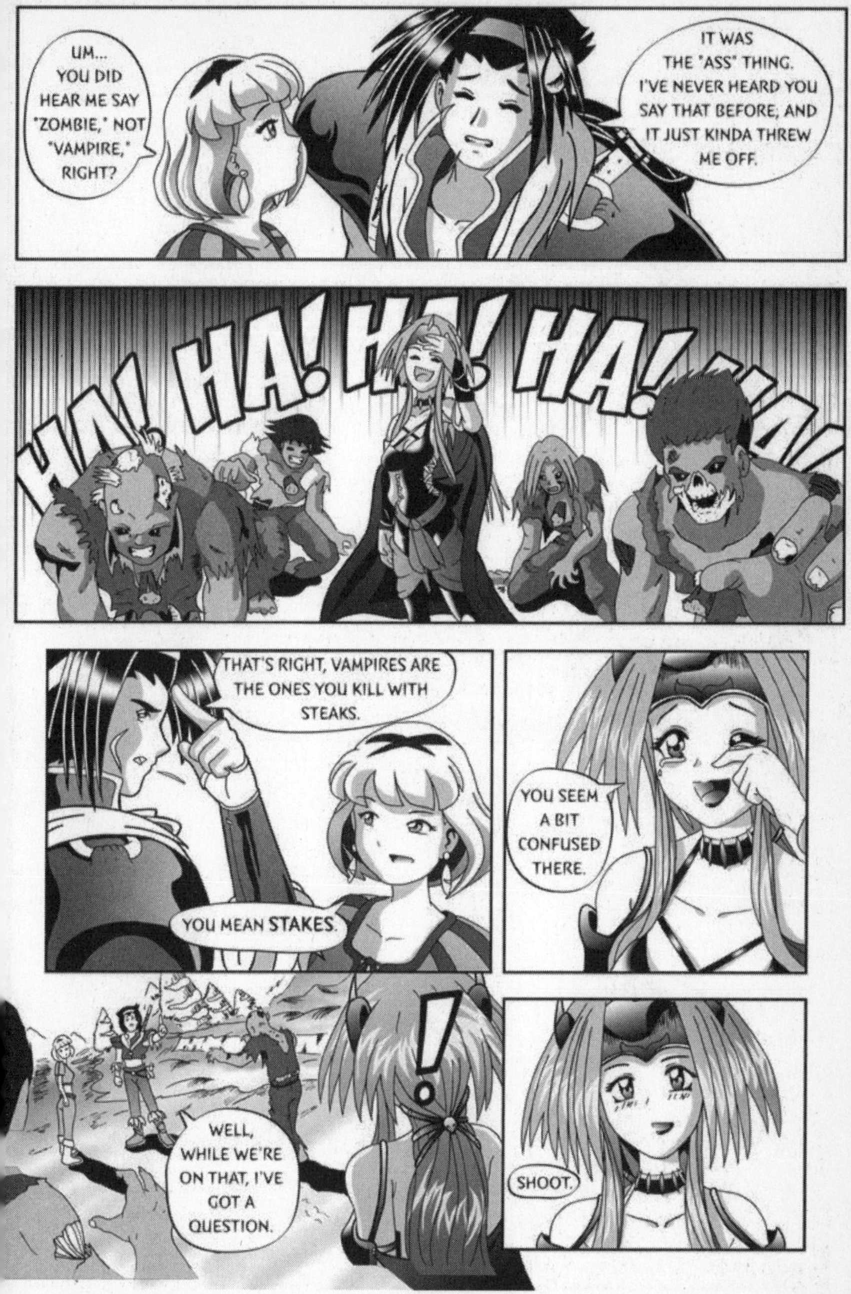
UM... YOU DID HEAR ME SAY "ZOMBIE," NOT "VAMPIRE," RIGHT?
IT WAS THE "ASS" THING. I'VE NEVER HEARD YOU SAY THAT BEFORE, AND IT JUST KINDA THREW ME OFF.
HA! HA! HA! HA!
THAT'S RIGHT, VAMPIRES ARE THE ONES YOU KILL WITH STEAKS.
YOU MEAN STAKES.
YOU SEEM A BIT CONFUSED THERE.
!
WELL, WHILE WE'RE ON THAT, I'VE GOT A QUESTION.
SHOOT.

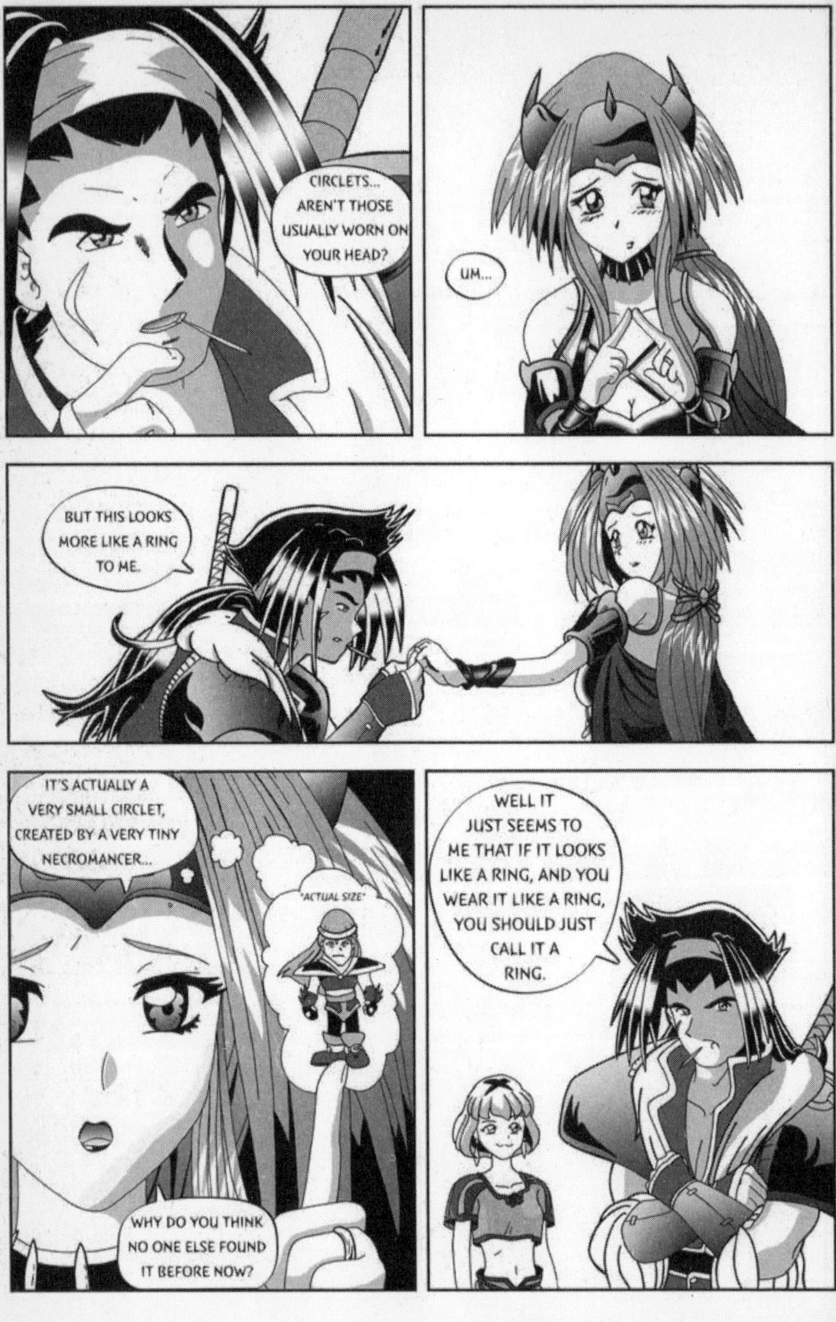
CIRCLETS... AREN'T THOSE USUALLY WORN ON YOUR HEAD?
UM...
BUT THIS LOOKS MORE LIKE A RING TO ME.
IT'S ACTUALLY A VERY SMALL CIRCLET, CREATED BY A VERY TINY NECROMANCER...
ACTUAL SIZE
WHY DO YOU THINK NO ONE ELSE FOUND IT BEFORE NOW?
WELL IT JUST SEEMS TO ME THAT IF IT LOOKS LIKE A RING, AND YOU WEAR IT LIKE A RING, YOU SHOULD JUST CALL IT A RING.

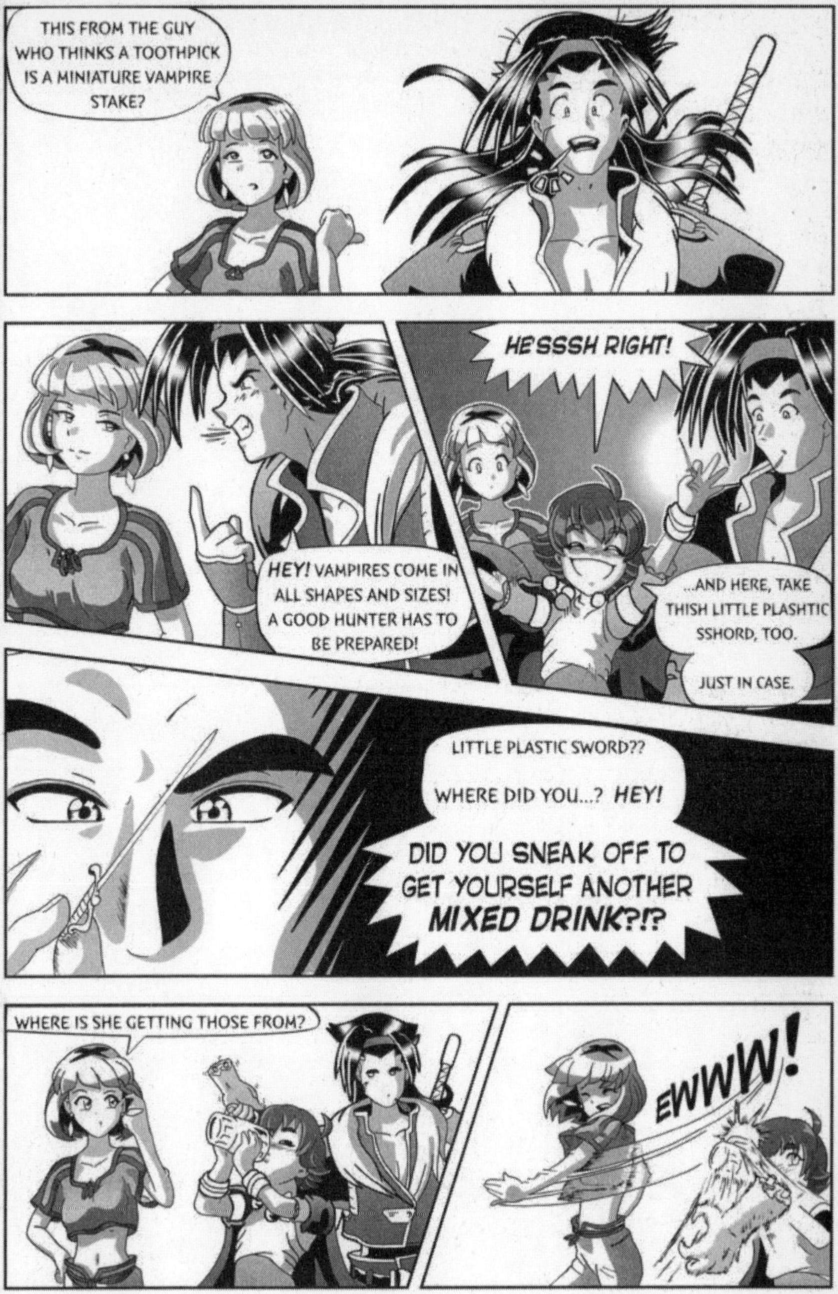

THIS FROM THE GUY WHO THINKS A TOOTHPICK IS A MINIATURE VAMPIRE STAKE?
HEY! VAMPIRES COME IN ALL SHAPES AND SIZES! A GOOD HUNTER HAS TO BE PREPARED!
HE'SSSH RIGHT!
...AND HERE, TAKE THISH LITTLE PLASHTIC SSHORD, TOO.
JUST IN CASE.
LITTLE PLASTIC SWORD??
WHERE DID YOU...? HEY!
DID YOU SNEAK OFF TO GET YOURSELF ANOTHER MIXED DRINK?!?
WHERE IS SHE GETTING THOSE FROM?
EWWW!

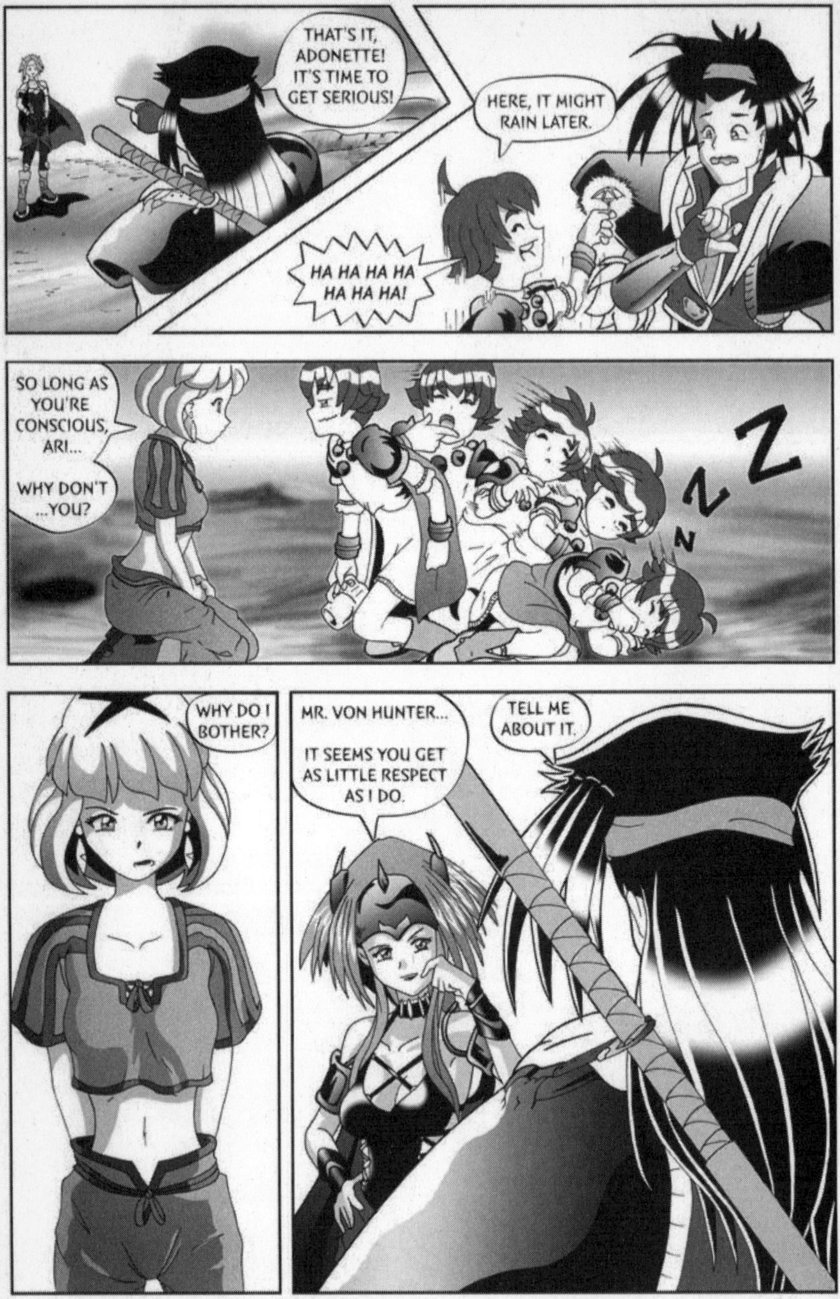
THAT'S IT, ADONETTE! IT'S TIME TO GET SERIOUS!
HERE, IT MIGHT RAIN LATER.
HA HA HA HA HA HA HA!
SO LONG AS YOU'RE CONSCIOUS, ARI...
WHY DON'T ...YOU?
Z Z Z
WHY DO I BOTHER?
MR. VON HUNTER...
IT SEEMS YOU GET AS LITTLE RESPECT AS I DO.
TELL ME ABOUT IT.

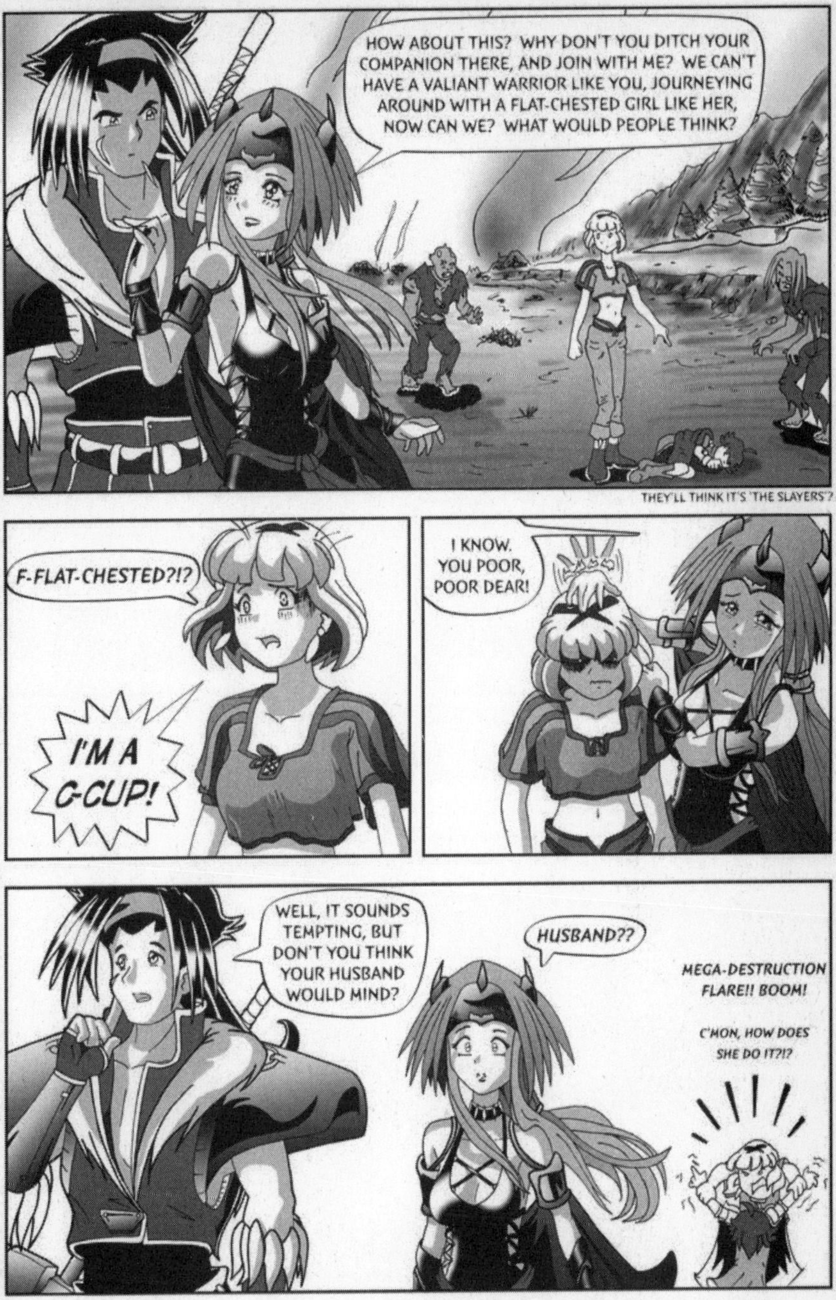
HOW ABOUT THIS? WHY DON'T YOU DITCH YOUR COMPANION THERE, AND JOIN WITH ME? WE CAN'T HAVE A VALIANT WARRIOR LIKE YOU, JOURNEYING AROUND WITH A FLAT-CHESTED GIRL LIKE HER, NOW CAN WE? WHAT WOULD PEOPLE THINK?
THEY'LL THINK IT'S 'THE SLAYERS'?
F-FLAT-CHESTED?!?
I'M A C-CUP!
I KNOW. YOU POOR, POOR DEAR!
WELL, IT SOUNDS TEMPTING, BUT DON'T YOU THINK YOUR HUSBAND WOULD MIND?
HUSBAND??
MEGA-DESTRUCTION FLARE!! BOOM!
C'MON, HOW DOES SHE DO IT?!?

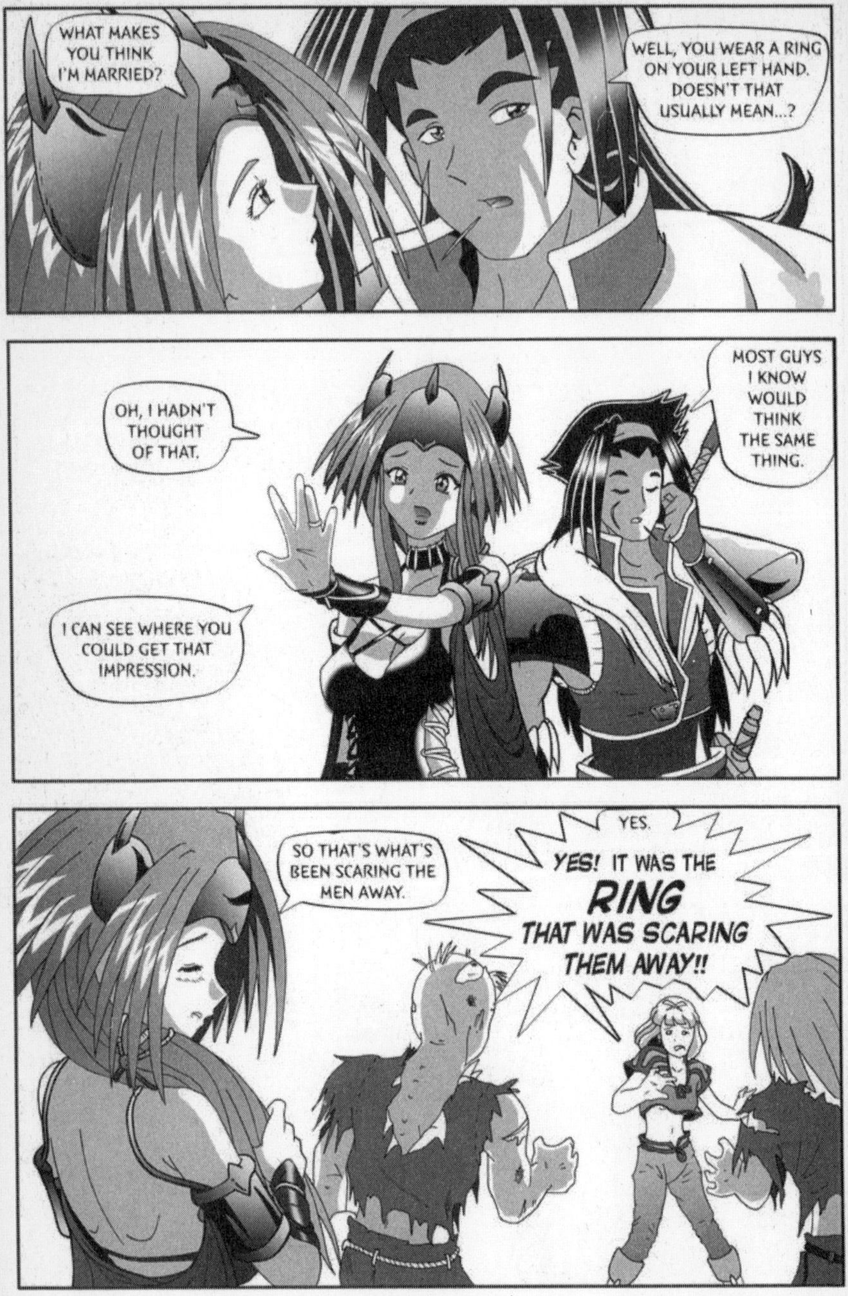
WHAT MAKES YOU THINK I'M MARRIED?
WELL, YOU WEAR A RING ON YOUR LEFT HAND. DOESN'T THAT USUALLY MEAN...?
OH, I HADN'T THOUGHT OF THAT.
MOST GUYS I KNOW WOULD THINK THE SAME THING.
I CAN SEE WHERE YOU COULD GET THAT IMPRESSION.
SO THAT'S WHAT'S BEEN SCARING THE MEN AWAY.
YES.
YES! IT WAS THE RING THAT WAS SCARING THEM AWAY!!

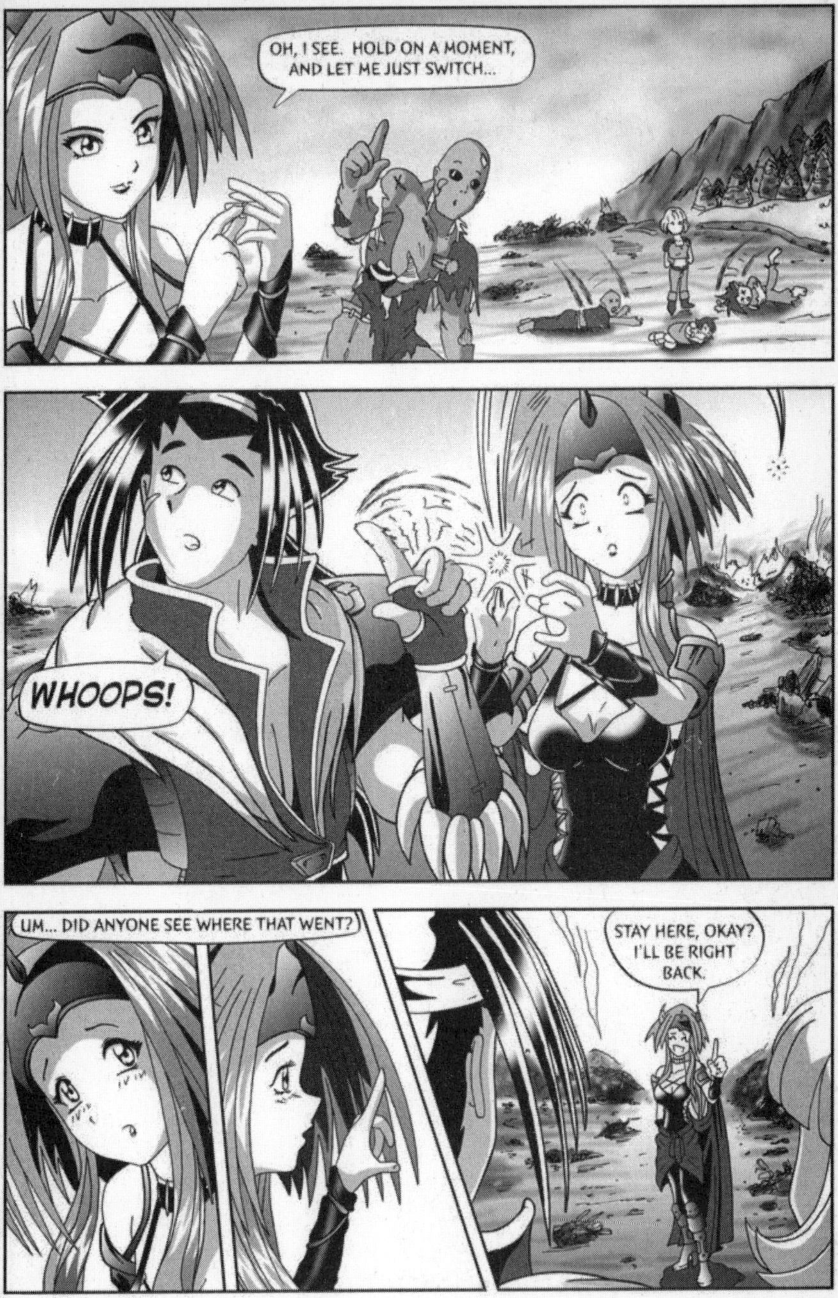

OH, I SEE. HOLD ON A MOMENT, AND LET ME JUST SWITCH...
WHOOPS!
UM... DID ANYONE SEE WHERE THAT WENT?
STAY HERE, OKAY? I'LL BE RIGHT BACK.

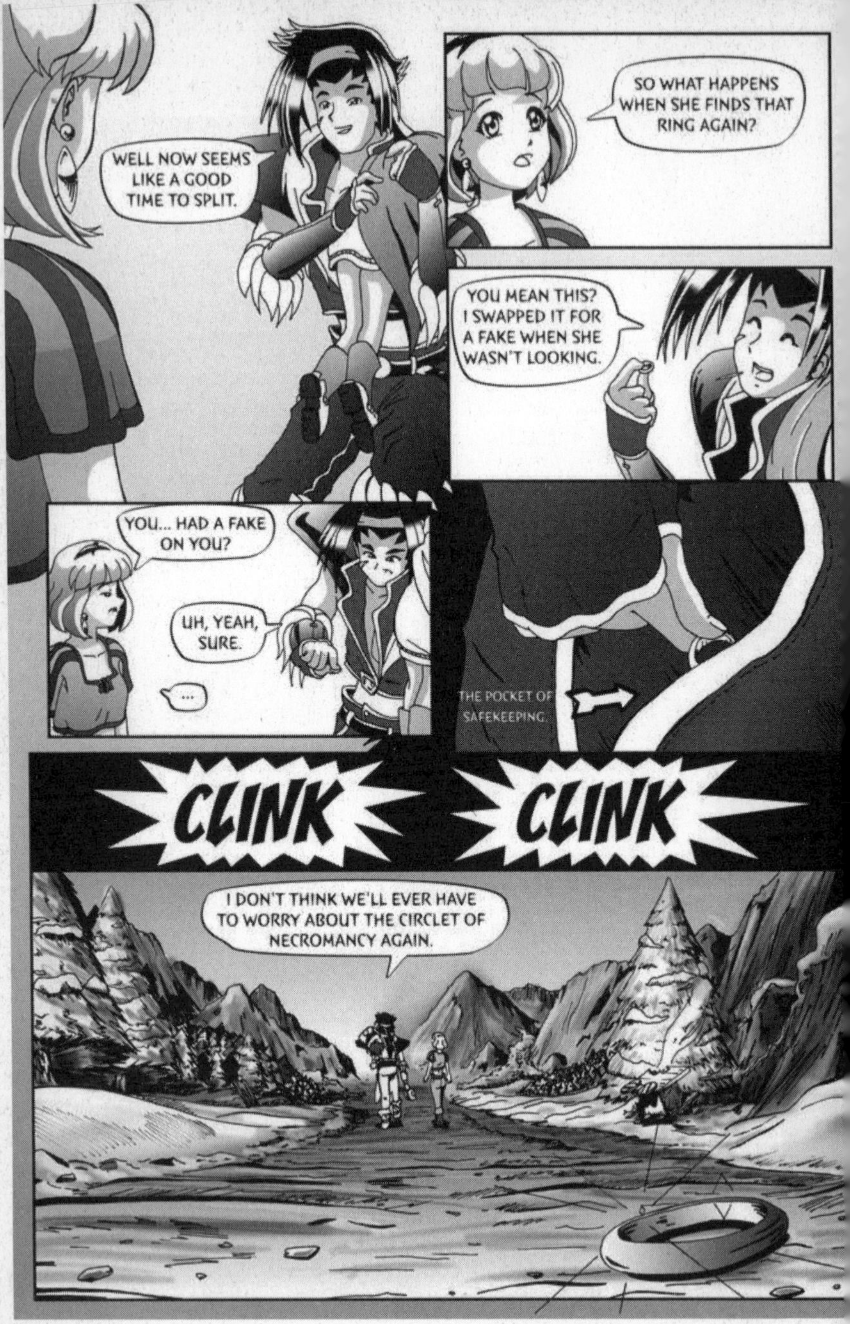
WELL NOW SEEMS LIKE A GOOD TIME TO SPLIT.
SO WHAT HAPPENS WHEN SHE FINDS THAT RING AGAIN?
YOU MEAN THIS? I SWAPPED IT FOR A FAKE WHEN SHE WASN'T LOOKING.
YOU... HAD A FAKE ON YOU?
UH, YEAH, SURE.
...
THE POCKET OF SAFEKEEPING.
CLINK
CLINK
I DON'T THINK WE'LL EVER HAVE TO WORRY ABOUT THE CIRCLET OF NECROMANCY AGAIN.

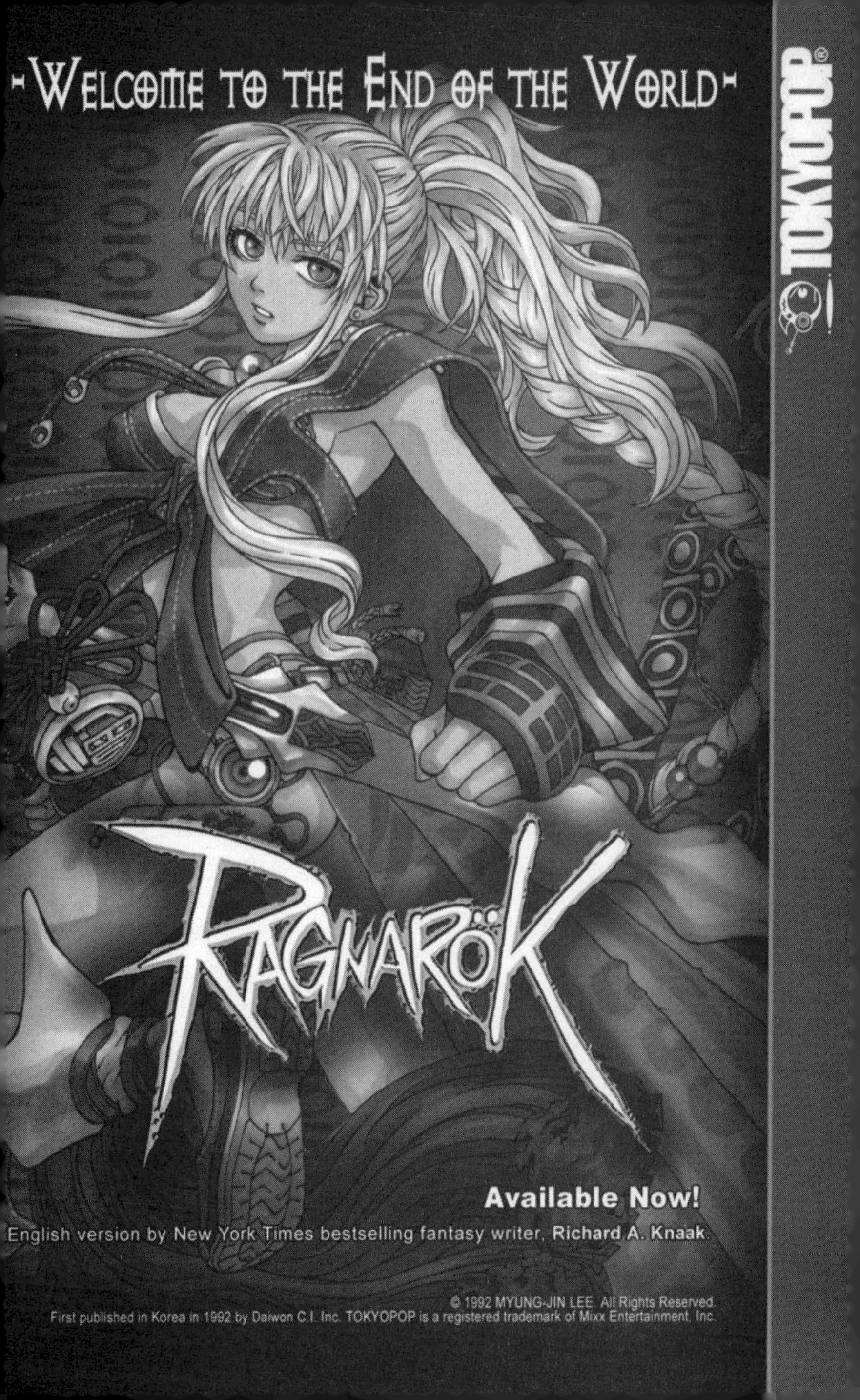

~WELCOME TO THE END OF THE WORLD~

TOKYOPOP

RAGNARÖK

Available Now!

English version by New York Times bestselling fantasy writer, **Richard A. Knaak**.

::

THE LITTLE MATCH GIRL :: RUNNER UP ::

Hans Tseng was born in Taipei, Taiwan, in 1986 and now lives in Orange, California. You can check out weekly updates on his graphic novel at http://destiny.slimemansion.com.

Inspiration for this story:
I remembered hearing the story when I was a child and how it made me sad.

Favorite Manga:
Hikaru no Go, Kareshi Kanojo no Jijou

Favorite Manga Artist:
CLAMP

....

Judge's Comments:
For over a century, Hans Christian Andersen's tale of a young street peddler has moved many readers but the powerful visual style of this entry almost brought a tear to our eyes. What struck us most about Hans Tseng's adaptation of this classic tale was his unique approach to story telling and how it took the tale to whole other level.

First, his page compositions showed not only strength in design—with the use of white space, inset panels and balance—but also an understanding of pacing and mood. Because the reader's eyes flow naturally from panel to panel, not distracted by unnecessary background information or awkward layout, a visual rhythm is created that moves the story in near real-time beats.

Second was the economy of images and the way each panel revealed important information to the reader. Each detail not only helps to guide you through the story but also brings you inside the world of the little match girl: a close up of a lone slipper, a cold brick wall, an empty rocking chair. Through their silhouettes alone, I knew the passers-by were lost in their own worlds—an amazing feat of subtlety. In the end, I was touched by this entry and it had much to do with Tseng's ability as a visual storyteller.
-Mark Paniccia

::

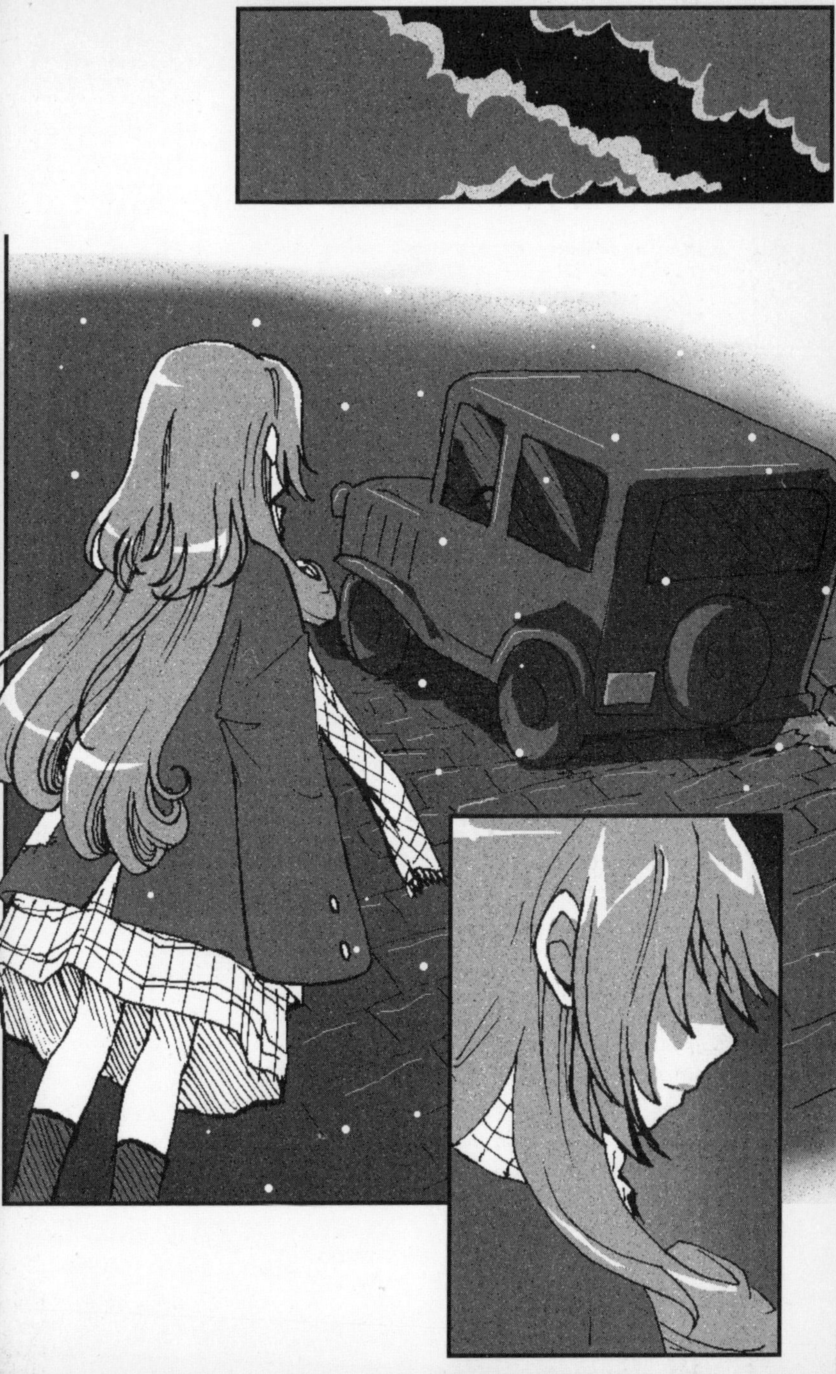

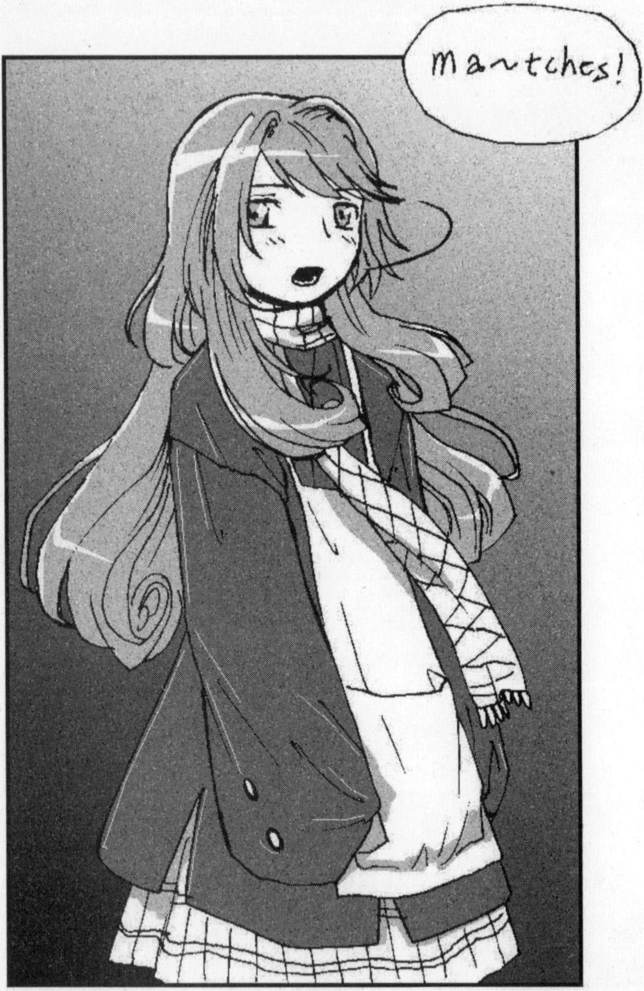
ma~tches!

the Little match Girl

by Hans Tseng

based on a short story by
Hans Christian Andersen

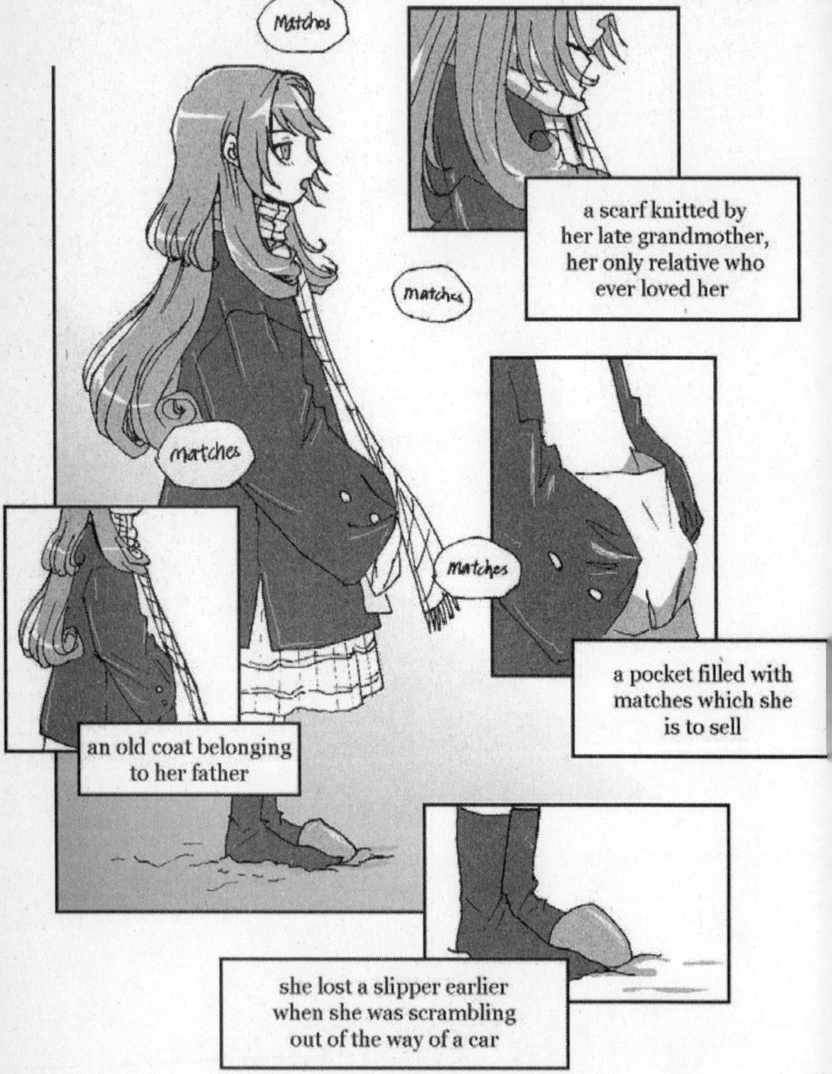
Matches
a scarf knitted by her late grandmother, her only relative who ever loved her
matches
matches
Matches
a pocket filled with matches which she is to sell
an old coat belonging to her father
she lost a slipper earlier when she was scrambling out of the way of a car

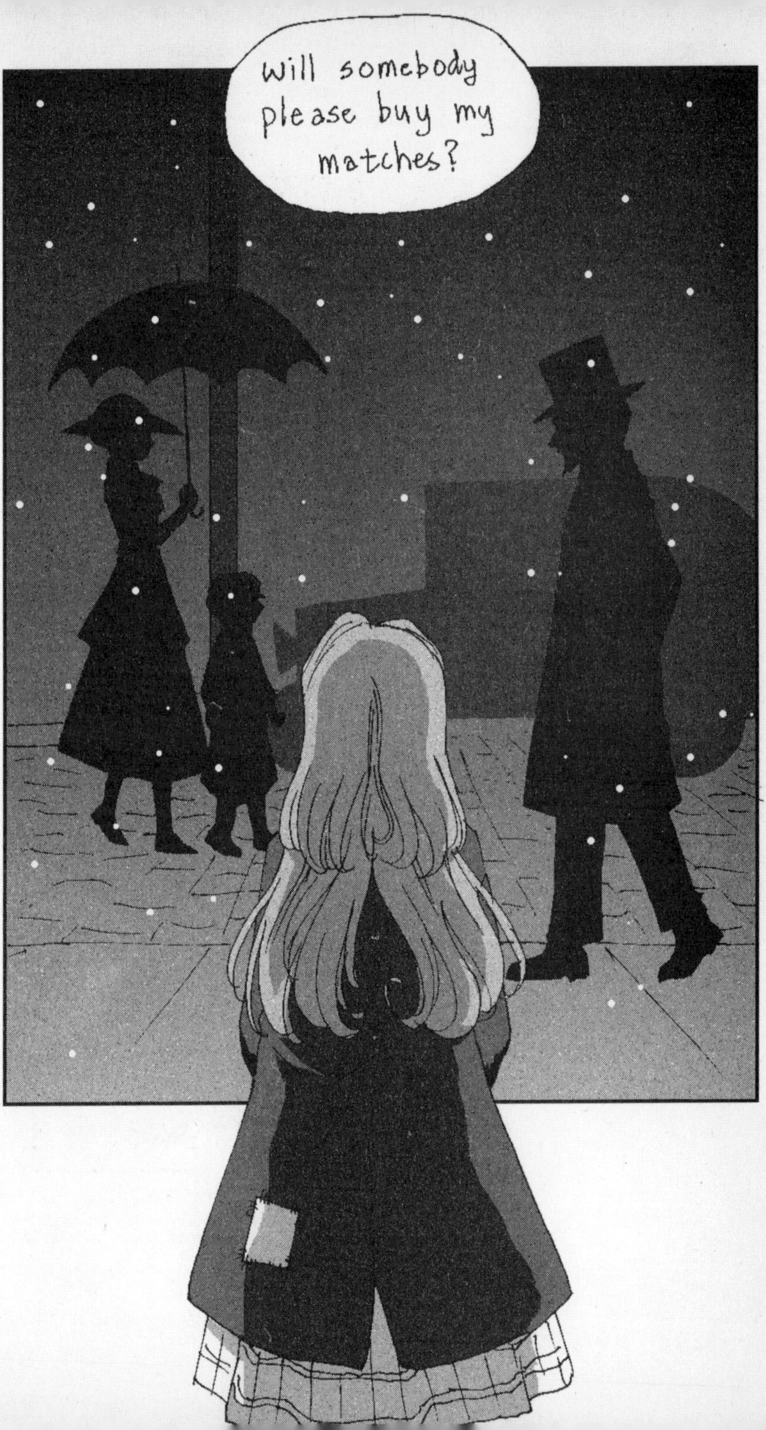
will somebody please buy my matches?

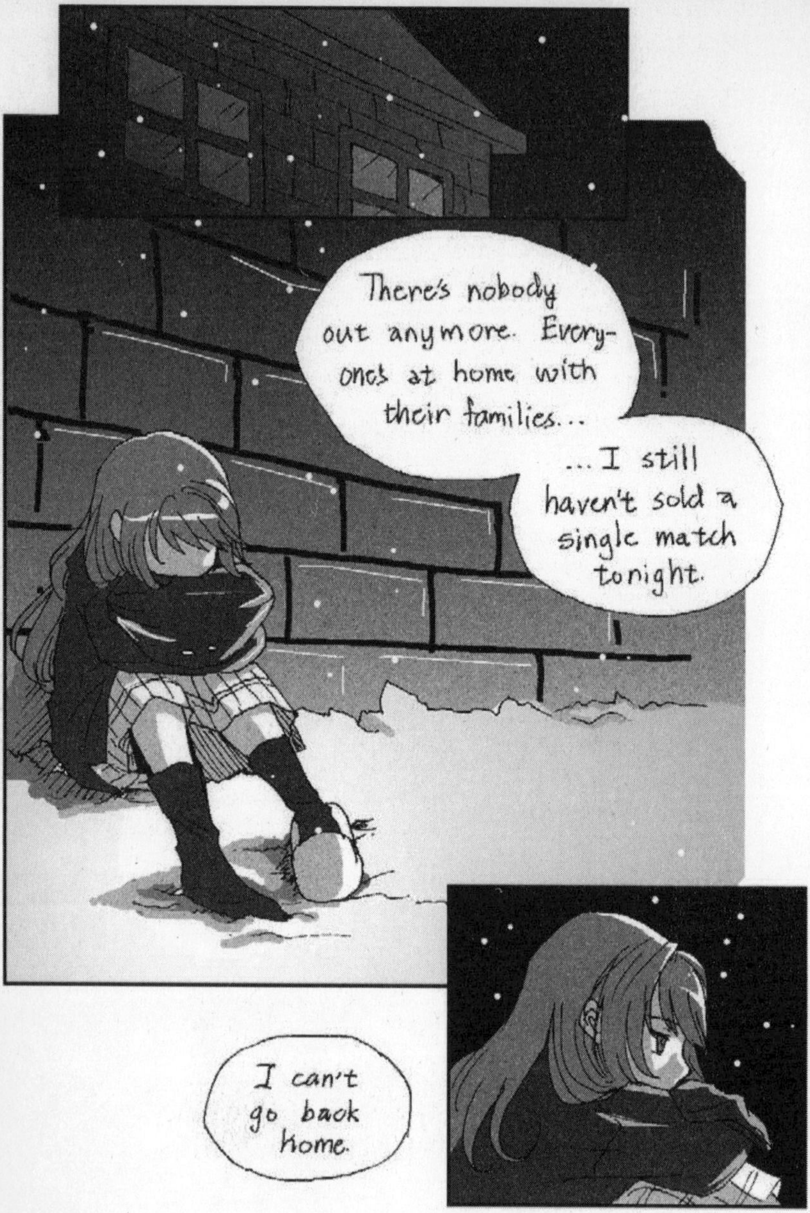
There's nobody out anymore. Every-ones at home with their families...
...I still haven't sold a single match tonight.
I can't go back home.

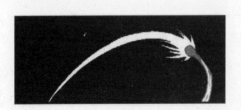

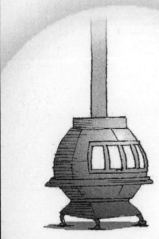

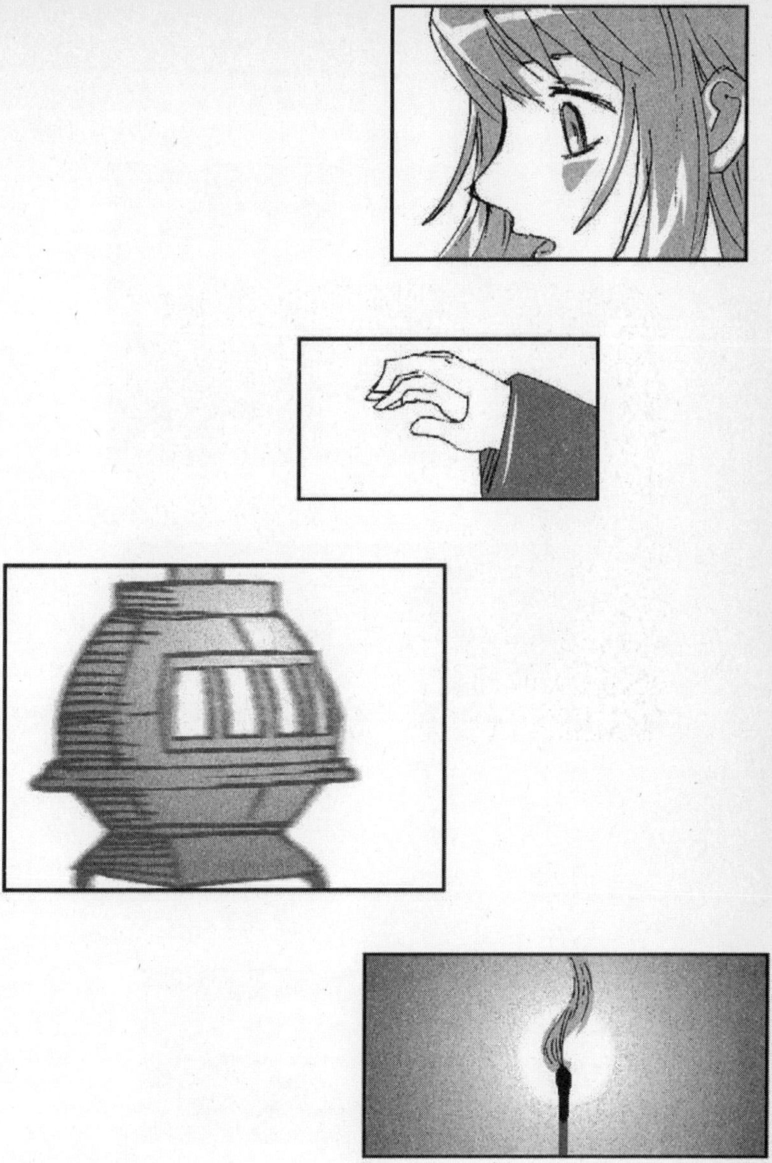

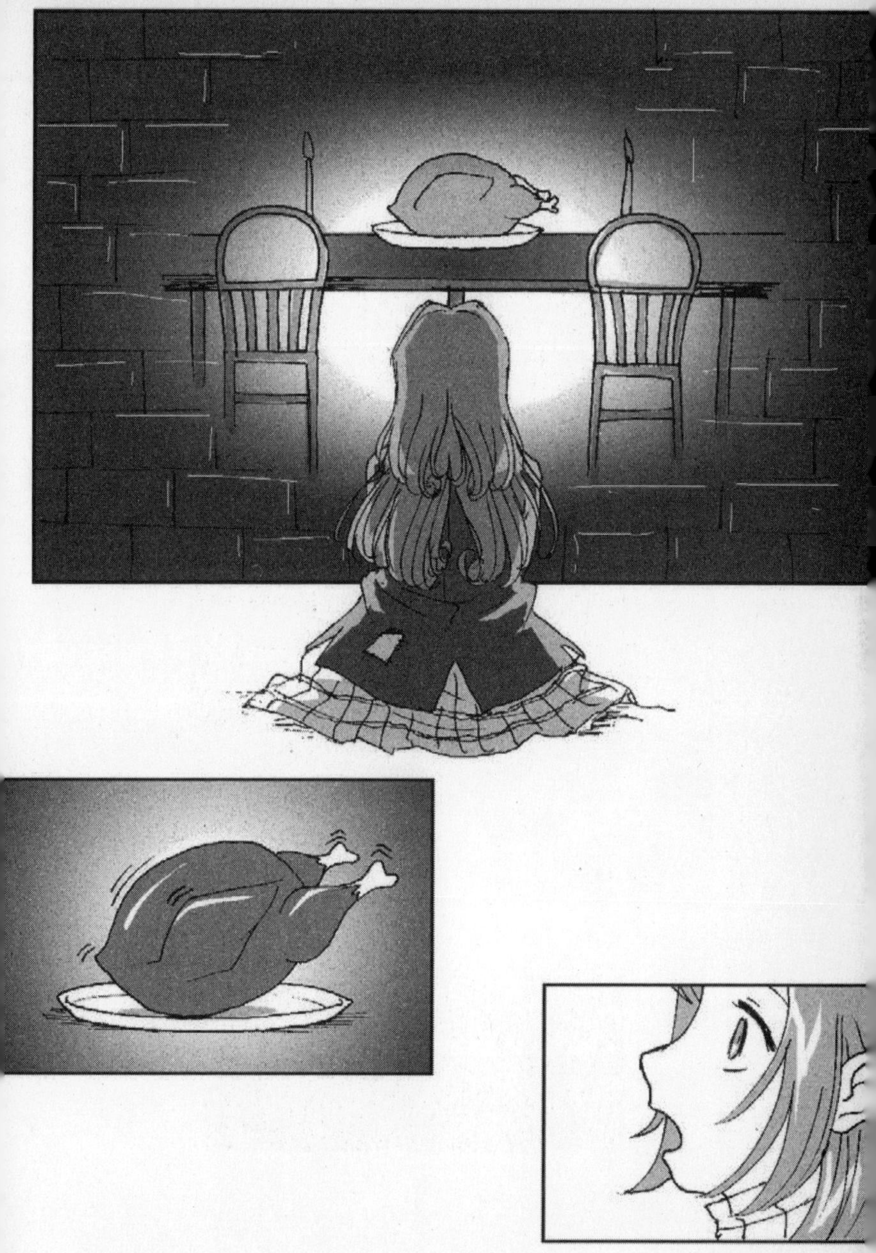

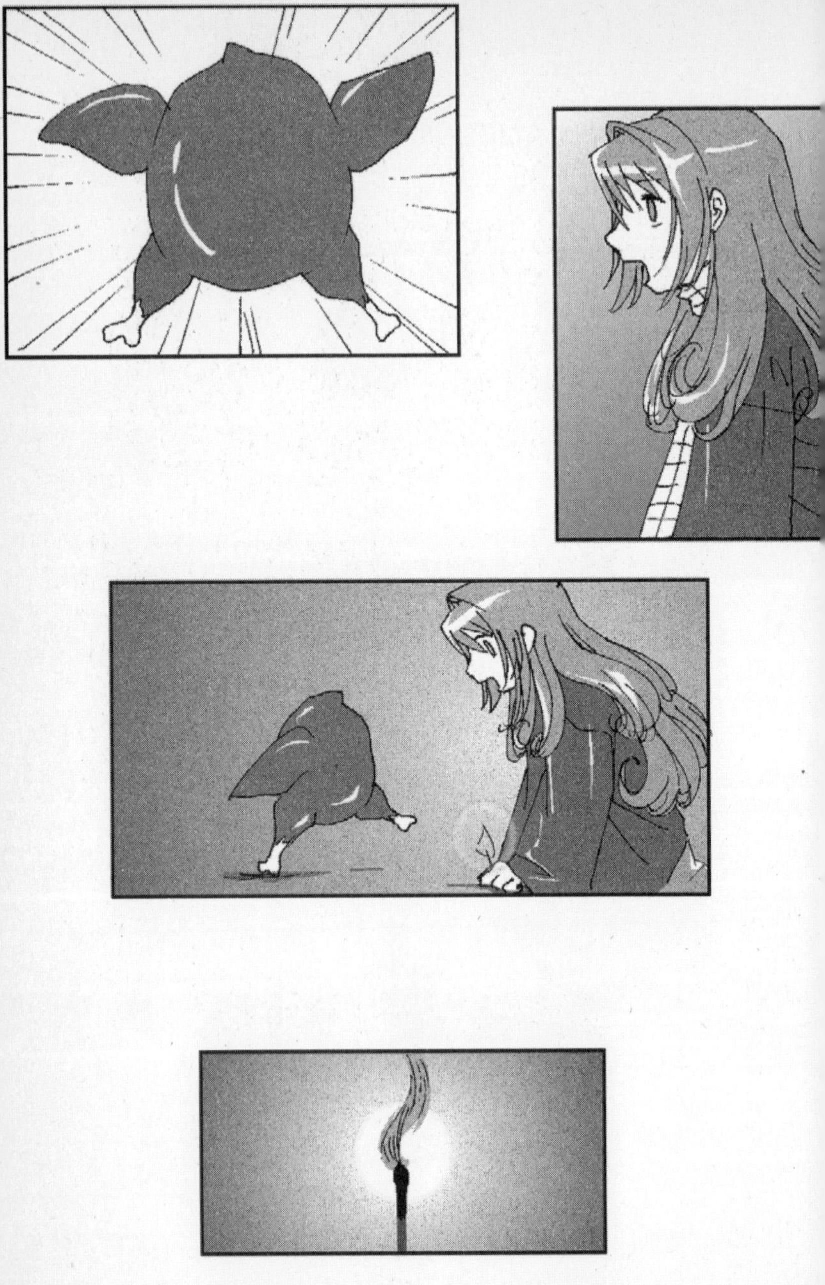

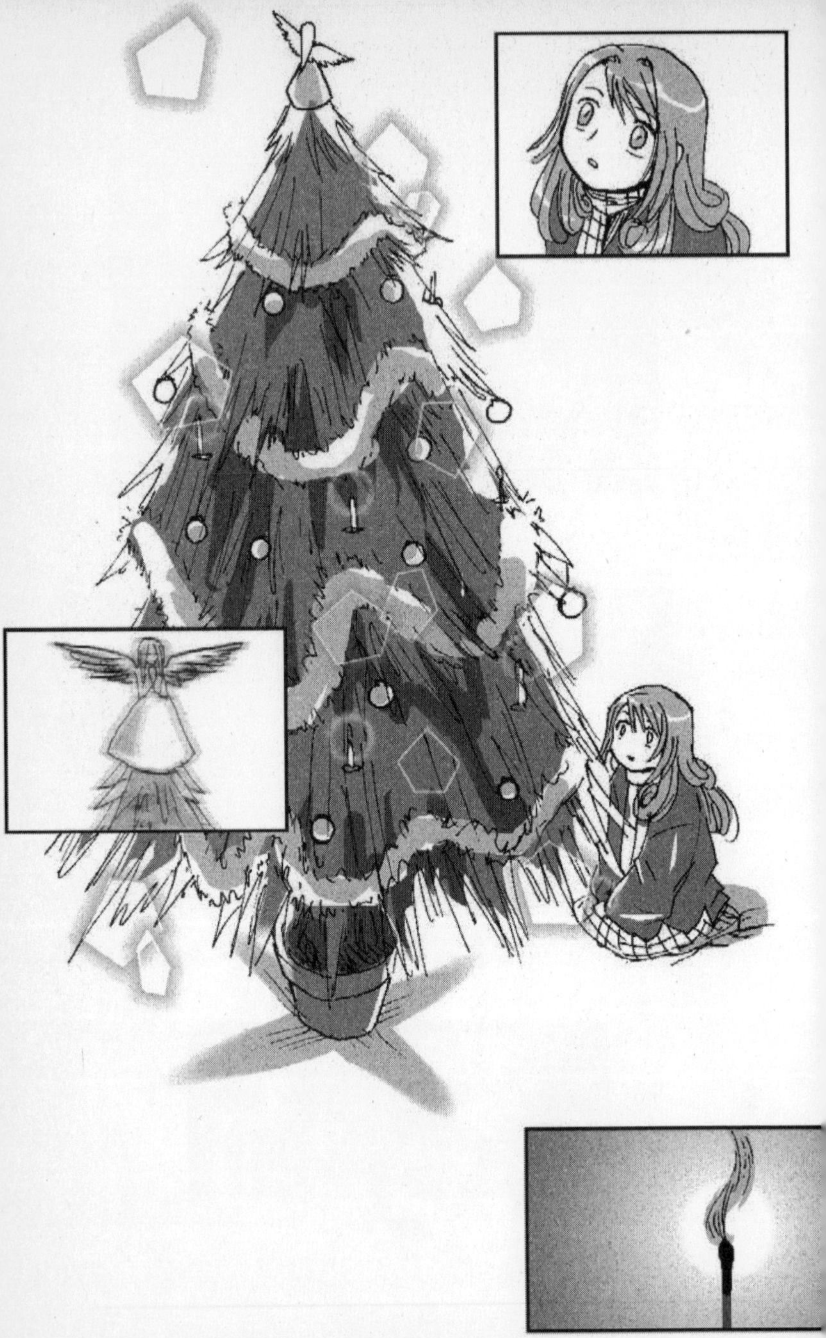

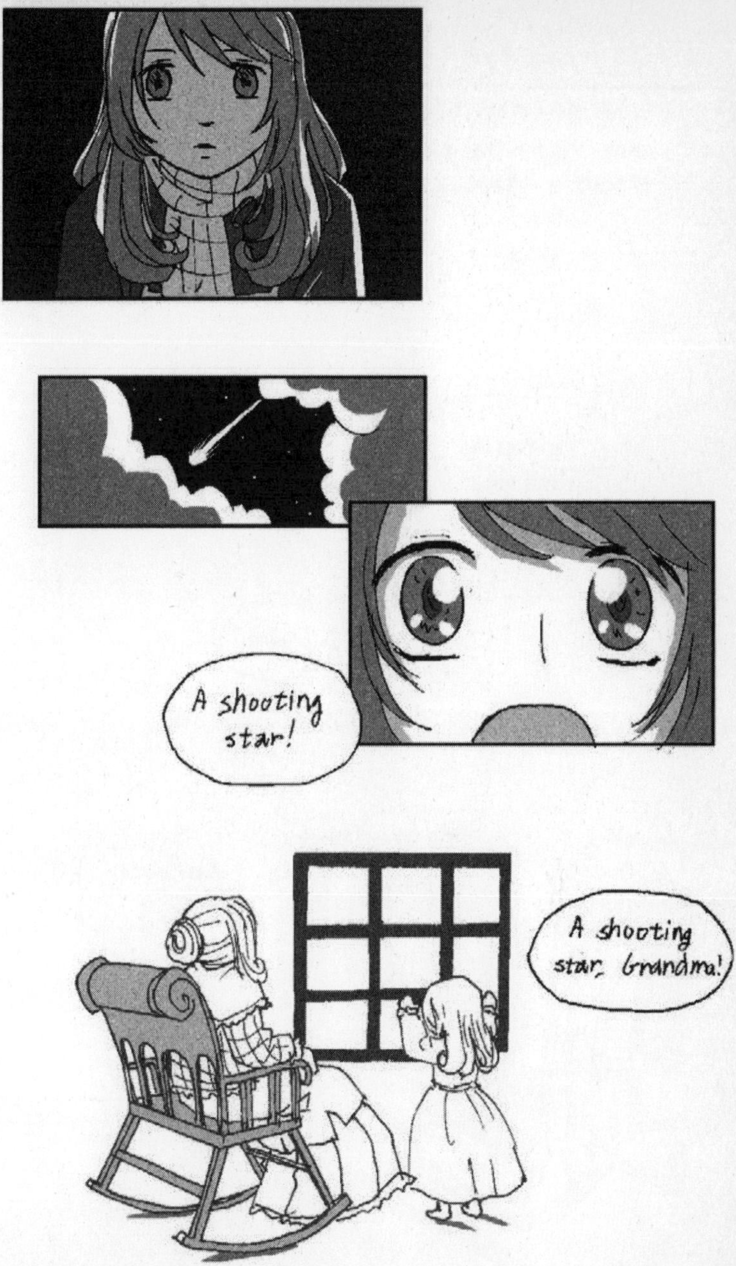
A shooting star!
A shooting star, Grandma!

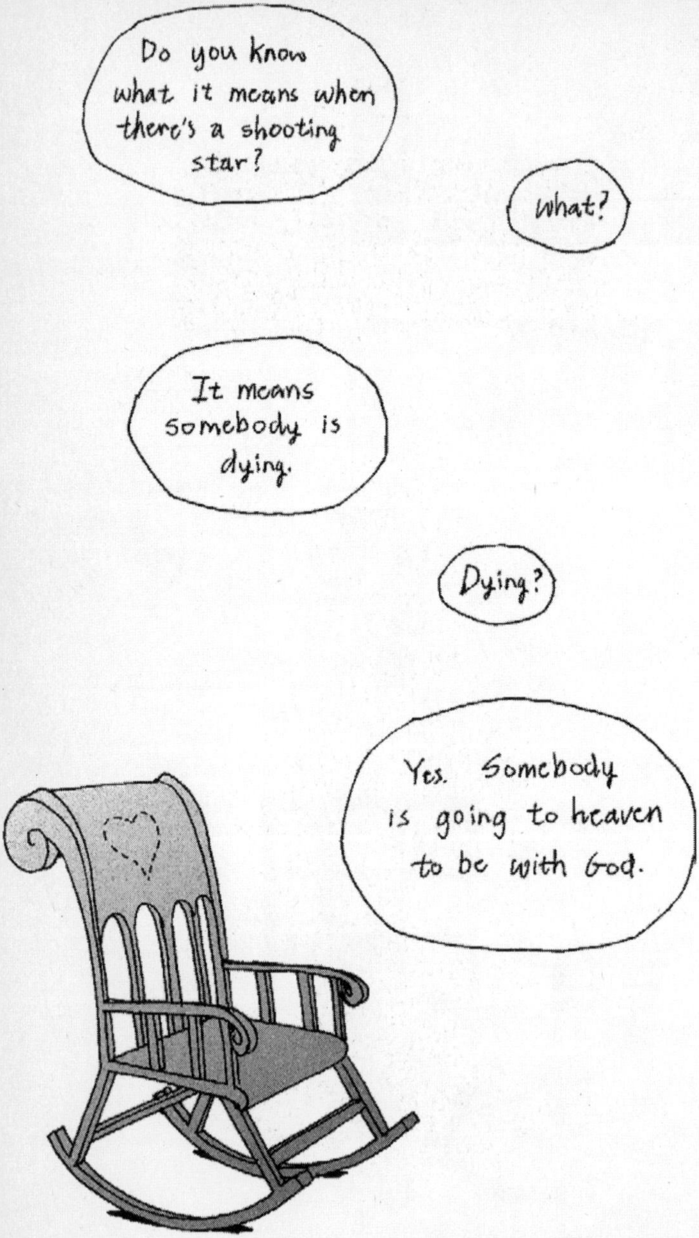
Do you know what it means when there's a shooting star?
What?
It means somebody is dying.
Dying?
Yes. Somebody is going to heaven to be with God.

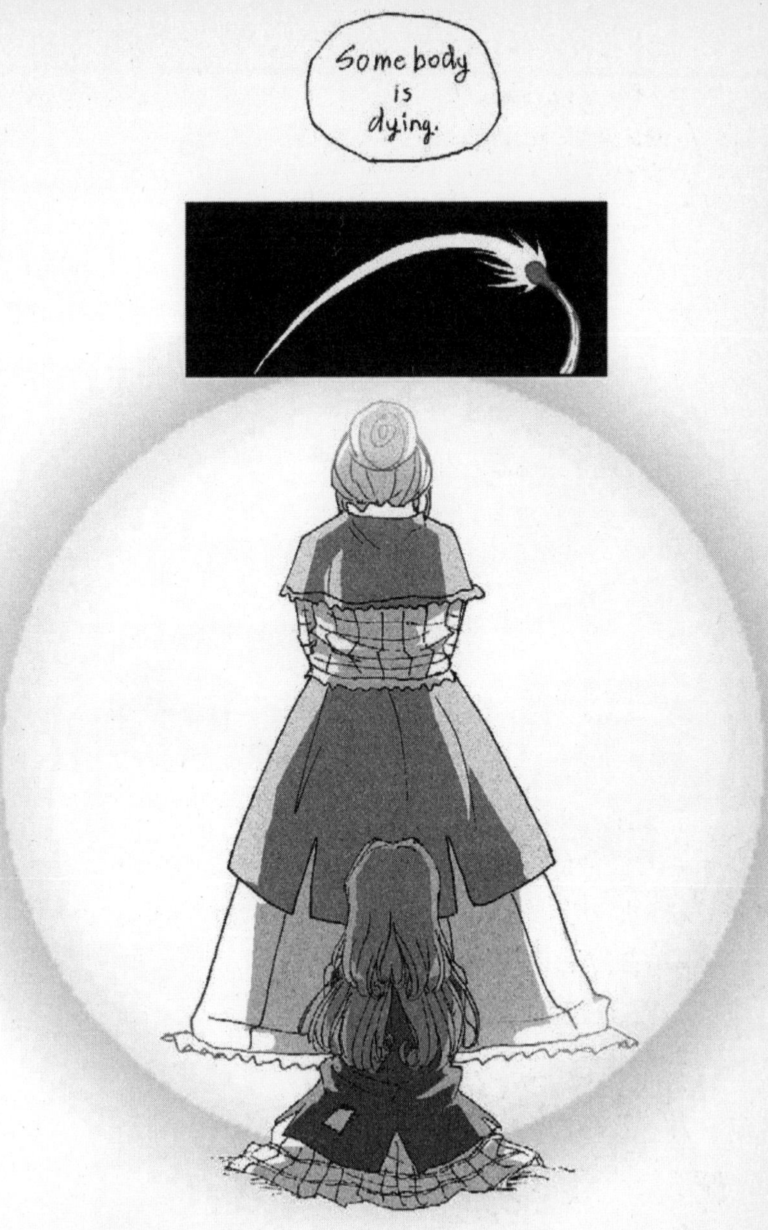
Somebody is dying.

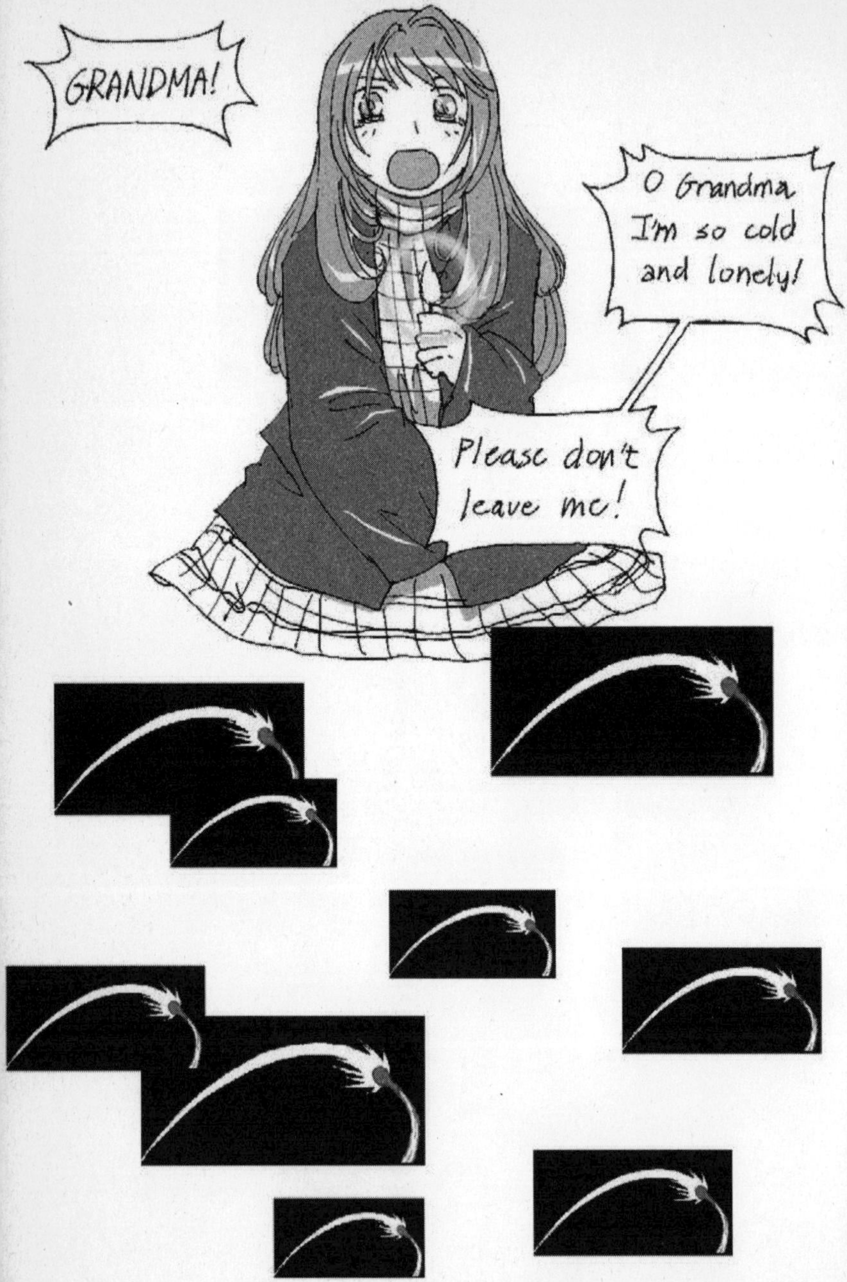
GRANDMA!
O Grandma I'm so cold and lonely!
Please don't leave me!

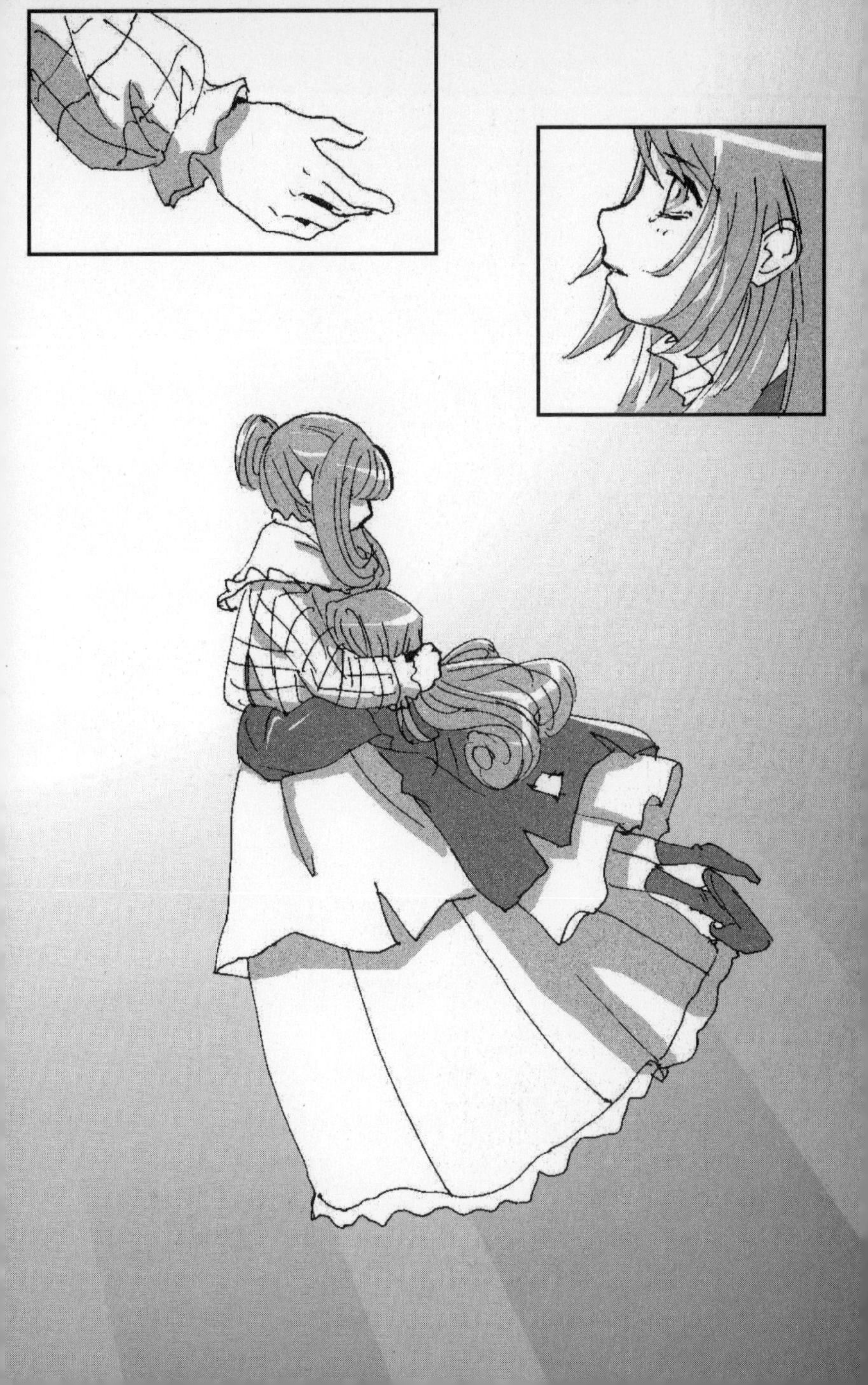

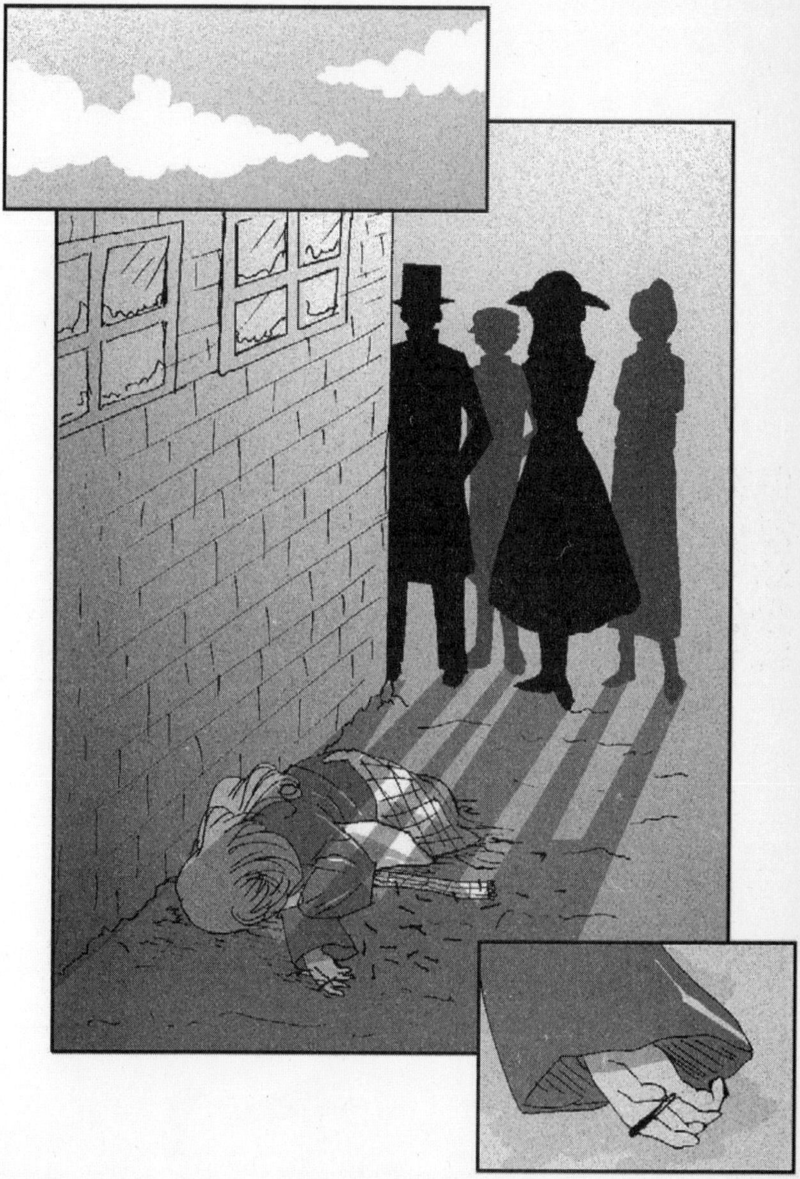

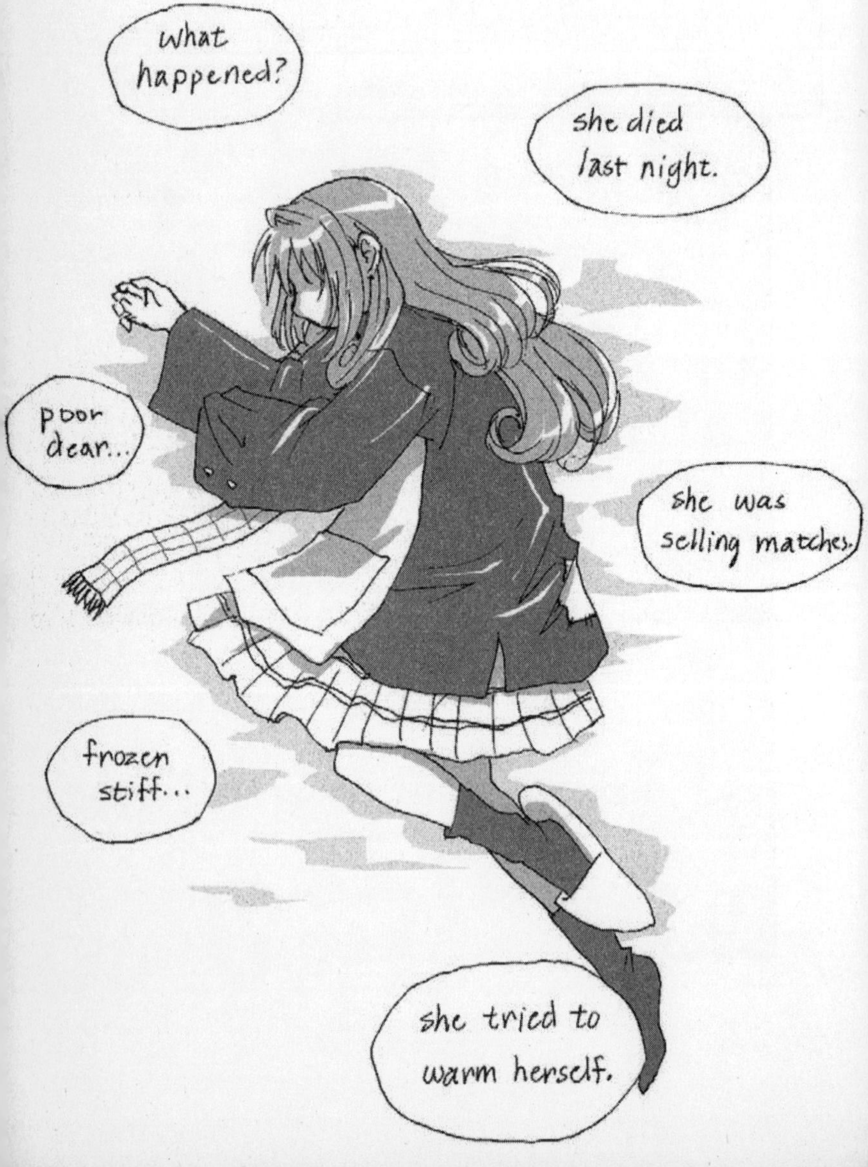
what happened?
she died last night.
poor dear...
she was selling matches.
frozen stiff...
she tried to warm herself.

fin

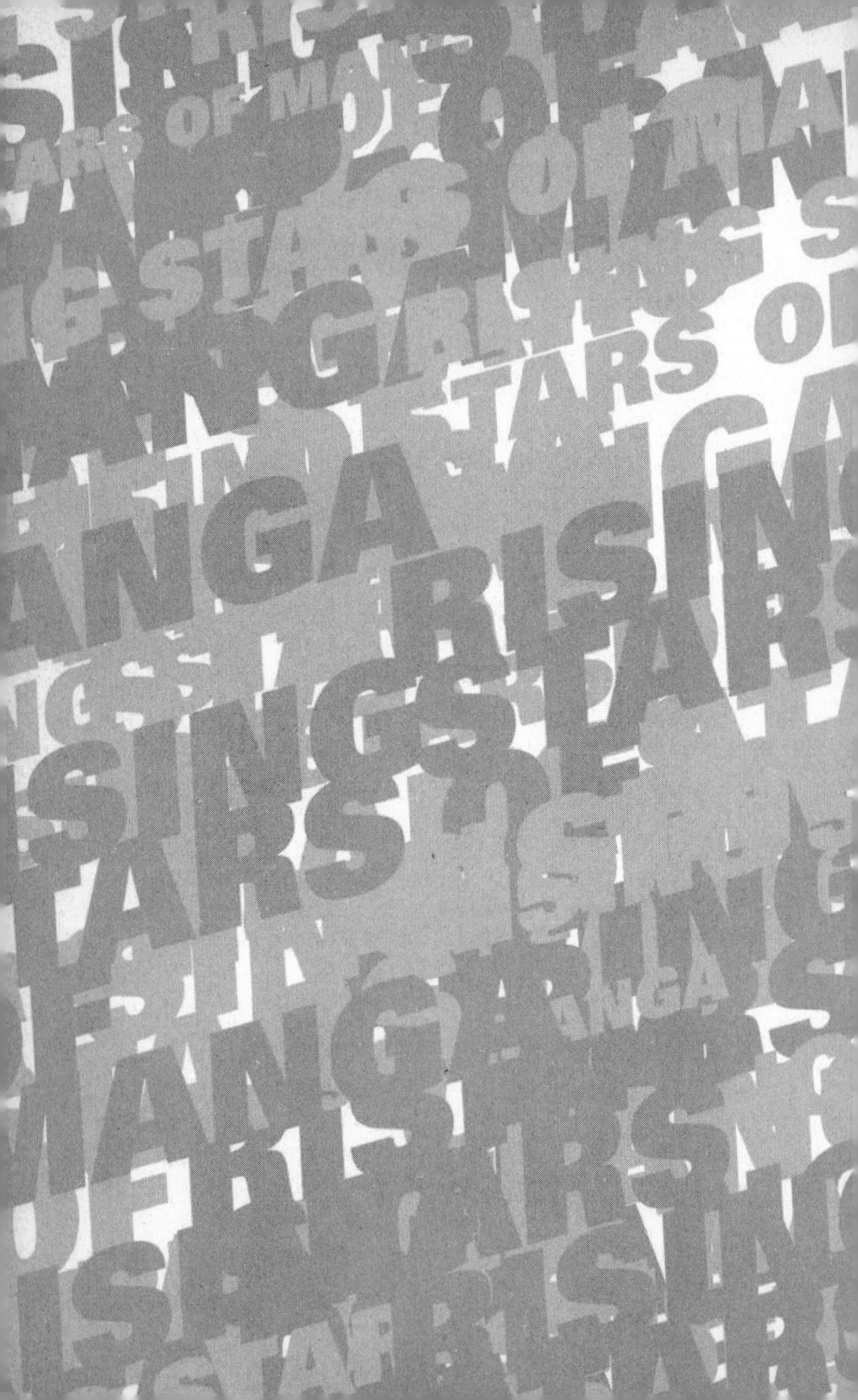

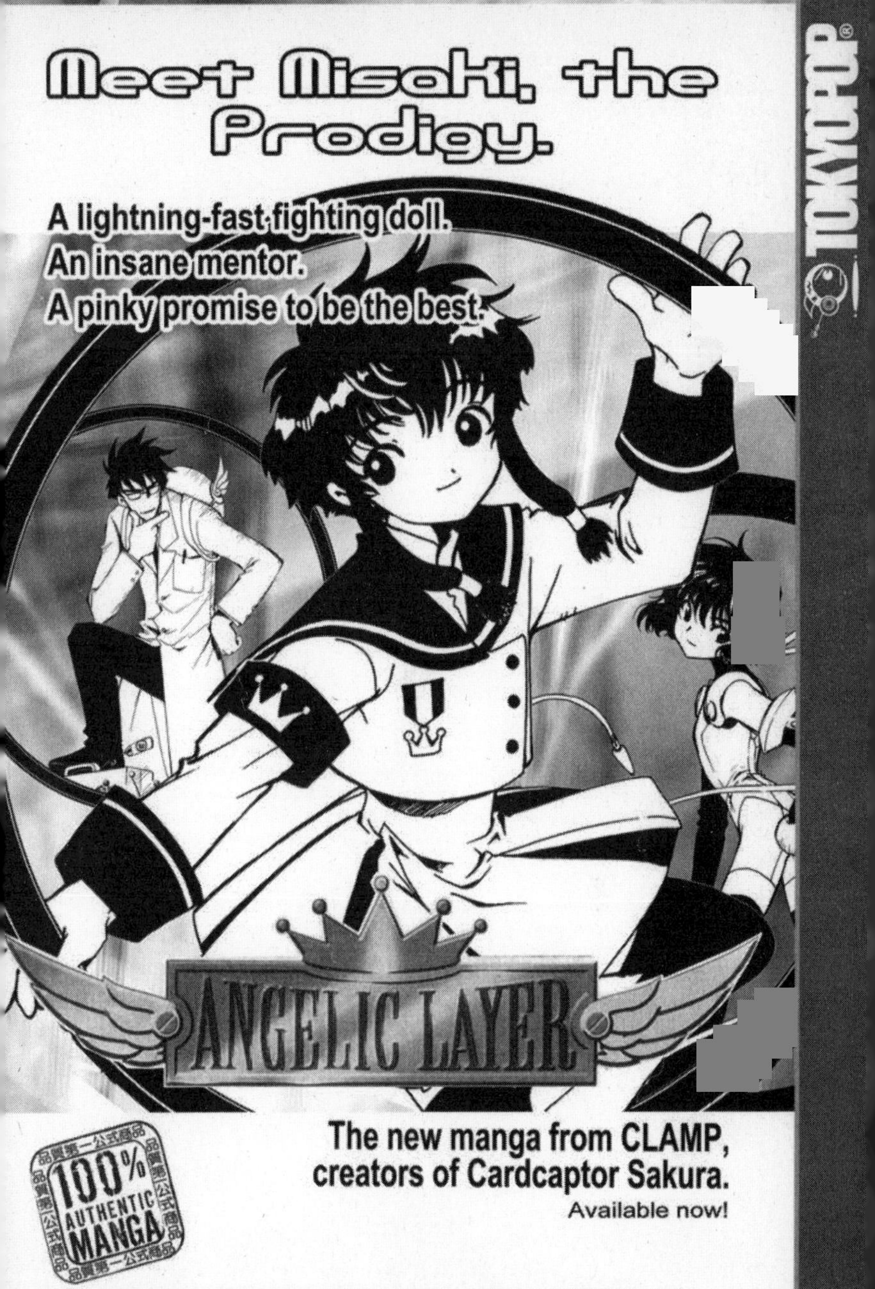
Meet Misaki, the Prodigy.
A lightning-fast fighting doll.
An insane mentor.
A pinky promise to be the best.
ANGELIC LAYER
100% AUTHENTIC MANGA
The new manga from CLAMP, creators of Cardcaptor Sakura.
Available now!
TOKYOPOP

TRICKSTER :: RUNNER UP ::

Bridget E. Wilde was born in 1972 in Marshall, Minnesota, and now lives in Tucson, Arizona, where she's a freelance artist and mom of two daughters, Rachel and Madeline. She spent two years at the University of New Orleans as a fine arts major, but through subsequent years of self-teaching, she's "managed to recover from the damage." Bridget also did the artwork for the first two issues of the fan comic *Purrsia*, published by Purrsia Press Comics.

Inspiration for this story:
I live in Tucson and have a strong interest in folktales and mythology, particularly the "trickster" archetype which is present in so many cultures. I was wondering what modern-day Tricksters might do, and came up with the idea that civil service would allow them to do the most damage. The characters and story grew from there.

Favorite Manga:
Ranma 1/2, Inuyasha, Fruits Basket, Maison Ikkoku, Yami no Matsuei, Video Girl Ai, Detective Conan, Ushio and Tora, Hyper Police

Favorite Manga Artists:
Rumiko Takahashi, Masakazu Katsura, Natsuki Takaya, Youko Matsushita

....

Judge's Comments:
Shojo is a tricky genre to master, but Bridget E. Wilde makes it look effortless in Trickster, her witty, coming-of-age manga short. This promising manga-ka used a nice variety of close-ups and wide-angle shots, and mixed things up by employing a variety of panel shapes and sizes. Her use of screen tones and shading adds even more depth and complexity to her already unique style.

Perhaps the one thing above all else that made Wilde's entry stand out is how she winningly captures the awkwardness of the high school experience. And Trickster features the best kiss of any of our entries. Smooch!
-Julie Taylor

::

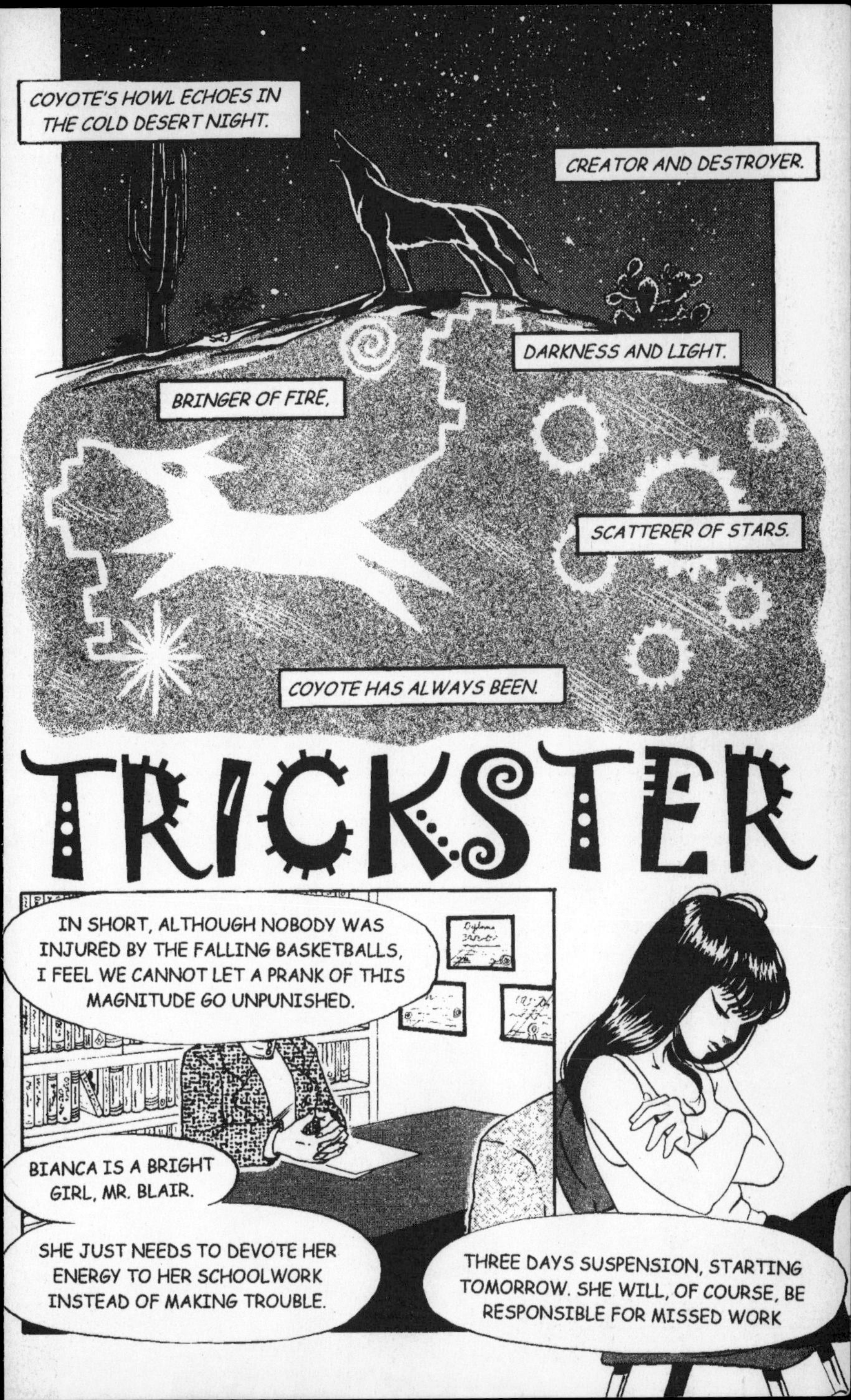
COYOTE'S HOWL ECHOES IN THE COLD DESERT NIGHT.
CREATOR AND DESTROYER.
DARKNESS AND LIGHT.
BRINGER OF FIRE.
SCATTERER OF STARS.
COYOTE HAS ALWAYS BEEN.
TRICKSTER
IN SHORT, ALTHOUGH NOBODY WAS INJURED BY THE FALLING BASKETBALLS, I FEEL WE CANNOT LET A PRANK OF THIS MAGNITUDE GO UNPUNISHED.
BIANCA IS A BRIGHT GIRL, MR. BLAIR.
SHE JUST NEEDS TO DEVOTE HER ENERGY TO HER SCHOOLWORK INSTEAD OF MAKING TROUBLE.
THREE DAYS SUSPENSION, STARTING TOMORROW. SHE WILL, OF COURSE, BE RESPONSIBLE FOR MISSED WORK

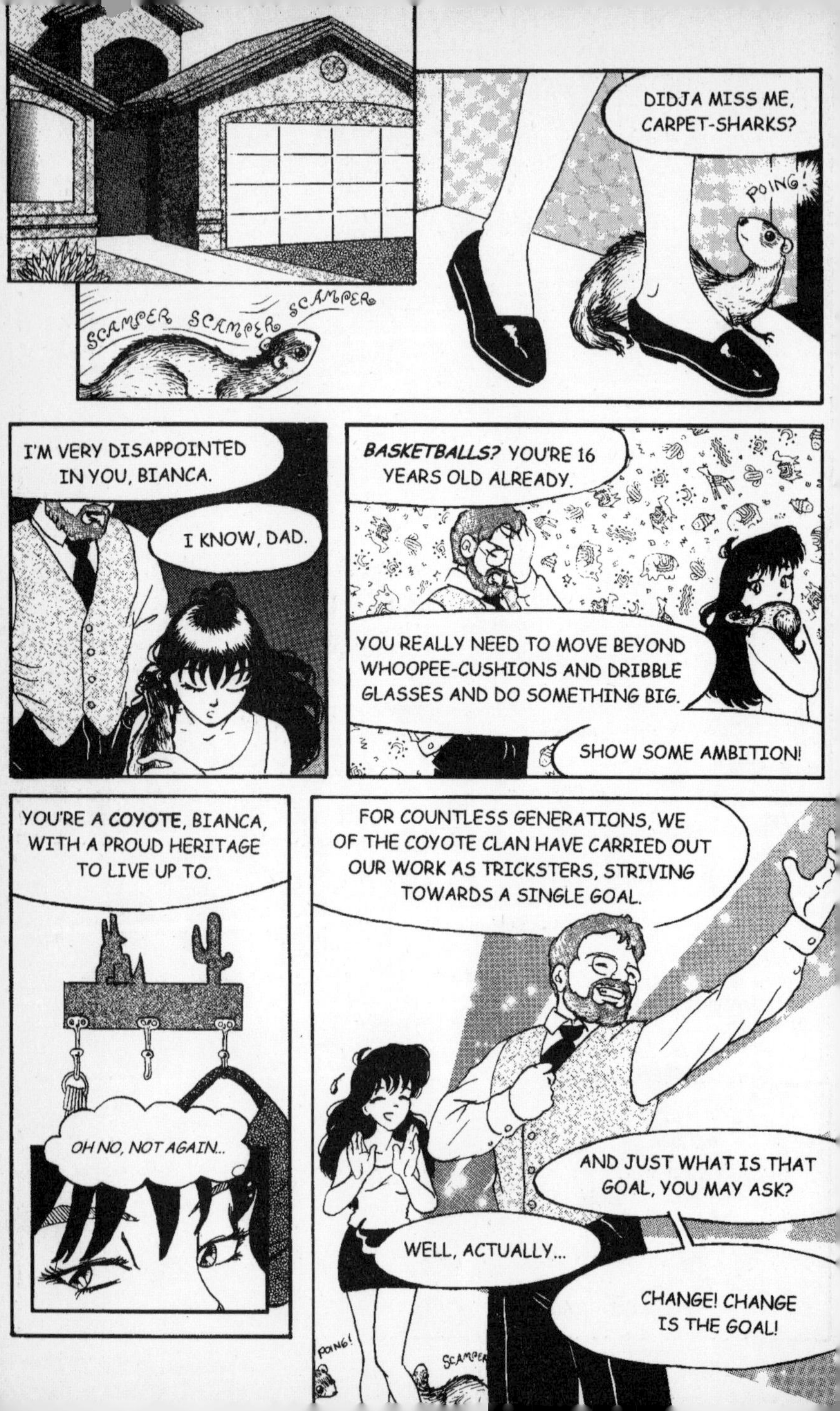
SCAMPER SCAMPER SCAMPER
DIDJA MISS ME, CARPET-SHARKS?
POING!
I'M VERY DISAPPOINTED IN YOU, BIANCA.
I KNOW, DAD.
BASKETBALLS? YOU'RE 16 YEARS OLD ALREADY.
YOU REALLY NEED TO MOVE BEYOND WHOOPEE-CUSHIONS AND DRIBBLE GLASSES AND DO SOMETHING BIG.
SHOW SOME AMBITION!
YOU'RE A **COYOTE**, BIANCA, WITH A PROUD HERITAGE TO LIVE UP TO.
OH NO, NOT AGAIN...
FOR COUNTLESS GENERATIONS, WE OF THE COYOTE CLAN HAVE CARRIED OUT OUR WORK AS TRICKSTERS, STRIVING TOWARDS A SINGLE GOAL.
AND JUST WHAT IS THAT GOAL, YOU MAY ASK?
WELL, ACTUALLY...
CHANGE! CHANGE IS THE GOAL!
POING!
SCAMPER

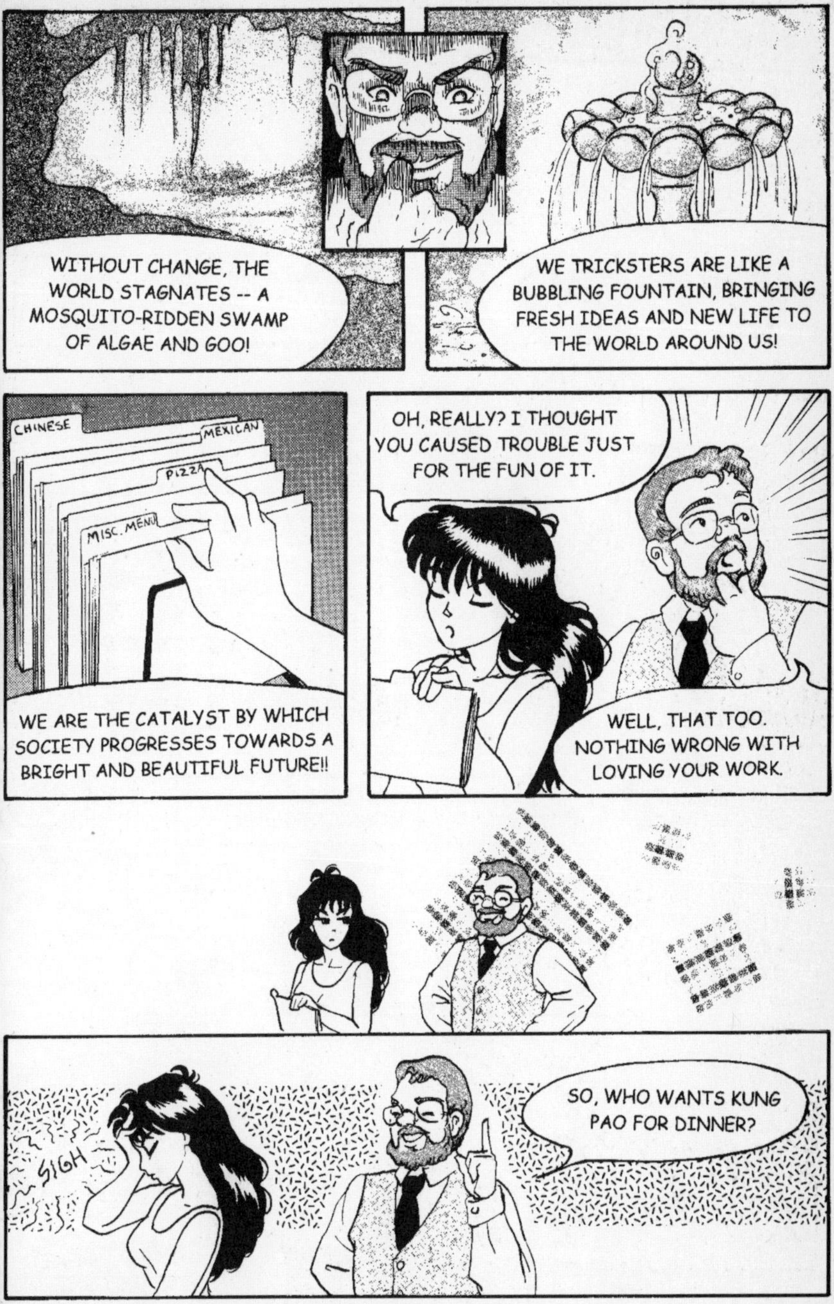
WITHOUT CHANGE, THE WORLD STAGNATES -- A MOSQUITO-RIDDEN SWAMP OF ALGAE AND GOO!
WE TRICKSTERS ARE LIKE A BUBBLING FOUNTAIN, BRINGING FRESH IDEAS AND NEW LIFE TO THE WORLD AROUND US!
CHINESE
MEXICAN
PIZZA
MISC. MENU
WE ARE THE CATALYST BY WHICH SOCIETY PROGRESSES TOWARDS A BRIGHT AND BEAUTIFUL FUTURE!!
OH, REALLY? I THOUGHT YOU CAUSED TROUBLE JUST FOR THE FUN OF IT.
WELL, THAT TOO. NOTHING WRONG WITH LOVING YOUR WORK.
SIGH
SO, WHO WANTS KUNG PAO FOR DINNER?

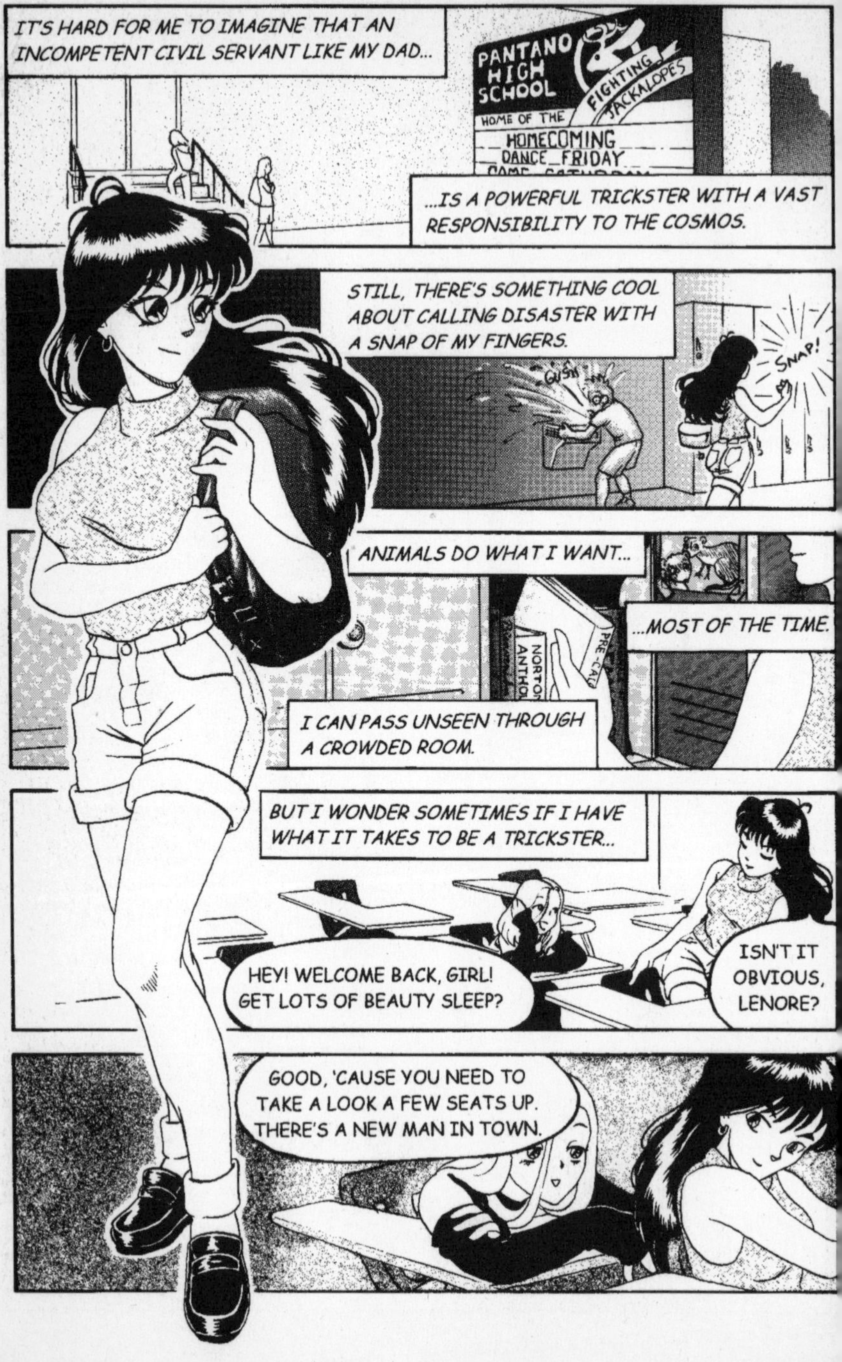
IT'S HARD FOR ME TO IMAGINE THAT AN INCOMPETENT CIVIL SERVANT LIKE MY DAD...
PANTANO HIGH SCHOOL
HOME OF THE FIGHTING JACKALOPES
HOMECOMING
DANCE FRIDAY
...IS A POWERFUL TRICKSTER WITH A VAST RESPONSIBILITY TO THE COSMOS.
STILL, THERE'S SOMETHING COOL ABOUT CALLING DISASTER WITH A SNAP OF MY FINGERS.
GUSH
SNAP!
ANIMALS DO WHAT I WANT...
...MOST OF THE TIME.
I CAN PASS UNSEEN THROUGH A CROWDED ROOM.
BUT I WONDER SOMETIMES IF I HAVE WHAT IT TAKES TO BE A TRICKSTER...
HEY! WELCOME BACK, GIRL! GET LOTS OF BEAUTY SLEEP?
ISN'T IT OBVIOUS, LENORE?
GOOD, 'CAUSE YOU NEED TO TAKE A LOOK A FEW SEATS UP. THERE'S A NEW MAN IN TOWN.

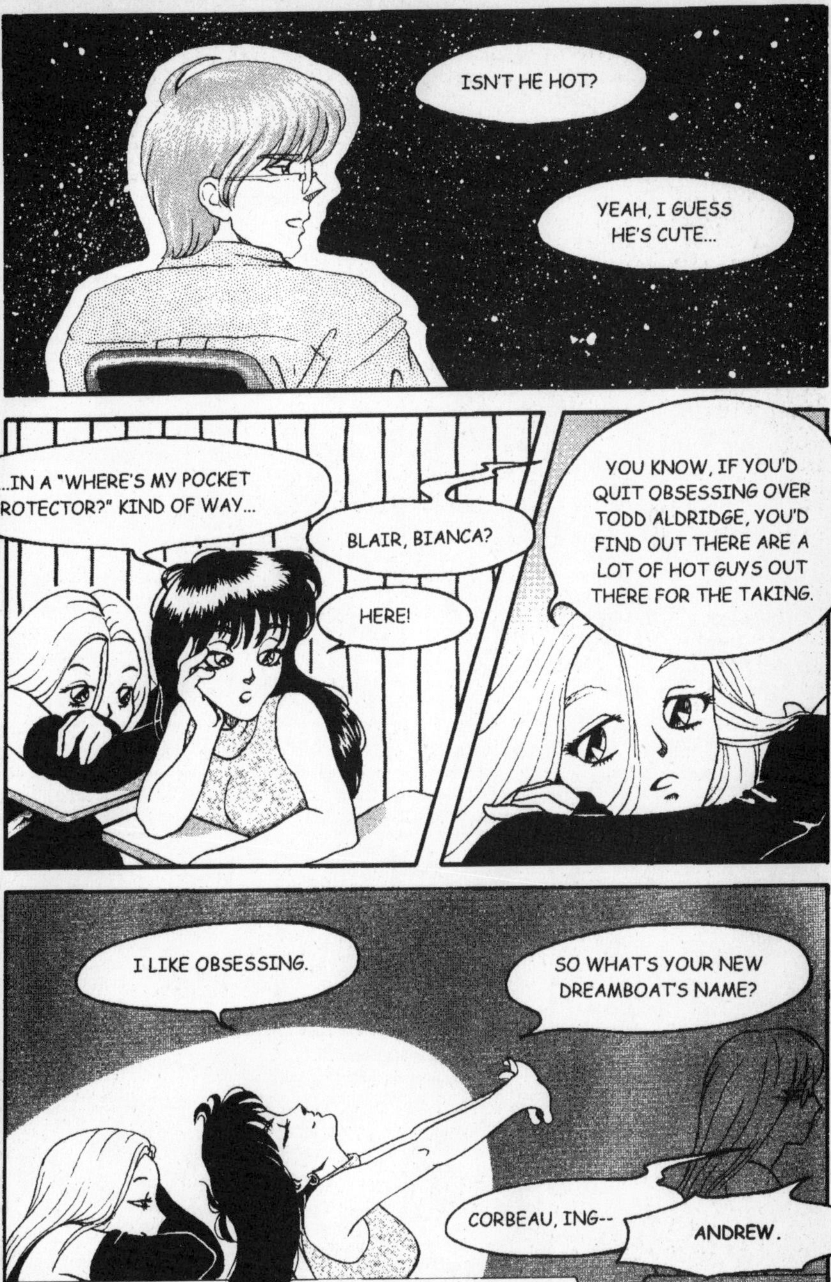
ISN'T HE HOT?
YEAH, I GUESS HE'S CUTE...
...IN A "WHERE'S MY POCKET PROTECTOR?" KIND OF WAY...
BLAIR, BIANCA?
HERE!
YOU KNOW, IF YOU'D QUIT OBSESSING OVER TODD ALDRIDGE, YOU'D FIND OUT THERE ARE A LOT OF HOT GUYS OUT THERE FOR THE TAKING.
I LIKE OBSESSING.
SO WHAT'S YOUR NEW DREAMBOAT'S NAME?
CORBEAU, ING--
ANDREW.

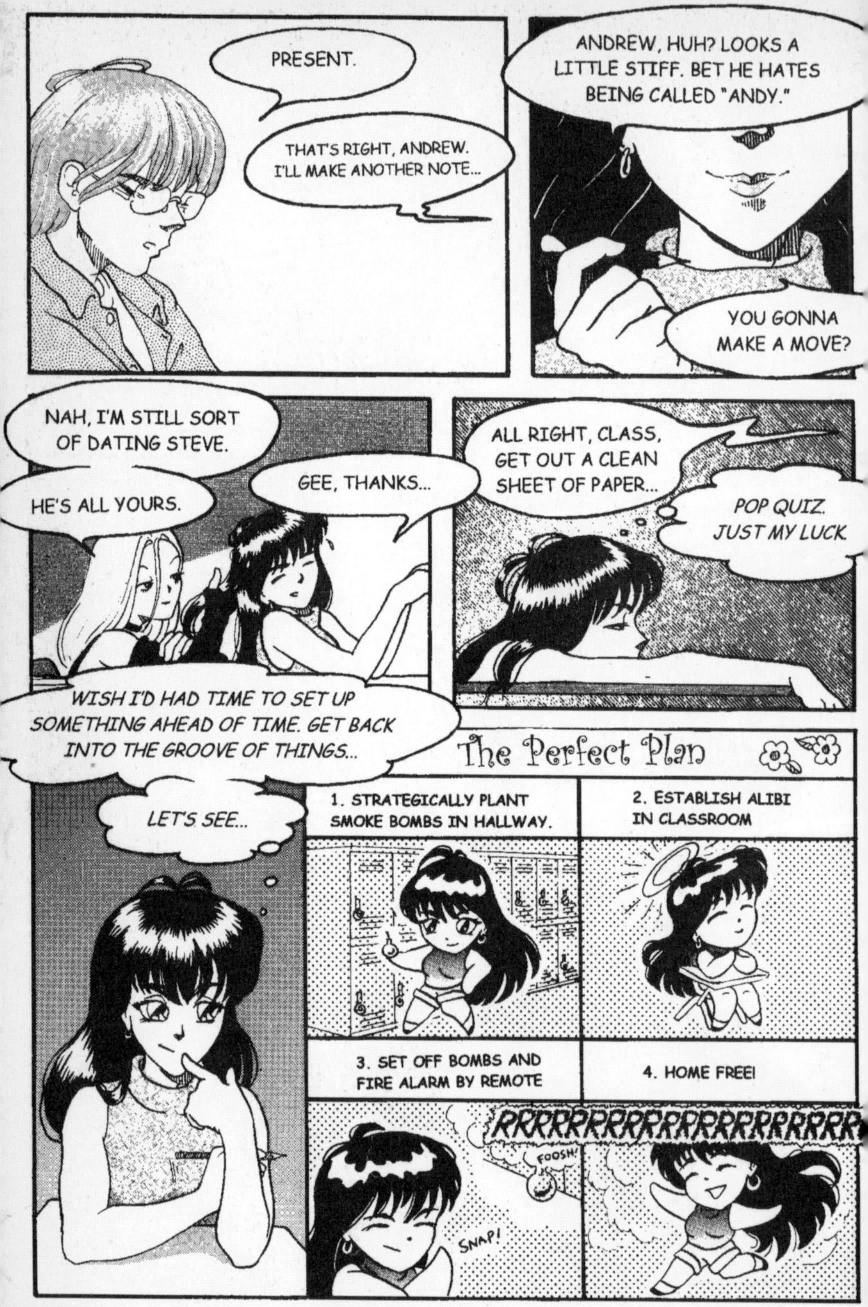
PRESENT.
THAT'S RIGHT, ANDREW. I'LL MAKE ANOTHER NOTE...
ANDREW, HUH? LOOKS A LITTLE STIFF. BET HE HATES BEING CALLED "ANDY."
YOU GONNA MAKE A MOVE?
NAH, I'M STILL SORT OF DATING STEVE.
HE'S ALL YOURS.
GEE, THANKS...
ALL RIGHT, CLASS, GET OUT A CLEAN SHEET OF PAPER...
POP QUIZ. JUST MY LUCK.
WISH I'D HAD TIME TO SET UP SOMETHING AHEAD OF TIME. GET BACK INTO THE GROOVE OF THINGS...
LET'S SEE...
The Perfect Plan
1. STRATEGICALLY PLANT SMOKE BOMBS IN HALLWAY.
2. ESTABLISH ALIBI IN CLASSROOM
3. SET OFF BOMBS AND FIRE ALARM BY REMOTE
4. HOME FREE!
RRRRRRRRRRRRRRRRRRRRRR
FOOSH!
SNAP!

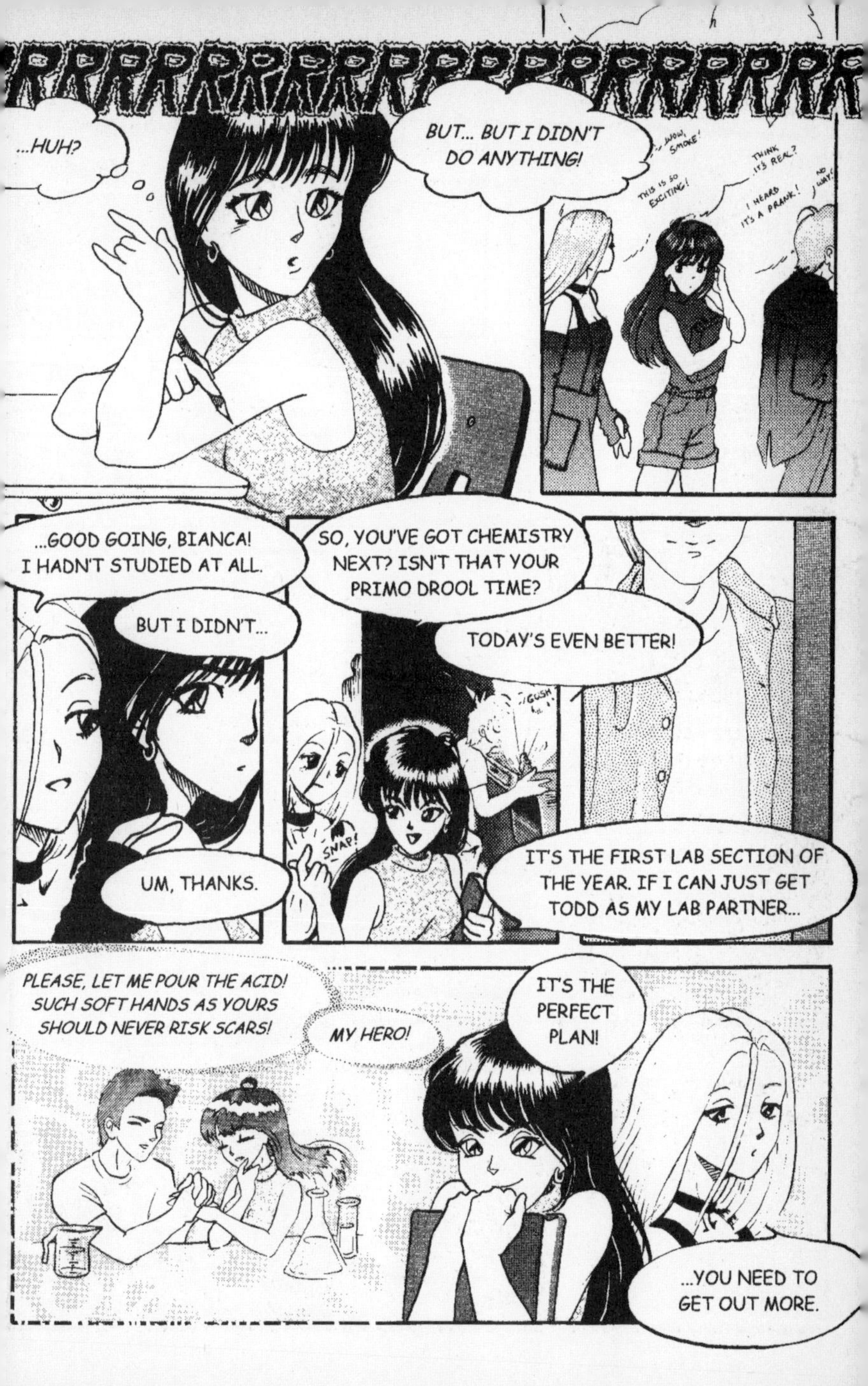
RRRRRRRRRRRRRRRRRRRRRRRR
...HUH?
BUT... BUT I DIDN'T DO ANYTHING!
WOW, SMOKE!
THIS IS SO EXCITING!
THINK IT'S REAL?
I HEARD IT'S A PRANK!
NO WAY!
...GOOD GOING, BIANCA! I HADN'T STUDIED AT ALL.
BUT I DIDN'T...
UM, THANKS.
SO, YOU'VE GOT CHEMISTRY NEXT? ISN'T THAT YOUR PRIMO DROOL TIME?
SNAP!
GUSH
TODAY'S EVEN BETTER!
IT'S THE FIRST LAB SECTION OF THE YEAR. IF I CAN JUST GET TODD AS MY LAB PARTNER...
PLEASE, LET ME POUR THE ACID! SUCH SOFT HANDS AS YOURS SHOULD NEVER RISK SCARS!
MY HERO!
IT'S THE PERFECT PLAN!
...YOU NEED TO GET OUT MORE.

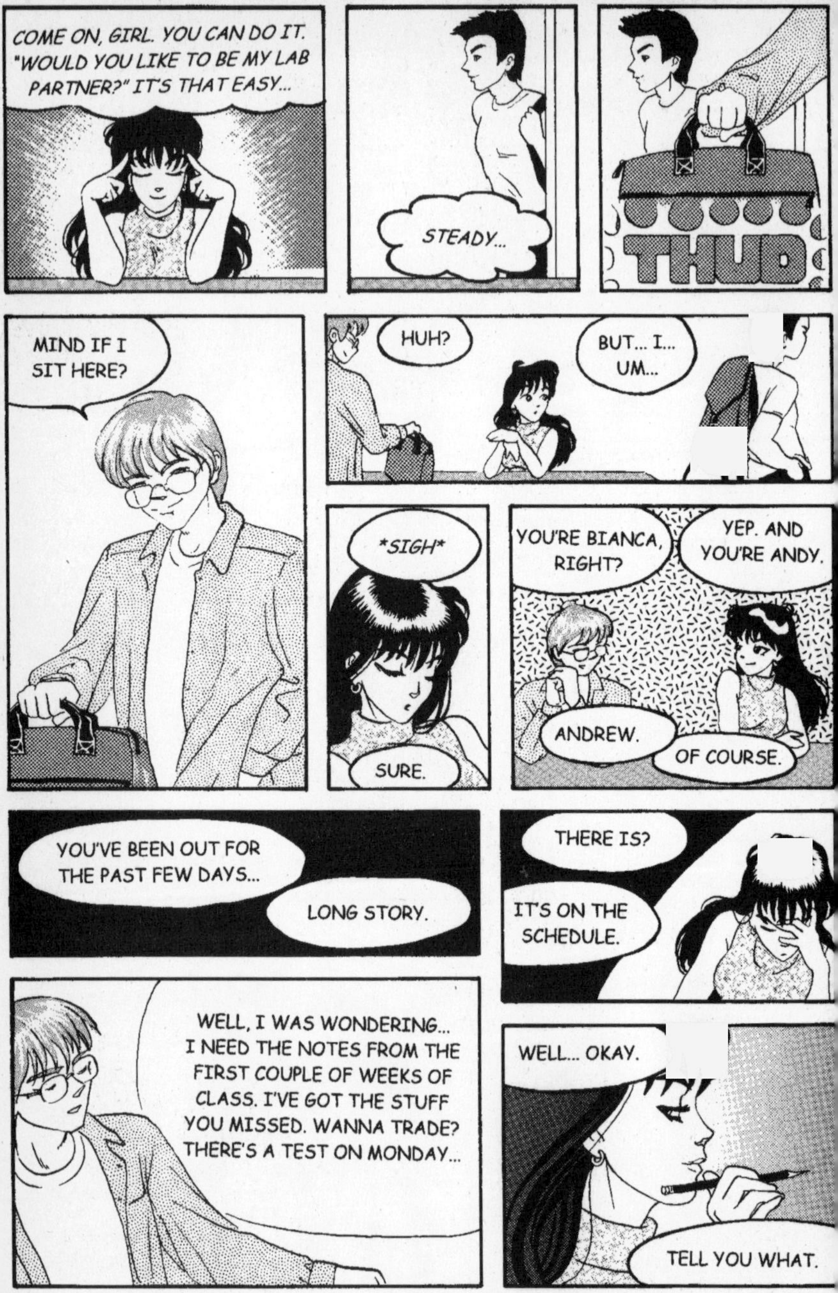
COME ON, GIRL. YOU CAN DO IT. "WOULD YOU LIKE TO BE MY LAB PARTNER?" IT'S THAT EASY...
STEADY...
THUD
MIND IF I SIT HERE?
HUH?
BUT... I... UM...
SIGH
SURE.
YOU'RE BIANCA, RIGHT?
YEP. AND YOU'RE ANDY.
ANDREW.
OF COURSE.
YOU'VE BEEN OUT FOR THE PAST FEW DAYS...
LONG STORY.
WELL, I WAS WONDERING... I NEED THE NOTES FROM THE FIRST COUPLE OF WEEKS OF CLASS. I'VE GOT THE STUFF YOU MISSED. WANNA TRADE? THERE'S A TEST ON MONDAY...
THERE IS?
IT'S ON THE SCHEDULE.
WELL... OKAY.
TELL YOU WHAT.

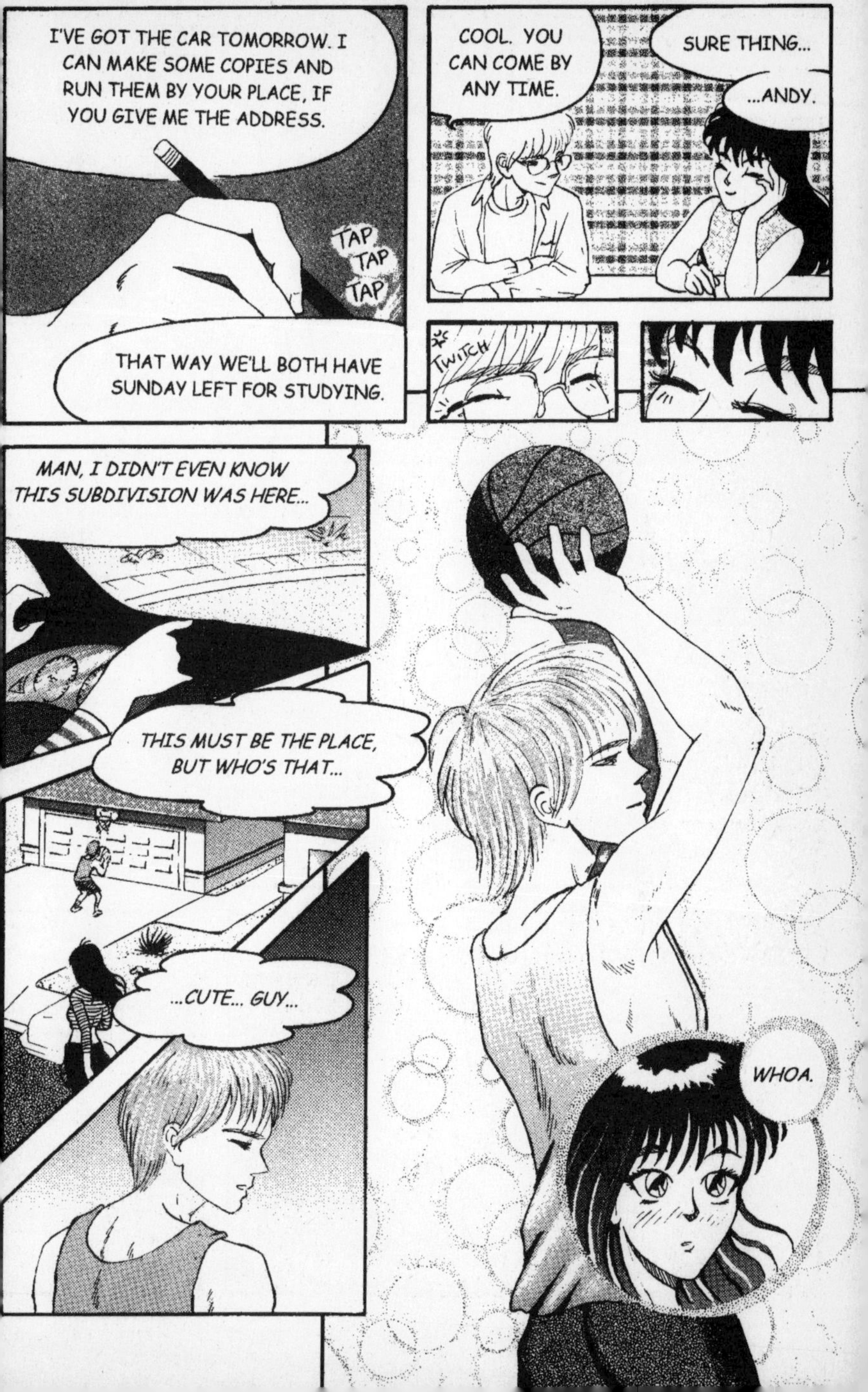
I'VE GOT THE CAR TOMORROW. I CAN MAKE SOME COPIES AND RUN THEM BY YOUR PLACE, IF YOU GIVE ME THE ADDRESS.
TAP TAP TAP
THAT WAY WE'LL BOTH HAVE SUNDAY LEFT FOR STUDYING.
COOL. YOU CAN COME BY ANY TIME.
SURE THING...
...ANDY.
TWITCH
MAN, I DIDN'T EVEN KNOW THIS SUBDIVISION WAS HERE...
THIS MUST BE THE PLACE, BUT WHO'S THAT...
...CUTE... GUY...
WHOA.

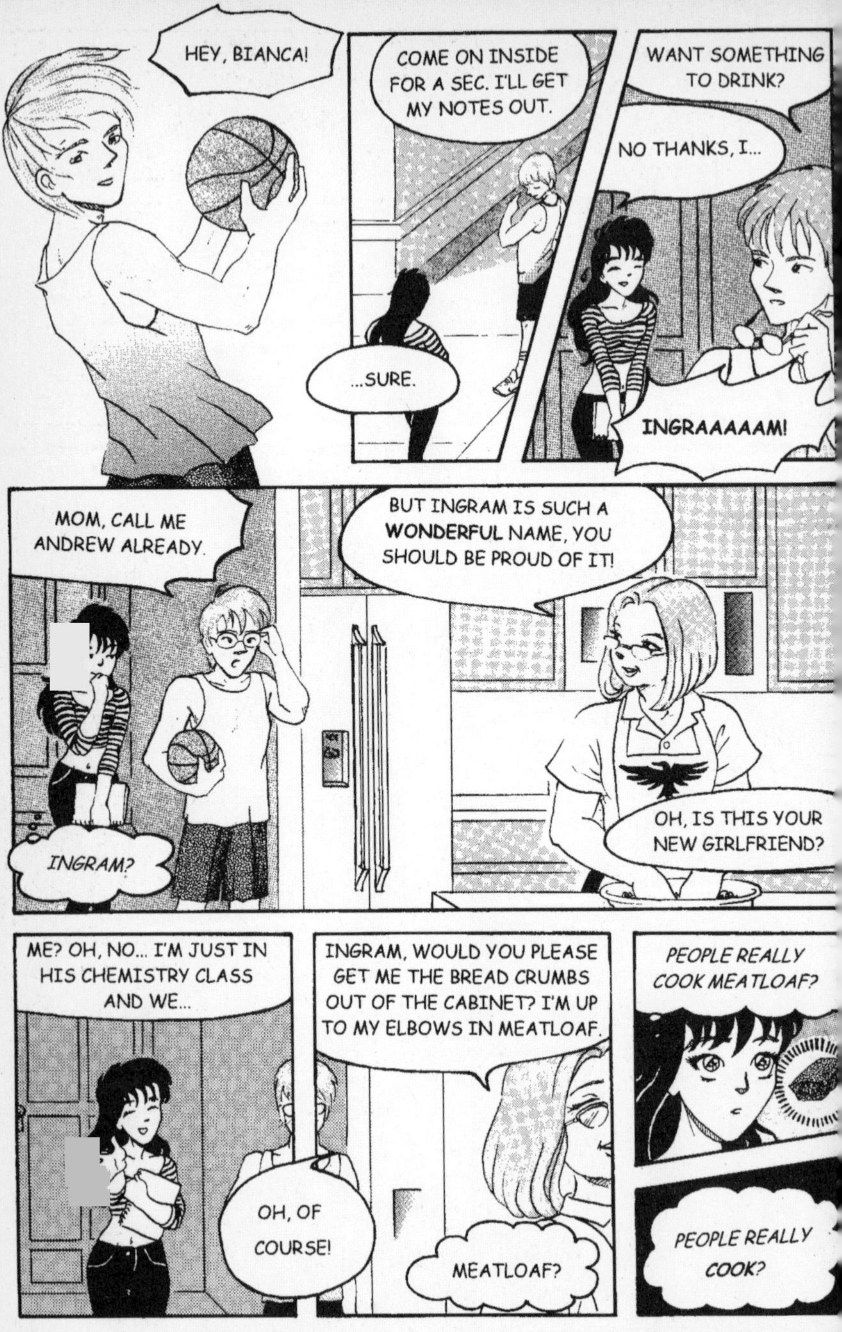
HEY, BIANCA!
COME ON INSIDE FOR A SEC. I'LL GET MY NOTES OUT.
...SURE.
WANT SOMETHING TO DRINK?
NO THANKS, I...
INGRAAAAAM!
MOM, CALL ME ANDREW ALREADY.
INGRAM?
BUT INGRAM IS SUCH A WONDERFUL NAME, YOU SHOULD BE PROUD OF IT!
OH, IS THIS YOUR NEW GIRLFRIEND?
ME? OH, NO... I'M JUST IN HIS CHEMISTRY CLASS AND WE...
INGRAM, WOULD YOU PLEASE GET ME THE BREAD CRUMBS OUT OF THE CABINET? I'M UP TO MY ELBOWS IN MEATLOAF.
OH, OF COURSE!
MEATLOAF?
PEOPLE REALLY COOK MEATLOAF?
PEOPLE REALLY COOK?

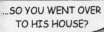

...SO YOU WENT OVER TO HIS HOUSE?
DON'T GET TOO EXCITED ABOUT IT. WE WERE JUST EXCHANGING NOTES.
ANYHOW, MIND BEING MY ALIBI FOR TONIGHT? I'VE GOT A LITTLE PROJECT TO PULL OFF...
MORE BASKETBALLS?
NO, SOMETHING MUCH MORE **VISIONARY** AND **AMBITIOUS**...
...YET DECEPTIVELY SIMPLE.
I'VE GOT ALL THE STUFF RIGHT HERE.
...A RUBBER DUCKY, FISHING LINE, DUCT TAPE, THREE BOBBY PINS, THREE DOZEN EGGS...
...AND A LITTLE MOOD MUSIC.
Stunt
IT'S THE PERFECT PLAN!
CLICK!
PSSSSSSSSHHHT!
CHARLOTT
PRINC
THAT LOOKS DANGEROUS.

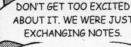

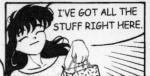

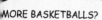

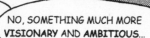

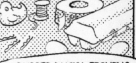

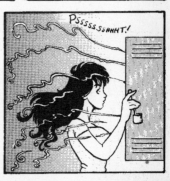

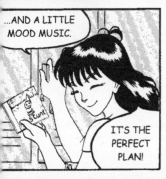

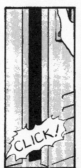

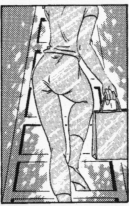

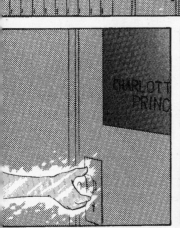

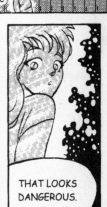

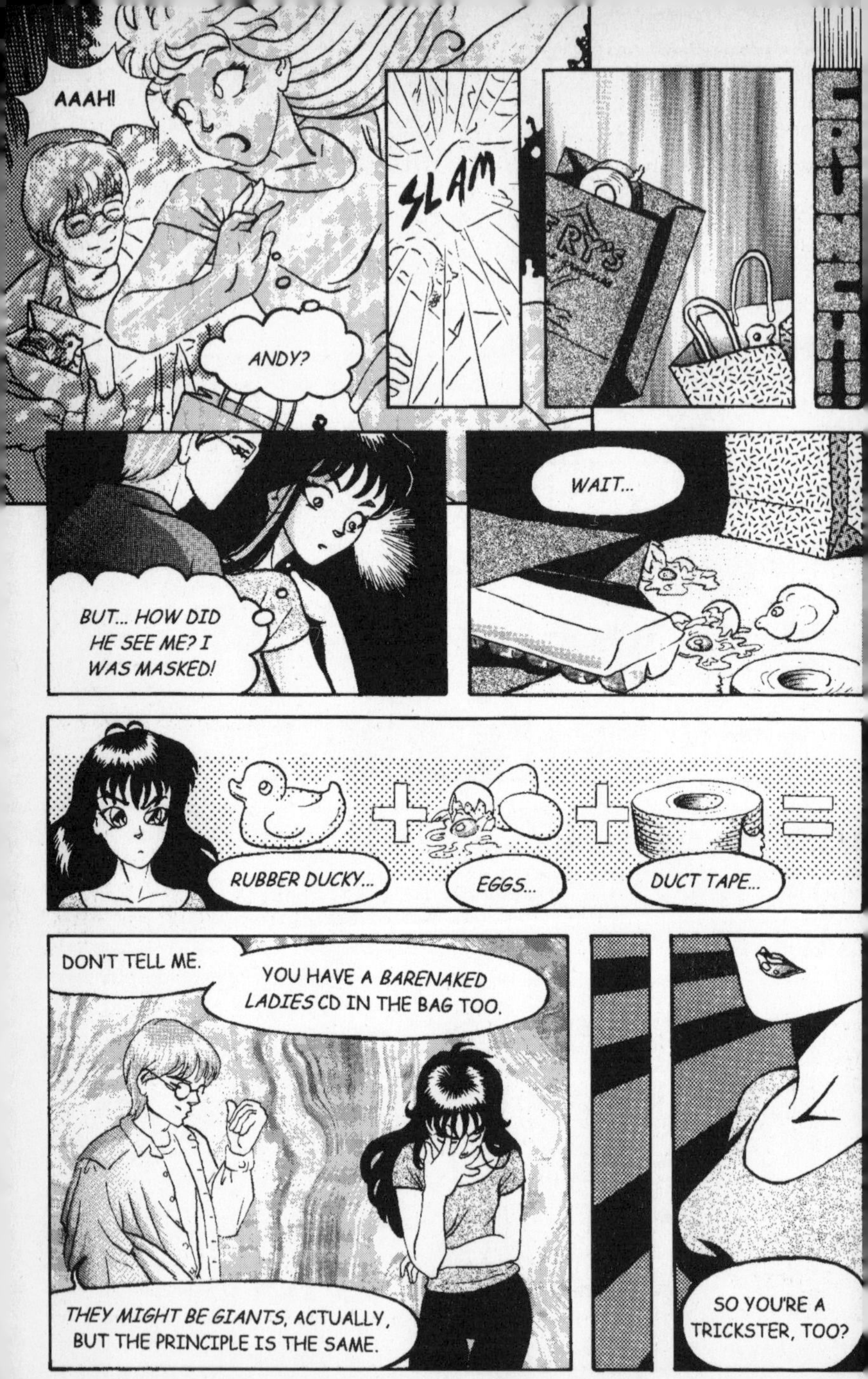
AAAH!
ANDY?
SLAM
CRUNCH!
BUT... HOW DID HE SEE ME? I WAS MASKED!
WAIT...
RUBBER DUCKY...
EGGS...
DUCT TAPE...
DON'T TELL ME.
YOU HAVE A BARENAKED LADIES CD IN THE BAG TOO.
THEY MIGHT BE GIANTS, ACTUALLY, BUT THE PRINCIPLE IS THE SAME.
SO YOU'RE A TRICKSTER, TOO?

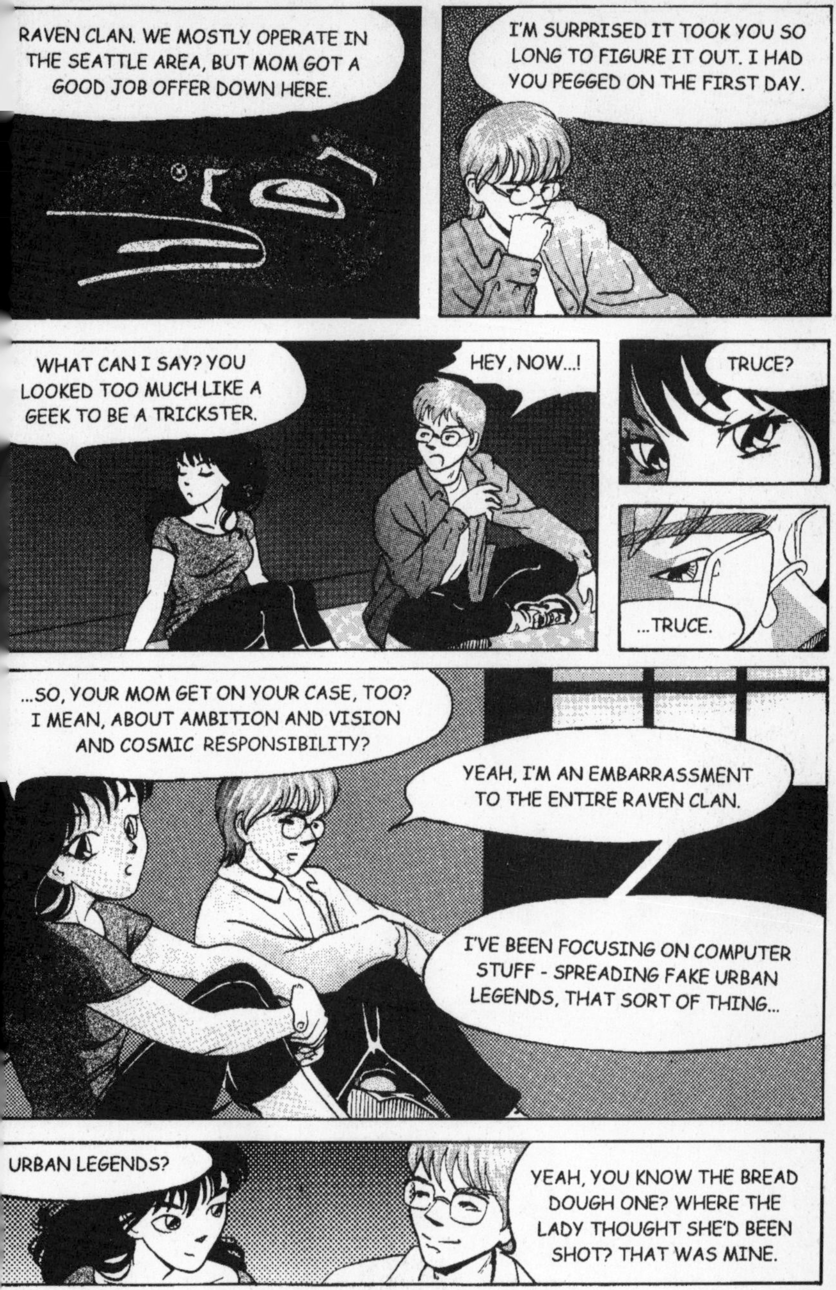
RAVEN CLAN. WE MOSTLY OPERATE IN THE SEATTLE AREA, BUT MOM GOT A GOOD JOB OFFER DOWN HERE.
I'M SURPRISED IT TOOK YOU SO LONG TO FIGURE IT OUT. I HAD YOU PEGGED ON THE FIRST DAY.
WHAT CAN I SAY? YOU LOOKED TOO MUCH LIKE A GEEK TO BE A TRICKSTER.
HEY, NOW...!
TRUCE?
...TRUCE.
...SO, YOUR MOM GET ON YOUR CASE, TOO? I MEAN, ABOUT AMBITION AND VISION AND COSMIC RESPONSIBILITY?
YEAH, I'M AN EMBARRASSMENT TO THE ENTIRE RAVEN CLAN.
I'VE BEEN FOCUSING ON COMPUTER STUFF - SPREADING FAKE URBAN LEGENDS, THAT SORT OF THING...
URBAN LEGENDS?
YEAH, YOU KNOW THE BREAD DOUGH ONE? WHERE THE LADY THOUGHT SHE'D BEEN SHOT? THAT WAS MINE.

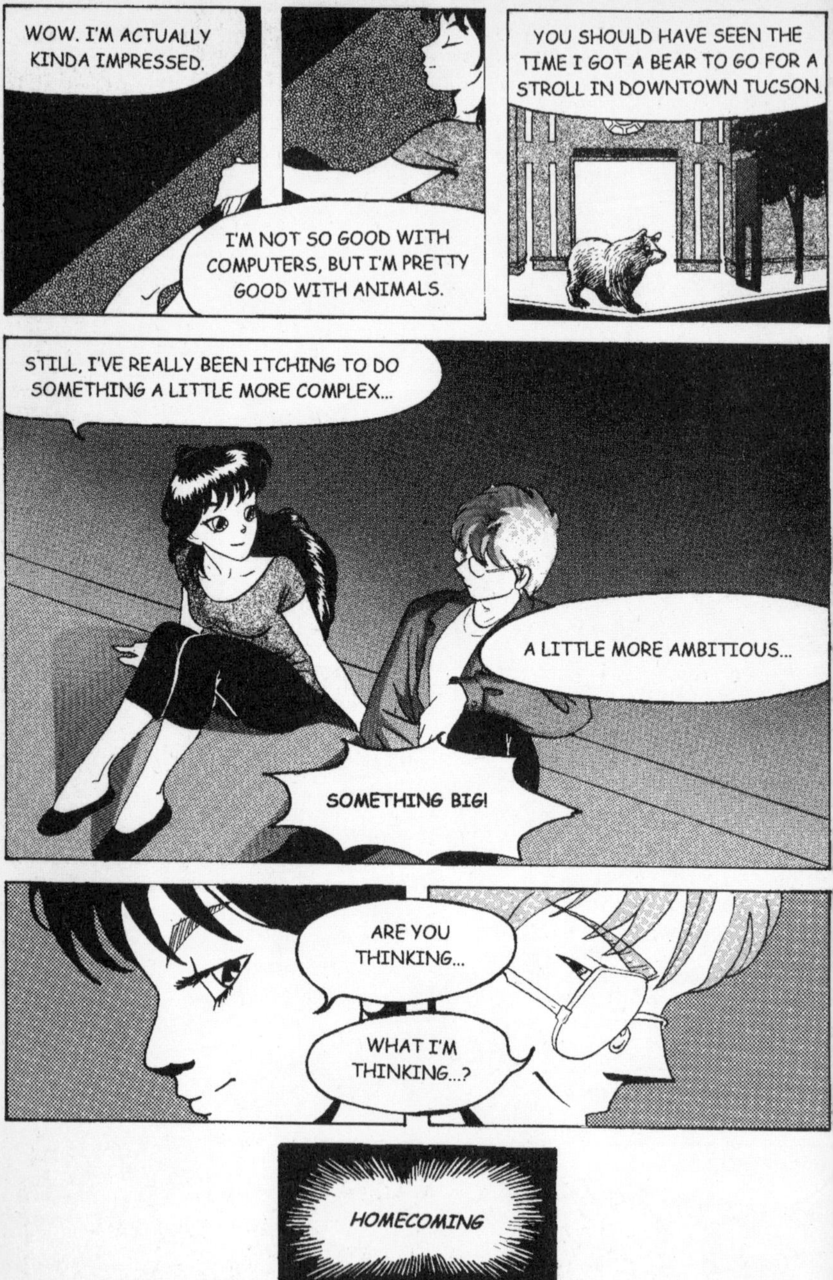
WOW. I'M ACTUALLY KINDA IMPRESSED.
I'M NOT SO GOOD WITH COMPUTERS, BUT I'M PRETTY GOOD WITH ANIMALS.
YOU SHOULD HAVE SEEN THE TIME I GOT A BEAR TO GO FOR A STROLL IN DOWNTOWN TUCSON.
STILL, I'VE REALLY BEEN ITCHING TO DO SOMETHING A LITTLE MORE COMPLEX...
A LITTLE MORE AMBITIOUS...
SOMETHING BIG!
ARE YOU THINKING...
WHAT I'M THINKING...?
HOMECOMING

DAD, WHY **EXACTLY** ARE YOU CLEANING YOUR GUN ON THE COUCH?

OH, DON'T MIND ME. YOU JUST GET READY FOR YOUR DATE.

DING DONG ♪

HEY, BIANCA.

ANDY! COME ON IN. I'LL GET MY PURSE.

DON'T PAY ANY ATTENTION TO MY DAD. HE'S A LOONY.

OH, UH...HERE. THIS IS FOR YOU.

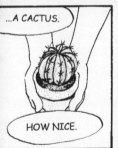

...A CACTUS.

HOW NICE.

THEY WERE OUT OF CORSAGES.

LET ME JUST GO PUT THIS IN MY ROOM...

I GUESS DAD'S NOT THE ONLY LOONY AROUND...

...SO WHILE THE BLACK POWDER .45-70 CARTRIDGE WAS CAPABLE OF DROPPING A HALF-TON BUFFALO IN ITS TRACKS FROM FIVE HUNDRED YARDS AWAY BACK IN THE 1870s, YOU CAN JUST **IMAGINE** THE GRISLY CRUSHING STOPPING POWER OF THE .45-70 USING MODERN SMOKELESS POWDER...

DAAAAD!

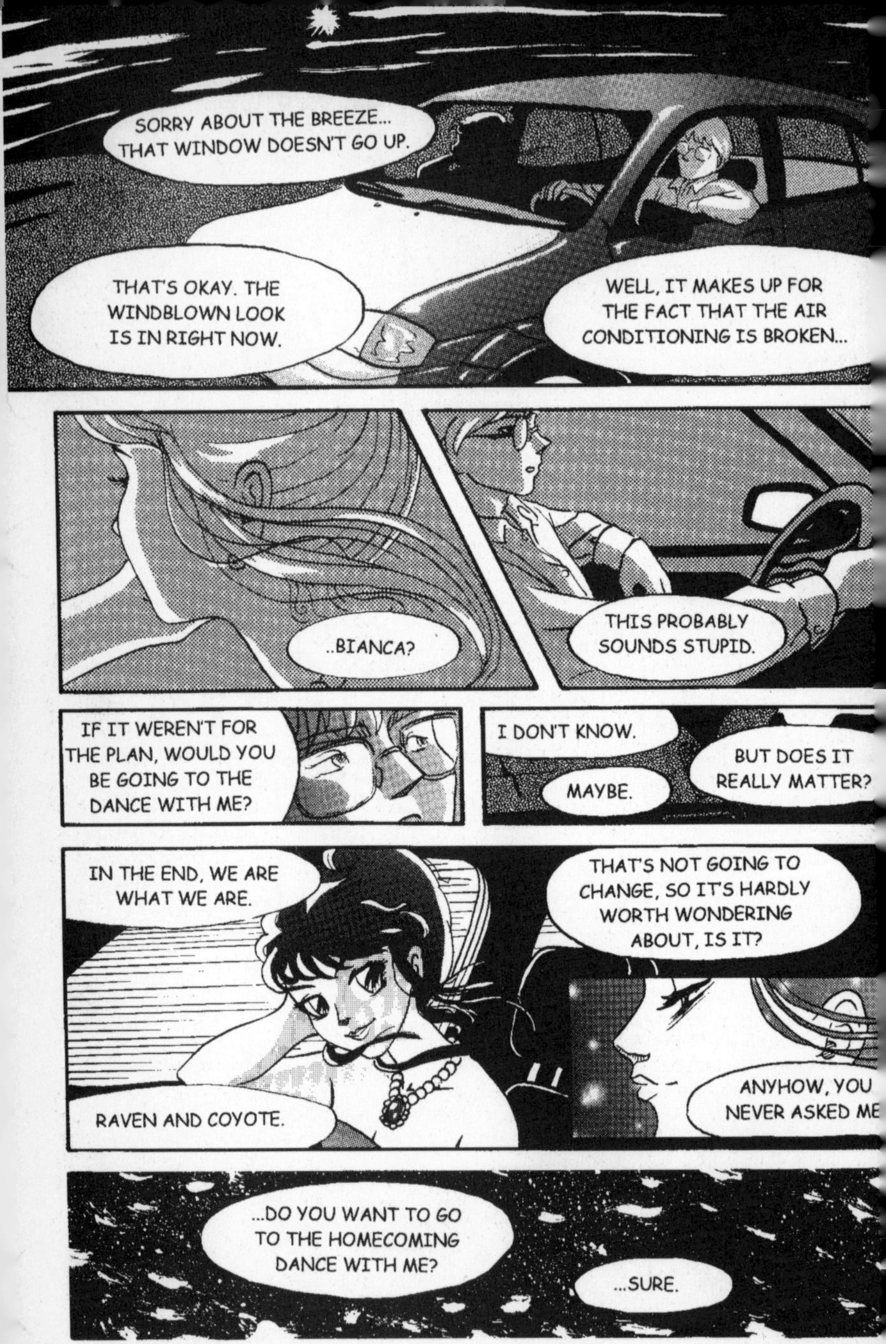
SORRY ABOUT THE BREEZE... THAT WINDOW DOESN'T GO UP.
THAT'S OKAY. THE WINDBLOWN LOOK IS IN RIGHT NOW.
WELL, IT MAKES UP FOR THE FACT THAT THE AIR CONDITIONING IS BROKEN...
..BIANCA?
THIS PROBABLY SOUNDS STUPID.
IF IT WEREN'T FOR THE PLAN, WOULD YOU BE GOING TO THE DANCE WITH ME?
I DON'T KNOW.
MAYBE.
BUT DOES IT REALLY MATTER?
IN THE END, WE ARE WHAT WE ARE.
RAVEN AND COYOTE.
THAT'S NOT GOING TO CHANGE, SO IT'S HARDLY WORTH WONDERING ABOUT, IS IT?
ANYHOW, YOU NEVER ASKED ME
...DO YOU WANT TO GO TO THE HOMECOMING DANCE WITH ME?
...SURE.

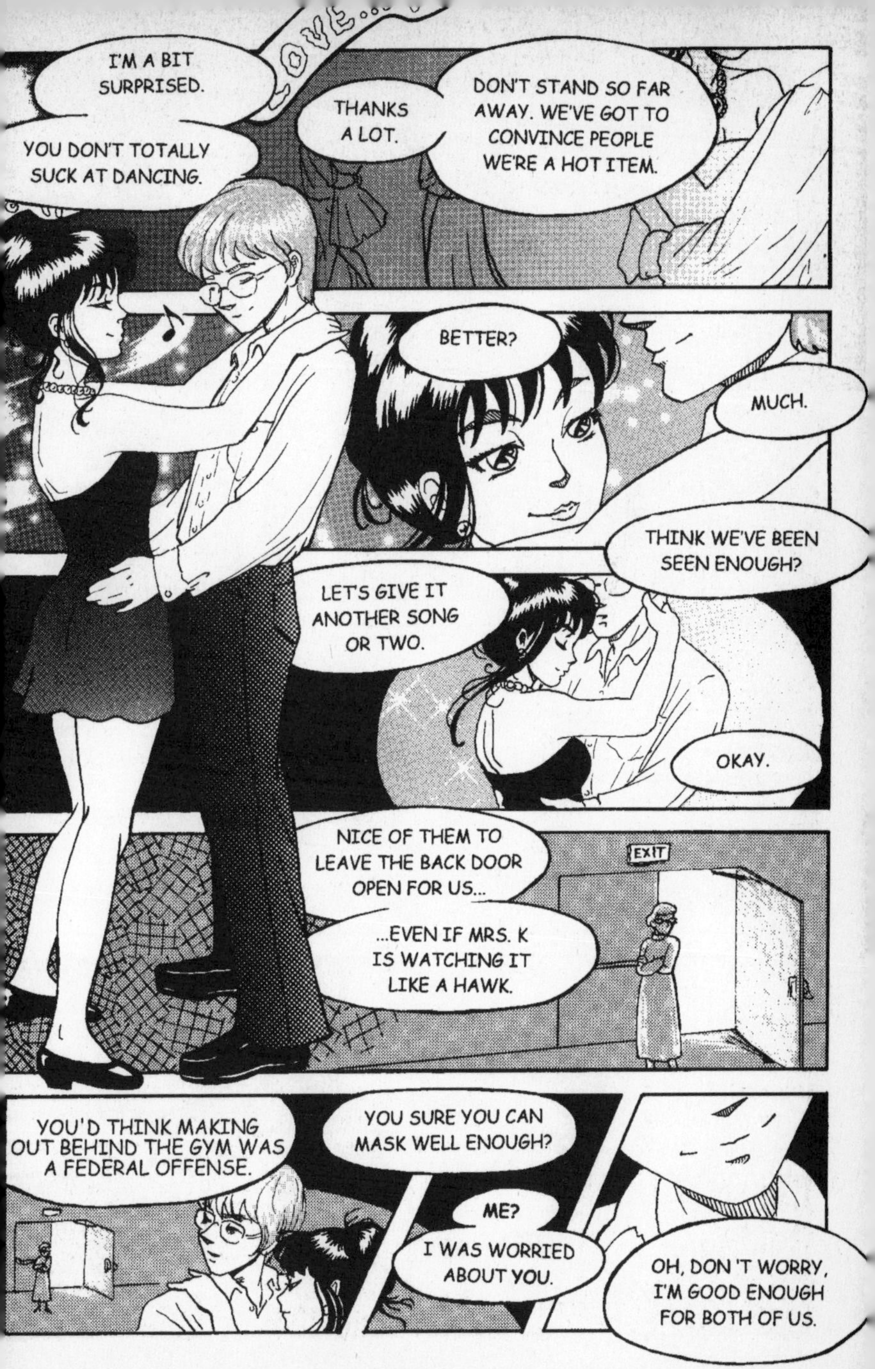
LOVE...
I'M A BIT SURPRISED.
YOU DON'T TOTALLY SUCK AT DANCING.
THANKS A LOT.
DON'T STAND SO FAR AWAY. WE'VE GOT TO CONVINCE PEOPLE WE'RE A HOT ITEM.
BETTER?
MUCH.
THINK WE'VE BEEN SEEN ENOUGH?
LET'S GIVE IT ANOTHER SONG OR TWO.
OKAY.
NICE OF THEM TO LEAVE THE BACK DOOR OPEN FOR US...
EXIT
...EVEN IF MRS. K IS WATCHING IT LIKE A HAWK.
YOU'D THINK MAKING OUT BEHIND THE GYM WAS A FEDERAL OFFENSE.
YOU SURE YOU CAN MASK WELL ENOUGH?
ME?
I WAS WORRIED ABOUT YOU.
OH, DON'T WORRY, I'M GOOD ENOUGH FOR BOTH OF US.

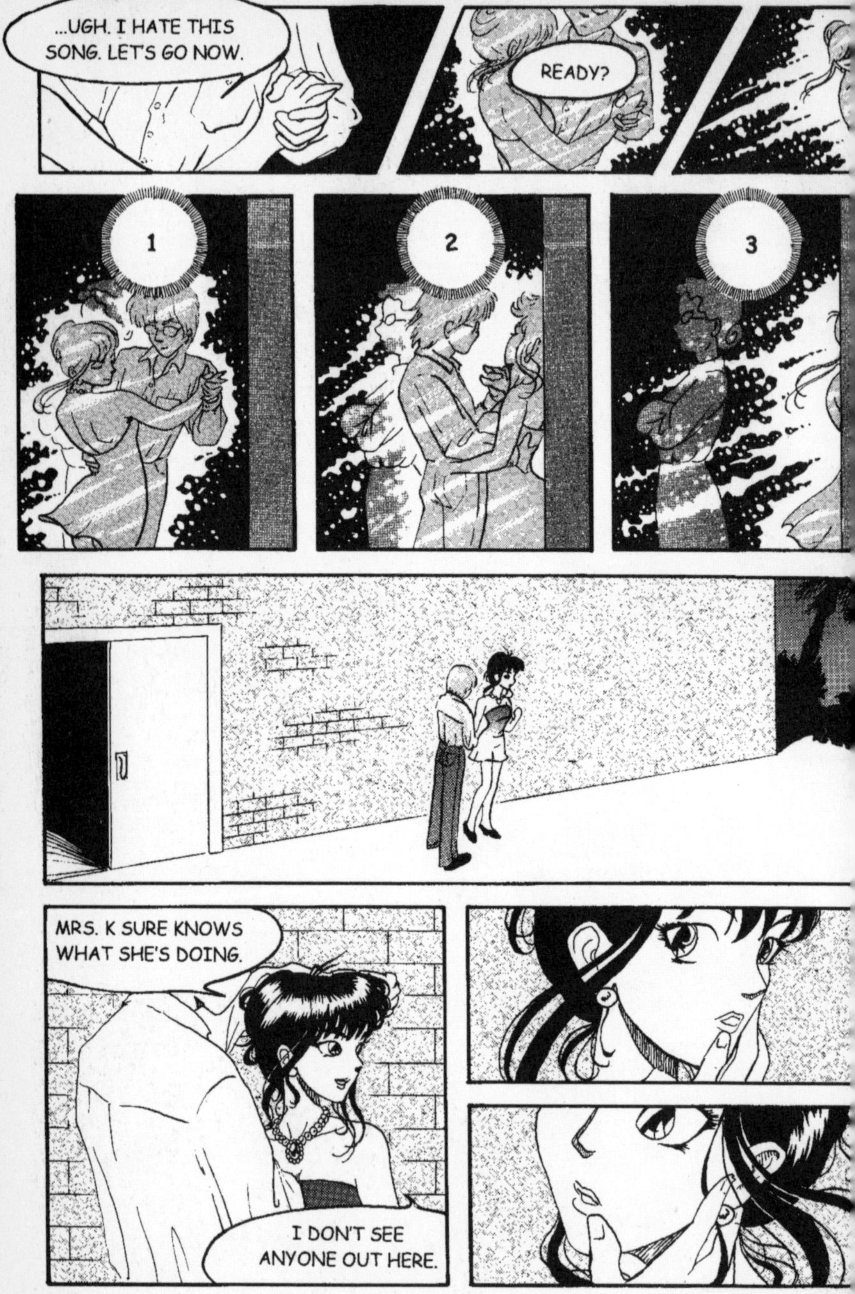
...UGH. I HATE THIS SONG. LET'S GO NOW.
READY?
1
2
3
MRS. K SURE KNOWS WHAT SHE'S DOING.
I DON'T SEE ANYONE OUT HERE.

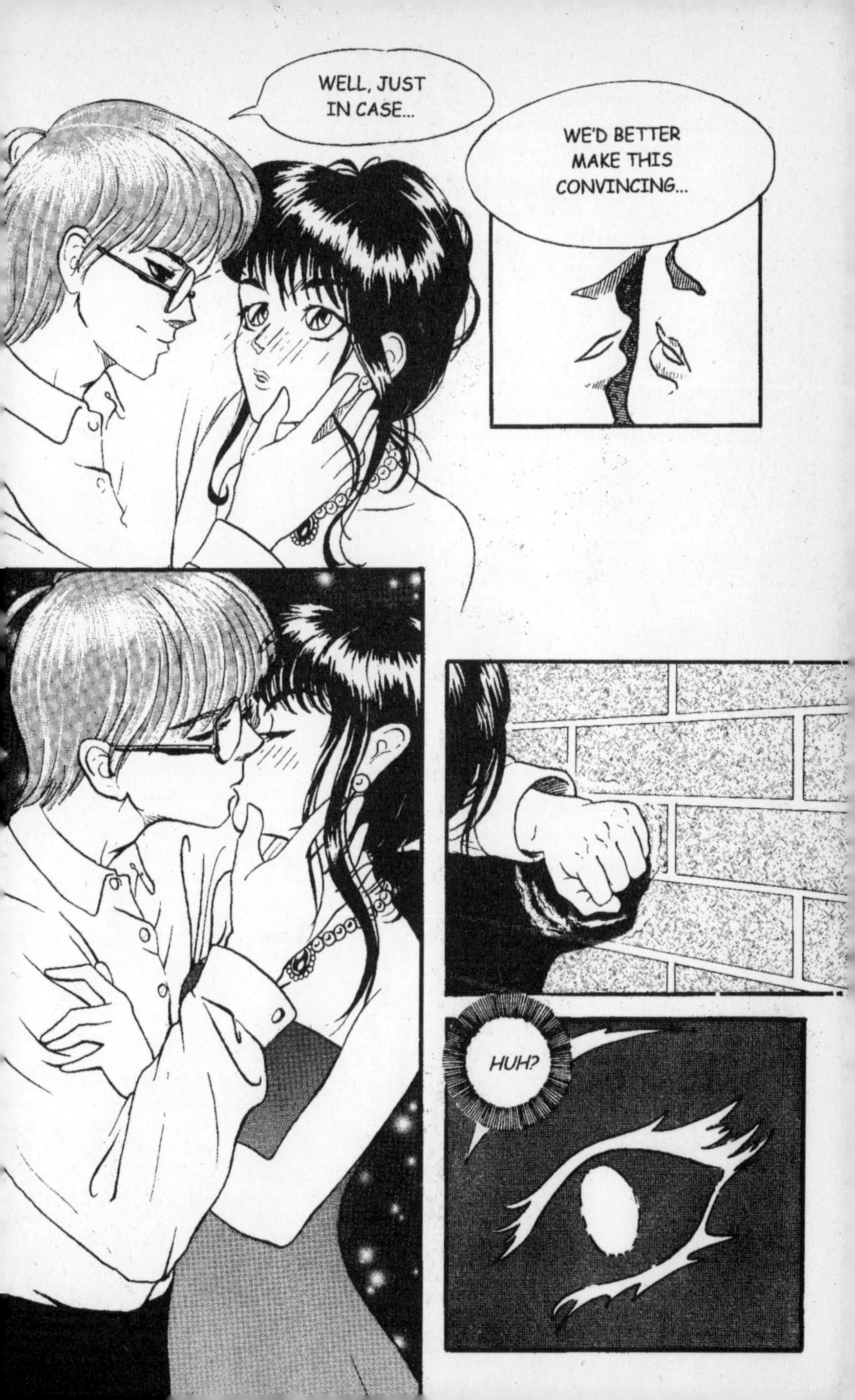
WELL, JUST IN CASE...
WE'D BETTER MAKE THIS CONVINCING...
HUH?

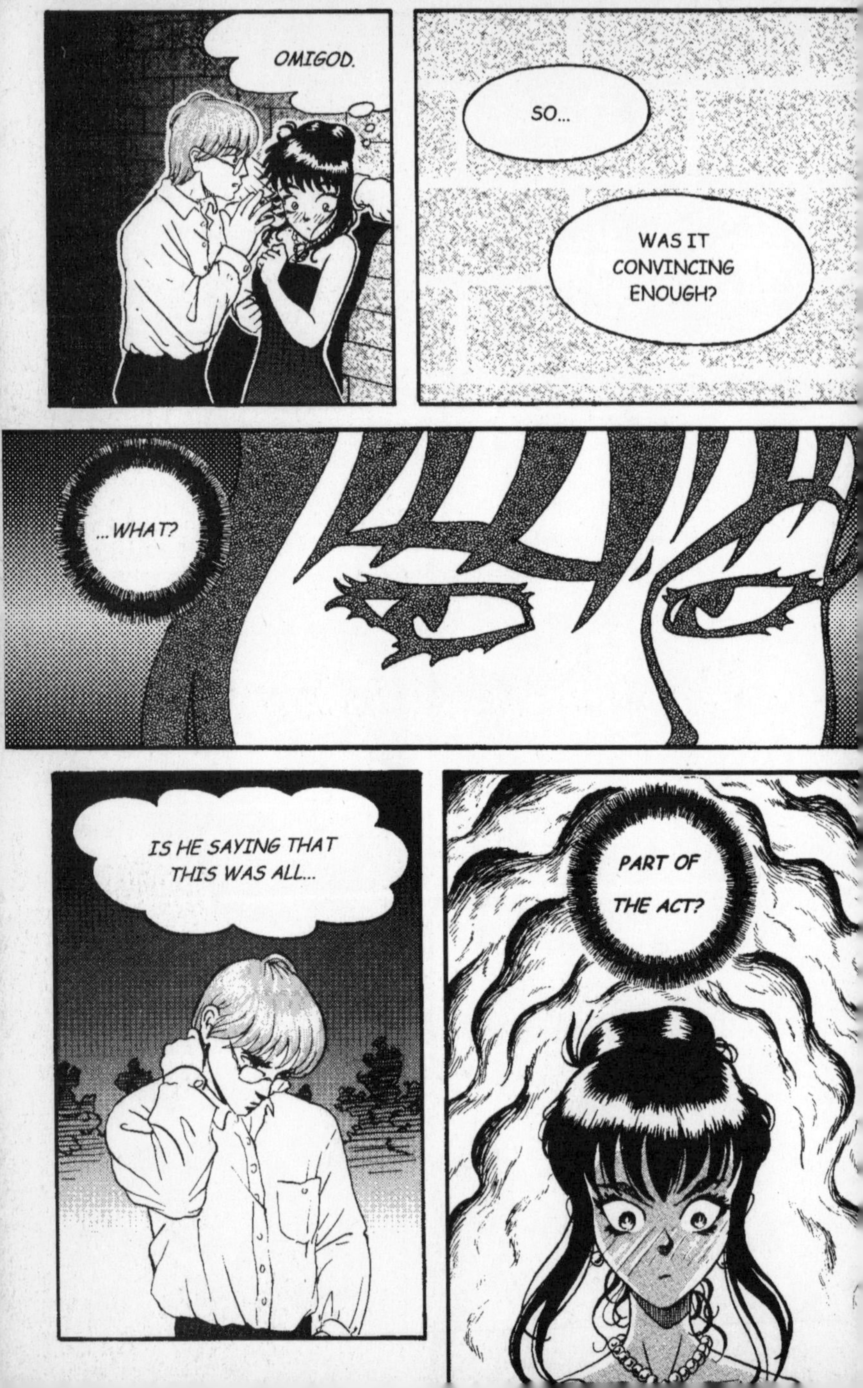
OMIGOD.
SO...
WAS IT CONVINCING ENOUGH?
...WHAT?
IS HE SAYING THAT THIS WAS ALL...
PART OF THE ACT?

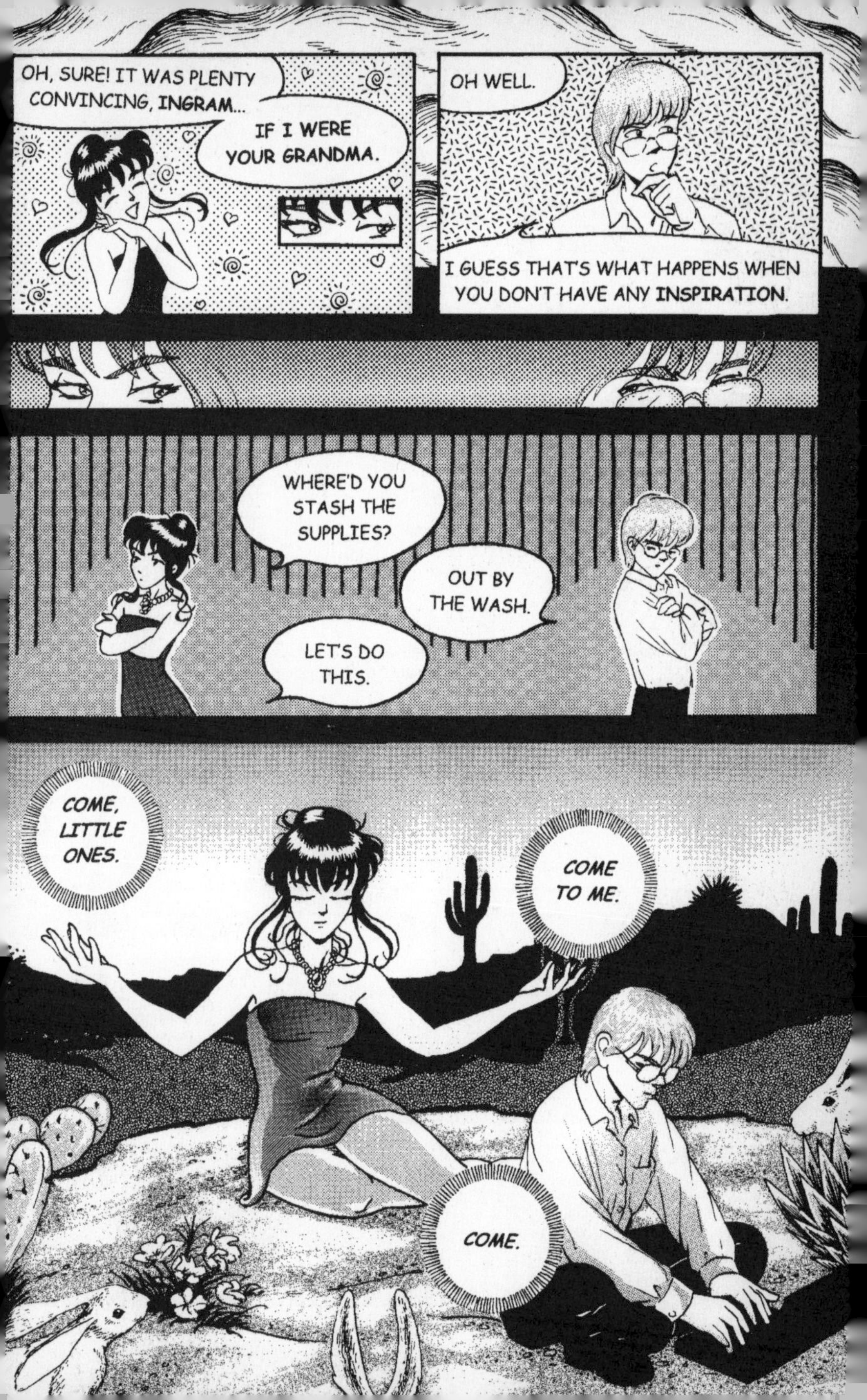
OH, SURE! IT WAS PLENTY CONVINCING, INGRAM...
IF I WERE YOUR GRANDMA.
OH WELL.
I GUESS THAT'S WHAT HAPPENS WHEN YOU DON'T HAVE ANY INSPIRATION.
WHERE'D YOU STASH THE SUPPLIES?
OUT BY THE WASH.
LET'S DO THIS.
COME, LITTLE ONES.
COME TO ME.
COME.

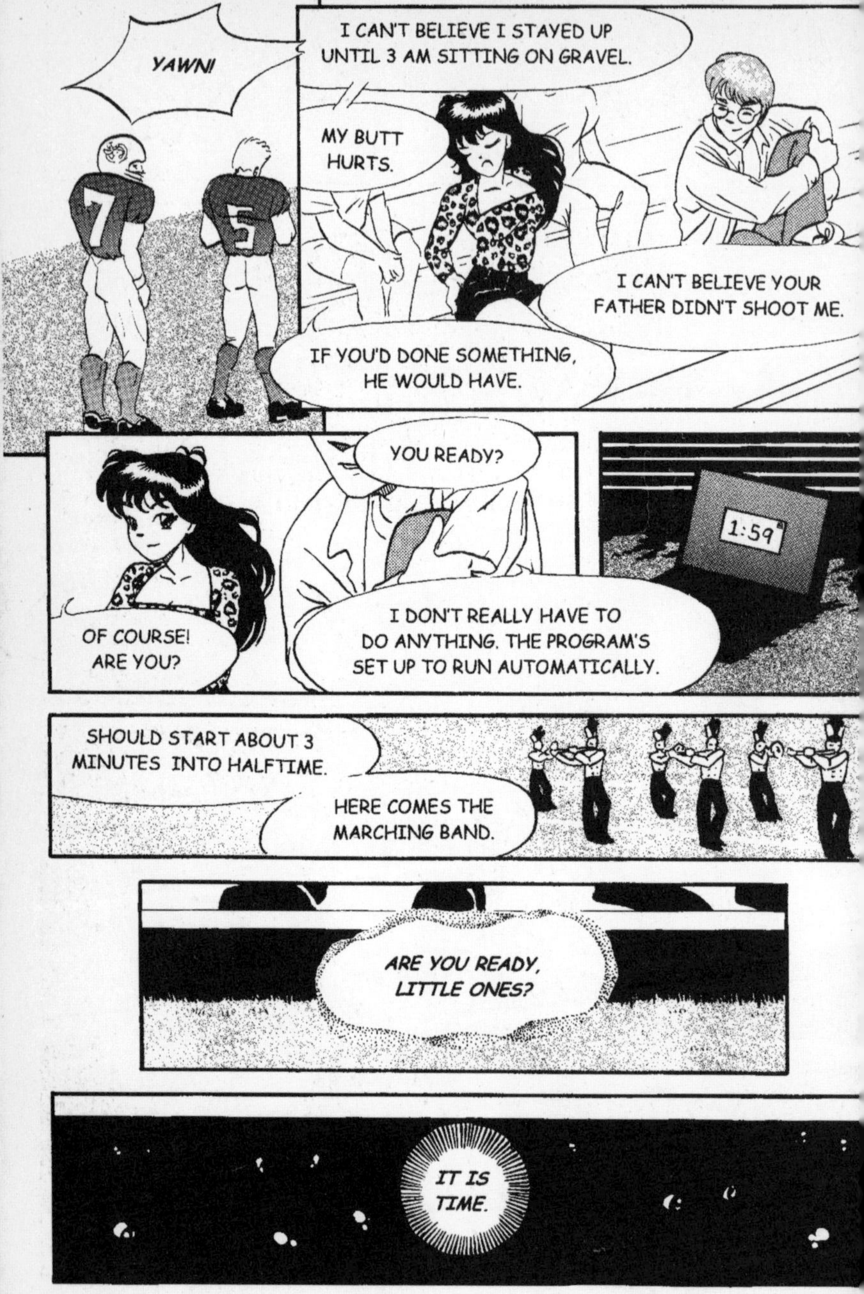
YAWN!
I CAN'T BELIEVE I STAYED UP UNTIL 3 AM SITTING ON GRAVEL.
MY BUTT HURTS.
I CAN'T BELIEVE YOUR FATHER DIDN'T SHOOT ME.
IF YOU'D DONE SOMETHING, HE WOULD HAVE.
YOU READY?
OF COURSE! ARE YOU?
I DON'T REALLY HAVE TO DO ANYTHING. THE PROGRAM'S SET UP TO RUN AUTOMATICALLY.
1:59
SHOULD START ABOUT 3 MINUTES INTO HALFTIME.
HERE COMES THE MARCHING BAND.
ARE YOU READY, LITTLE ONES?
IT IS TIME.

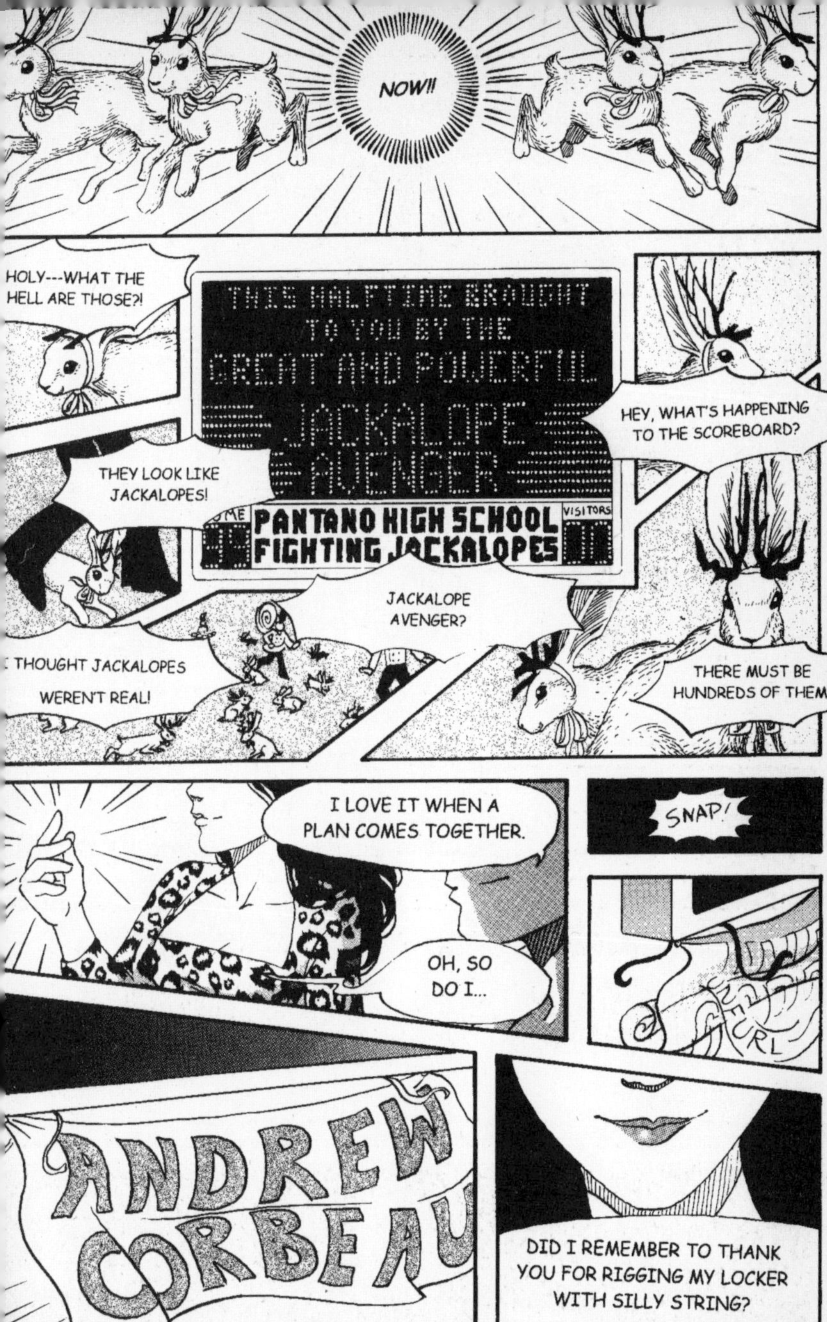
NOW!!
HOLY---WHAT THE HELL ARE THOSE?!
THIS HALFTIME BROUGHT TO YOU BY THE GREAT AND POWERFUL JACKALOPE AVENGER
PANTANO HIGH SCHOOL FIGHTING JACKALOPES
VISITORS
THEY LOOK LIKE JACKALOPES!
I THOUGHT JACKALOPES WEREN'T REAL!
JACKALOPE AVENGER?
HEY, WHAT'S HAPPENING TO THE SCOREBOARD?
THERE MUST BE HUNDREDS OF THEM!
I LOVE IT WHEN A PLAN COMES TOGETHER.
OH, SO DO I...
SNAP!
UNFURL
ANDREW CORBEAU
DID I REMEMBER TO THANK YOU FOR RIGGING MY LOCKER WITH SILLY STRING?

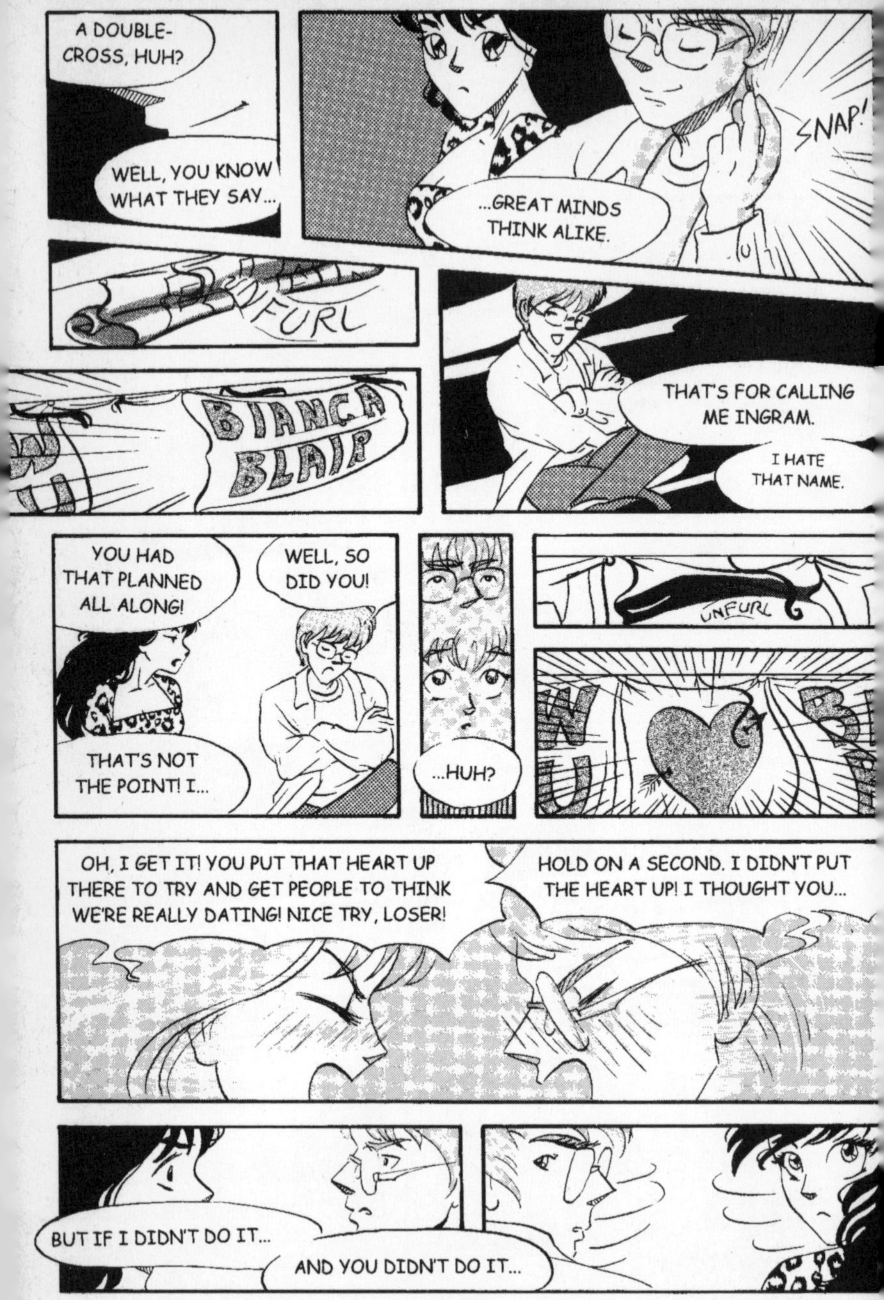
A DOUBLE-CROSS, HUH?
WELL, YOU KNOW WHAT THEY SAY...
...GREAT MINDS THINK ALIKE.
SNAP!
UNFURL
THAT'S FOR CALLING ME INGRAM.
I HATE THAT NAME.
BIANCA BLAIR
YOU HAD THAT PLANNED ALL ALONG!
WELL, SO DID YOU!
THAT'S NOT THE POINT! I...
...HUH?
UNFURL
OH, I GET IT! YOU PUT THAT HEART UP THERE TO TRY AND GET PEOPLE TO THINK WE'RE REALLY DATING! NICE TRY, LOSER!
HOLD ON A SECOND. I DIDN'T PUT THE HEART UP! I THOUGHT YOU...
BUT IF I DIDN'T DO IT...
AND YOU DIDN'T DO IT...

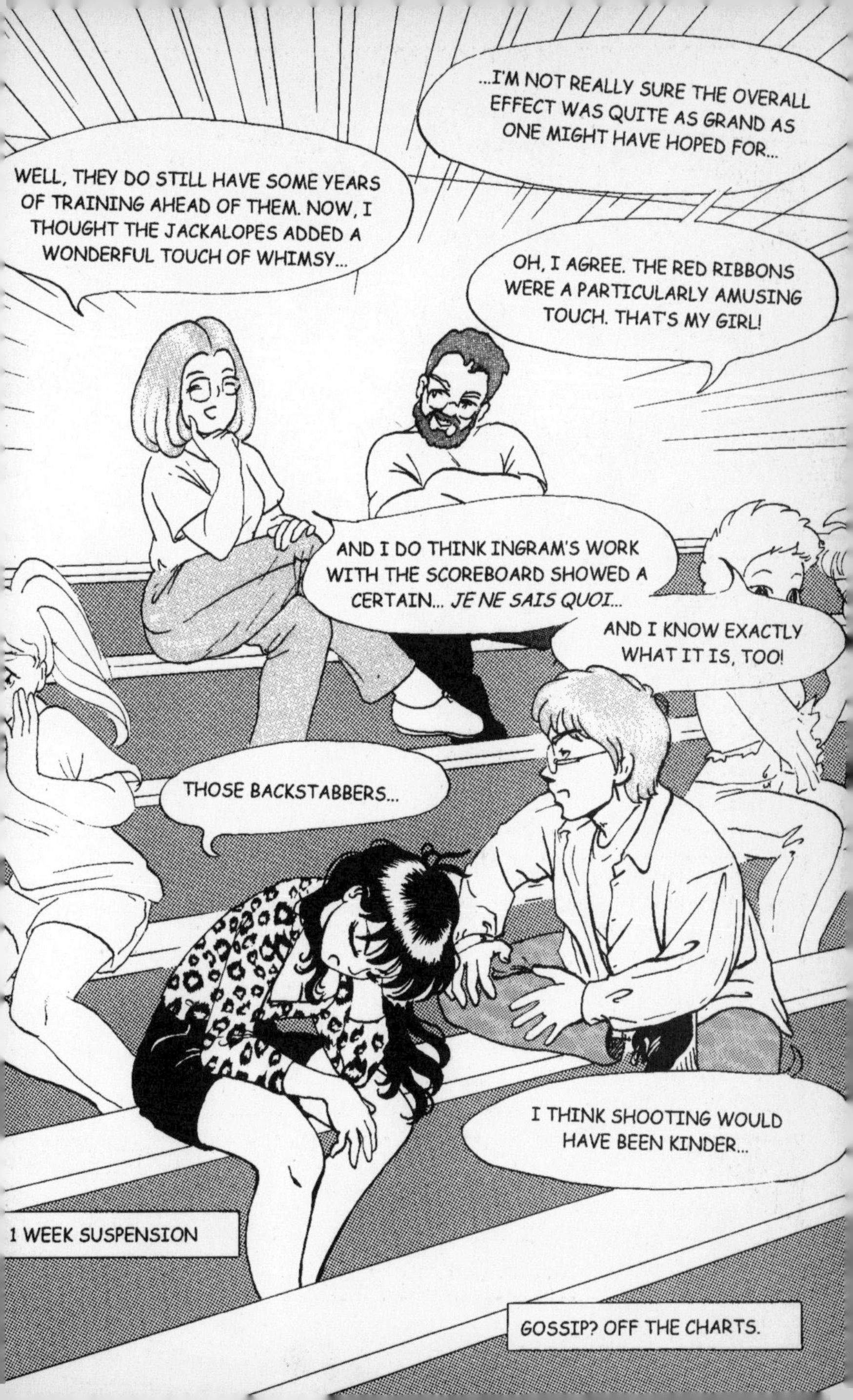
...I'M NOT REALLY SURE THE OVERALL EFFECT WAS QUITE AS GRAND AS ONE MIGHT HAVE HOPED FOR...
WELL, THEY DO STILL HAVE SOME YEARS OF TRAINING AHEAD OF THEM. NOW, I THOUGHT THE JACKALOPES ADDED A WONDERFUL TOUCH OF WHIMSY...
OH, I AGREE. THE RED RIBBONS WERE A PARTICULARLY AMUSING TOUCH. THAT'S MY GIRL!
AND I DO THINK INGRAM'S WORK WITH THE SCOREBOARD SHOWED A CERTAIN... *JE NE SAIS QUOI*...
AND I KNOW EXACTLY WHAT IT IS, TOO!
THOSE BACKSTABBERS...
I THINK SHOOTING WOULD HAVE BEEN KINDER...
1 WEEK SUSPENSION
GOSSIP? OFF THE CHARTS.

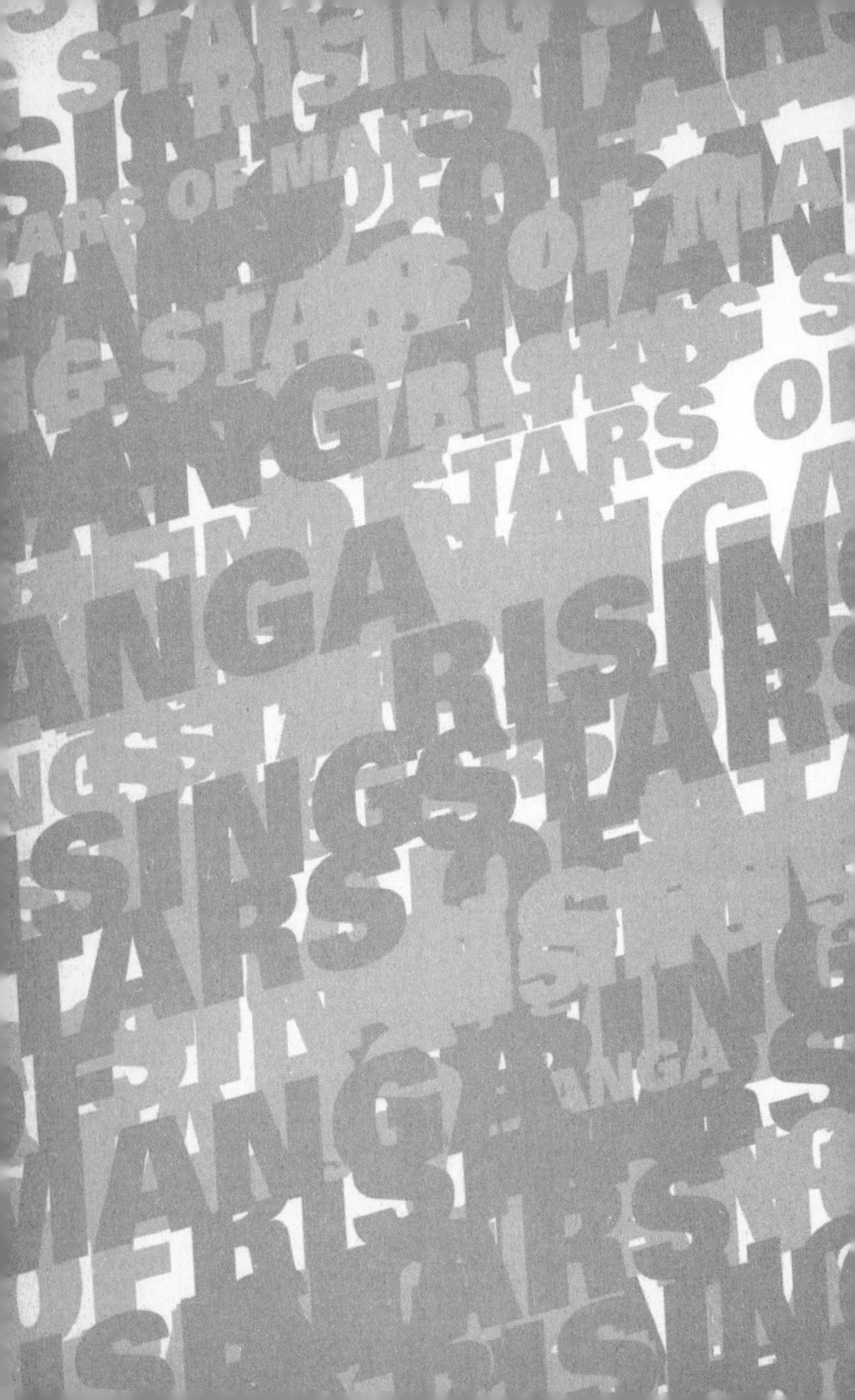

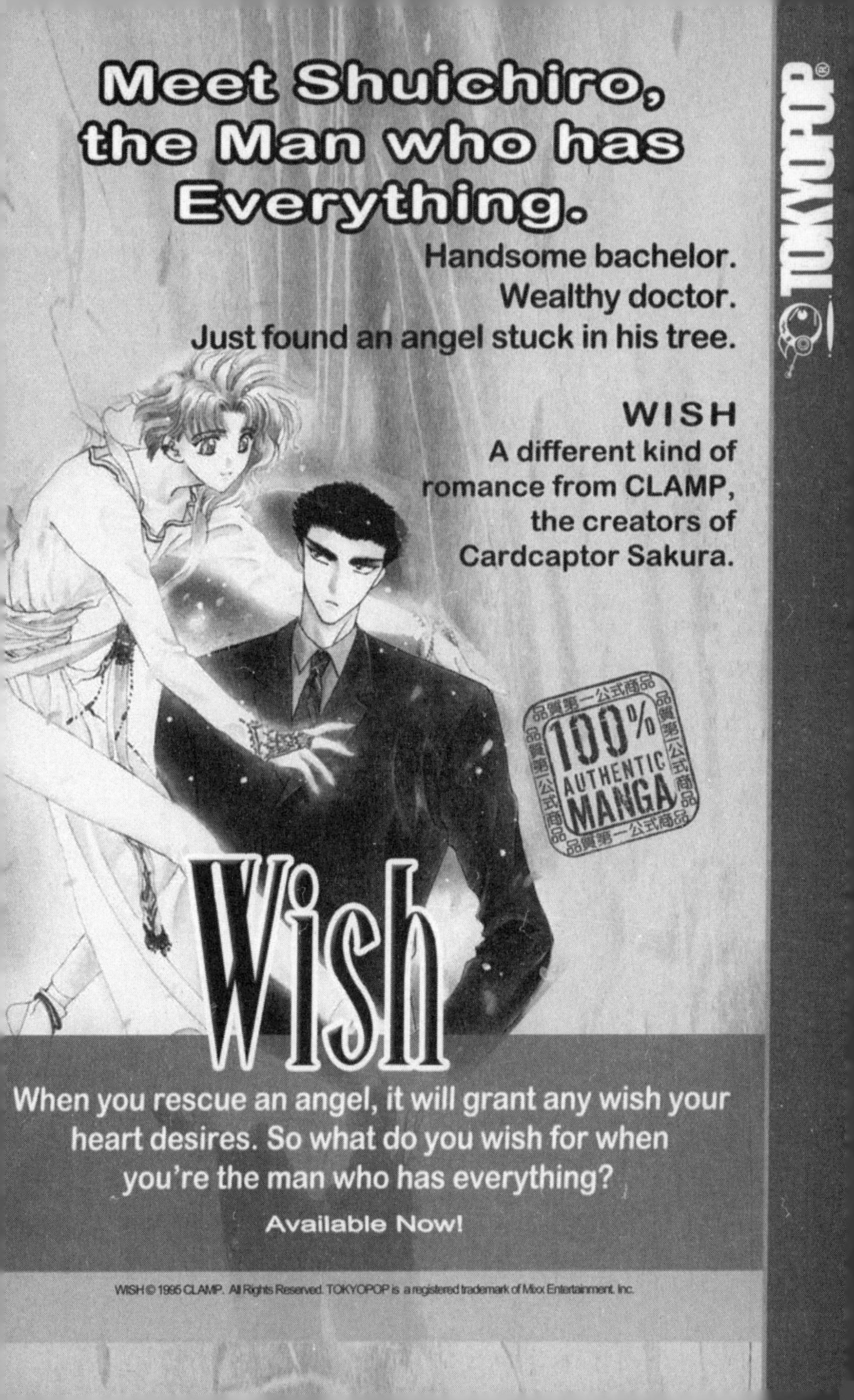
Meet Shuichiro, the Man who has Everything.
Handsome bachelor.
Wealthy doctor.
Just found an angel stuck in his tree.
WISH
A different kind of romance from CLAMP, the creators of Cardcaptor Sakura.
100% AUTHENTIC MANGA
Wish
When you rescue an angel, it will grant any wish your heart desires. So what do you wish for when you're the man who has everything?
Available Now!
WISH © 1995 CLAMP. All Rights Reserved. TOKYOPOP is a registered trademark of Mixx Entertainment, Inc.
TOKYOPOP®

EMMALYNE'S MANSION

RUNNER UP

RISING.STARS.OF.MANGA.2003

::

EMMALYNNE'S MANSION :: RUNNER UP ::

Michael Vega was born in 1977 in Victoria, Texas. He now lives in Bakersfield, California, where he works as a freelance illustrator. He has previously had his work (on Saiko & Lavender, Morning Glory, Gremlin and Monsters of Rock) published by Radio Comix, Anti-Ballistic Pixelation and Antarctic Press. More of his material is available at www.ghostcircles.com.

Inspiration for this story:
Emmalyne's Mansion came from an urge to do an all-ages comic—something fantasy that both children and adults could enjoy. I wanted to do something with a younger character where the world seems very large and overwhelming.

Favorite Manga:
Card Captor Sakura, Beast of the East, Sandland

Favorite Manga Artists:
Akira Toriyama, Oh! Great, CLAMP

....

Judge's Comments:
Michael Vega's *Emmalyne's Mansion* is like a breath of fresh air. It's a cute, inventive story that appeals to all ages. The black-and-white artwork gives it a retro vibe that delights, though the addition of screen tones could help add depth.

Emmalyne's Mansion is definitely a second-generation American manga in that it borrows from the best of the genre. Its design—particularly the eyes—and its moments of emotional extremes are truly manga-esque. But rather than imitating another style, Vega has adapted manga to create a style uniquely his own.

Vega's prominent mascot figure shows this guy can do great things in the world of character design for children's manga. And major props for creating an adorable mouse that could give *Card Captor's* Kero a run for his money!
-Julie Taylor

::

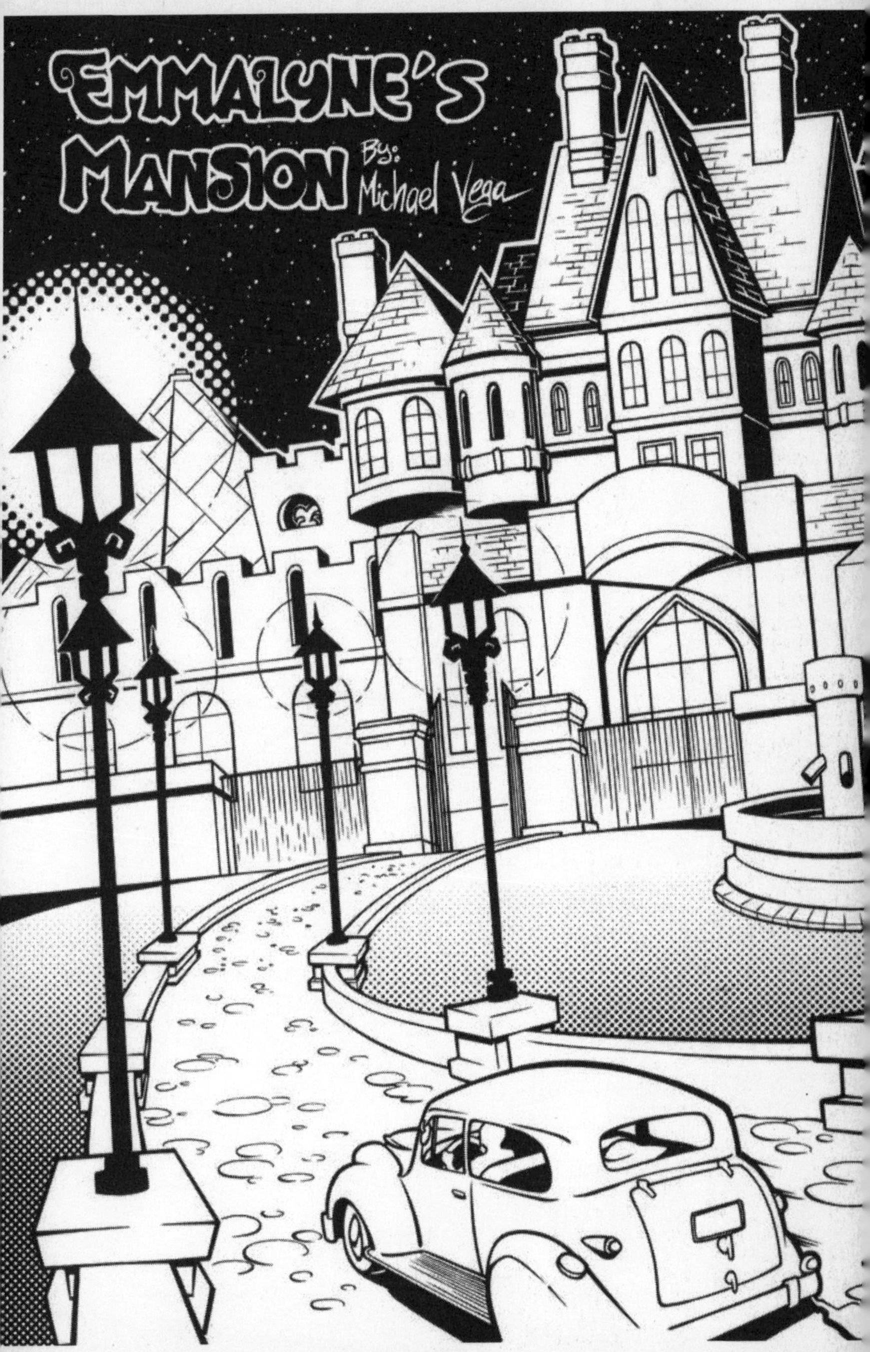
EMMALYNE'S
MANSION
By:
Michael Vega

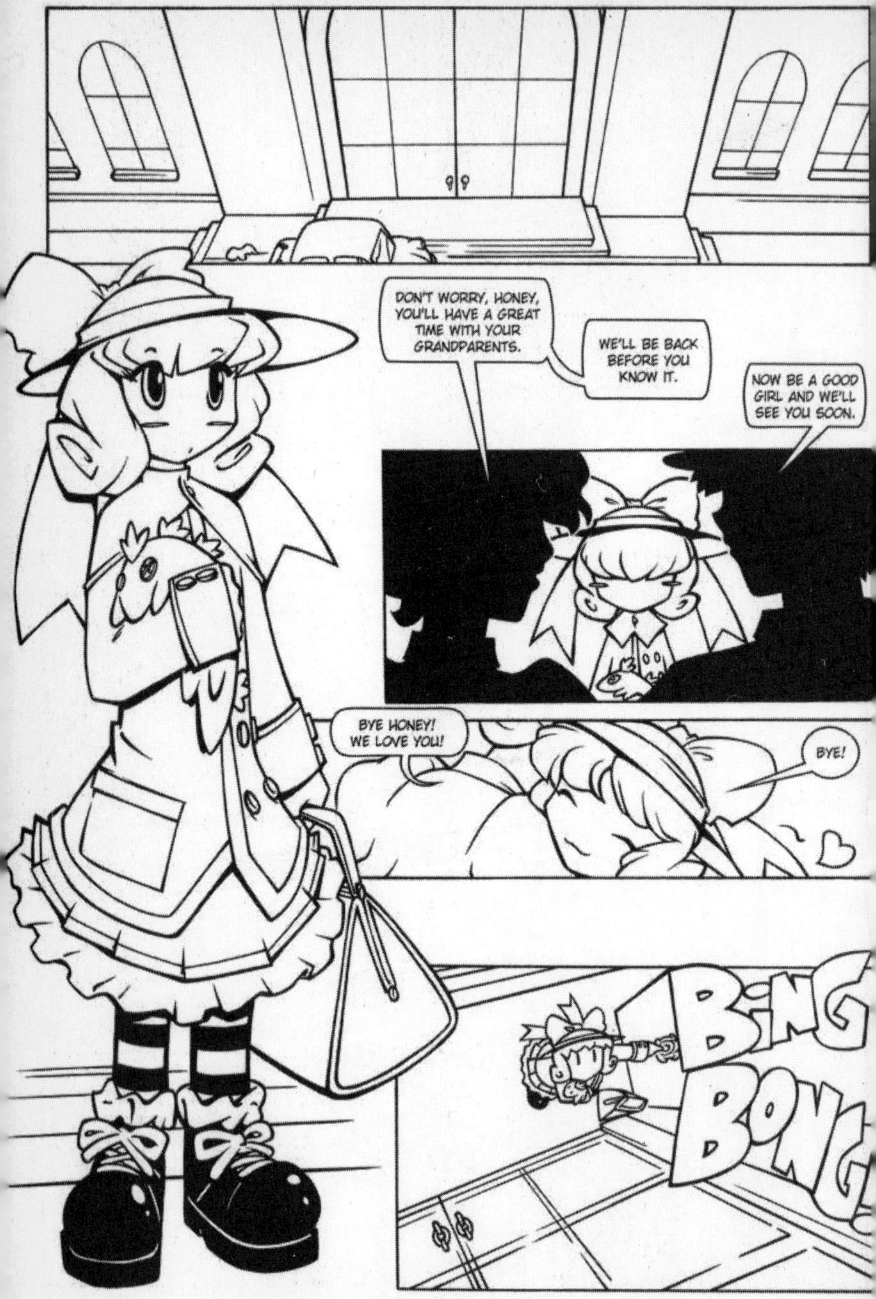
DON'T WORRY, HONEY, YOU'LL HAVE A GREAT TIME WITH YOUR GRANDPARENTS.
WE'LL BE BACK BEFORE YOU KNOW IT.
NOW BE A GOOD GIRL AND WE'LL SEE YOU SOON.
BYE HONEY! WE LOVE YOU!
BYE!
BING
BONG

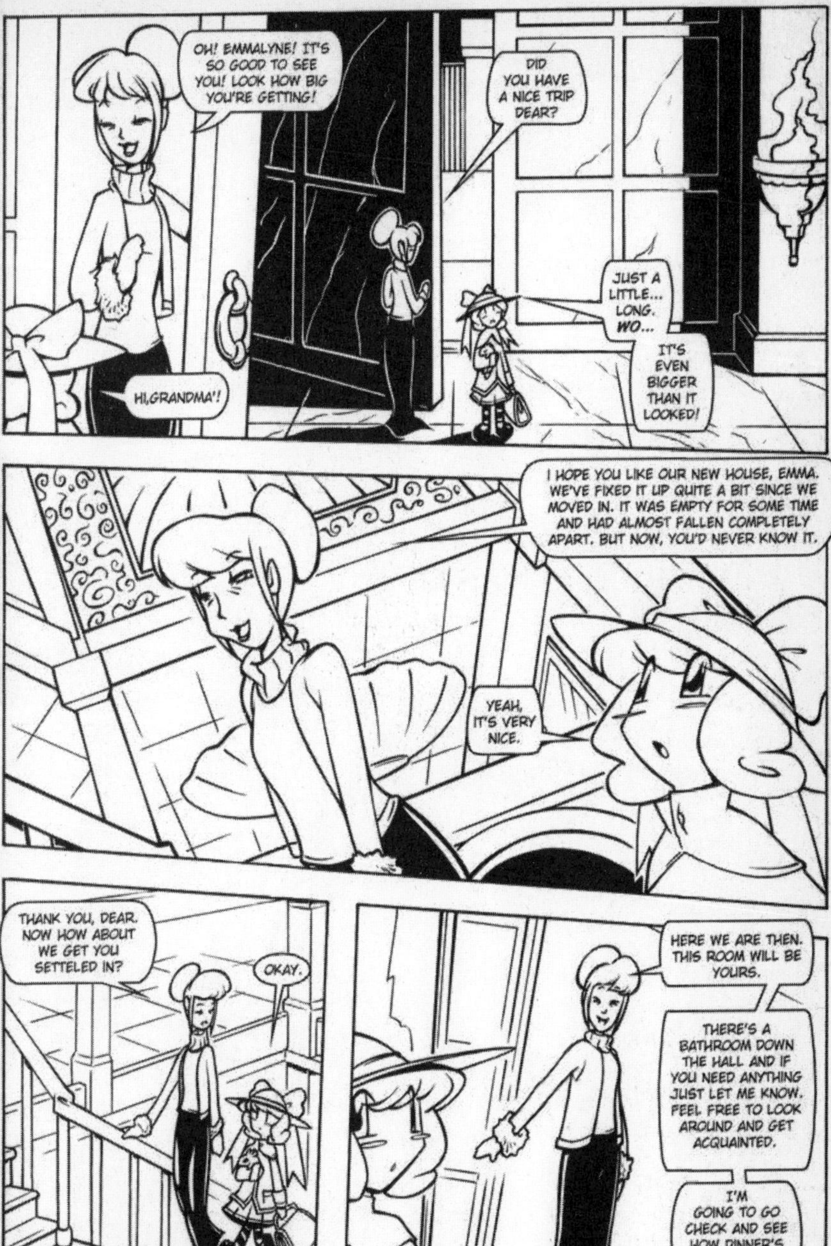
OH! EMMALYNE! IT'S SO GOOD TO SEE YOU! LOOK HOW BIG YOU'RE GETTING!
HI,GRANDMA'!
DID YOU HAVE A NICE TRIP DEAR?
JUST A LITTLE... LONG. WO...
IT'S EVEN BIGGER THAN IT LOOKED!
I HOPE YOU LIKE OUR NEW HOUSE, EMMA. WE'VE FIXED IT UP QUITE A BIT SINCE WE MOVED IN. IT WAS EMPTY FOR SOME TIME AND HAD ALMOST FALLEN COMPLETELY APART. BUT NOW, YOU'D NEVER KNOW IT.
YEAH, IT'S VERY NICE.
THANK YOU, DEAR. NOW HOW ABOUT WE GET YOU SETTELED IN?
OKAY.
HERE WE ARE THEN. THIS ROOM WILL BE YOURS.
THERE'S A BATHROOM DOWN THE HALL AND IF YOU NEED ANYTHING JUST LET ME KNOW. FEEL FREE TO LOOK AROUND AND GET ACQUAINTED.
I'M GOING TO GO CHECK AND SEE HOW DINNER'S COMING ALONG.

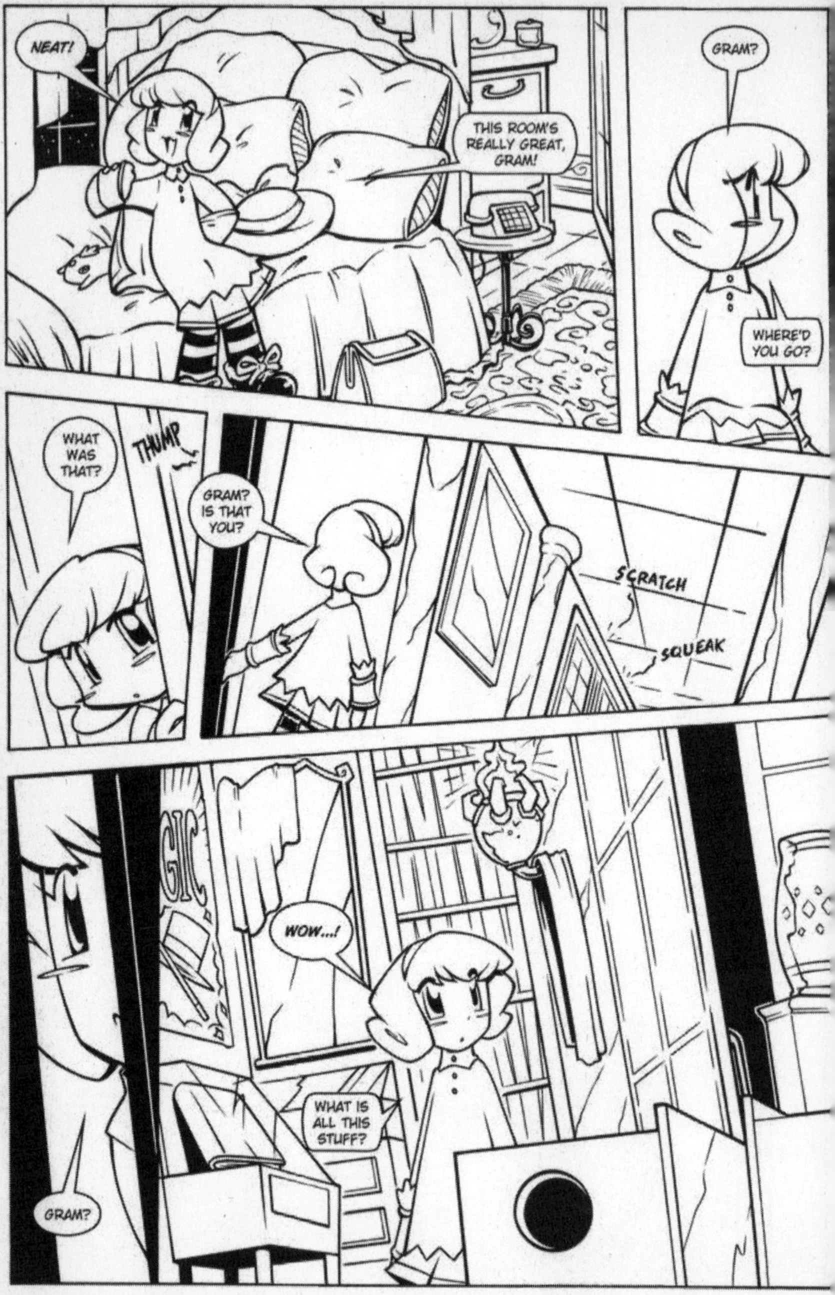
NEAT!
THIS ROOM'S REALLY GREAT, GRAM!
GRAM?
WHERE'D YOU GO?
WHAT WAS THAT?
THUMP
GRAM? IS THAT YOU?
SCRATCH
SQUEAK
WOW...!
WHAT IS ALL THIS STUFF?
GRAM?

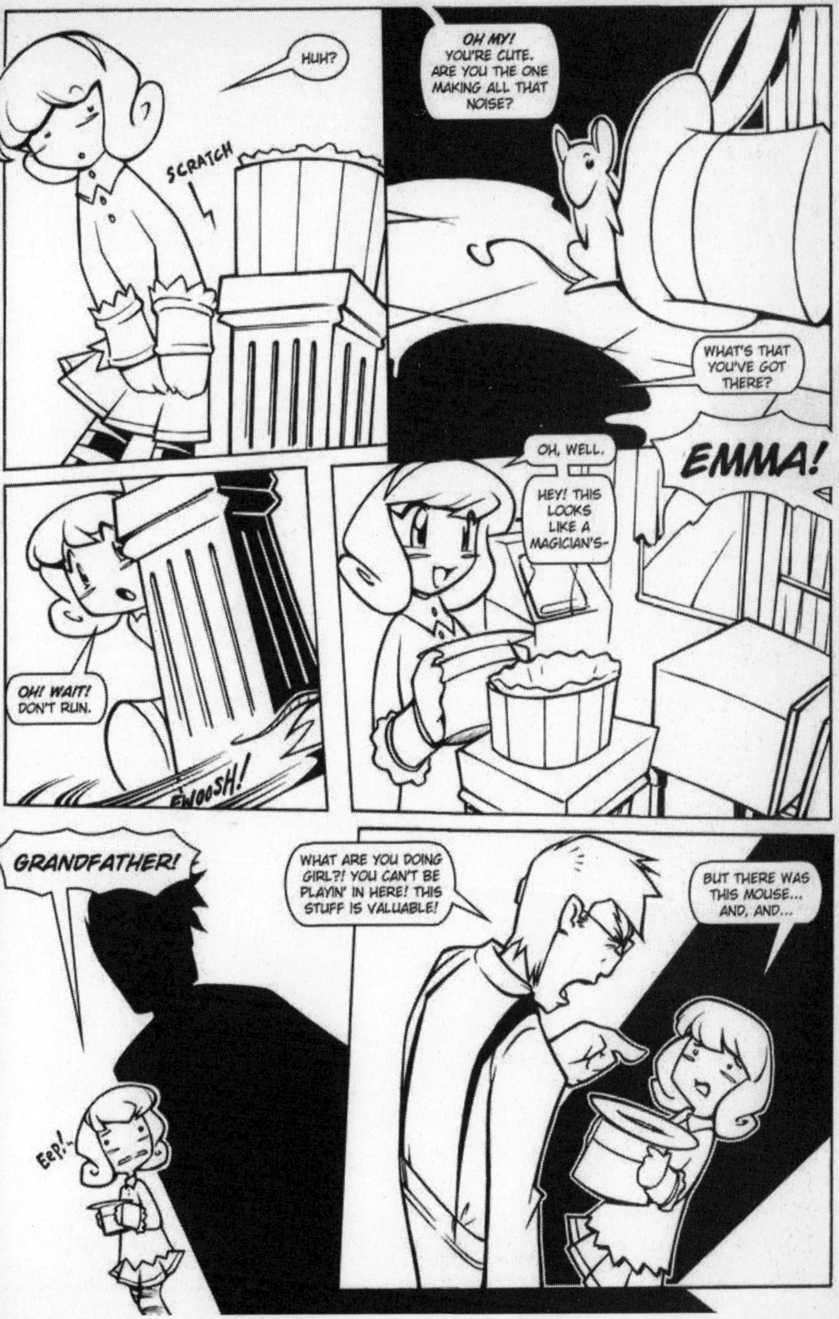
HUH?
SCRATCH
OH MY! YOU'RE CUTE. ARE YOU THE ONE MAKING ALL THAT NOISE?
WHAT'S THAT YOU'VE GOT THERE?
OH! WAIT! DON'T RUN.
FWOOSH!
OH, WELL.
HEY! THIS LOOKS LIKE A MAGICIAN'S-
EMMA!
GRANDFATHER!
Eep!
WHAT ARE YOU DOING GIRL?! YOU CAN'T BE PLAYIN' IN HERE! THIS STUFF IS VALUABLE!
BUT THERE WAS THIS MOUSE... AND, AND...

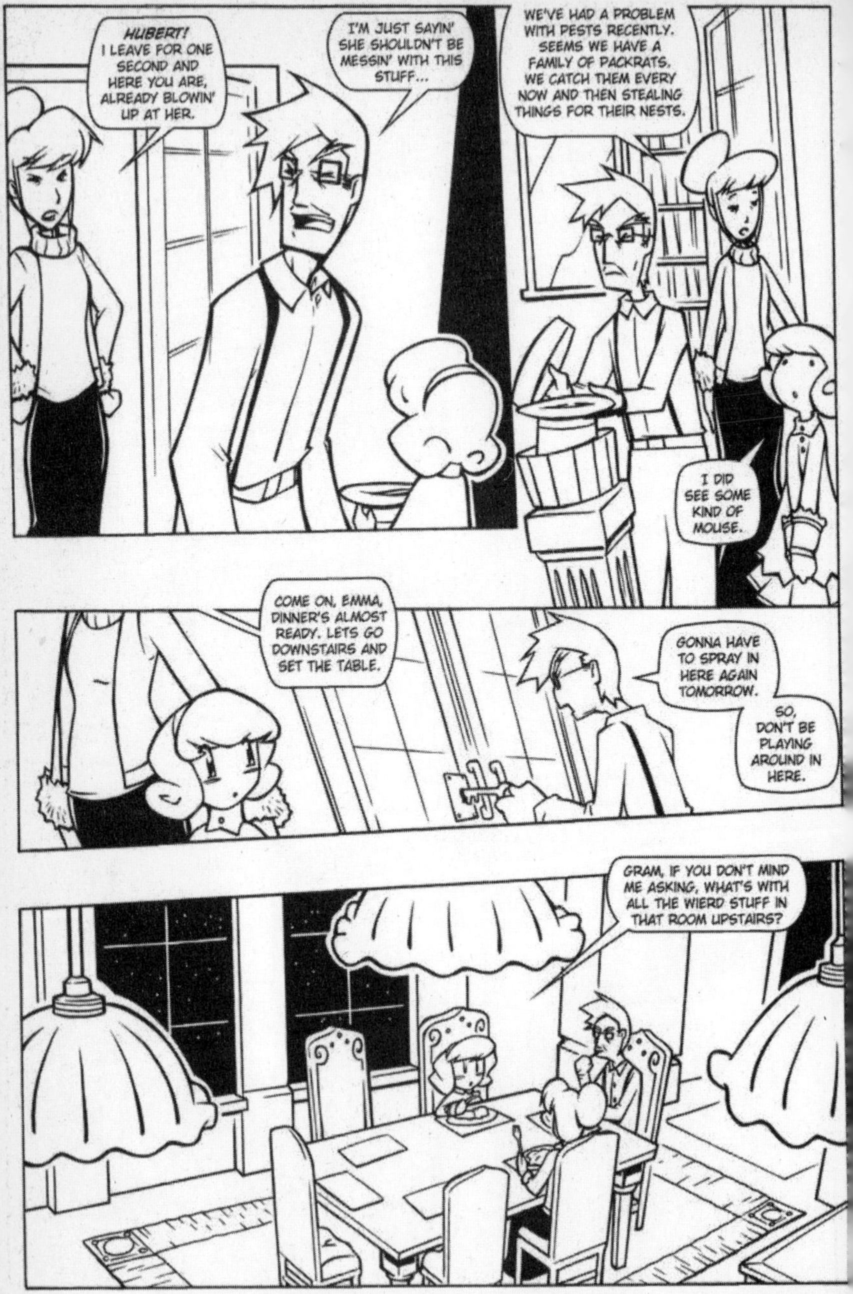
HUBERT! I LEAVE FOR ONE SECOND AND HERE YOU ARE, ALREADY BLOWIN' UP AT HER.
I'M JUST SAYIN' SHE SHOULDN'T BE MESSIN' WITH THIS STUFF...
WE'VE HAD A PROBLEM WITH PESTS RECENTLY. SEEMS WE HAVE A FAMILY OF PACKRATS. WE CATCH THEM EVERY NOW AND THEN STEALING THINGS FOR THEIR NESTS.
I DID SEE SOME KIND OF MOUSE.
COME ON, EMMA, DINNER'S ALMOST READY. LETS GO DOWNSTAIRS AND SET THE TABLE.
GONNA HAVE TO SPRAY IN HERE AGAIN TOMORROW.
SO, DON'T BE PLAYING AROUND IN HERE.
GRAM, IF YOU DON'T MIND ME ASKING, WHAT'S WITH ALL THE WIERD STUFF IN THAT ROOM UPSTAIRS?

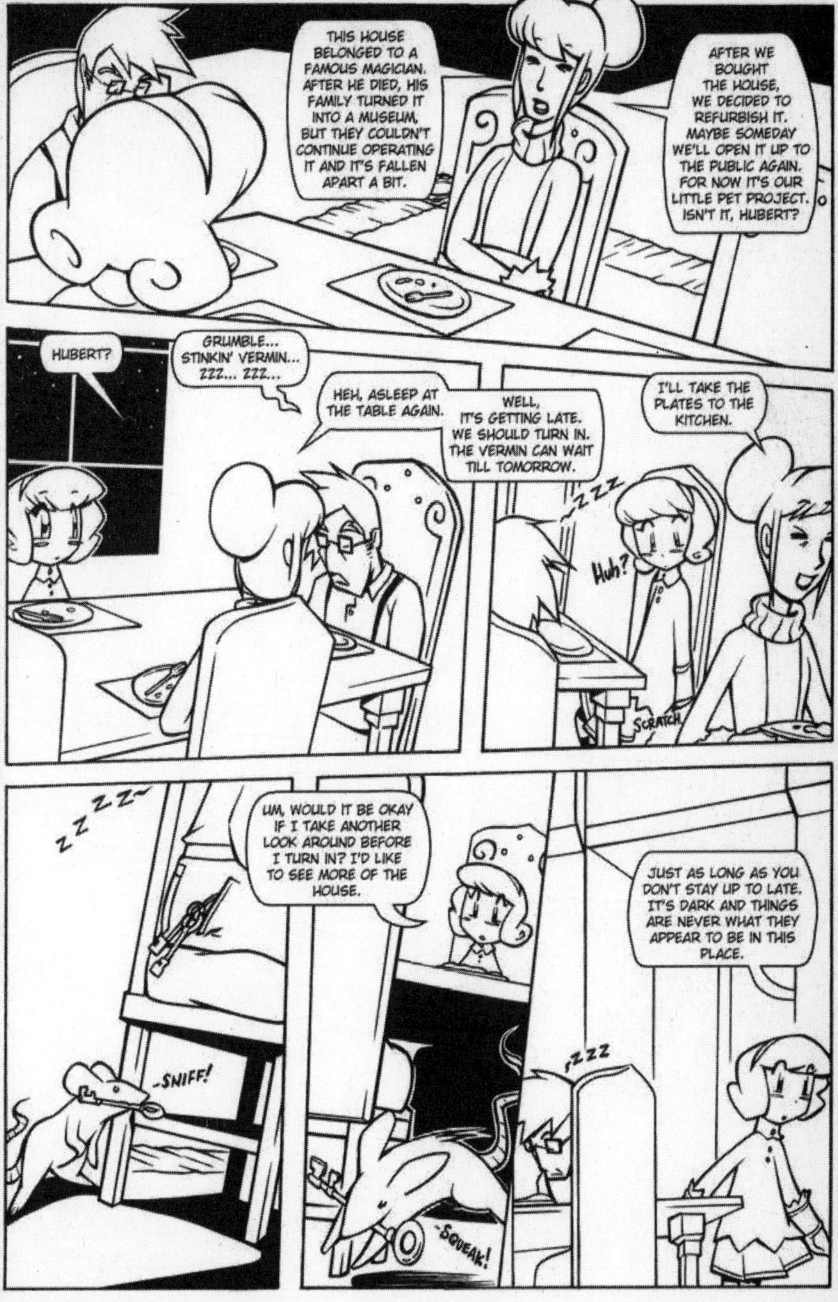
THIS HOUSE BELONGED TO A FAMOUS MAGICIAN. AFTER HE DIED, HIS FAMILY TURNED IT INTO A MUSEUM, BUT THEY COULDN'T CONTINUE OPERATING IT AND IT'S FALLEN APART A BIT.
AFTER WE BOUGHT THE HOUSE, WE DECIDED TO REFURBISH IT. MAYBE SOMEDAY WE'LL OPEN IT UP TO THE PUBLIC AGAIN. FOR NOW IT'S OUR LITTLE PET PROJECT. ISN'T IT, HUBERT?
HUBERT?
GRUMBLE... STINKIN' VERMIN... ZZZ... ZZZ...
HEH, ASLEEP AT THE TABLE AGAIN.
WELL, IT'S GETTING LATE. WE SHOULD TURN IN. THE VERMIN CAN WAIT TILL TOMORROW.
I'LL TAKE THE PLATES TO THE KITCHEN.
ZZZ
Huh?
SCRATCH
Z Z Z Z~
UM, WOULD IT BE OKAY IF I TAKE ANOTHER LOOK AROUND BEFORE I TURN IN? I'D LIKE TO SEE MORE OF THE HOUSE.
-SNIFF!
JUST AS LONG AS YOU DON'T STAY UP TO LATE. IT'S DARK AND THINGS ARE NEVER WHAT THEY APPEAR TO BE IN THIS PLACE.
ZZZ
-SQUEAK!

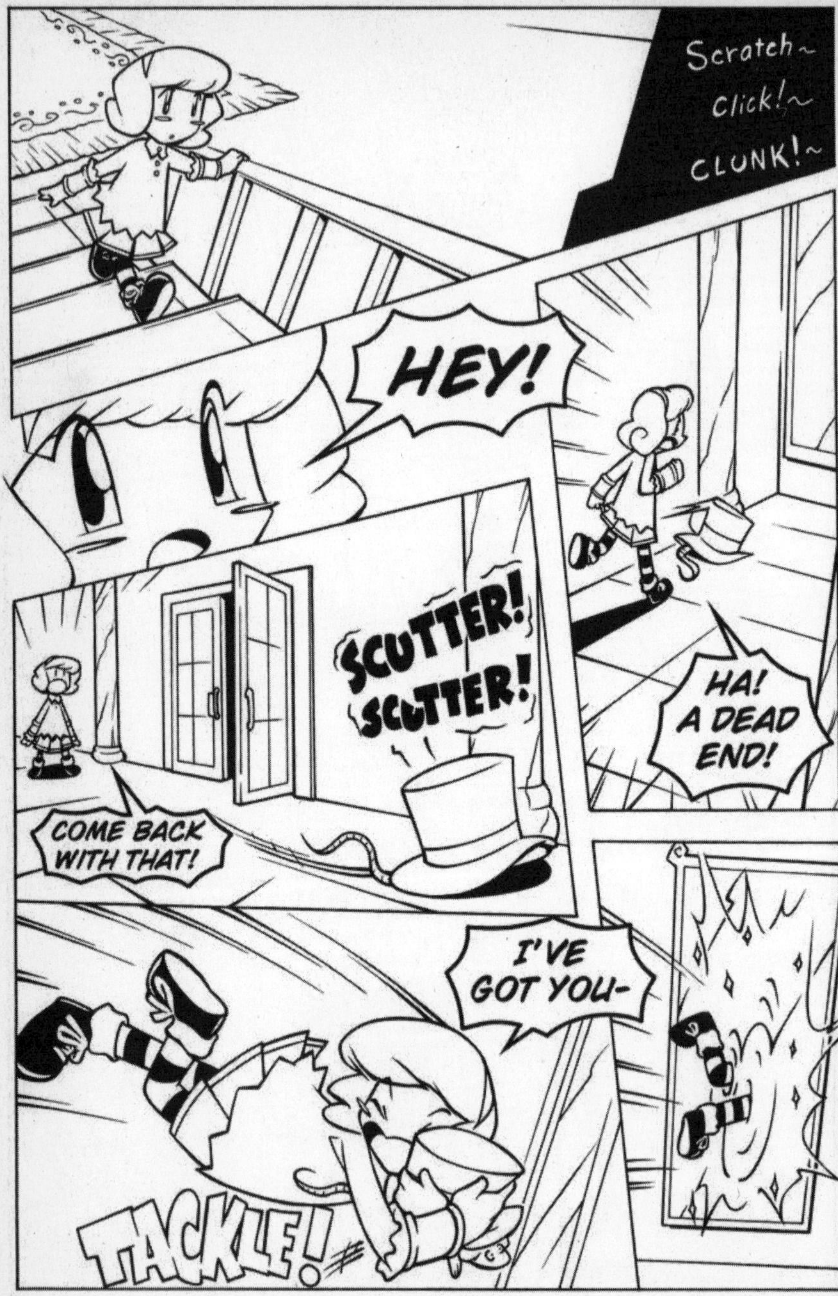
Scratch~
Click!~
CLUNK!~
HEY!
SCUTTER! SCUTTER!
COME BACK WITH THAT!
HA! A DEAD END!
I'VE GOT YOU-
TACKLE!

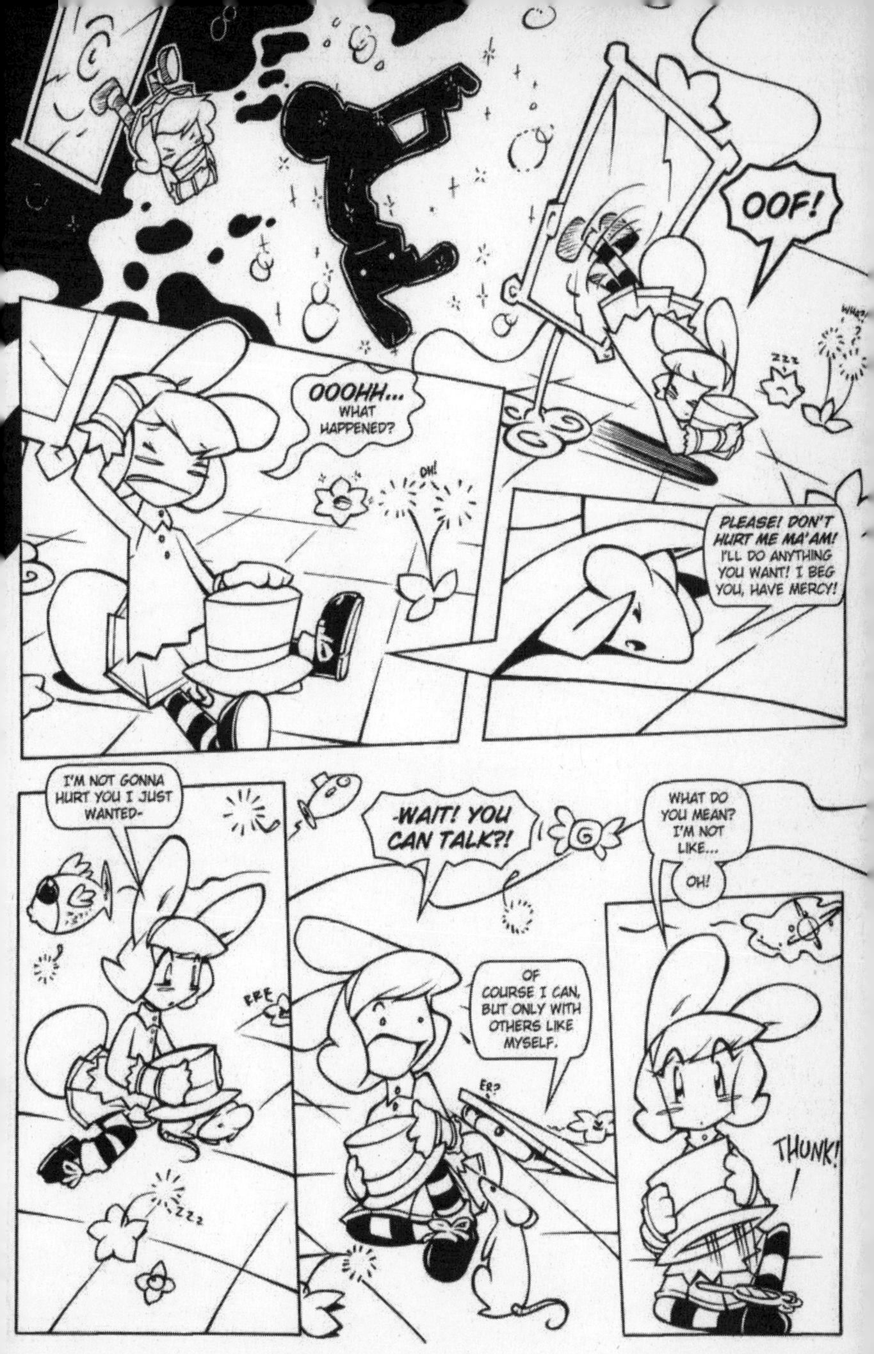
OOF!
WHAT?
ZZZ
OOOHH... WHAT HAPPENED?
OH!
PLEASE! DON'T HURT ME MA'AM! I'LL DO ANYTHING YOU WANT! I BEG YOU, HAVE MERCY!
I'M NOT GONNA HURT YOU I JUST WANTED-
EEE
ZZZ
-WAIT! YOU CAN TALK?!
OF COURSE I CAN, BUT ONLY WITH OTHERS LIKE MYSELF.
ER?
WHAT DO YOU MEAN? I'M NOT LIKE...
OH!
THUNK!

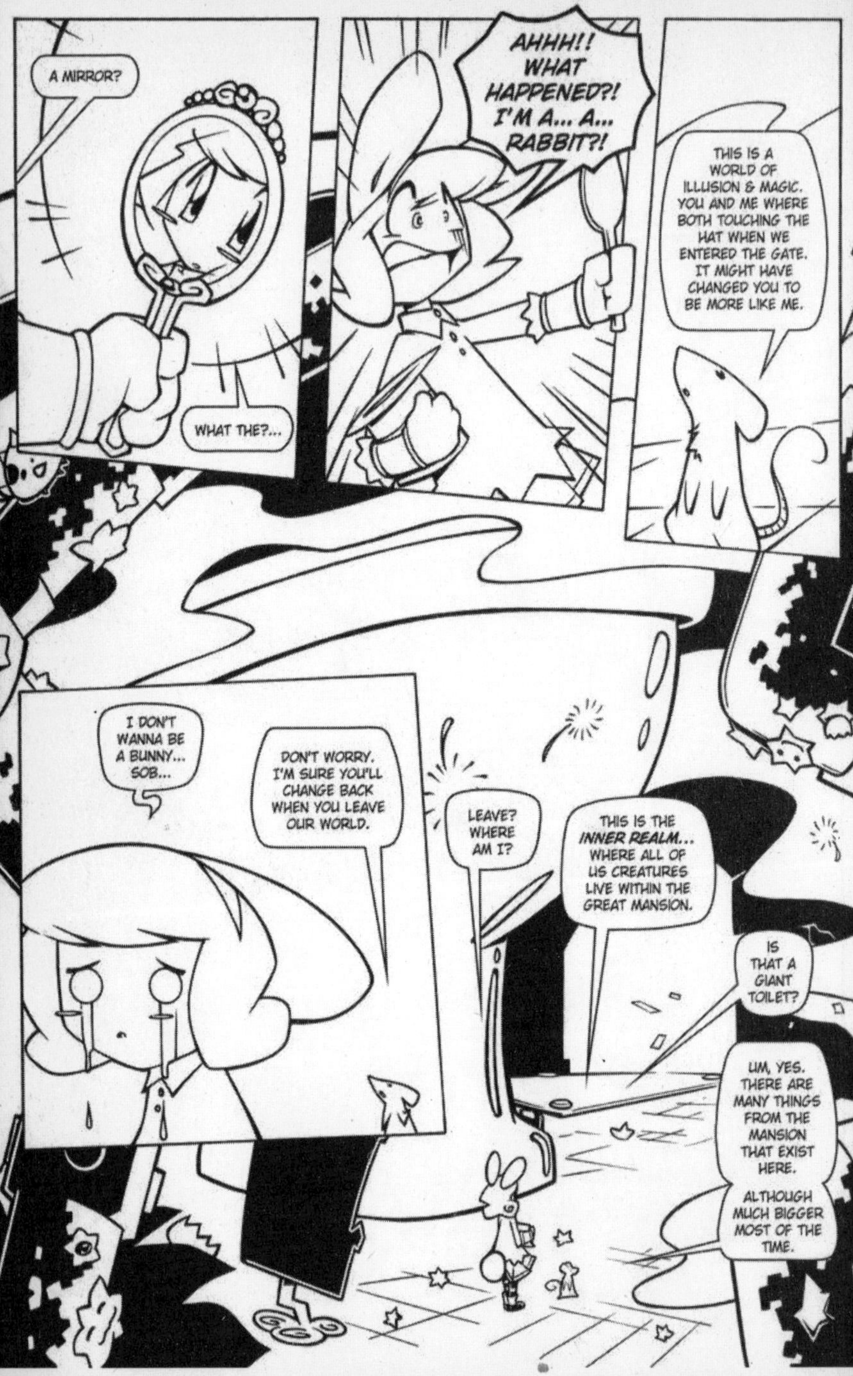
A MIRROR?
WHAT THE?...
AHHH!! WHAT HAPPENED?! I'M A... A... RABBIT?!
THIS IS A WORLD OF ILLUSION & MAGIC. YOU AND ME WHERE BOTH TOUCHING THE HAT WHEN WE ENTERED THE GATE. IT MIGHT HAVE CHANGED YOU TO BE MORE LIKE ME.
I DON'T WANNA BE A BUNNY... SOB...
DON'T WORRY. I'M SURE YOU'LL CHANGE BACK WHEN YOU LEAVE OUR WORLD.
LEAVE? WHERE AM I?
THIS IS THE ***INNER REALM...*** WHERE ALL OF US CREATURES LIVE WITHIN THE GREAT MANSION.
IS THAT A GIANT TOILET?
UM, YES. THERE ARE MANY THINGS FROM THE MANSION THAT EXIST HERE.
ALTHOUGH MUCH BIGGER MOST OF THE TIME.

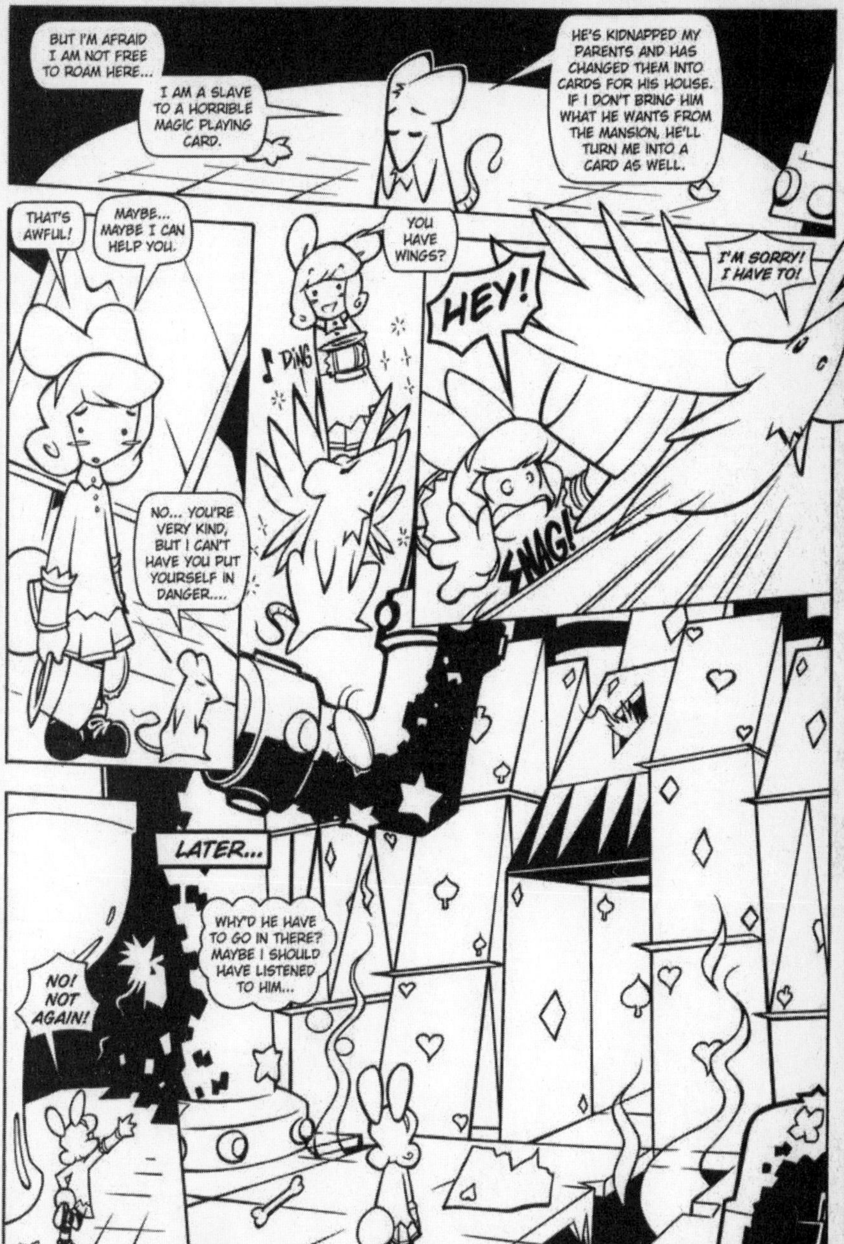
BUT I'M AFRAID I AM NOT FREE TO ROAM HERE...
I AM A SLAVE TO A HORRIBLE MAGIC PLAYING CARD.
HE'S KIDNAPPED MY PARENTS AND HAS CHANGED THEM INTO CARDS FOR HIS HOUSE. IF I DON'T BRING HIM WHAT HE WANTS FROM THE MANSION, HE'LL TURN ME INTO A CARD AS WELL.
THAT'S AWFUL!
MAYBE... MAYBE I CAN HELP YOU.
NO... YOU'RE VERY KIND, BUT I CAN'T HAVE YOU PUT YOURSELF IN DANGER....
YOU HAVE WINGS?
DING
HEY!
I'M SORRY! I HAVE TO!
SNAG!
LATER...
NO! NOT AGAIN!
WHY'D HE HAVE TO GO IN THERE? MAYBE I SHOULD HAVE LISTENED TO HIM...

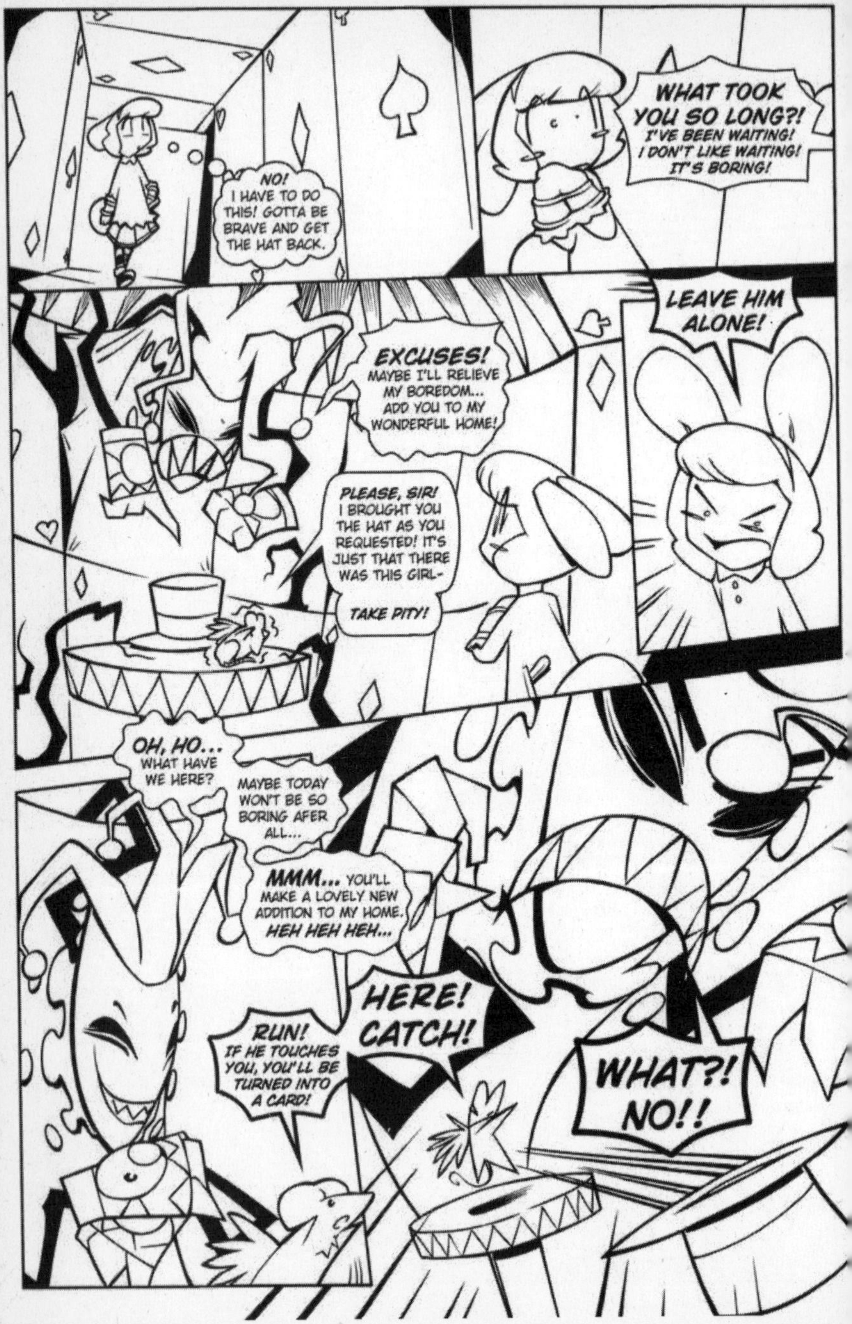
NO! I HAVE TO DO THIS! GOTTA BE BRAVE AND GET THE HAT BACK.
WHAT TOOK YOU SO LONG?! I'VE BEEN WAITING! I DON'T LIKE WAITING! IT'S BORING!
EXCUSES! MAYBE I'LL RELIEVE MY BOREDOM... ADD YOU TO MY WONDERFUL HOME!
PLEASE, SIR! I BROUGHT YOU THE HAT AS YOU REQUESTED! IT'S JUST THAT THERE WAS THIS GIRL-
TAKE PITY!
LEAVE HIM ALONE!
OH, HO... WHAT HAVE WE HERE?
MAYBE TODAY WON'T BE SO BORING AFER ALL...
MMM... YOU'LL MAKE A LOVELY NEW ADDITION TO MY HOME. HEH HEH HEH...
RUN! IF HE TOUCHES YOU, YOU'LL BE TURNED INTO A CARD!
HERE! CATCH!
WHAT?! NO!!

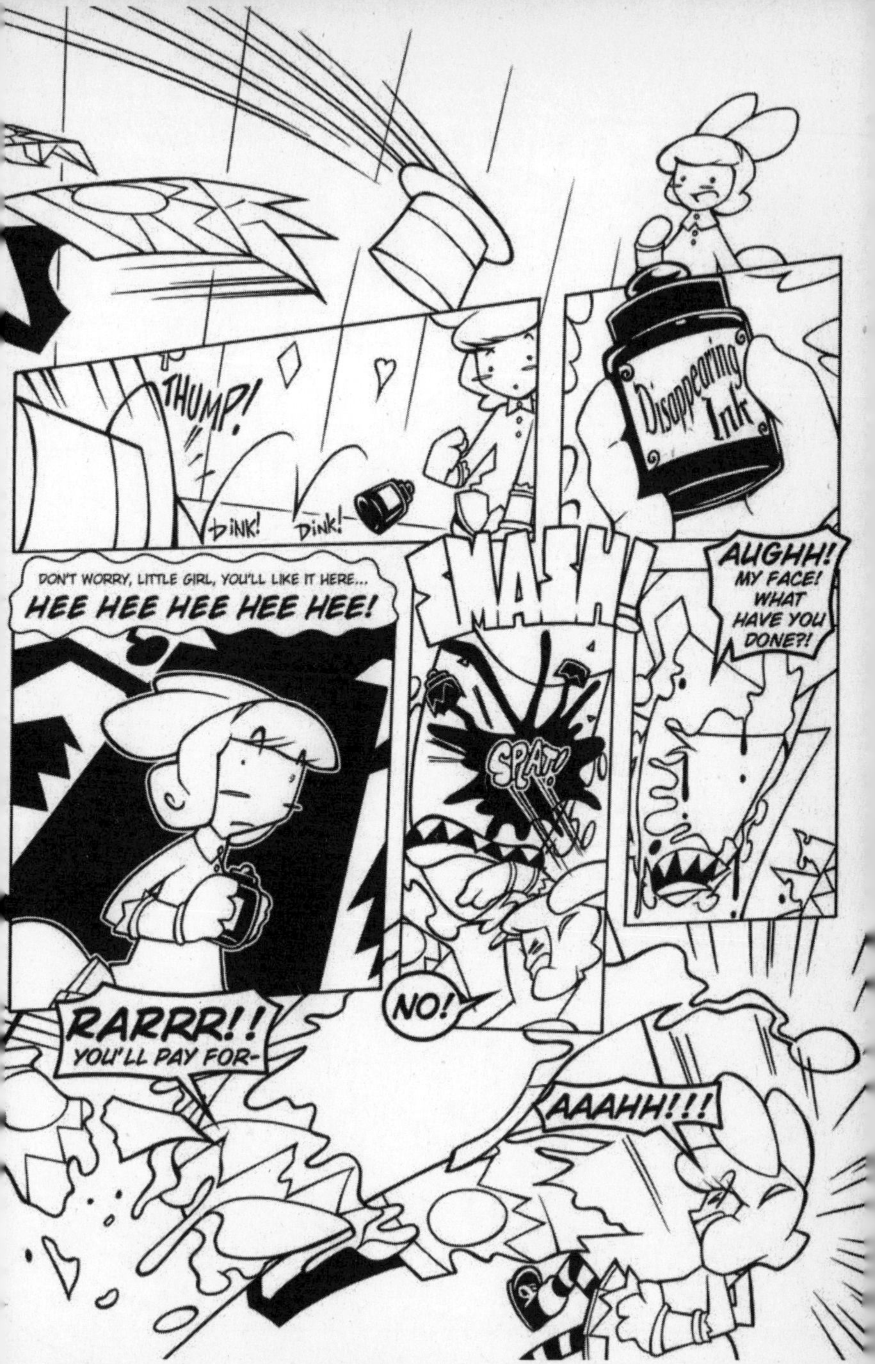
THUMP!
DINK!
DINK!
Disappearing Ink
DON'T WORRY, LITTLE GIRL, YOU'LL LIKE IT HERE...
HEE HEE HEE HEE HEE!
SMASH!
SPLAT!
AUGHH! MY FACE! WHAT HAVE YOU DONE?!
RARRR!! YOU'LL PAY FOR-
NO!
AAAHH!!!

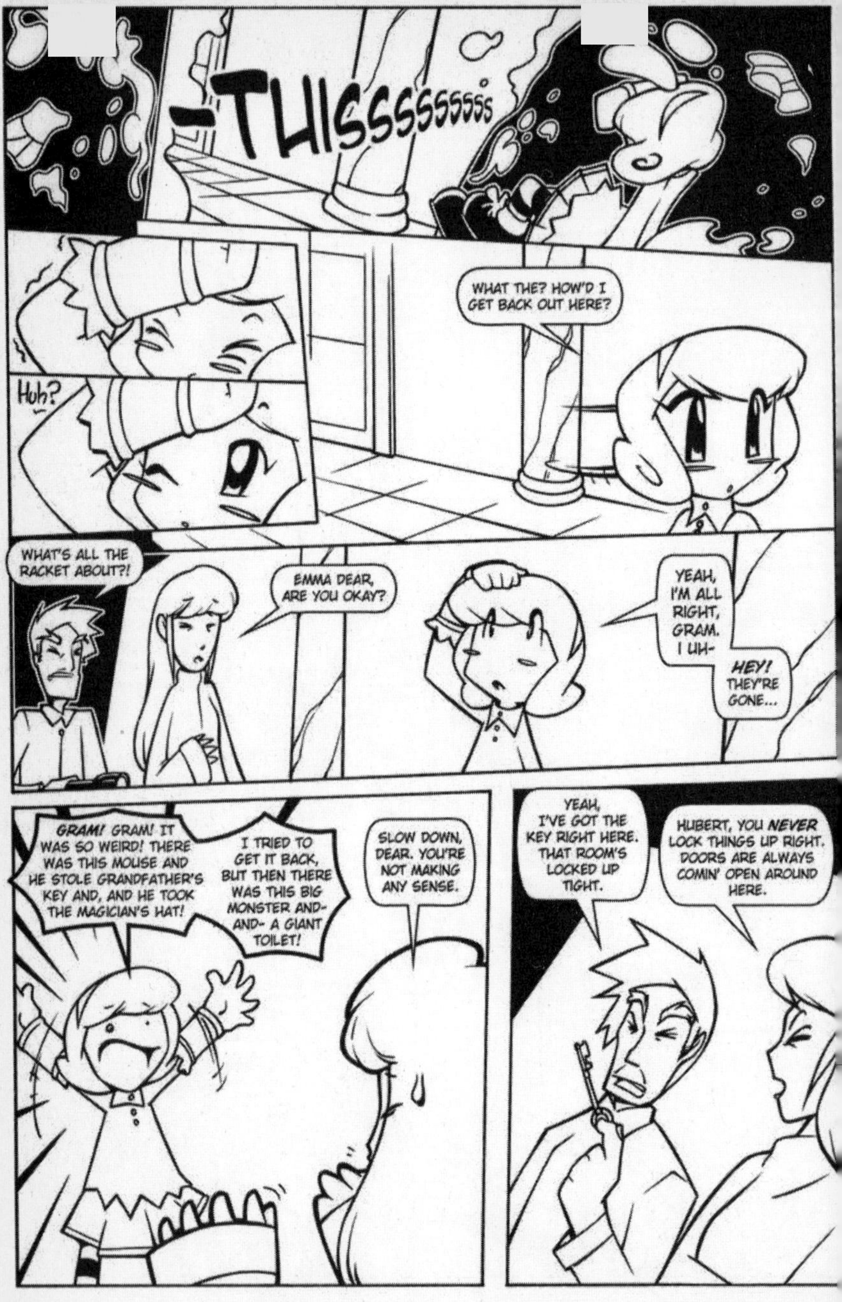
THISSSSSSSS
WHAT THE? HOW'D I GET BACK OUT HERE?
Huh?
WHAT'S ALL THE RACKET ABOUT?!
EMMA DEAR, ARE YOU OKAY?
YEAH, I'M ALL RIGHT, GRAM. I UH-
HEY! THEY'RE GONE...
GRAM! GRAM! IT WAS SO WEIRD! THERE WAS THIS MOUSE AND HE STOLE GRANDFATHER'S KEY AND, AND HE TOOK THE MAGICIAN'S HAT!
I TRIED TO GET IT BACK, BUT THEN THERE WAS THIS BIG MONSTER AND- AND- A GIANT TOILET!
SLOW DOWN, DEAR. YOU'RE NOT MAKING ANY SENSE.
YEAH, I'VE GOT THE KEY RIGHT HERE. THAT ROOM'S LOCKED UP TIGHT.
HUBERT, YOU NEVER LOCK THINGS UP RIGHT. DOORS ARE ALWAYS COMIN' OPEN AROUND HERE.

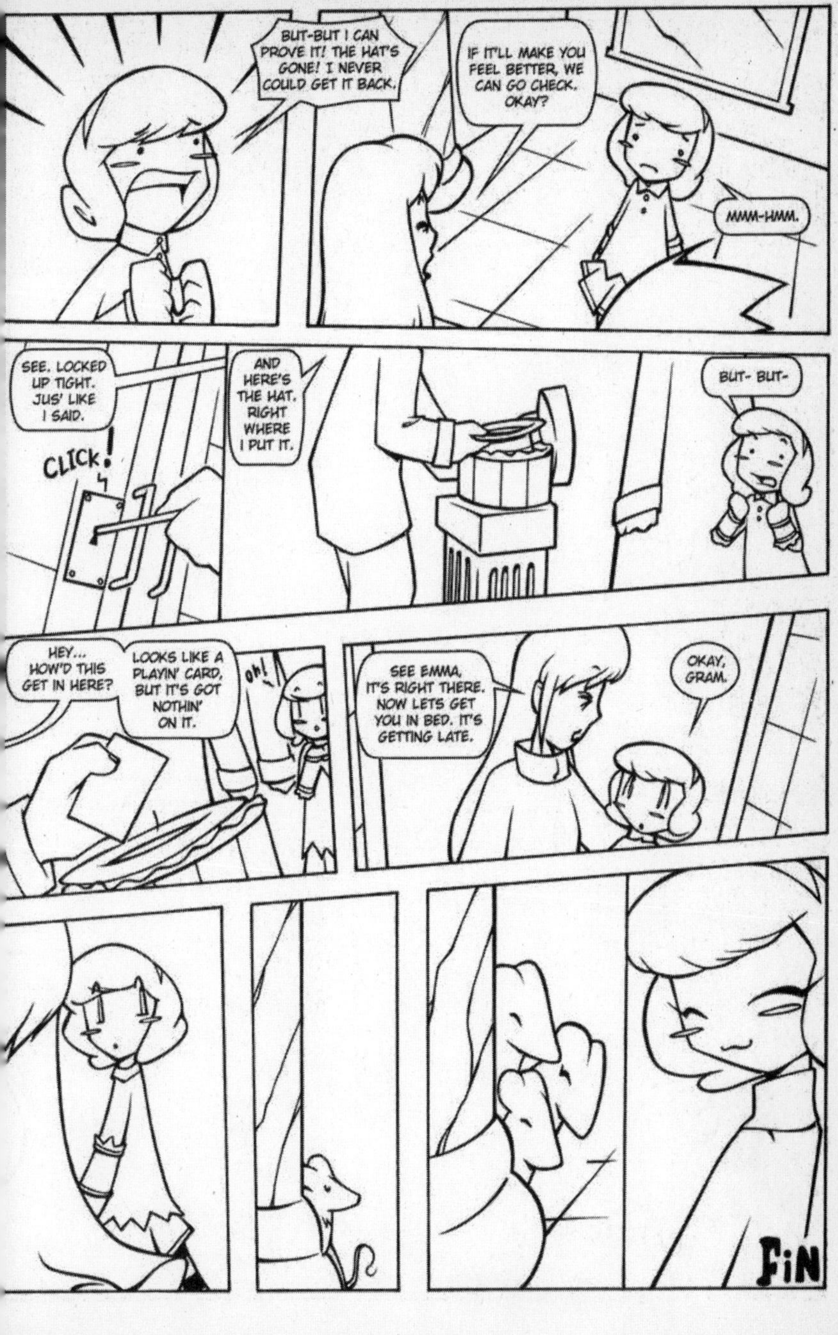
BUT-BUT I CAN PROVE IT! THE HAT'S GONE! I NEVER COULD GET IT BACK.
IF IT'LL MAKE YOU FEEL BETTER, WE CAN GO CHECK. OKAY?
MMM-HMM.
SEE. LOCKED UP TIGHT. JUS' LIKE I SAID.
CLICK!
AND HERE'S THE HAT, RIGHT WHERE I PUT IT.
BUT- BUT-
HEY... HOW'D THIS GET IN HERE?
LOOKS LIKE A PLAYIN' CARD, BUT IT'S GOT NOTHIN' ON IT.
oh!
SEE EMMA, IT'S RIGHT THERE. NOW LETS GET YOU IN BED. IT'S GETTING LATE.
OKAY, GRAM.
FiN

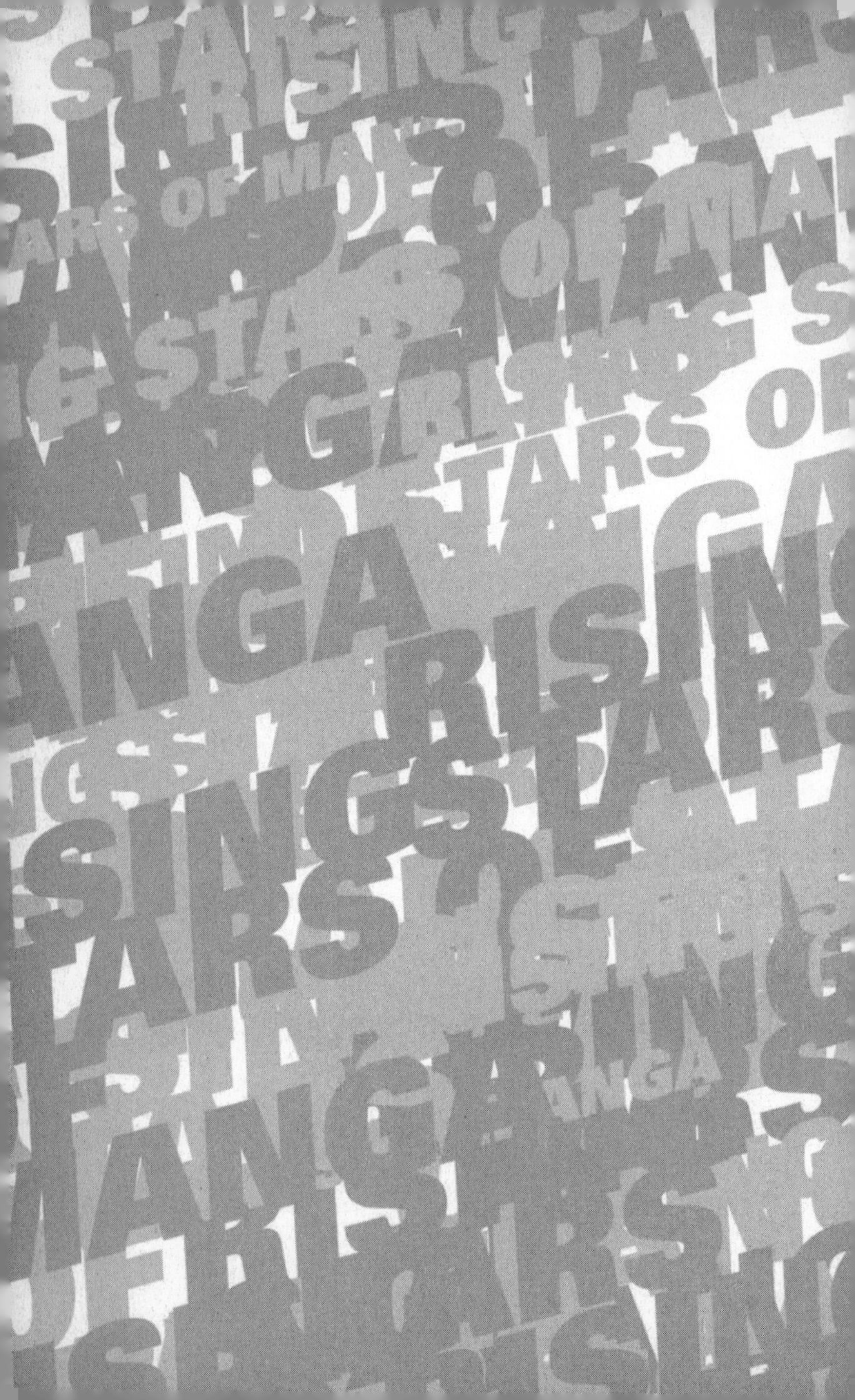

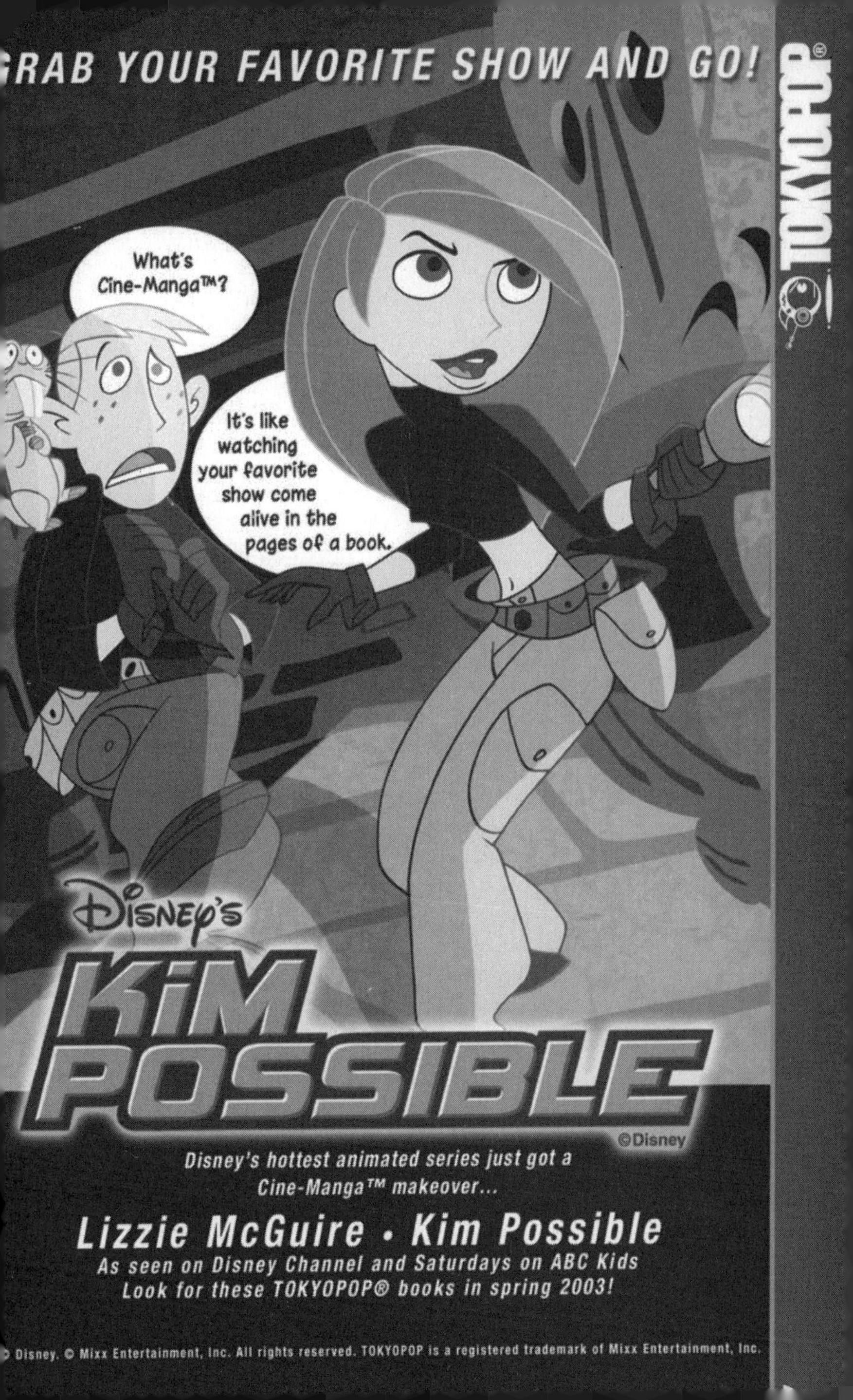
GRAB YOUR FAVORITE SHOW AND GO!
TOKYOPOP®
What's Cine-Manga™?
It's like watching your favorite show come alive in the pages of a book.
Disney's
KIM POSSIBLE
©Disney
Disney's hottest animated series just got a Cine-Manga™ makeover...
Lizzie McGuire • Kim Possible
As seen on Disney Channel and Saturdays on ABC Kids
Look for these TOKYOPOP® books in spring 2003!
© Disney. © Mixx Entertainment, Inc. All rights reserved. TOKYOPOP is a registered trademark of Mixx Entertainment, Inc.

PEST

RUNNER UP

::

PEST :: RUNNER UP ::

Kyle Hoyt was born in 1974 in Erie, Pennsylvania, and currently works as a graphic designer in San Francisco. He went to art school at the University of Cincinnati's School of Design, Architecture, Art and Planning (DAAP), although he notes that his professors would probably bristle at his using that training to produce comic art. You can see more of his work at www.stationzero.org.

Inspiration for this story:
My life, exaggerated beyond recognition. The monster is, of course, my cat, who has truly earned the moniker of "Pest" through a consistent program of property destruction, gluttony and bellyaching. The setting is actually my neighborhood in lovely downtown San Francisco, although there are no cable cars or glamour shots of the Golden Gate Bridge here--just perpetual construction, bums and tiny, tiny apartments. And yes, I actually have had people I don't know come through my apartment by way of the fire escape. Truth is stranger than fiction.

Favorite Manga:
Urusei Yatsura, Spirit of Wonder, Nausicaa

Favorite Manga Artists:
Rumiko Takahashi, Kenji Tsuruta, Kosuke Fujishima

....

Judge's Comments:
This seductively charming tale makes light of the challenges faced by a teen that has just moved to the big city. Hitting the streets means running a gauntlet of weirdoes, and without a good job it's even hard to get a decent meal. After an encounter in a dark alley, this teen gathers her wits and ends up making the best of a surprising situation.

Kyle Hoyt's stark and simple artwork supports an ominous yet witty tone for this story. Realistic backgrounds with stylized characters, page layouts with varied panel shapes and a good assortment of angles shows that Hoyt has been doing his homework. Pest is one flavor of American manga that should have a strong future.
-Jeremy Ross

::

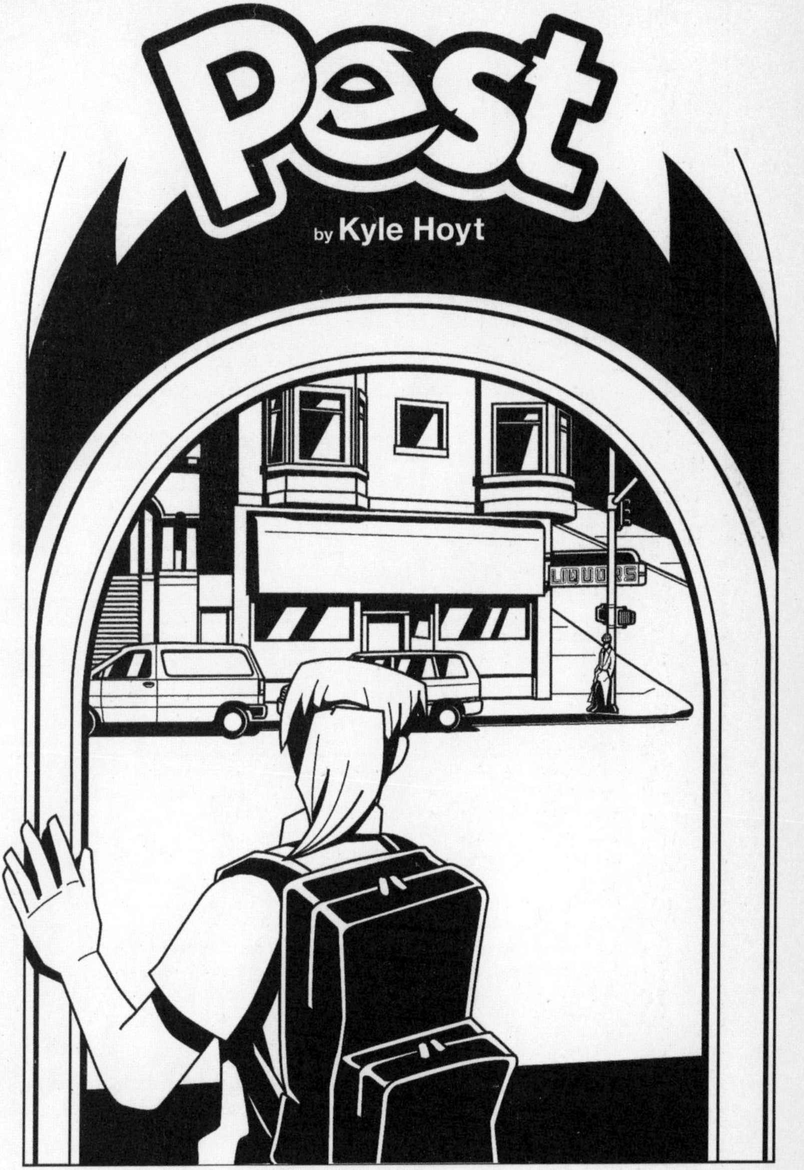
Pest
by Kyle Hoyt
LIQUORS

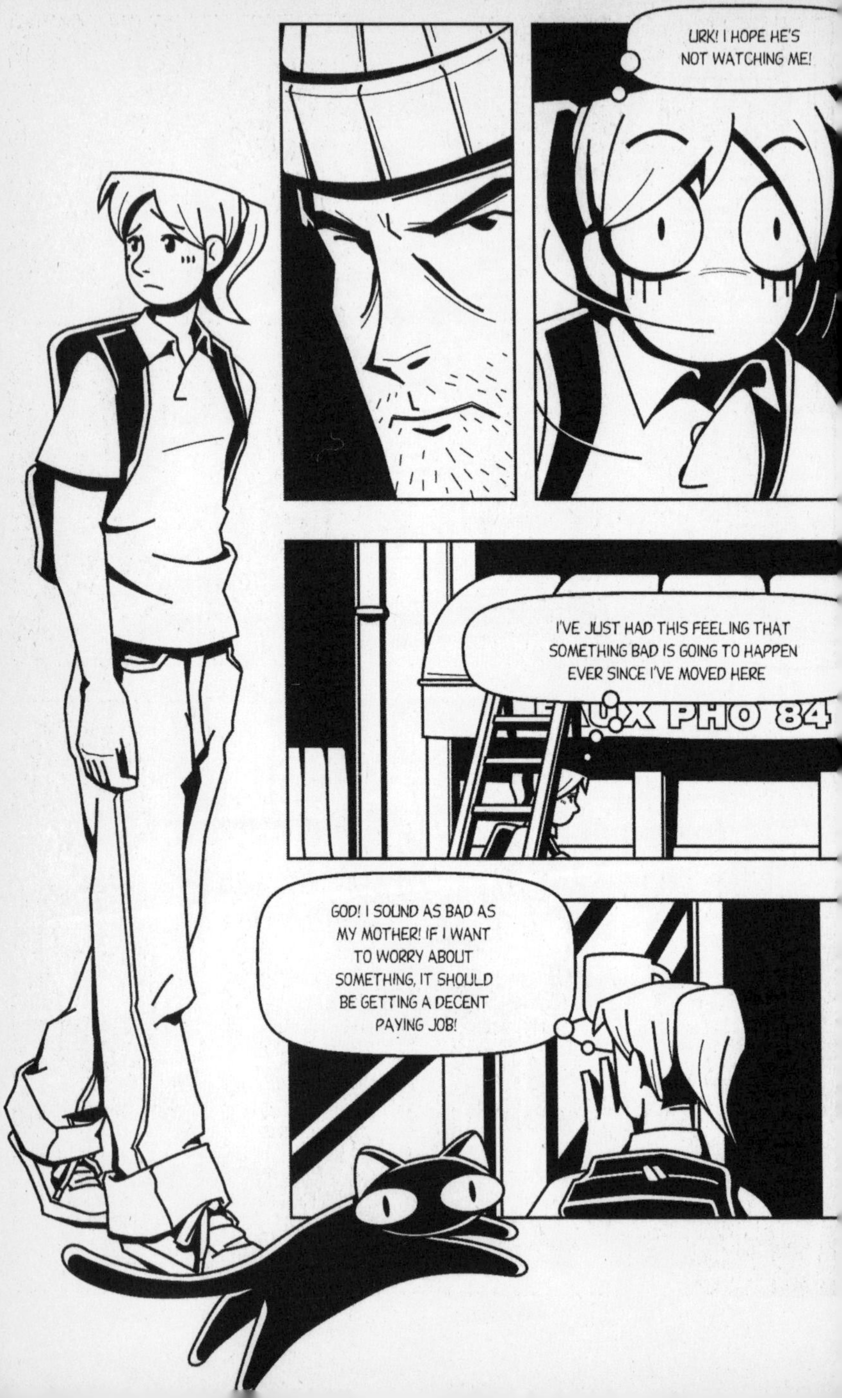
URK! I HOPE HE'S NOT WATCHING ME!
I'VE JUST HAD THIS FEELING THAT SOMETHING BAD IS GOING TO HAPPEN EVER SINCE I'VE MOVED HERE
X PHO 84
GOD! I SOUND AS BAD AS MY MOTHER! IF I WANT TO WORRY ABOUT SOMETHING, IT SHOULD BE GETTING A DECENT PAYING JOB!

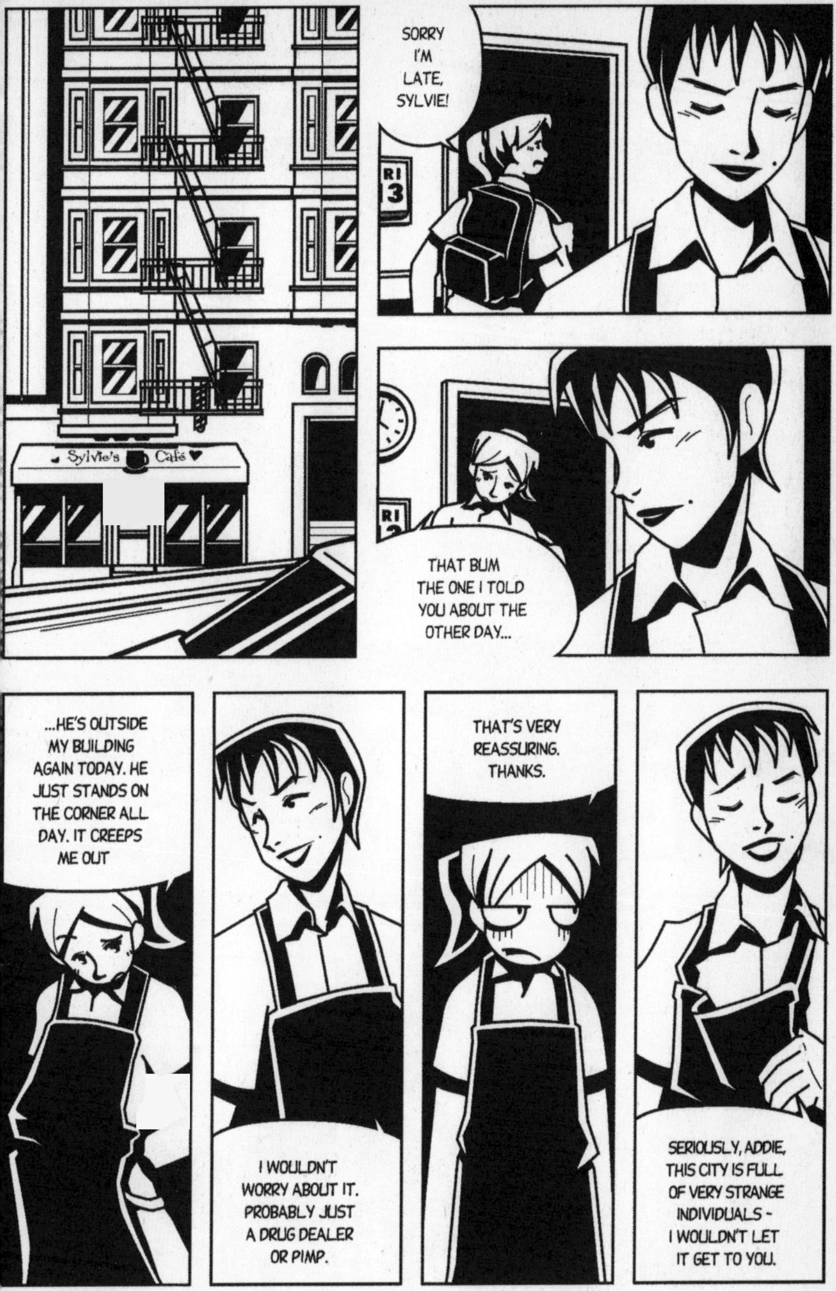
Sylvie's Café
SORRY I'M LATE, SYLVIE!
THAT BUM THE ONE I TOLD YOU ABOUT THE OTHER DAY...
...HE'S OUTSIDE MY BUILDING AGAIN TODAY. HE JUST STANDS ON THE CORNER ALL DAY. IT CREEPS ME OUT
I WOULDN'T WORRY ABOUT IT. PROBABLY JUST A DRUG DEALER OR PIMP.
THAT'S VERY REASSURING. THANKS.
SERIOUSLY, ADDIE, THIS CITY IS FULL OF VERY STRANGE INDIVIDUALS - I WOULDN'T LET IT GET TO YOU.

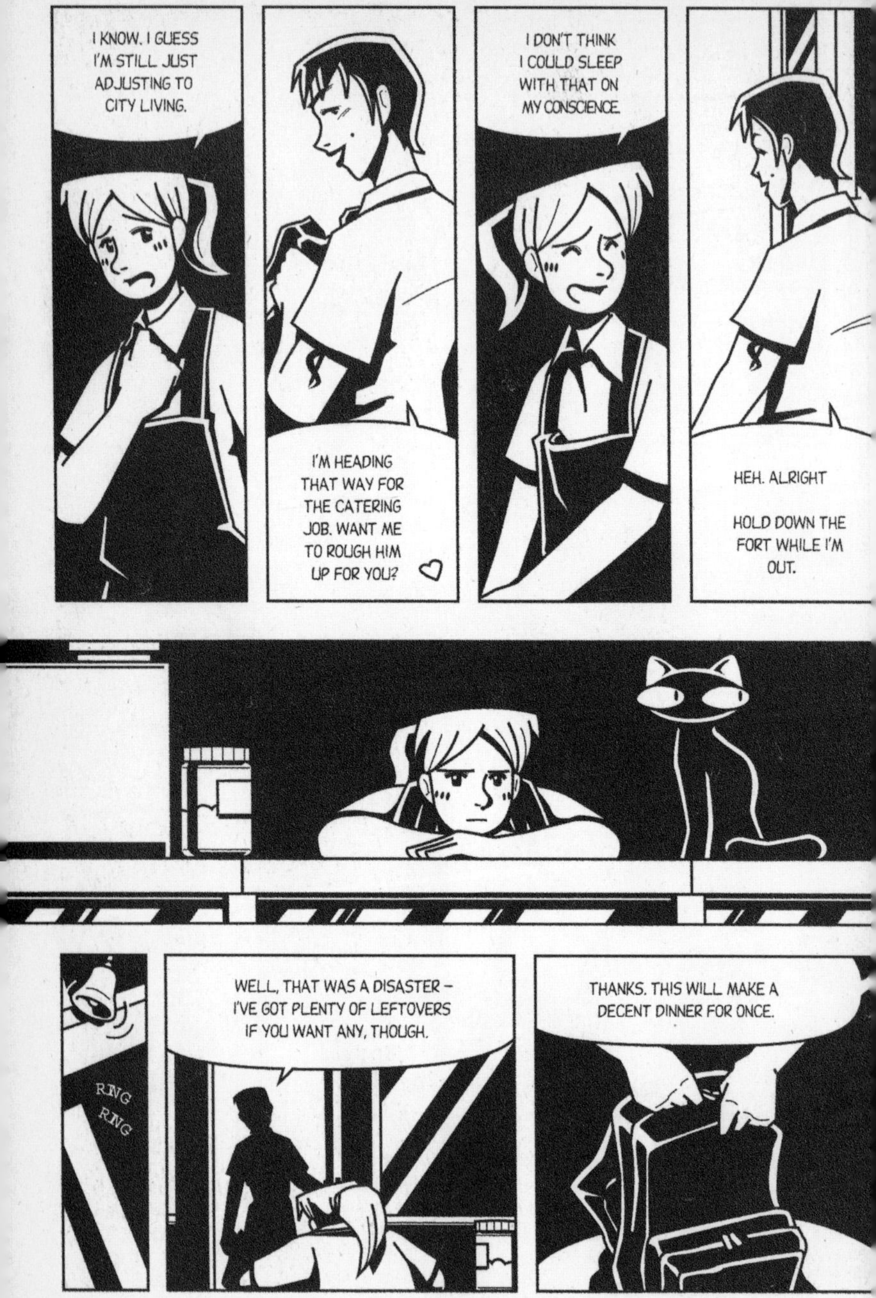
I KNOW. I GUESS I'M STILL JUST ADJUSTING TO CITY LIVING.
I'M HEADING THAT WAY FOR THE CATERING JOB. WANT ME TO ROUGH HIM UP FOR YOU? ♡
I DON'T THINK I COULD SLEEP WITH THAT ON MY CONSCIENCE.
HEH. ALRIGHT
HOLD DOWN THE FORT WHILE I'M OUT.
RING RING
WELL, THAT WAS A DISASTER - I'VE GOT PLENTY OF LEFTOVERS IF YOU WANT ANY, THOUGH.
THANKS. THIS WILL MAKE A DECENT DINNER FOR ONCE.

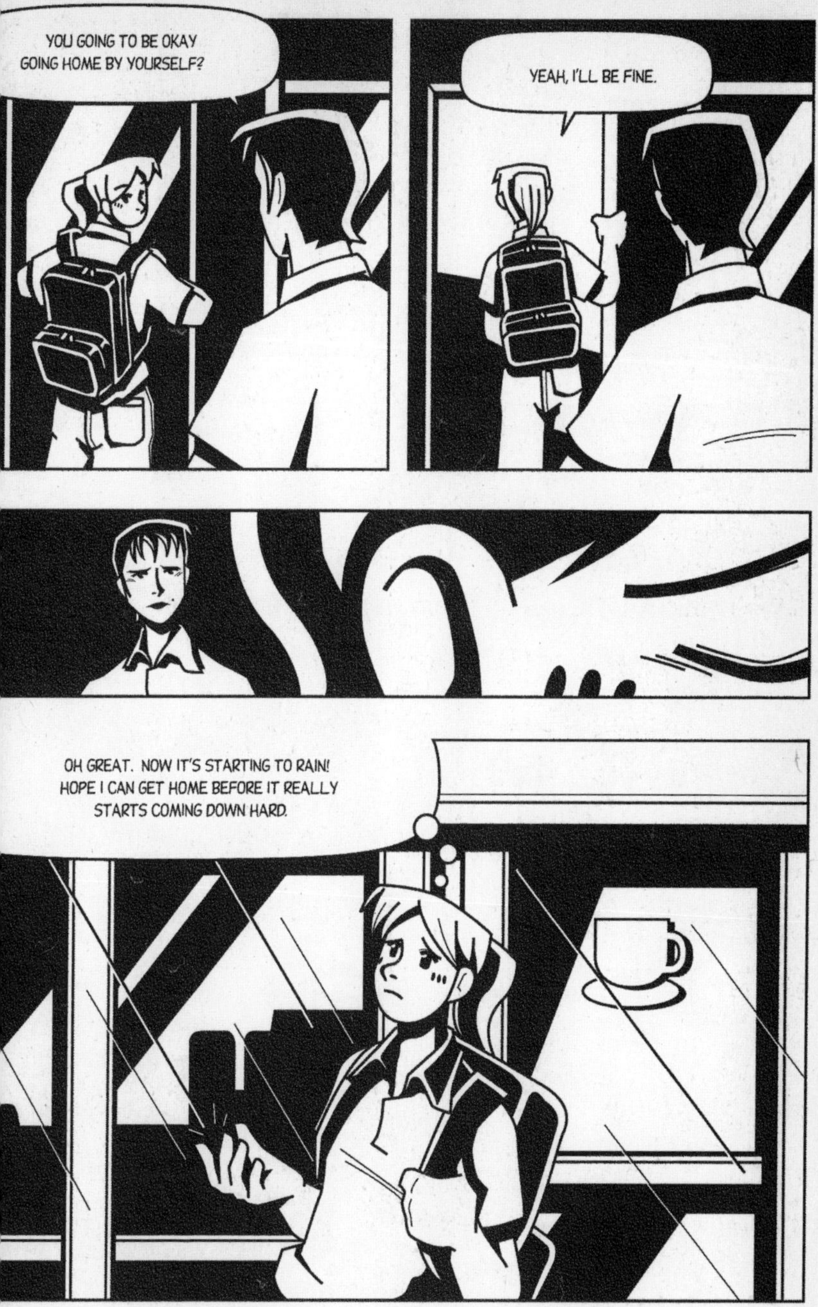
YOU GOING TO BE OKAY GOING HOME BY YOURSELF?
YEAH, I'LL BE FINE.
OH GREAT. NOW IT'S STARTING TO RAIN! HOPE I CAN GET HOME BEFORE IT REALLY STARTS COMING DOWN HARD.

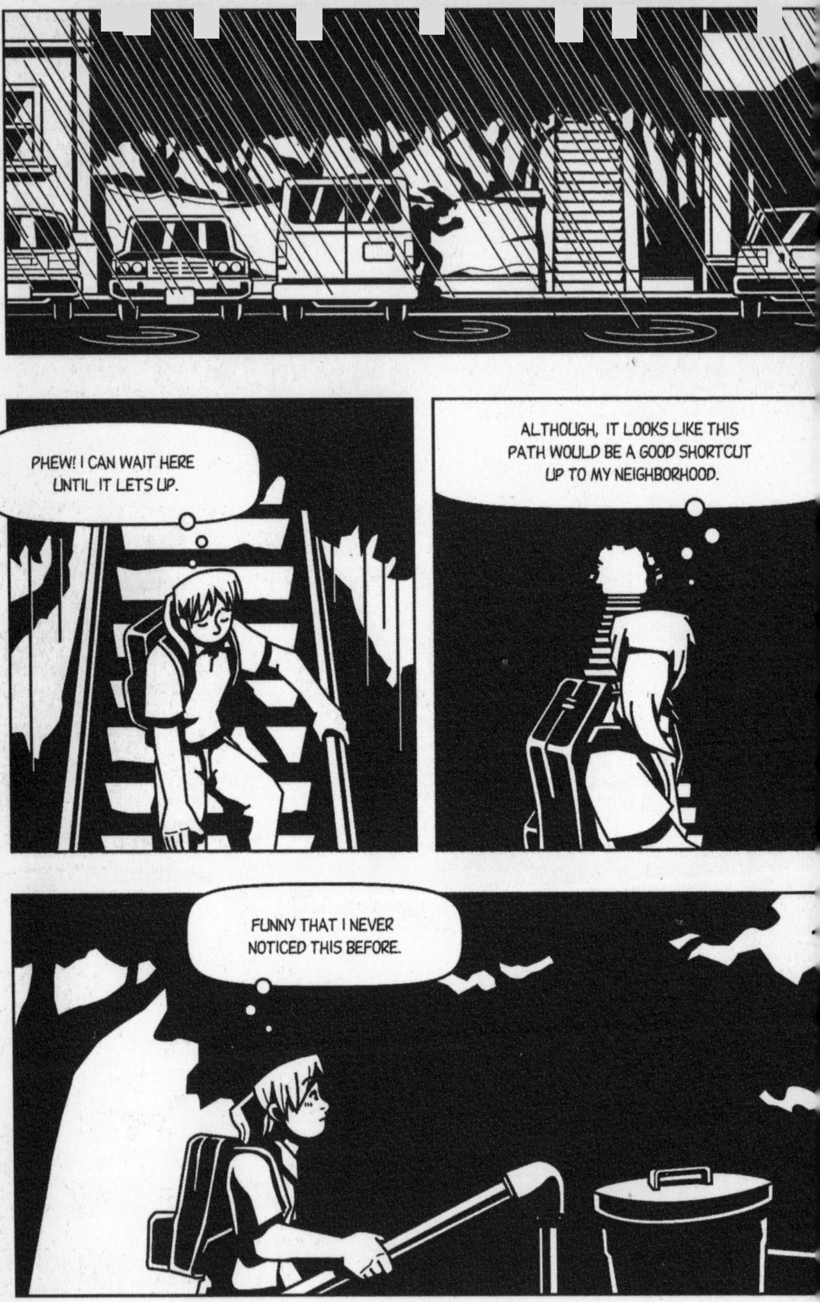
PHEW! I CAN WAIT HERE UNTIL IT LETS UP.
ALTHOUGH, IT LOOKS LIKE THIS PATH WOULD BE A GOOD SHORTCUT UP TO MY NEIGHBORHOOD.
FUNNY THAT I NEVER NOTICED THIS BEFORE.

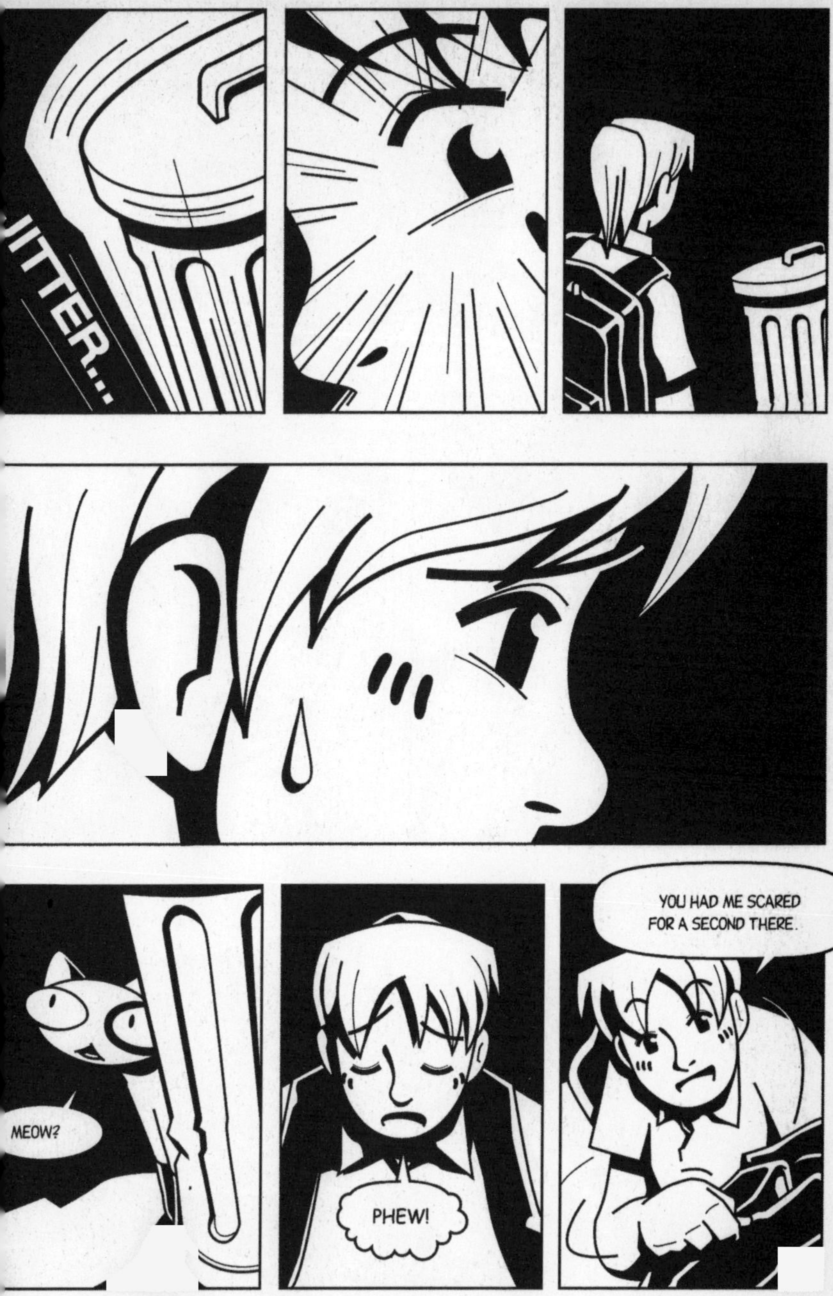
ITTER...
MEOW?
PHEW!
YOU HAD ME SCARED FOR A SECOND THERE.

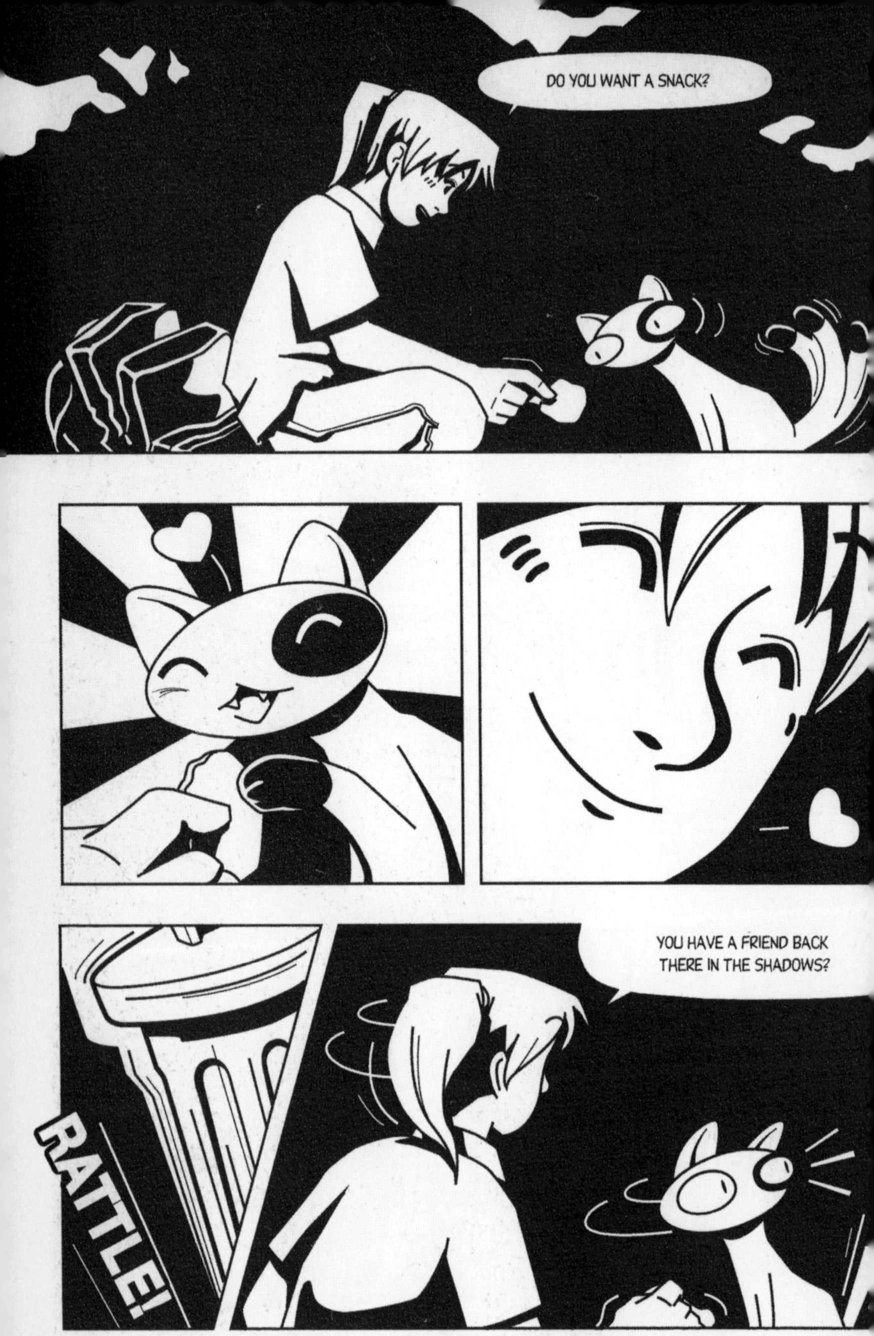

DO YOU WANT A SNACK?
YOU HAVE A FRIEND BACK THERE IN THE SHADOWS?
RATTLE!

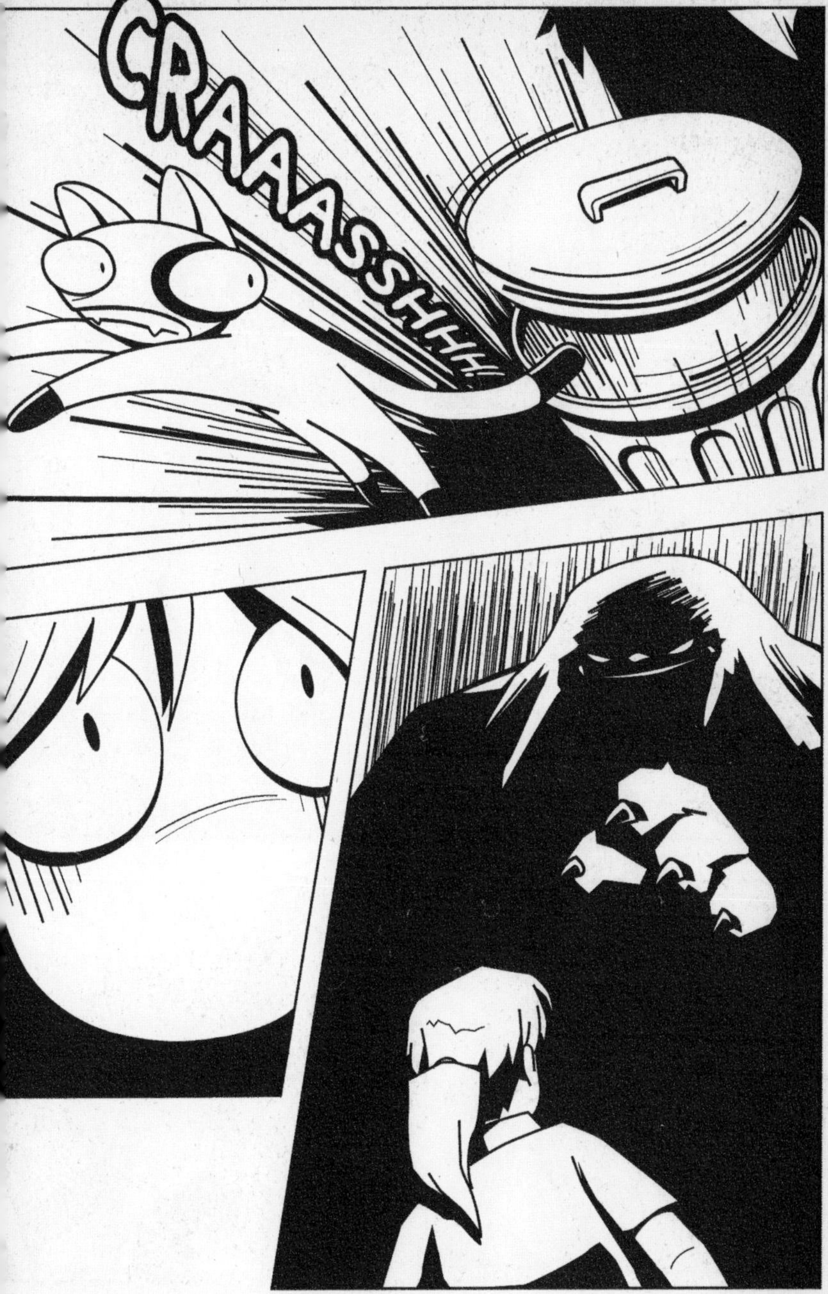
CRAAASSHHH!

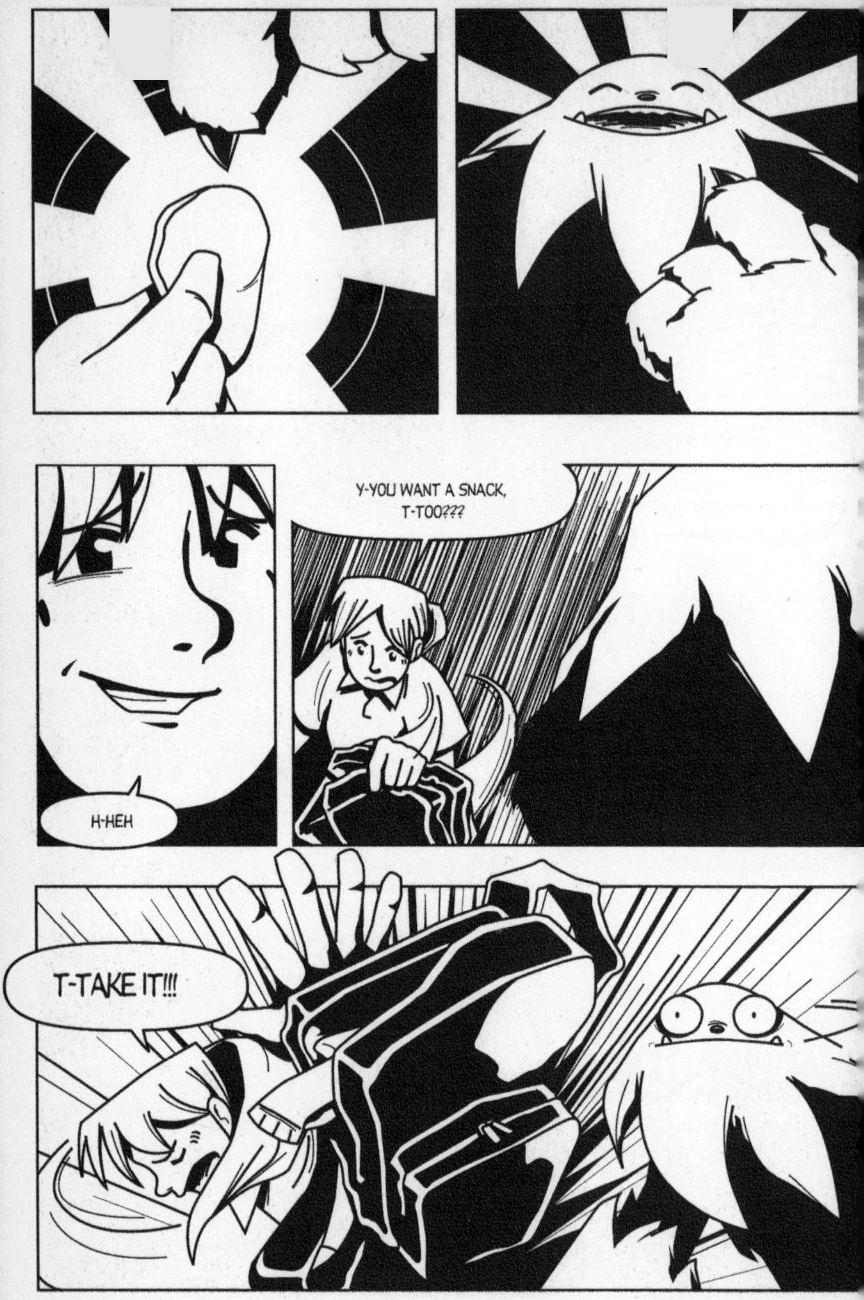
H-HEH
Y-YOU WANT A SNACK, T-TOO???
T-TAKE IT!!!

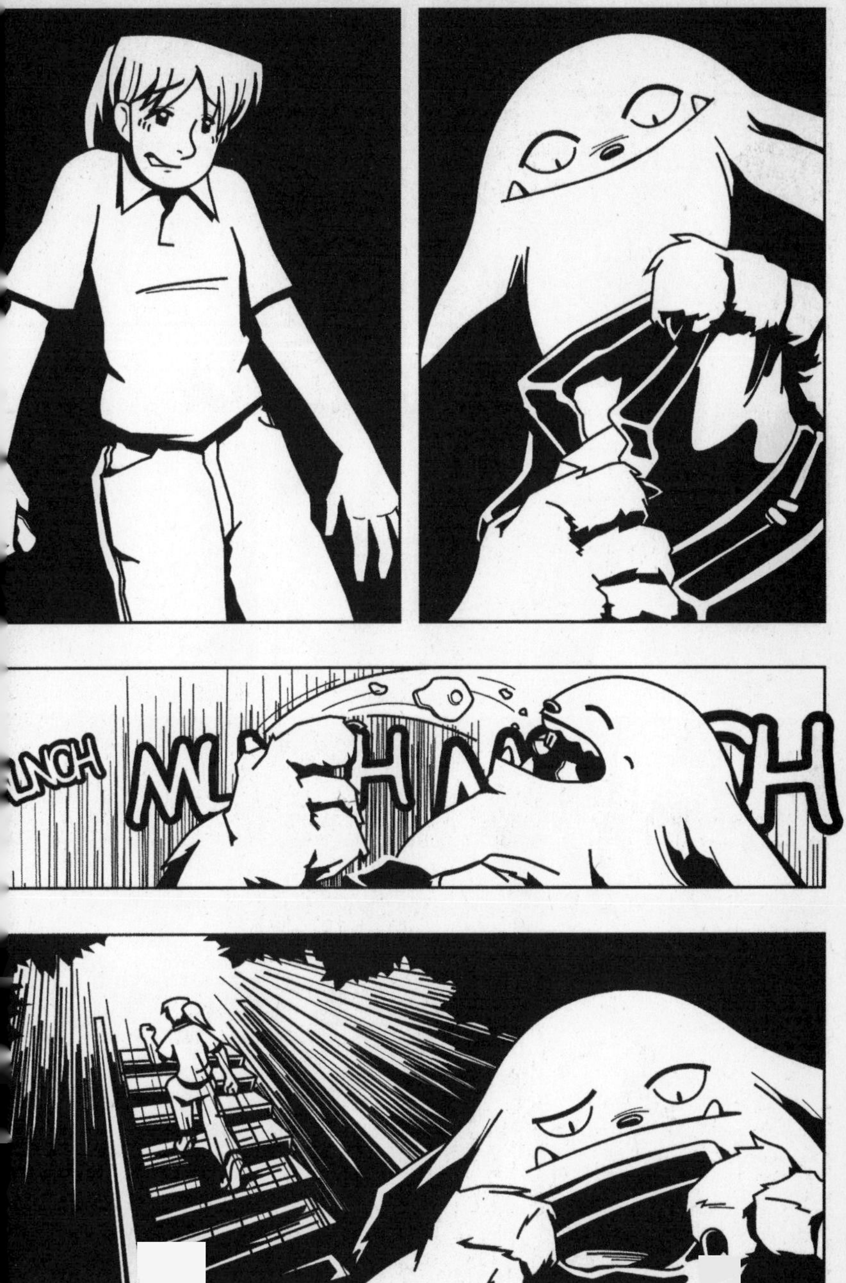

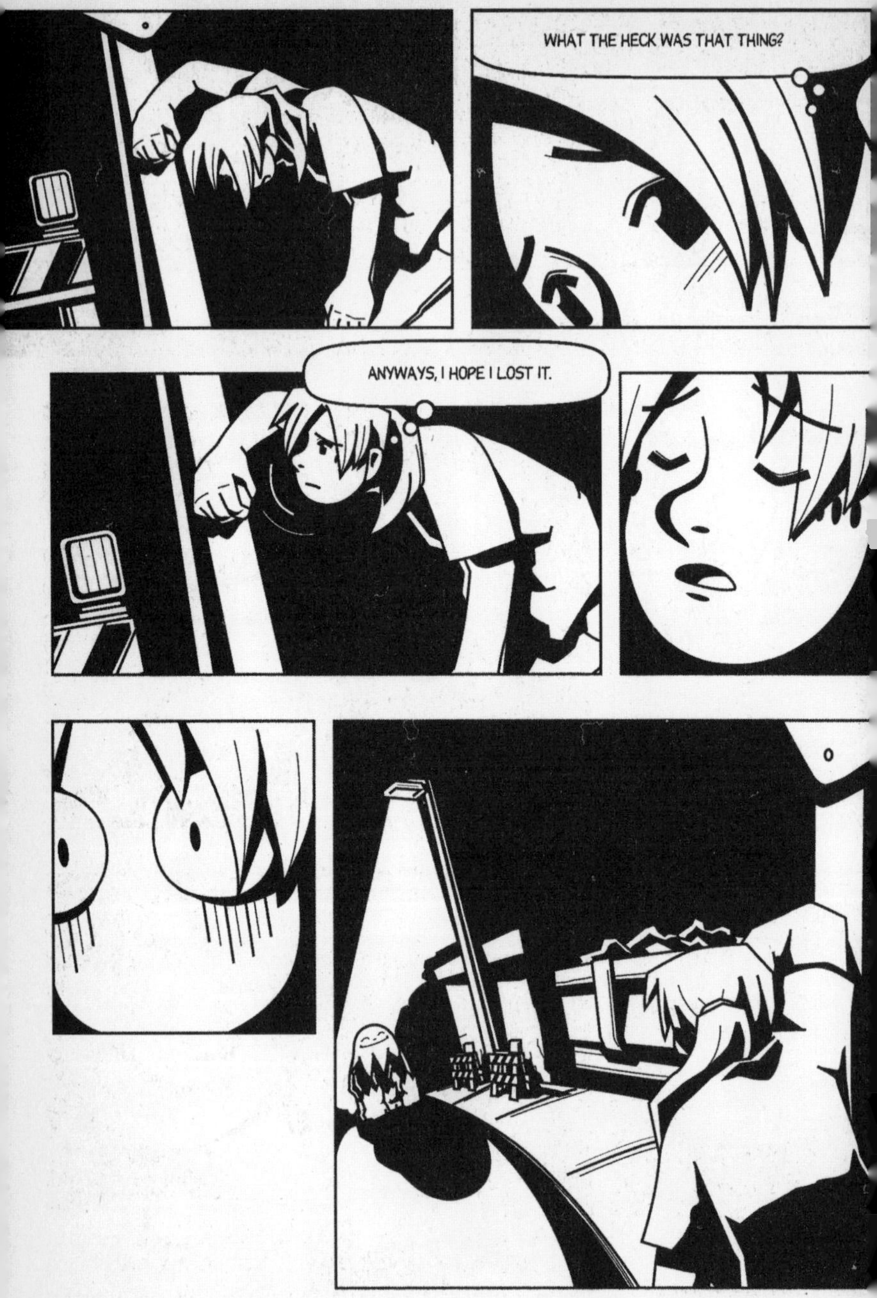
WHAT THE HECK WAS THAT THING?
ANYWAYS, I HOPE I LOST IT.

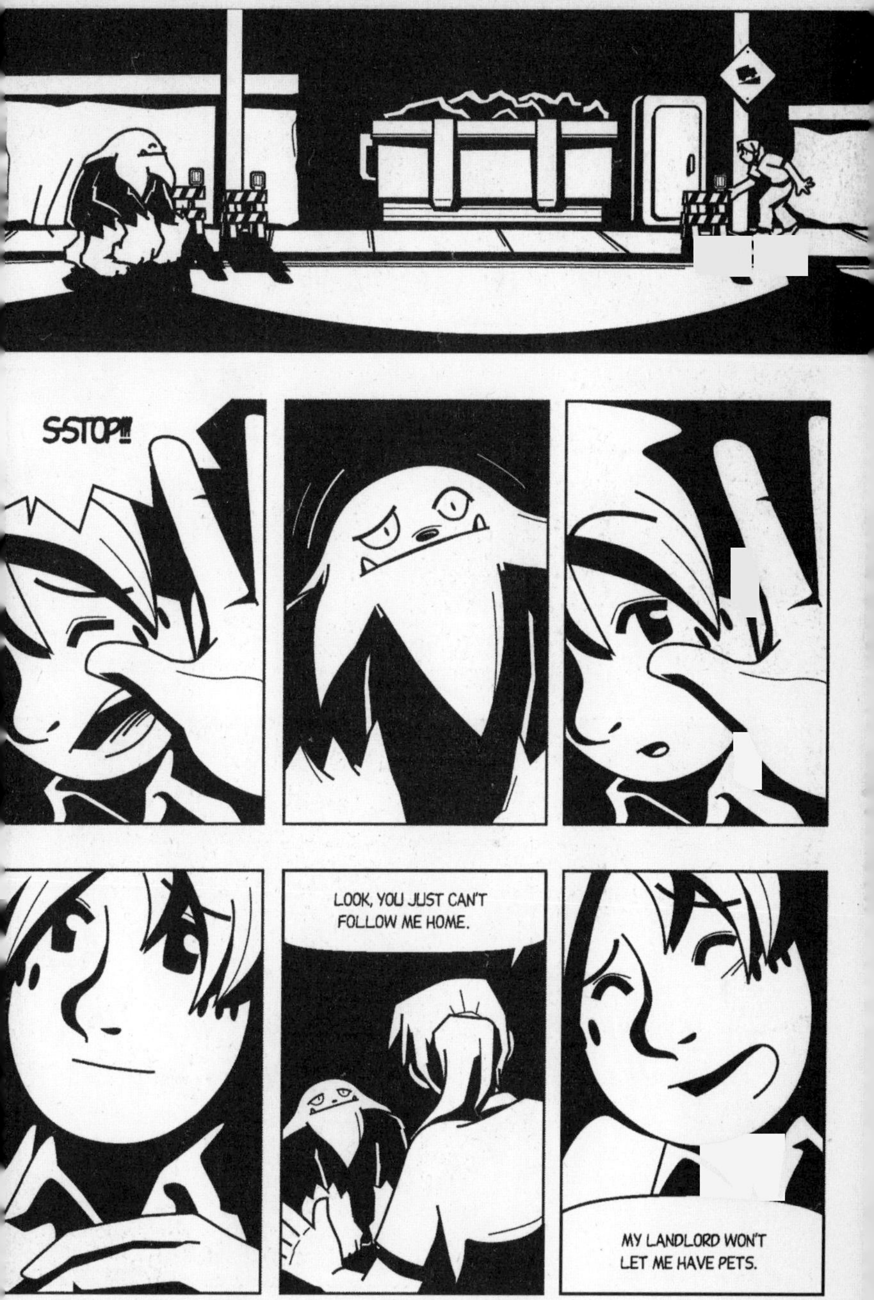
S-STOP!!!
LOOK, YOU JUST CAN'T FOLLOW ME HOME.
MY LANDLORD WON'T LET ME HAVE PETS.

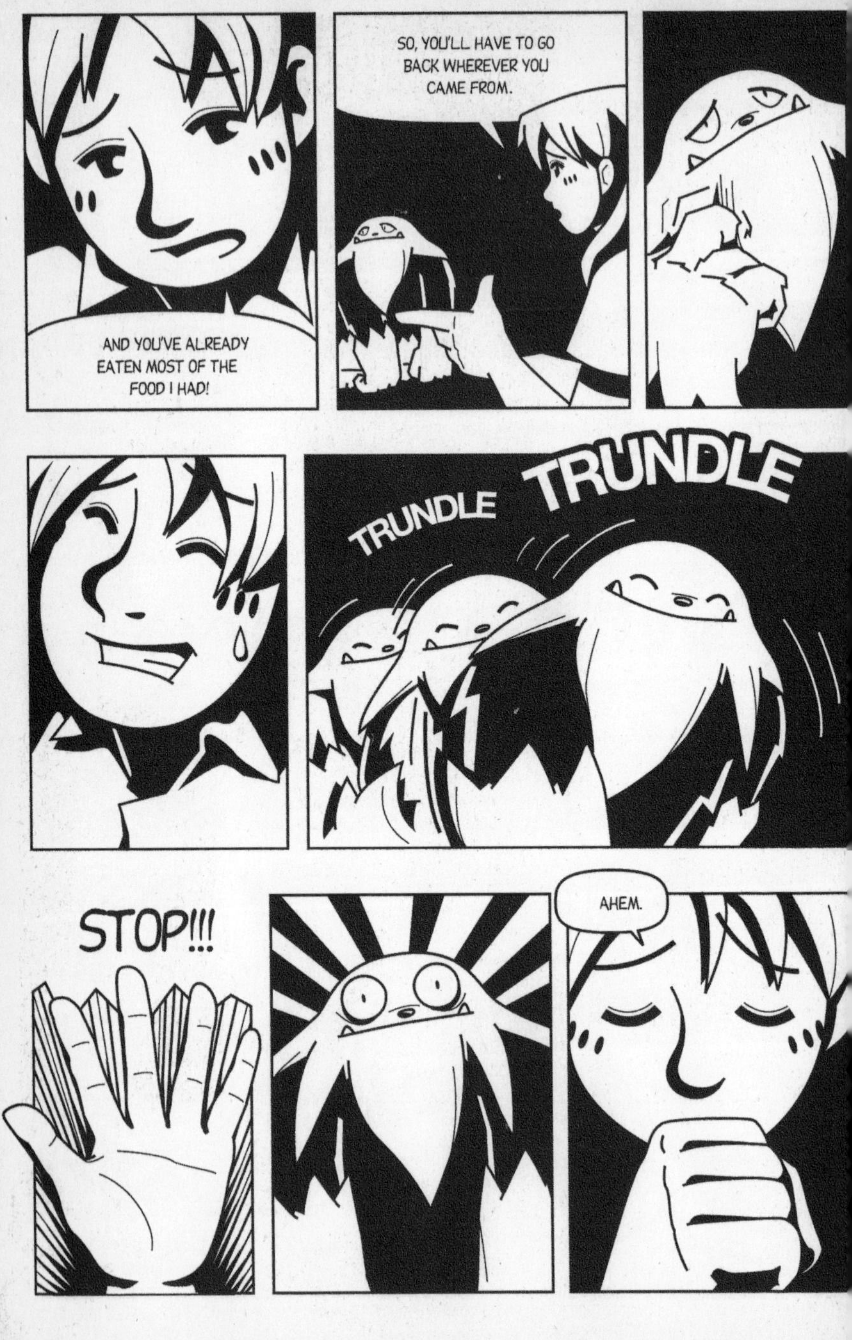
AND YOU'VE ALREADY EATEN MOST OF THE FOOD I HAD!
SO, YOU'LL HAVE TO GO BACK WHEREVER YOU CAME FROM.
TRUNDLE
TRUNDLE
STOP!!!
AHEM.

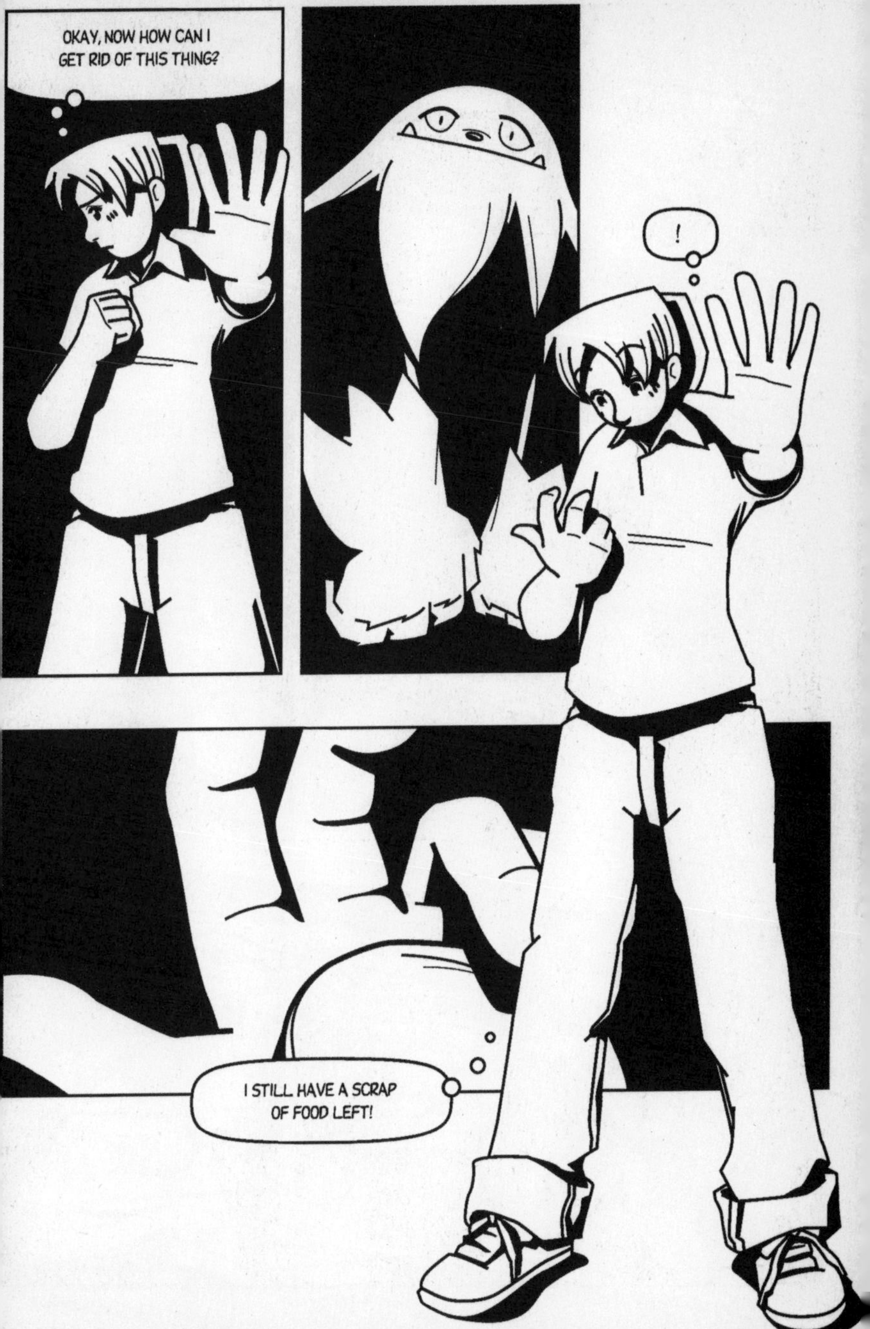
OKAY, NOW HOW CAN I GET RID OF THIS THING?
!
I STILL HAVE A SCRAP OF FOOD LEFT!

FETCH!

WHIIIIFFFA!

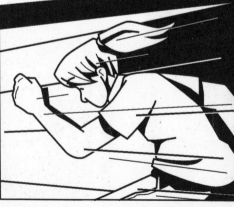

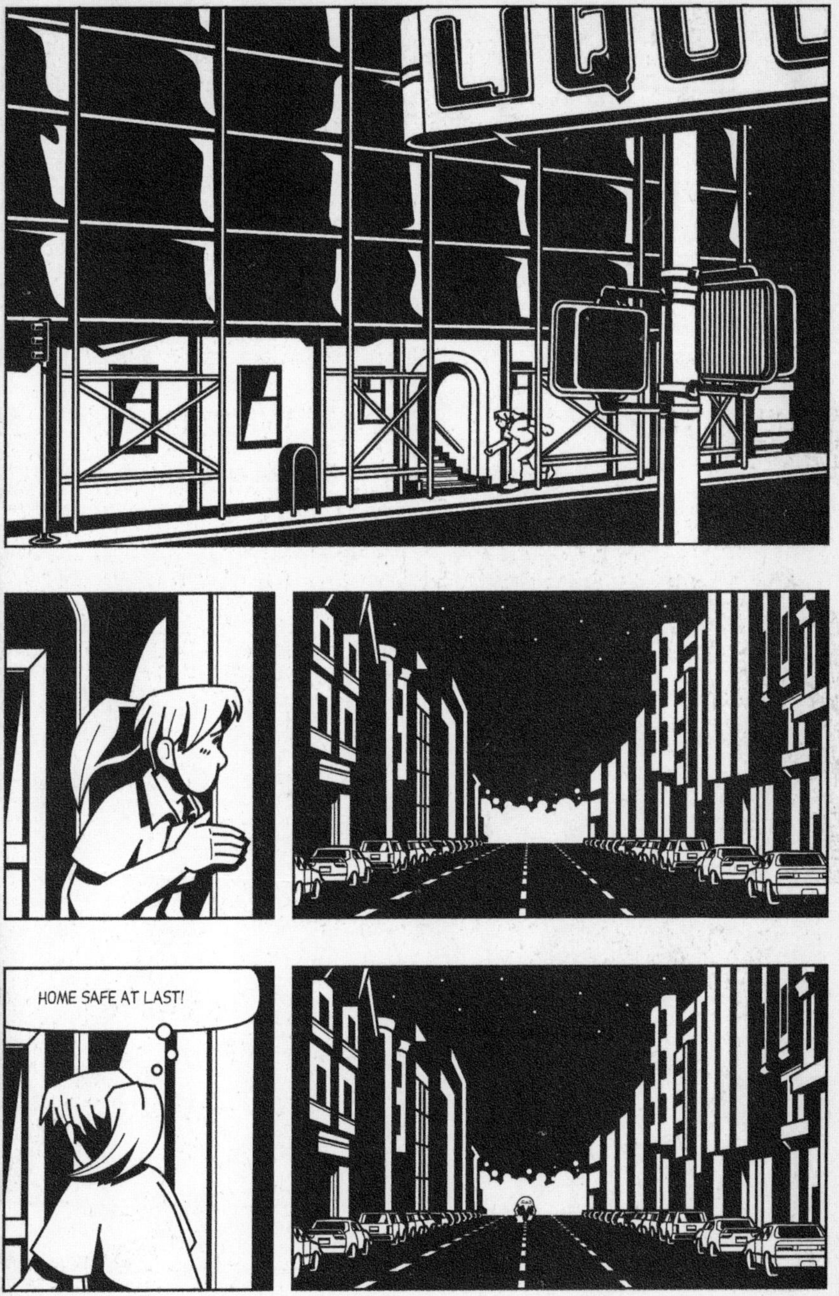
LIQU
HOME SAFE AT LAST!

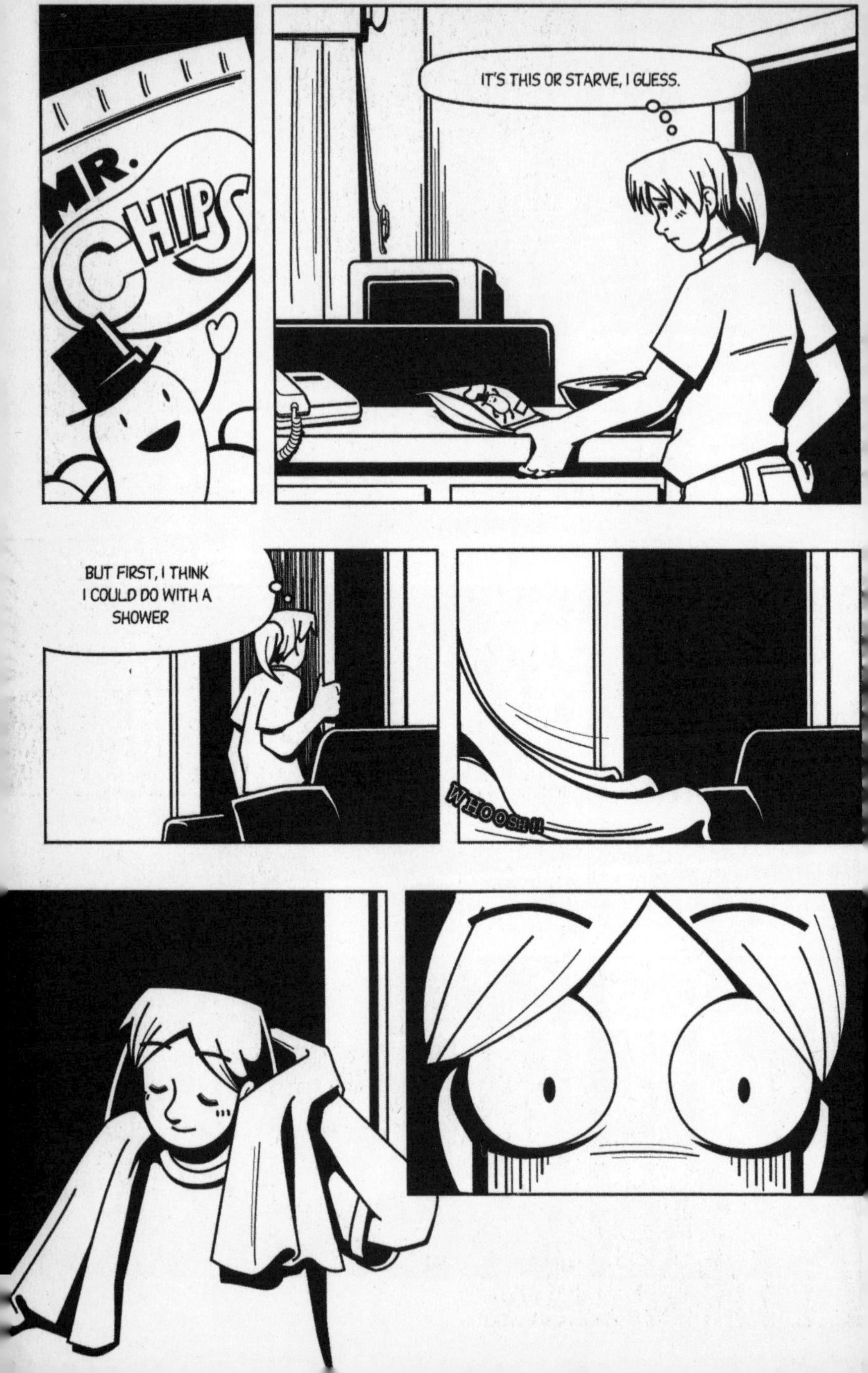
MR. CHIPS
IT'S THIS OR STARVE, I GUESS.
BUT FIRST, I THINK I COULD DO WITH A SHOWER
WHOOSH!!

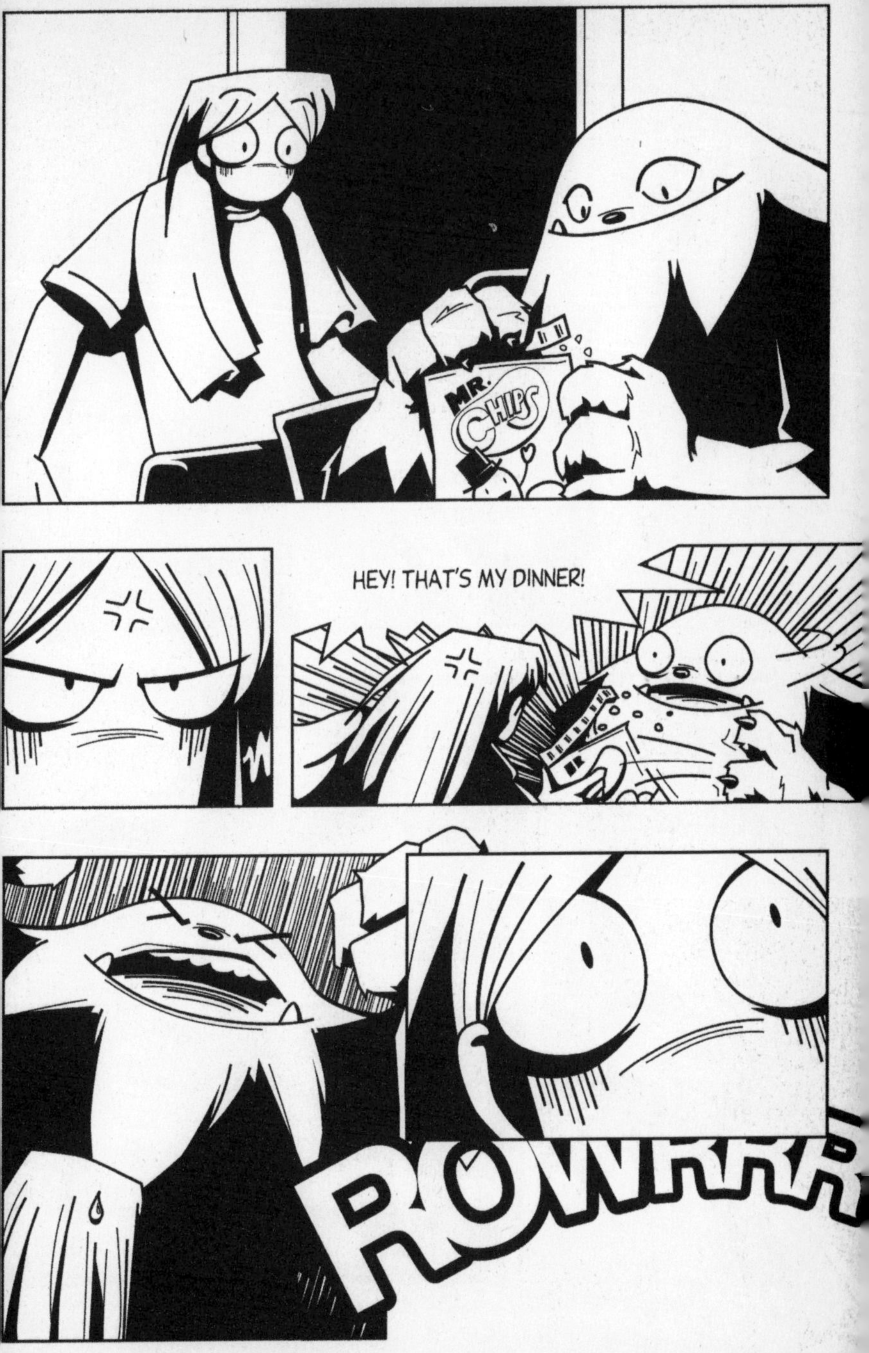
MR. CHIPS
HEY! THAT'S MY DINNER!
ROWRRR

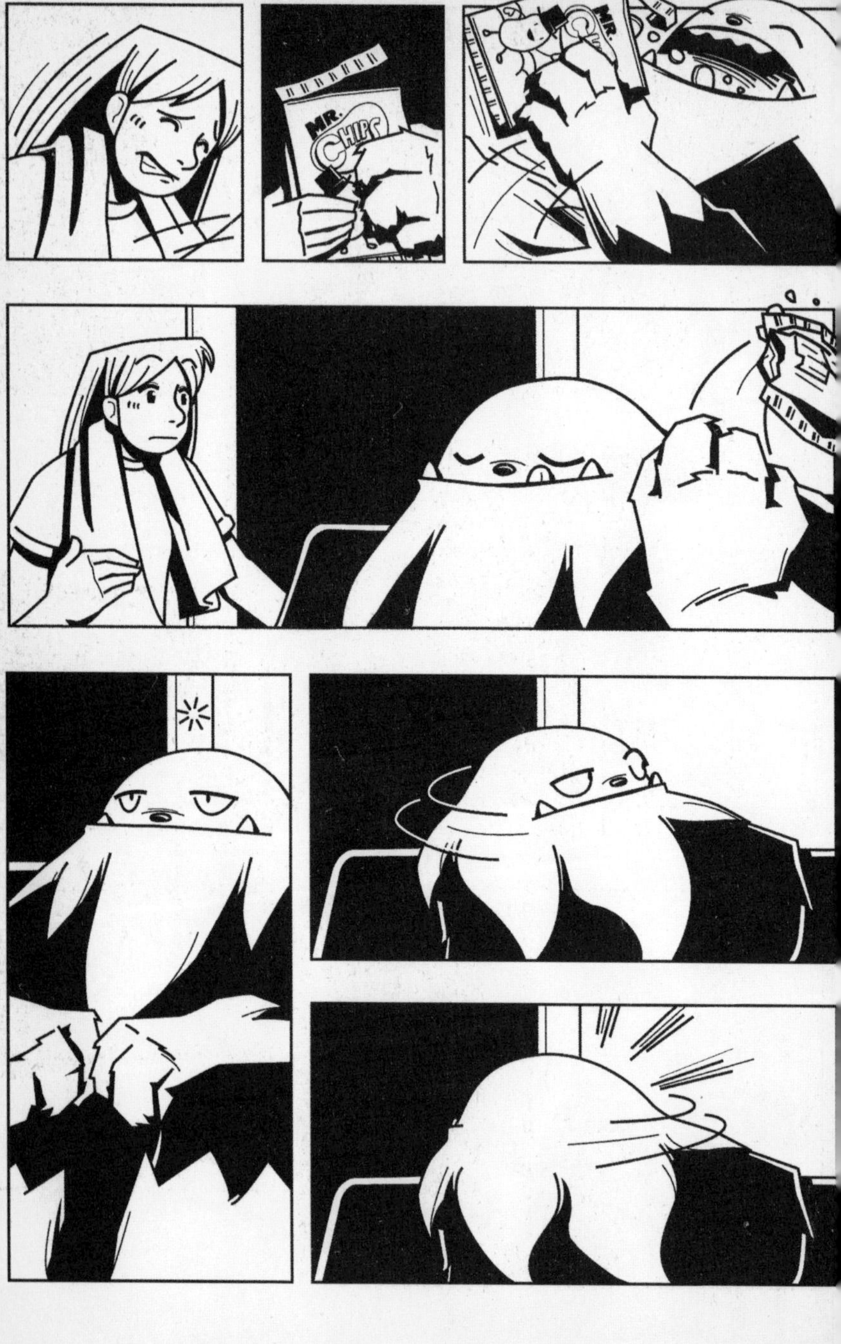
MR. CHIPS

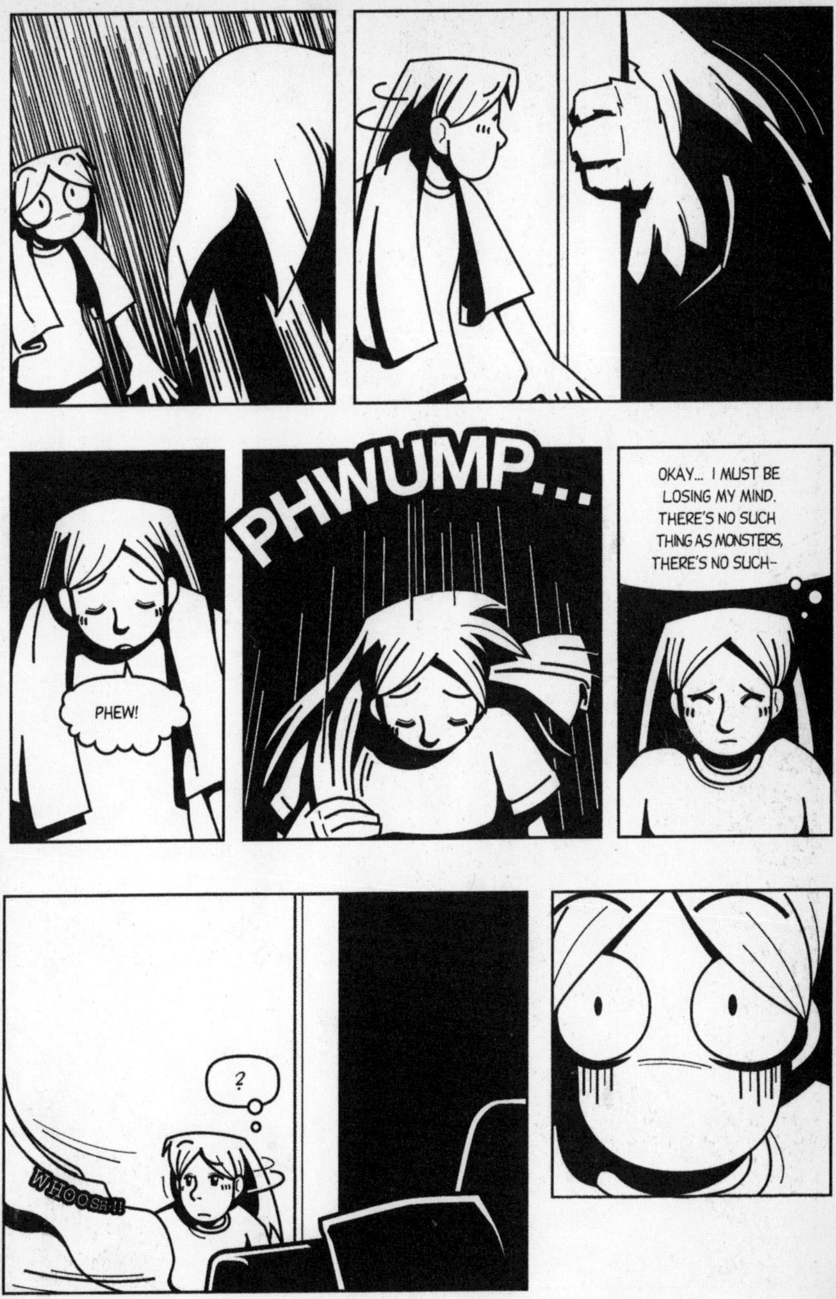
PHEW!
PHWUMP...
OKAY... I MUST BE LOSING MY MIND. THERE'S NO SUCH THING AS MONSTERS, THERE'S NO SUCH-
?
WHOOSH!!

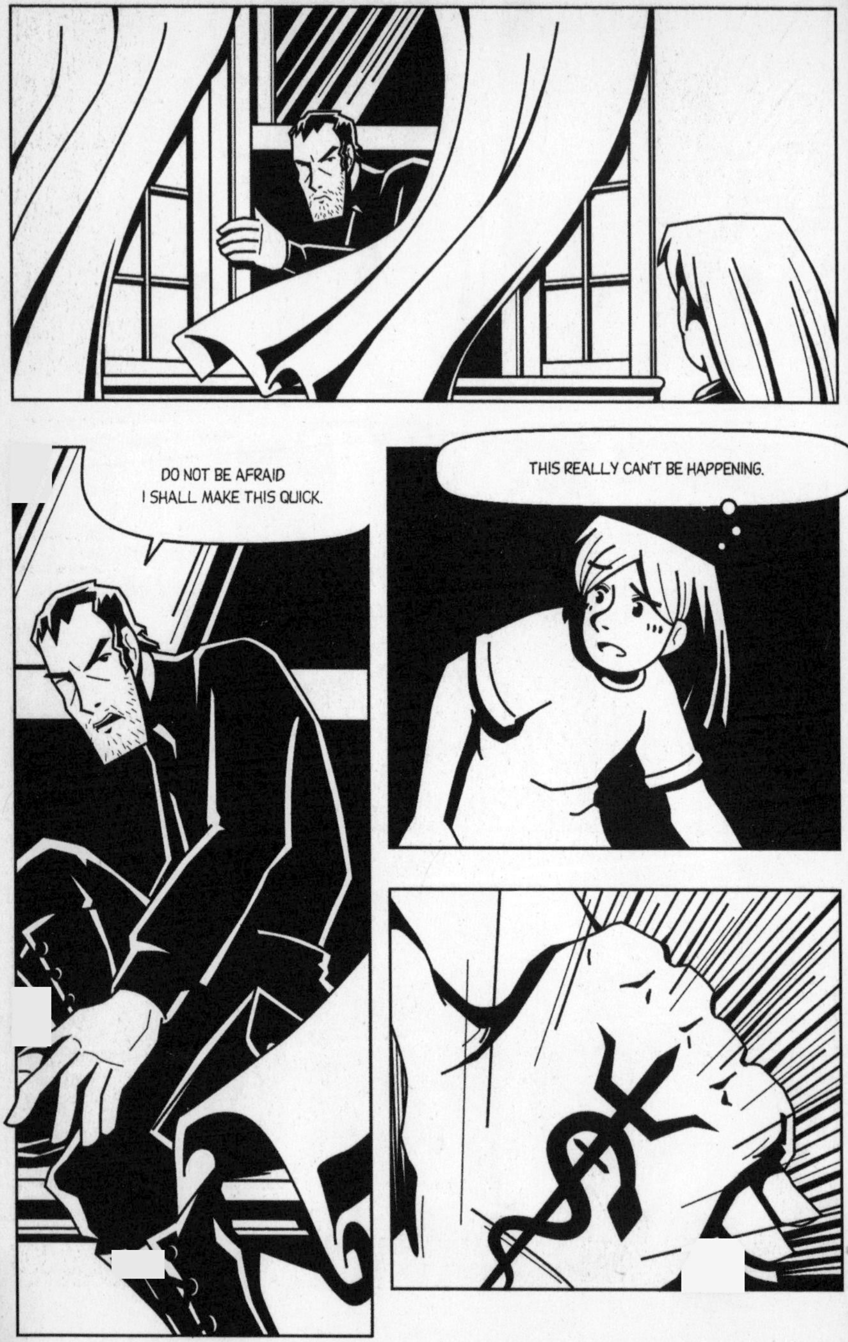
DO NOT BE AFRAID
I SHALL MAKE THIS QUICK.
THIS REALLY CAN'T BE HAPPENING.

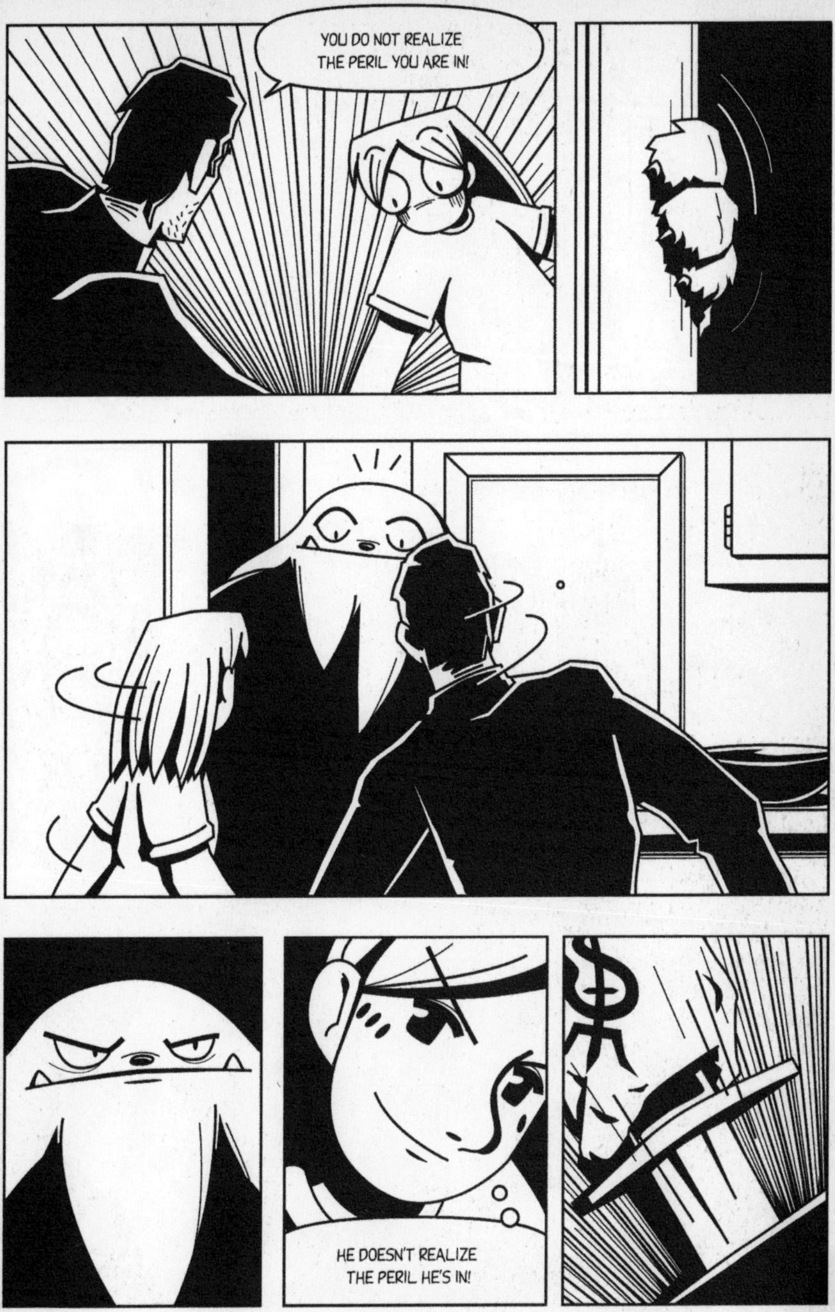
YOU DO NOT REALIZE THE PERIL YOU ARE IN!
HE DOESN'T REALIZE THE PERIL HE'S IN!

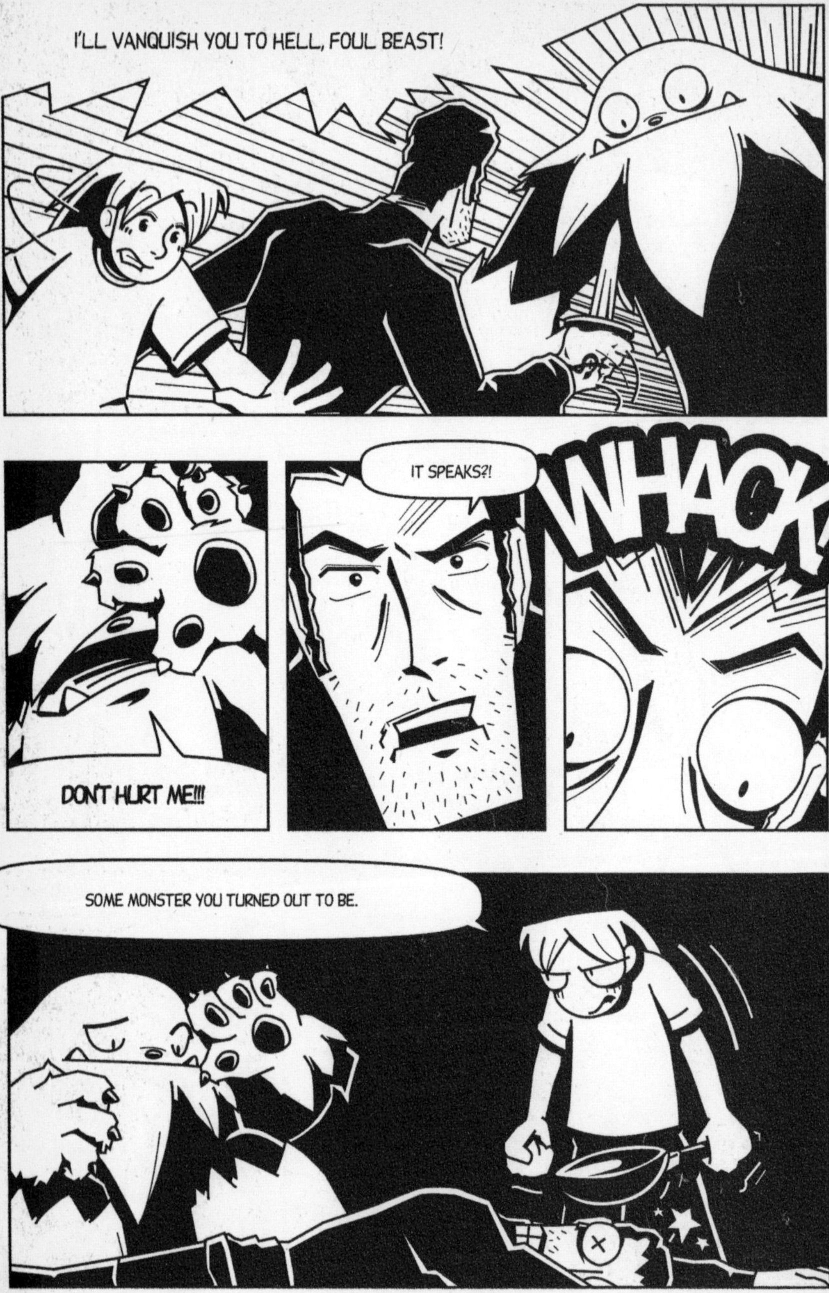
I'LL VANQUISH YOU TO HELL, FOUL BEAST!
DON'T HURT ME!!!
IT SPEAKS?!
WHACK!
SOME MONSTER YOU TURNED OUT TO BE.

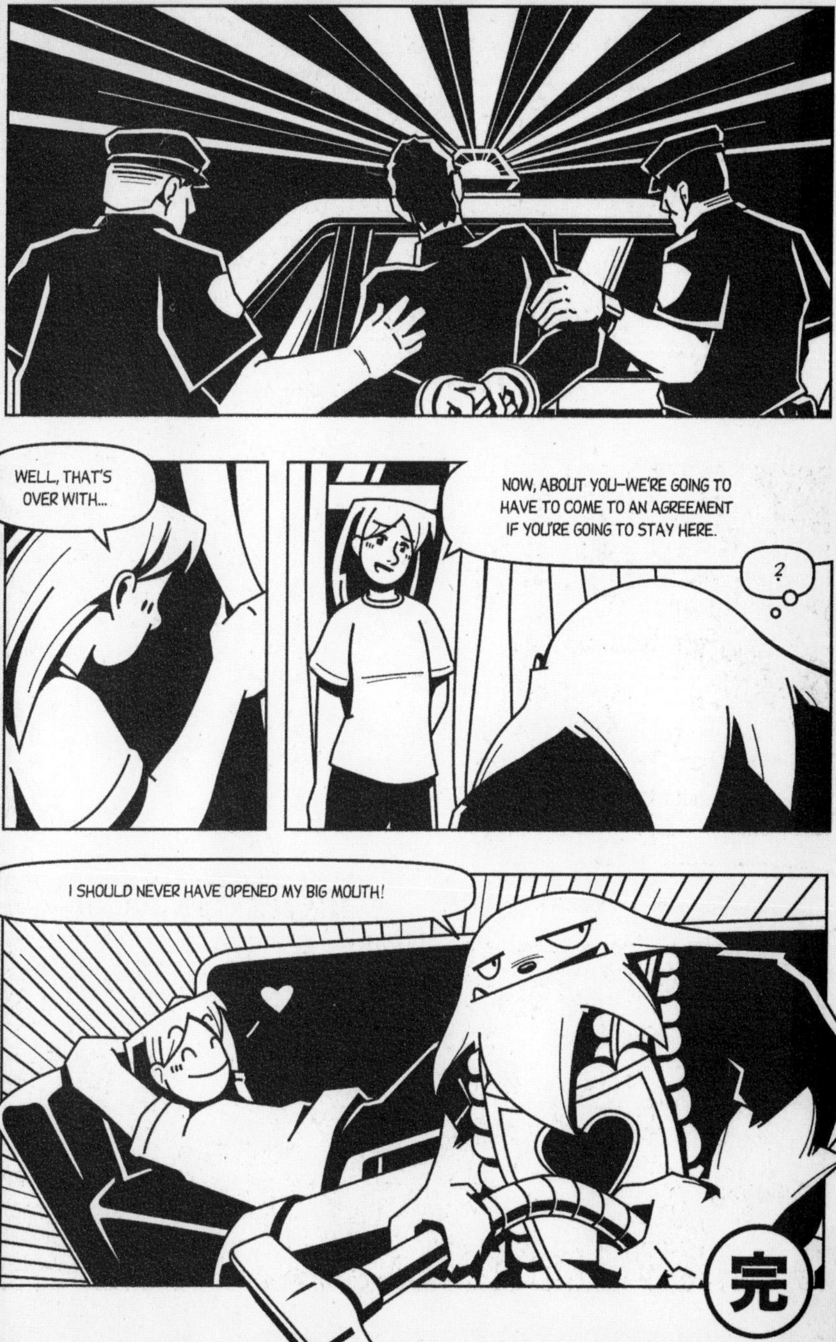
WELL, THAT'S OVER WITH...
NOW, ABOUT YOU—WE'RE GOING TO HAVE TO COME TO AN AGREEMENT IF YOU'RE GOING TO STAY HERE.
?
I SHOULD NEVER HAVE OPENED MY BIG MOUTH!
完

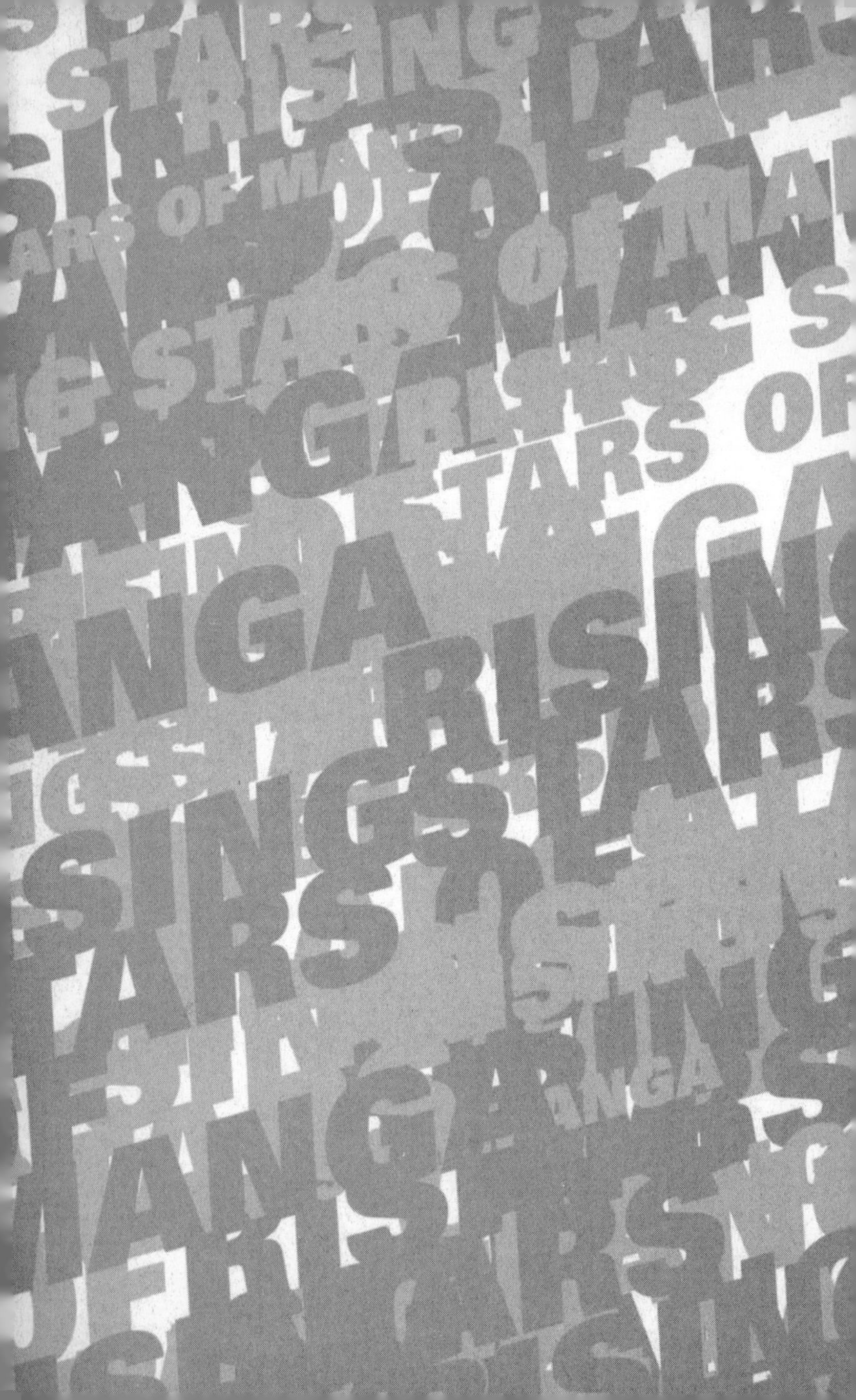

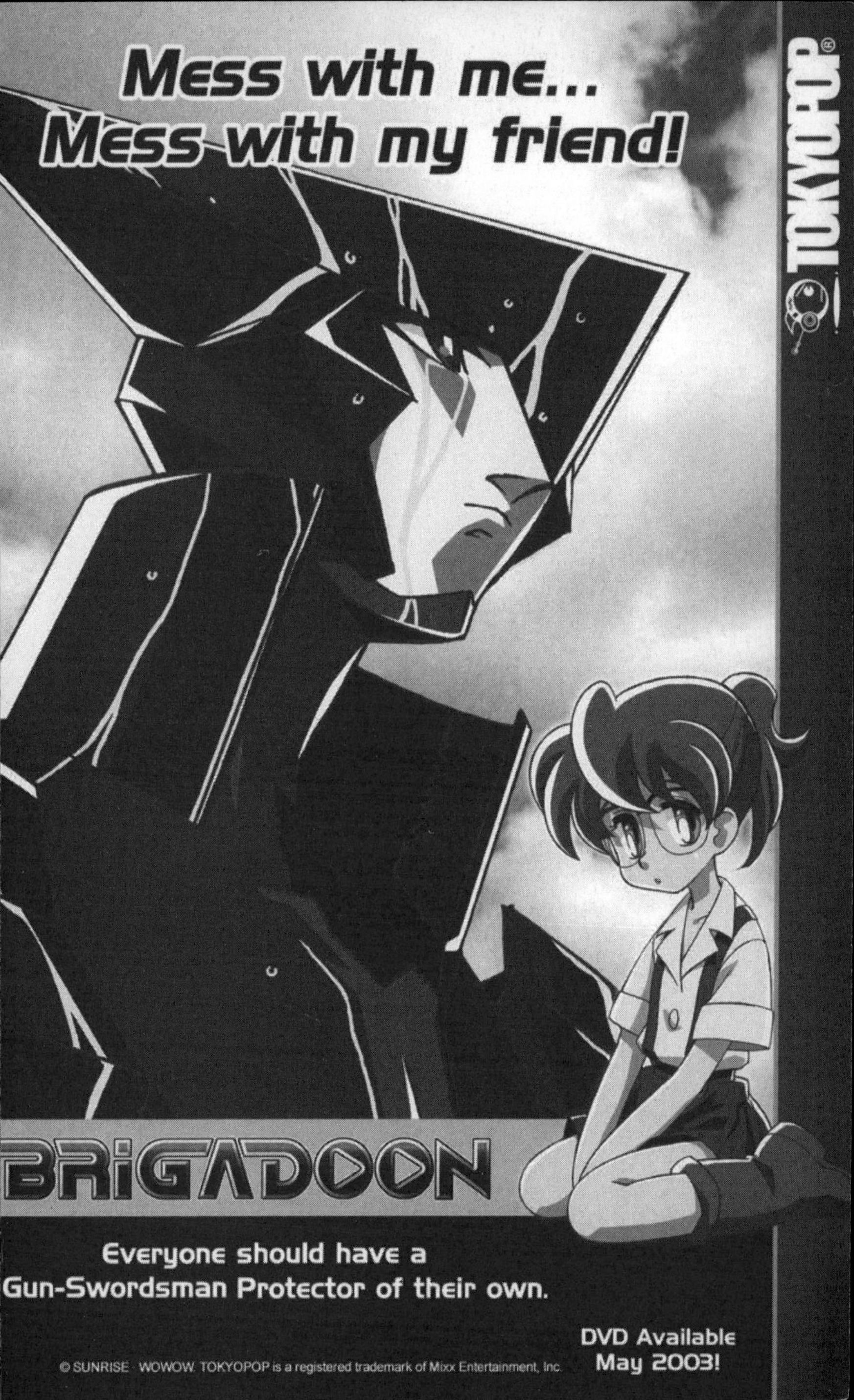

::

SITTING DUCKS :: RUNNER UP ::
Ben Seto was born in Oakland, California, in 1980 and now lives in Hayward, California. He also creates his own comic, *Waterfall*, and publishes it himself under the Black Sheep Comics label. You can check out some of his work at www.blacksheepcomics.com.

Inspiration for this story:
Some of my friends found out about TOKYOPOP's Rising Stars of Manga contest and suggested I take shot at it. I didn't want to enter, but my friends kept egging me on, so I eventually decided to do it. The reason I didn't want to participate in the contest was that I didn't have any ideas for a story... so I decided to make a story out of my problem.

Favorite Manga:
I don't have a favorite manga. I like almost everything I read, even ones I hate at first (until I've read it enough to eventually like it). I really enjoy manga magazines, which offer a bunch of stories at a time. Comics are one or the greatest forms of art there is, no matter where it's made.

Favorite Manga Artists:
Masamune Shirow, Rumiko Takahashi
....

Judge's Comments:
Creating an entry about not being able to come up with an entry could have been a really cheap gimmick in the hands of a lesser artist, but Benjamin Seto pulls off a miracle with his manga short "Sitting Ducks"—it's downright funny, and rings oh so true.

This is definitely an "American Manga" in both style and substance; from the comic convention scene, with its hilarious parody of Eri—um, some fictitious creator—to the indie-comic look of its supporting cast, to the moments of very Western lettering.

But it also borrows very competently from the manga canon. Notice the photo-real establishing shot at the beginning, the effective—if a little too infrequent—use of screen tone and the female lead Nole's moments of perfect manga emoting (especially the hand flapping and phone yelling). Reliance on dialog and head-and-shoulders shots grounds this tale a little more on the American side, but no other entry better captured the love of manga and the creative process. Ganbarre!
-Jake Forbes

::

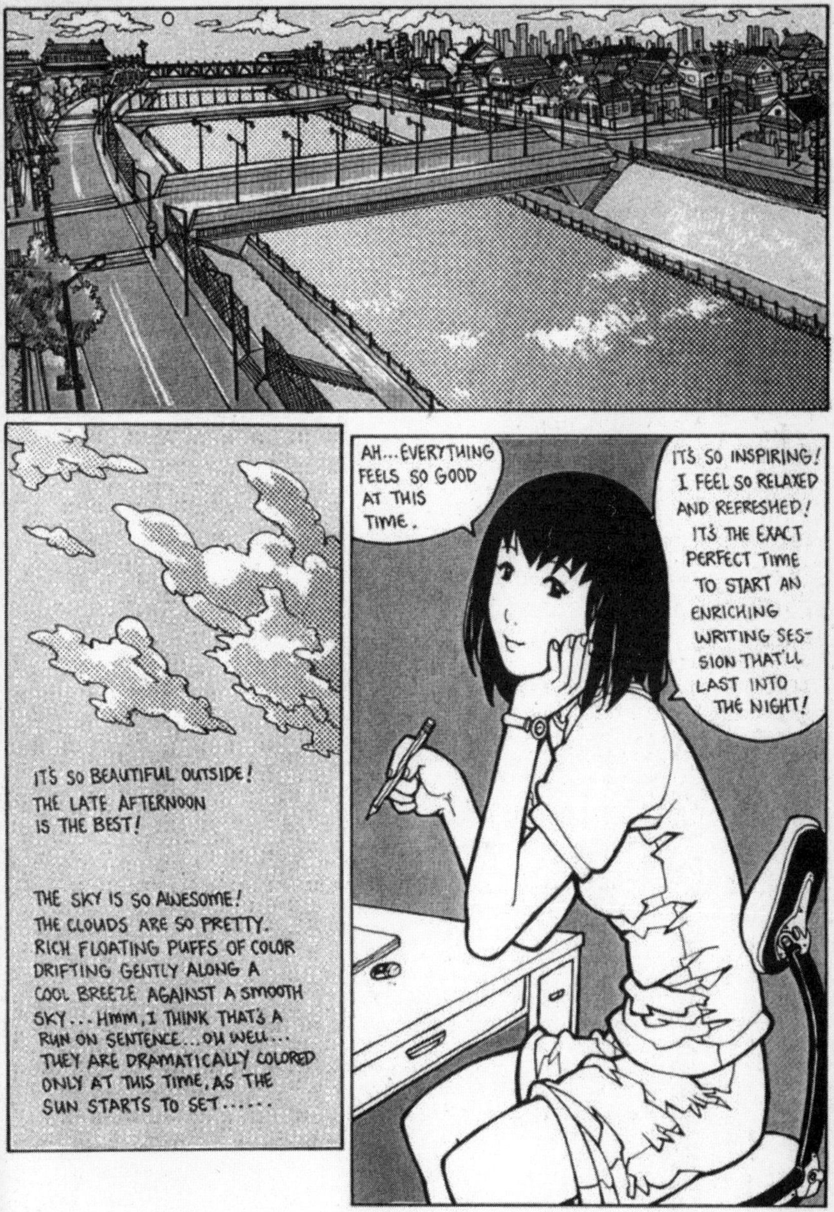
IT'S SO BEAUTIFUL OUTSIDE! THE LATE AFTERNOON IS THE BEST!
THE SKY IS SO AWESOME! THE CLOUDS ARE SO PRETTY. RICH FLOATING PUFFS OF COLOR DRIFTING GENTLY ALONG A COOL BREEZE AGAINST A SMOOTH SKY... HMM, I THINK THAT'S A RUN ON SENTENCE... OH WELL... THEY ARE DRAMATICALLY COLORED ONLY AT THIS TIME, AS THE SUN STARTS TO SET......
AH... EVERYTHING FEELS SO GOOD AT THIS TIME.
IT'S SO INSPIRING! I FEEL SO RELAXED AND REFRESHED! IT'S THE EXACT PERFECT TIME TO START AN ENRICHING WRITING SES-SION THAT'LL LAST INTO THE NIGHT!

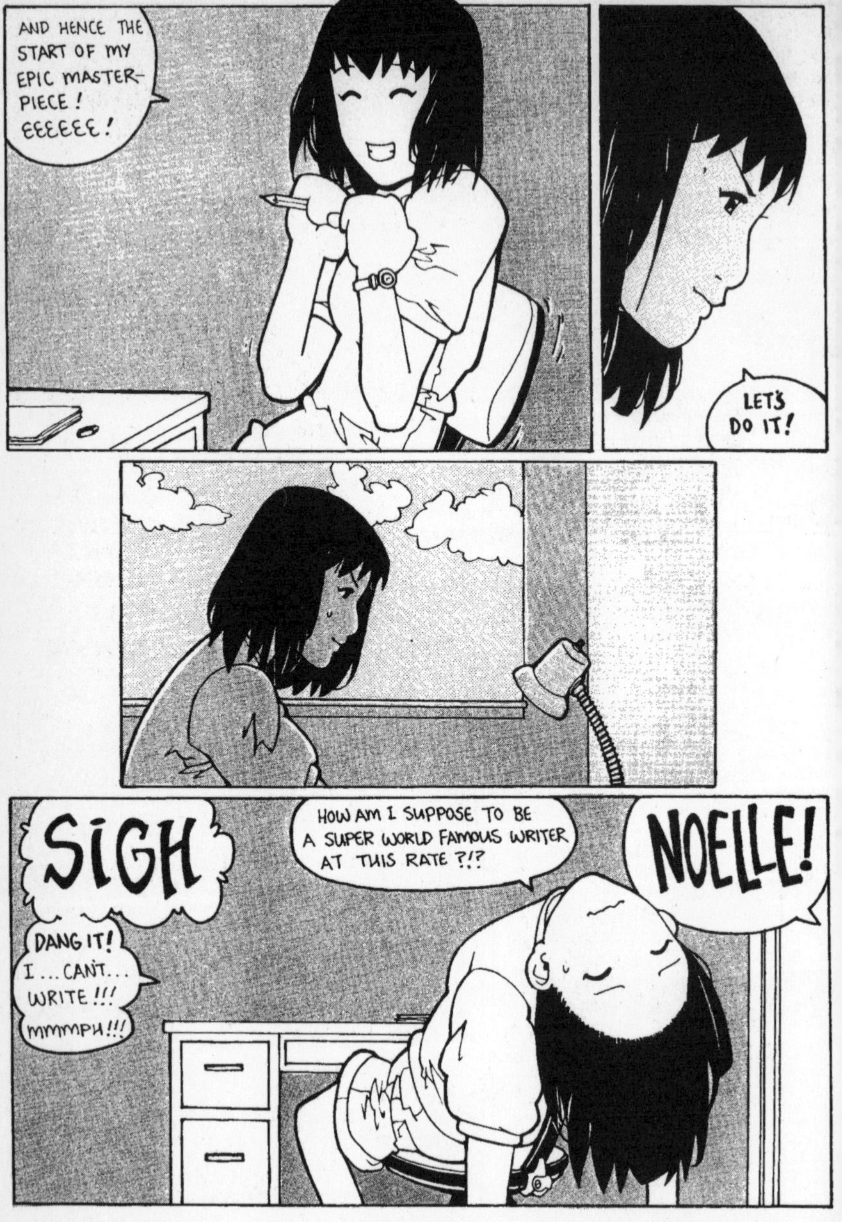
AND HENCE THE START OF MY EPIC MASTER-PIECE! EEEEEE!
LET'S DO IT!
SIGH
HOW AM I SUPPOSE TO BE A SUPER WORLD FAMOUS WRITER AT THIS RATE ?!?
NOELLE!
DANG IT! I... CAN'T... WRITE!!! MMMPH!!!

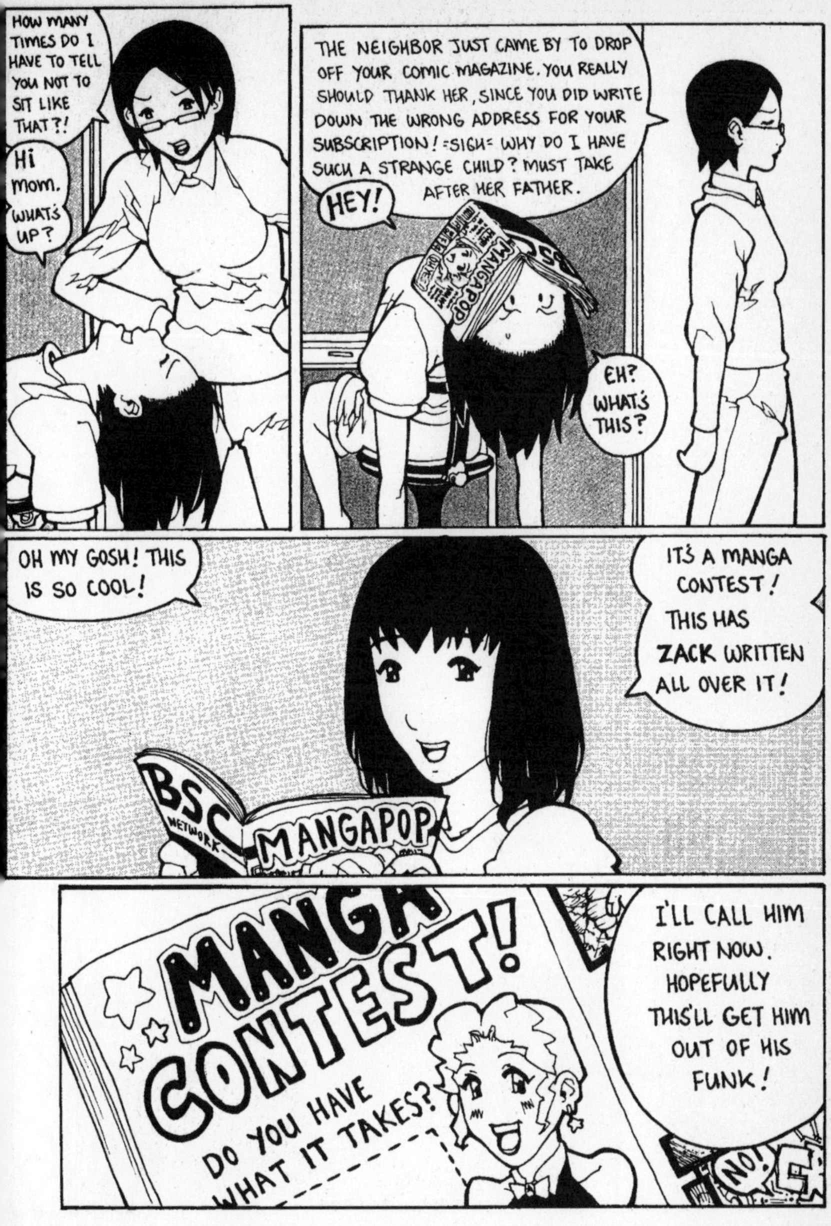
HOW MANY TIMES DO I HAVE TO TELL YOU NOT TO SIT LIKE THAT?!
Hi mom.
WHAT'S UP?
THE NEIGHBOR JUST CAME BY TO DROP OFF YOUR COMIC MAGAZINE. YOU REALLY SHOULD THANK HER, SINCE YOU DID WRITE DOWN THE WRONG ADDRESS FOR YOUR SUBSCRIPTION! =SIGH= WHY DO I HAVE SUCH A STRANGE CHILD? MUST TAKE AFTER HER FATHER.
HEY!
MANGAPOP
EH? WHAT'S THIS?
OH MY GOSH! THIS IS SO COOL!
IT'S A MANGA CONTEST! THIS HAS ZACK WRITTEN ALL OVER IT!
BSC NETWORK
MANGAPOP
MANGA CONTEST!
DO YOU HAVE WHAT IT TAKES?
I'LL CALL HIM RIGHT NOW. HOPEFULLY THIS'LL GET HIM OUT OF HIS FUNK!
NO!

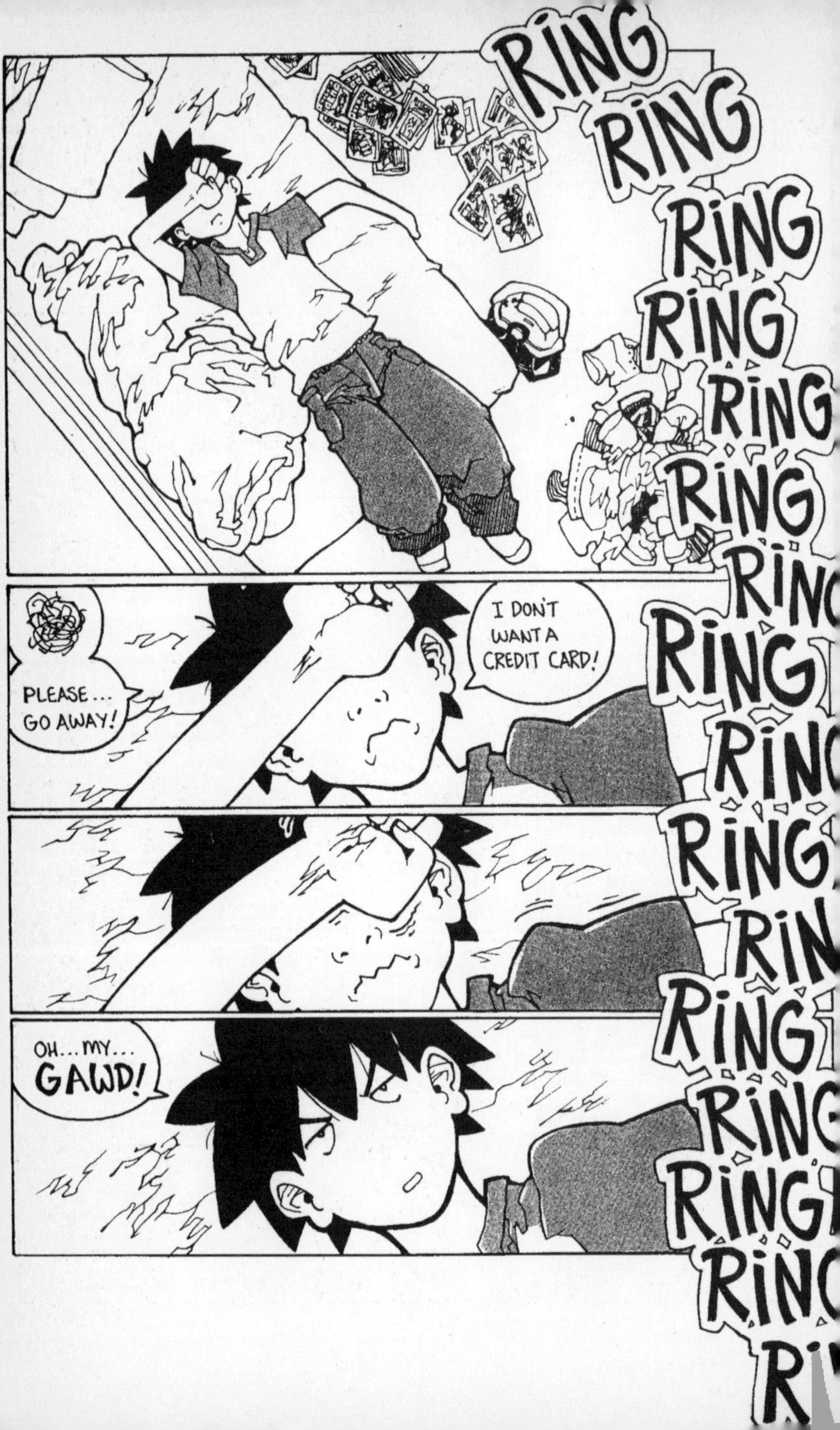
RING
RING
RING
RING
RING
RING
PLEASE... GO AWAY!
I DON'T WANT A CREDIT CARD!
RING
RING
RING
OH... MY... GAWD!
RING

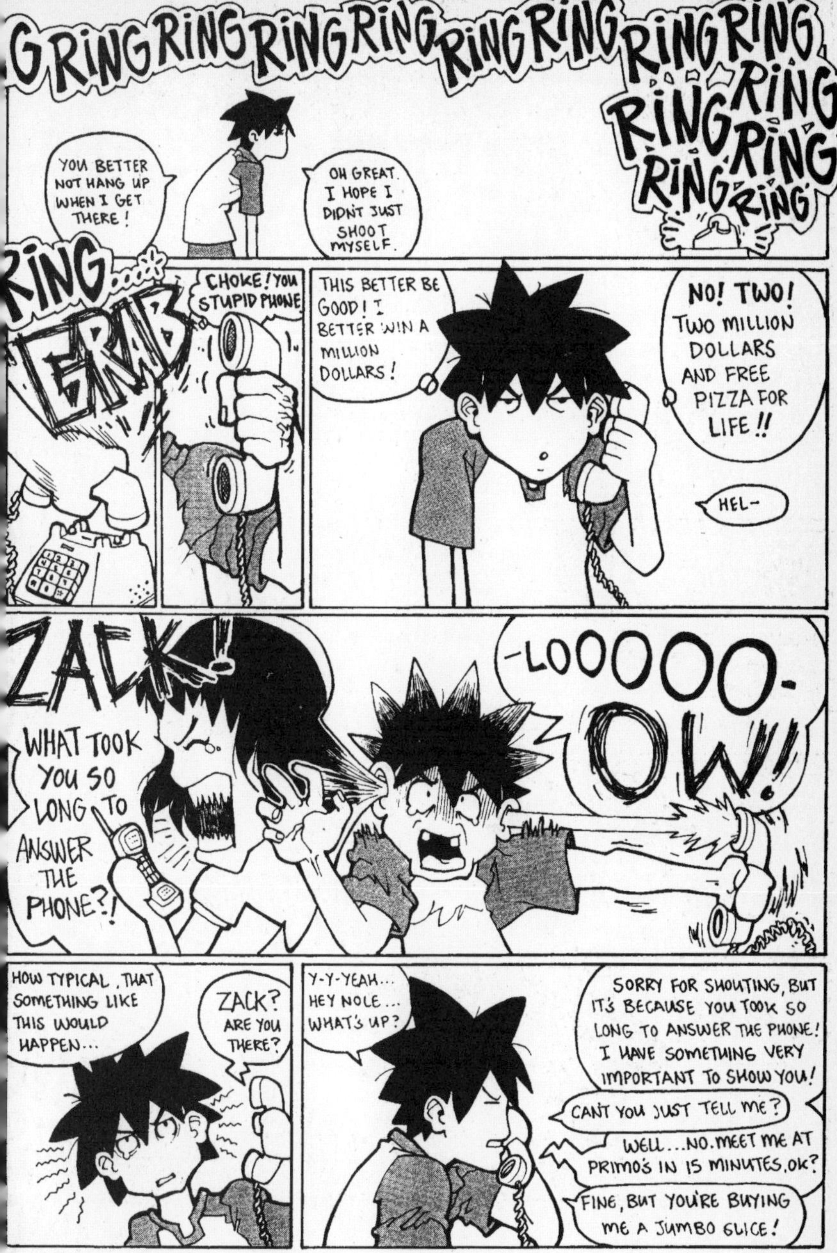
G RING RING RING RING RING RING RING RING
RING RING RING RING RING RING
YOU BETTER NOT HANG UP WHEN I GET THERE!
OH GREAT. I HOPE I DIDN'T JUST SHOOT MYSELF.
RING...*
GRAB
CHOKE! YOU STUPID PHONE
THIS BETTER BE GOOD! I BETTER WIN A MILLION DOLLARS!
NO! TWO! TWO MILLION DOLLARS AND FREE PIZZA FOR LIFE!!
HEL-
ZACK!
WHAT TOOK YOU SO LONG TO ANSWER THE PHONE?!
-LOOOOO-OW!
HOW TYPICAL, THAT SOMETHING LIKE THIS WOULD HAPPEN...
ZACK? ARE YOU THERE?
Y-Y-YEAH... HEY NOLE... WHAT'S UP?
SORRY FOR SHOUTING, BUT IT'S BECAUSE YOU TOOK SO LONG TO ANSWER THE PHONE! I HAVE SOMETHING VERY IMPORTANT TO SHOW YOU!
CAN'T YOU JUST TELL ME?
WELL...NO. MEET ME AT PRIMO'S IN 15 MINUTES, OK?
FINE, BUT YOU'RE BUYING ME A JUMBO SLICE!

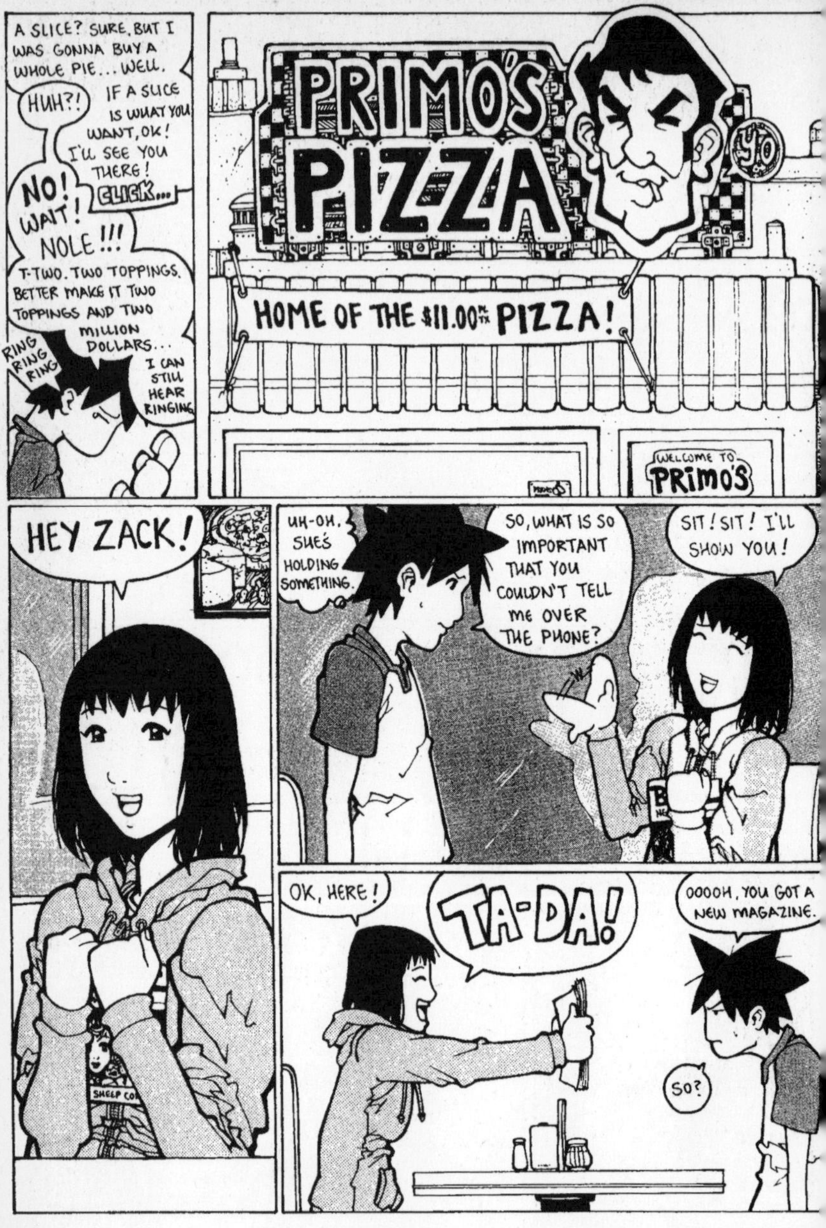
A SLICE? SURE, BUT I WAS GONNA BUY A WHOLE PIE... WELL,
HUH?!
IF A SLICE IS WHAT YOU WANT, OK! I'LL SEE YOU THERE!
CLICK...
NO! WAIT! NOLE!!!
T-TWO. TWO TOPPINGS. BETTER MAKE IT TWO TOPPINGS AND TWO MILLION DOLLARS...
RING RING RING
I CAN STILL HEAR RINGING
PRIMO'S PIZZA
YO
HOME OF THE $11.00 PIZZA!
WELCOME TO PRIMO'S
HEY ZACK!
UH-OH. SHE'S HOLDING SOMETHING.
SO, WHAT IS SO IMPORTANT THAT YOU COULDN'T TELL ME OVER THE PHONE?
SIT! SIT! I'LL SHOW YOU!
OK, HERE!
TA-DA!
OOOOH, YOU GOT A NEW MAGAZINE.
SO?

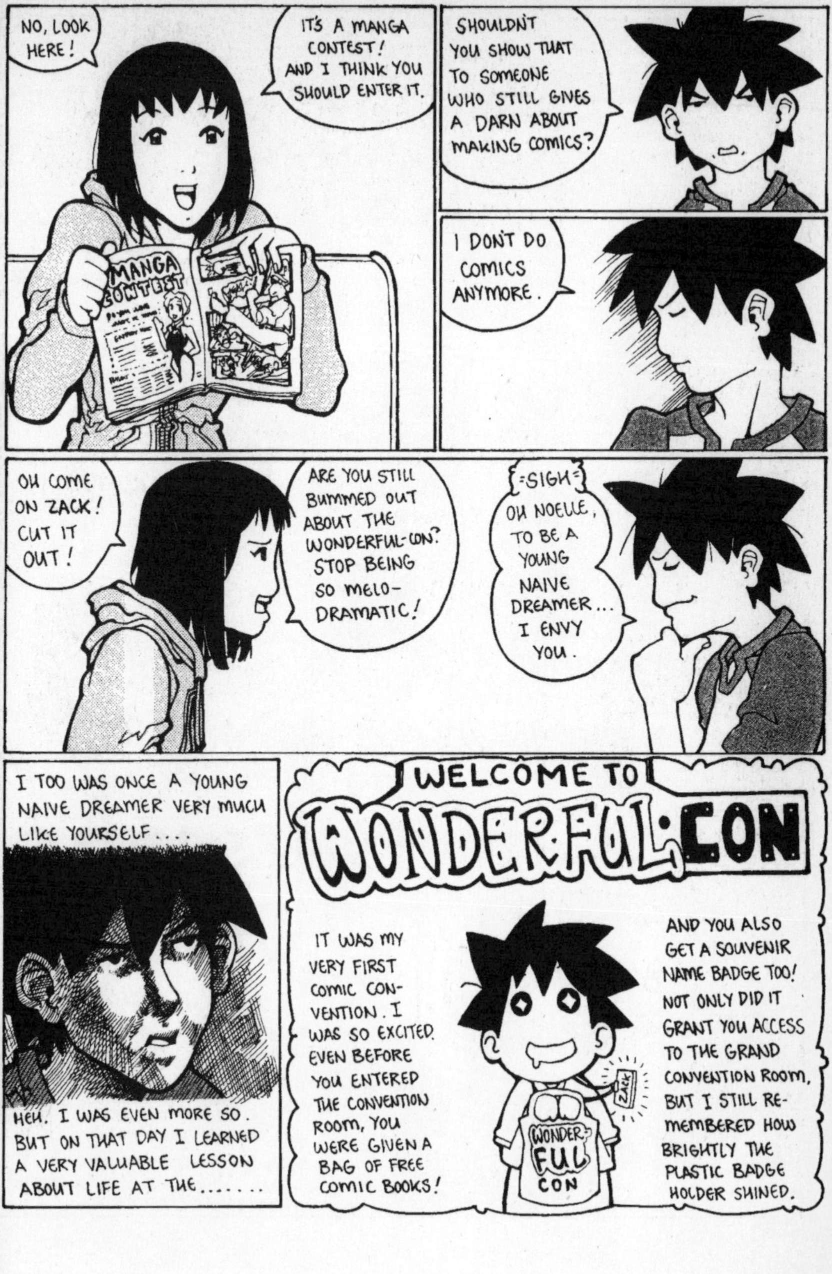
NO, LOOK HERE!
IT'S A MANGA CONTEST! AND I THINK YOU SHOULD ENTER IT.
MANGA CONTEST
SHOULDN'T YOU SHOW THAT TO SOMEONE WHO STILL GIVES A DARN ABOUT MAKING COMICS?
I DON'T DO COMICS ANYMORE.
OH COME ON ZACK! CUT IT OUT!
ARE YOU STILL BUMMED OUT ABOUT THE WONDERFUL-CON? STOP BEING SO MELO-DRAMATIC!
=SIGH=
OH NOELLE, TO BE A YOUNG NAIVE DREAMER... I ENVY YOU.
I TOO WAS ONCE A YOUNG NAIVE DREAMER VERY MUCH LIKE YOURSELF....
HEH. I WAS EVEN MORE SO. BUT ON THAT DAY I LEARNED A VERY VALUABLE LESSON ABOUT LIFE AT THE.......
WELCOME TO WONDERFUL:CON
IT WAS MY VERY FIRST COMIC CON-VENTION. I WAS SO EXCITED. EVEN BEFORE YOU ENTERED THE CONVENTION ROOM, YOU WERE GIVEN A BAG OF FREE COMIC BOOKS!
ZACK
WONDER FUL CON
AND YOU ALSO GET A SOUVENIR NAME BADGE TOO! NOT ONLY DID IT GRANT YOU ACCESS TO THE GRAND CONVENTION ROOM, BUT I STILL RE-MEMBERED HOW BRIGHTLY THE PLASTIC BADGE HOLDER SHINED.

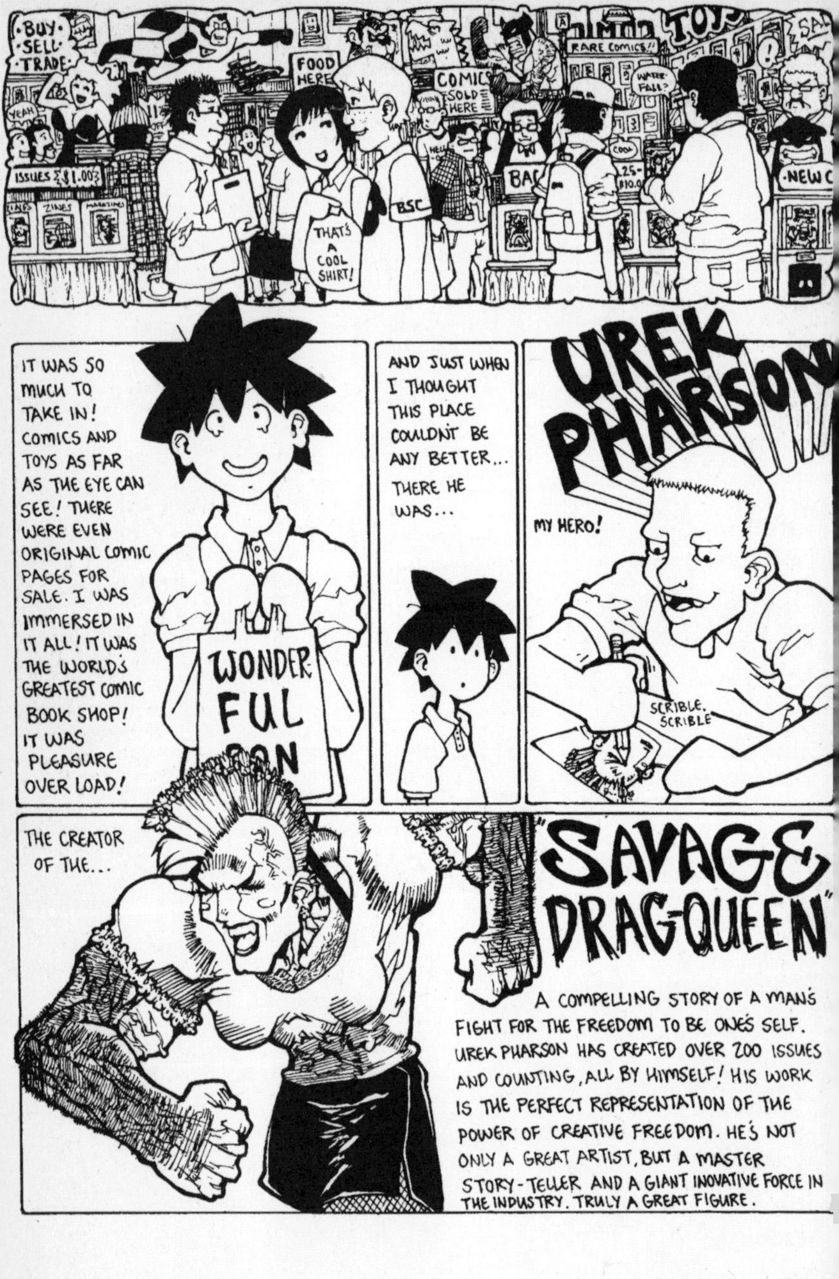

·BUY· ·SELL· ·TRADE·
FOOD HERE
COMICS SOLD HERE
RARE COMICS!!
TOYS
WATER-FALL?
YEAH
ISSUES $1.00
ZINES
THAT'S A COOL SHIRT!
BSC
COOL
·NEW C
IT WAS SO MUCH TO TAKE IN! COMICS AND TOYS AS FAR AS THE EYE CAN SEE! THERE WERE EVEN ORIGINAL COMIC PAGES FOR SALE. I WAS IMMERSED IN IT ALL! IT WAS THE WORLD'S GREATEST COMIC BOOK SHOP! IT WAS PLEASURE OVER LOAD!
WONDER-FUL
AND JUST WHEN I THOUGHT THIS PLACE COULDN'T BE ANY BETTER...
THERE HE WAS...
UREK PHARSON
MY HERO!
SCRIBLE, SCRIBLE
THE CREATOR OF THE...
"SAVAGE DRAG-QUEEN"
A COMPELLING STORY OF A MAN'S FIGHT FOR THE FREEDOM TO BE ONE'S SELF. UREK PHARSON HAS CREATED OVER 200 ISSUES AND COUNTING, ALL BY HIMSELF! HIS WORK IS THE PERFECT REPRESENTATION OF THE POWER OF CREATIVE FREEDOM. HE'S NOT ONLY A GREAT ARTIST, BUT A MASTER STORY-TELLER AND A GIANT INOVATIVE FORCE IN THE INDUSTRY. TRULY A GREAT FIGURE.

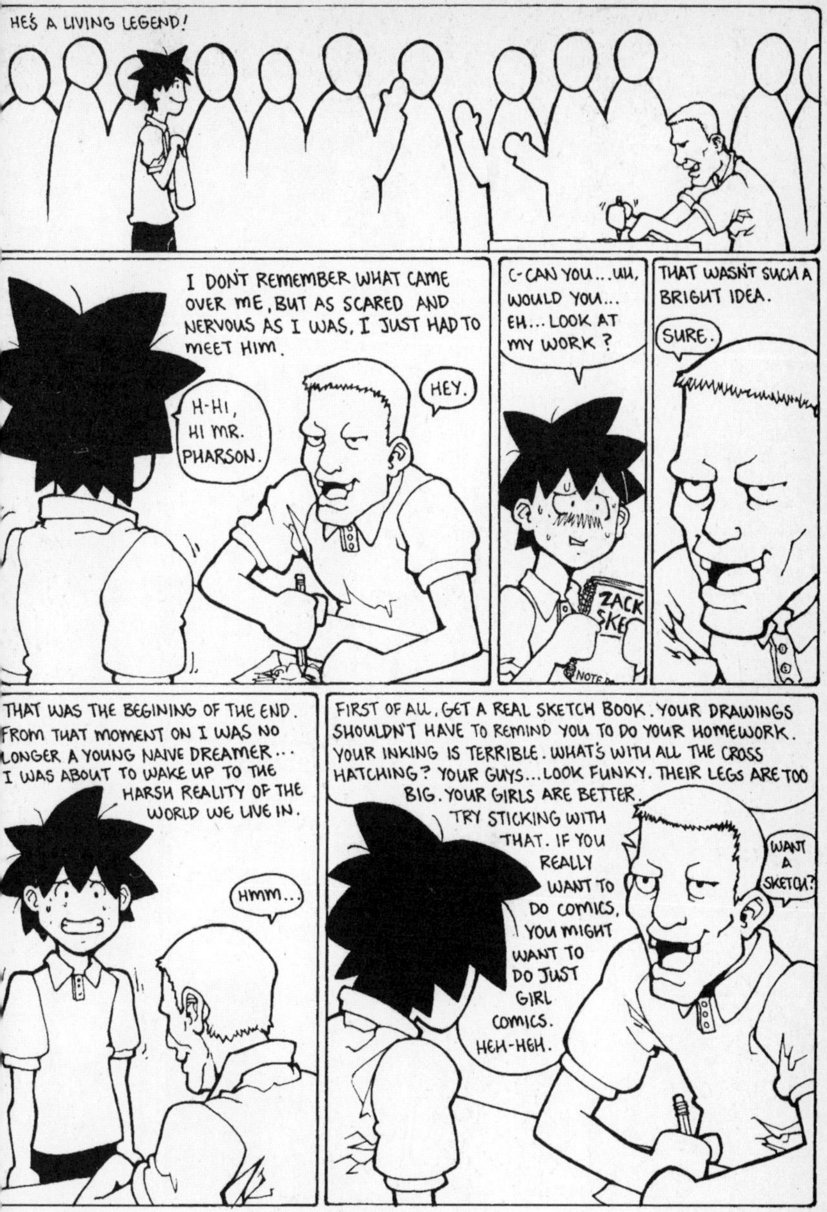
HE'S A LIVING LEGEND!
I DON'T REMEMBER WHAT CAME OVER ME, BUT AS SCARED AND NERVOUS AS I WAS, I JUST HAD TO MEET HIM.
H-HI, HI MR. PHARSON.
HEY.
C-CAN YOU... UH, WOULD YOU... EH... LOOK AT MY WORK?
ZACK SKE
NOTE
THAT WASN'T SUCH A BRIGHT IDEA.
SURE.
THAT WAS THE BEGINING OF THE END. FROM THAT MOMENT ON I WAS NO LONGER A YOUNG NAIVE DREAMER... I WAS ABOUT TO WAKE UP TO THE HARSH REALITY OF THE WORLD WE LIVE IN.
HMM...
FIRST OF ALL, GET A REAL SKETCH BOOK. YOUR DRAWINGS SHOULDN'T HAVE TO REMIND YOU TO DO YOUR HOMEWORK. YOUR INKING IS TERRIBLE. WHAT'S WITH ALL THE CROSS HATCHING? YOUR GUYS... LOOK FUNKY. THEIR LEGS ARE TOO BIG. YOUR GIRLS ARE BETTER. TRY STICKING WITH THAT. IF YOU REALLY WANT TO DO COMICS, YOU MIGHT WANT TO DO JUST GIRL COMICS. HEH-HEH.
WANT A SKETCH?

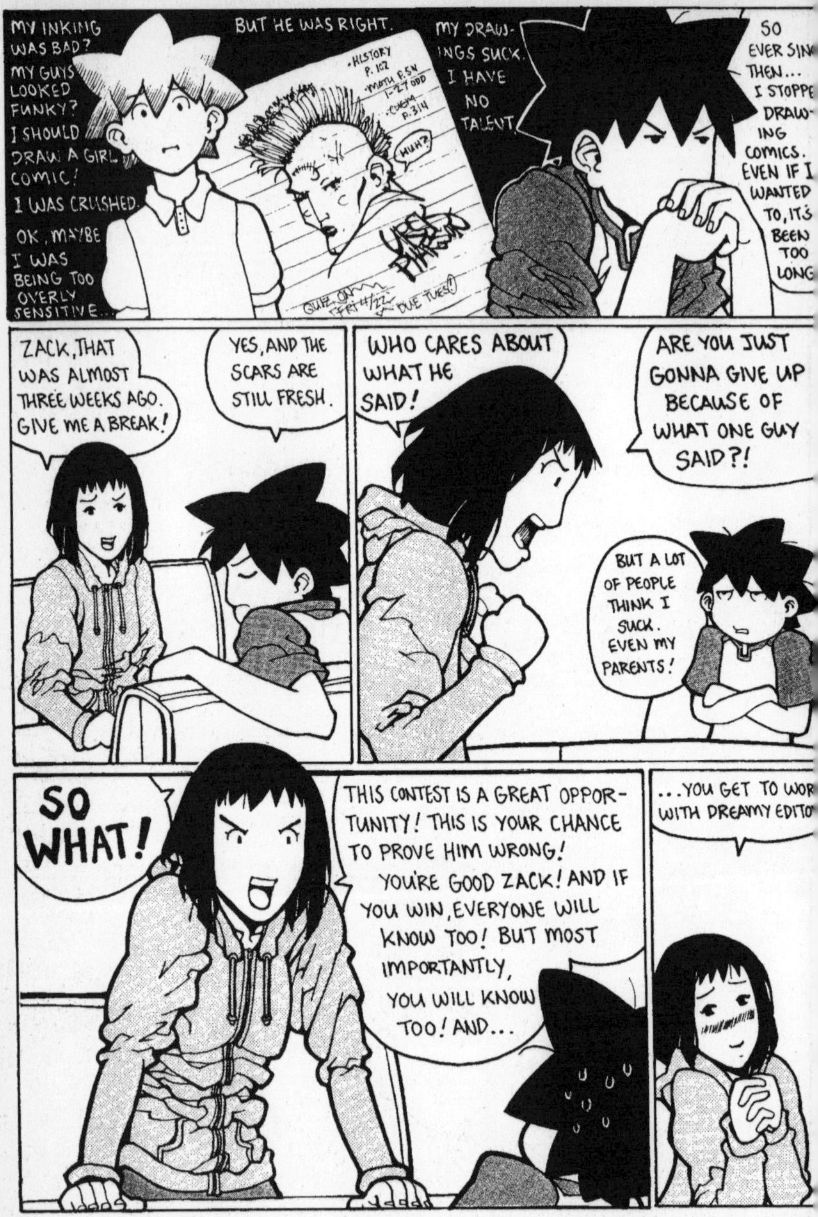
MY INKING WAS BAD? MY GUYS LOOKED FUNKY? I SHOULD DRAW A GIRL COMIC! I WAS CRUSHED.
OK, MAYBE I WAS BEING TOO OVERLY SENSITIVE...
BUT HE WAS RIGHT.
HISTORY P. 102
MATH P. 54 1-27 ODD
CHEM P. 314
HUH?
QUIZ ON FRI 4/22
DUE TUES!
MY DRAWINGS SUCK. I HAVE NO TALENT.
SO EVER SIN THEN... I STOPPE DRAWING COMICS. EVEN IF I WANTED TO, IT'S BEEN TOO LONG
ZACK, THAT WAS ALMOST THREE WEEKS AGO. GIVE ME A BREAK!
YES, AND THE SCARS ARE STILL FRESH.
WHO CARES ABOUT WHAT HE SAID!
ARE YOU JUST GONNA GIVE UP BECAUSE OF WHAT ONE GUY SAID?!
BUT A LOT OF PEOPLE THINK I SUCK. EVEN MY PARENTS!
SO WHAT!
THIS CONTEST IS A GREAT OPPORTUNITY! THIS IS YOUR CHANCE TO PROVE HIM WRONG! YOU'RE GOOD ZACK! AND IF YOU WIN, EVERYONE WILL KNOW TOO! BUT MOST IMPORTANTLY, YOU WILL KNOW TOO! AND...
...YOU GET TO WOR WITH DREAMY EDITO

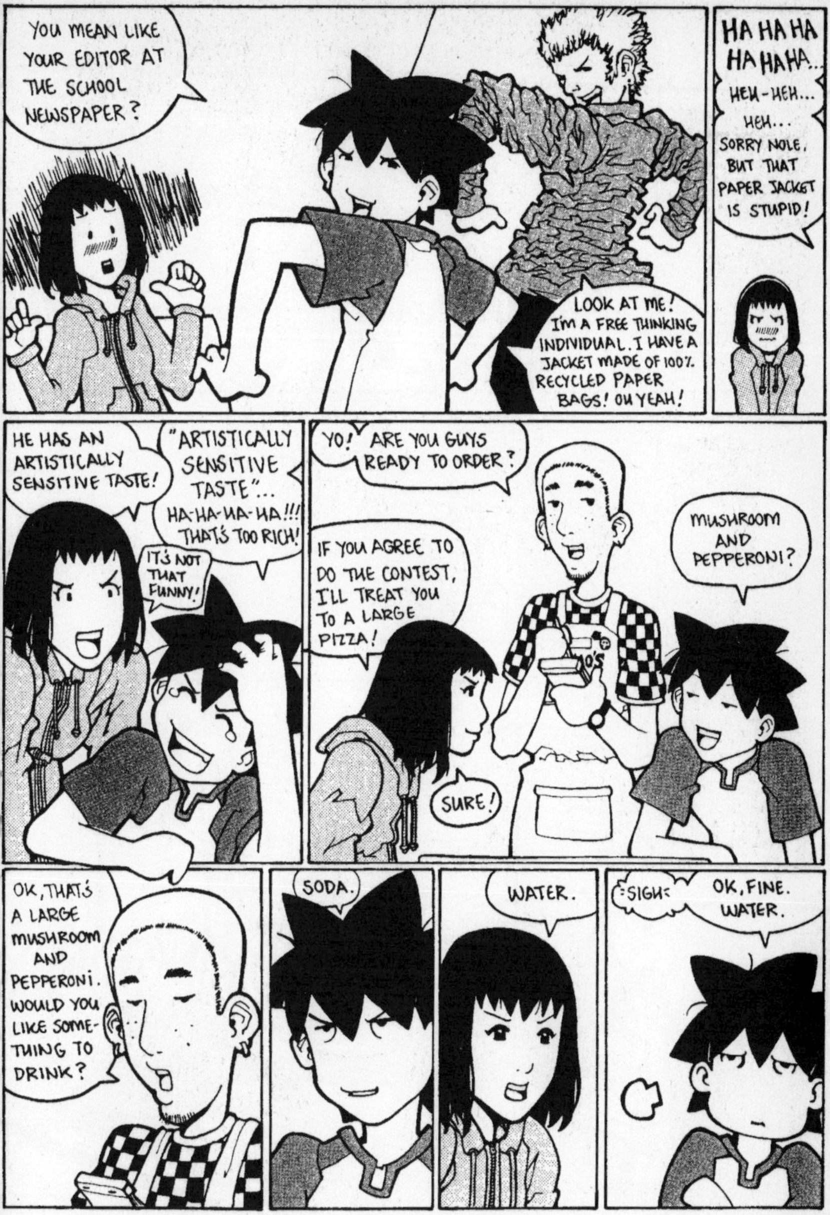
YOU MEAN LIKE YOUR EDITOR AT THE SCHOOL NEWSPAPER?
LOOK AT ME! I'M A FREE THINKING INDIVIDUAL. I HAVE A JACKET MADE OF 100% RECYCLED PAPER BAGS! OH YEAH!
HA HA HA HA HA HA...
HEH-HEH... HEH... SORRY NOLE, BUT THAT PAPER JACKET IS STUPID!
HE HAS AN ARTISTICALLY SENSITIVE TASTE!
"ARTISTICALLY SENSITIVE TASTE"... HA-HA-HA-HA!!! THAT'S TOO RICH!
IT'S NOT THAT FUNNY!
YO!
ARE YOU GUYS READY TO ORDER?
IF YOU AGREE TO DO THE CONTEST, I'LL TREAT YOU TO A LARGE PIZZA!
MUSHROOM AND PEPPERONI?
SURE!
OK, THAT'S A LARGE MUSHROOM AND PEPPERONI. WOULD YOU LIKE SOMETHING TO DRINK?
SODA.
WATER.
SIGH
OK, FINE. WATER.

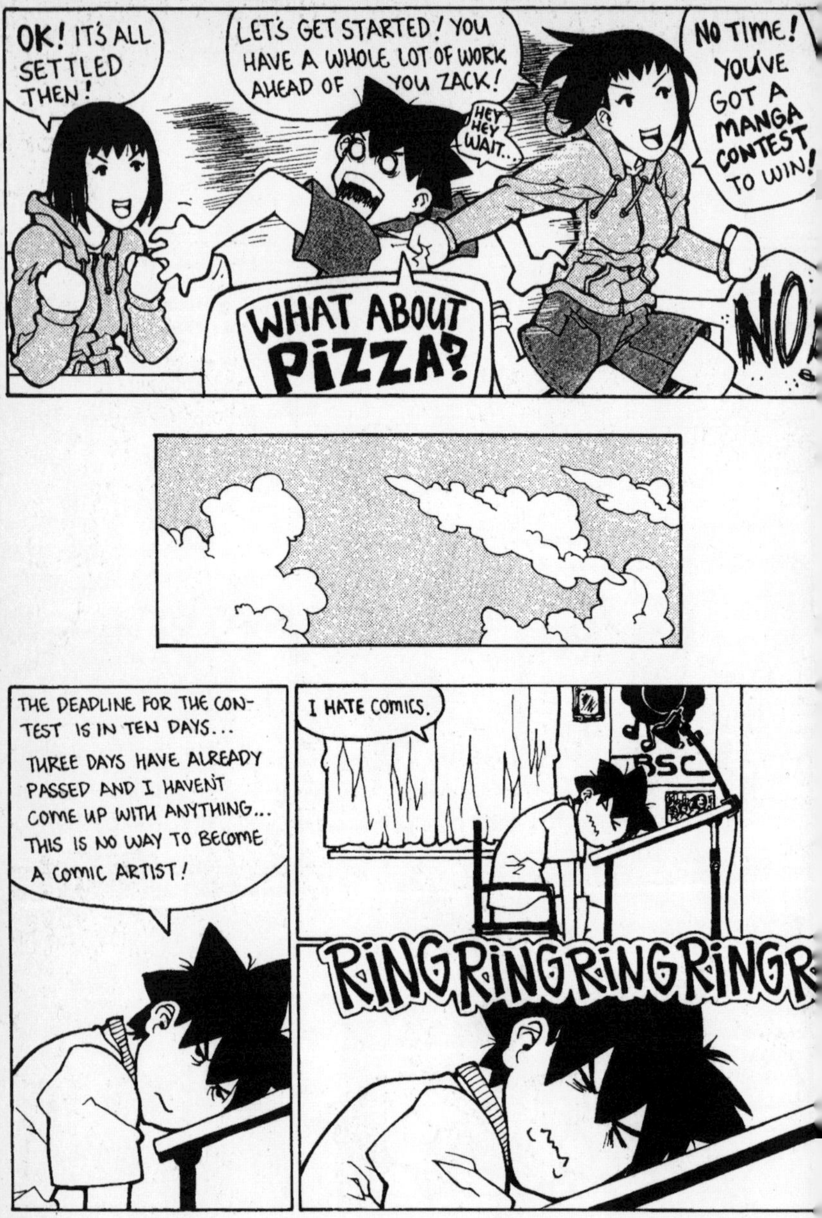
OK! IT'S ALL SETTLED THEN!
LET'S GET STARTED! YOU HAVE A WHOLE LOT OF WORK AHEAD OF YOU ZACK!
HEY HEY WAIT...
WHAT ABOUT PIZZA?
NO TIME! YOU'VE GOT A MANGA CONTEST TO WIN!
NO
THE DEADLINE FOR THE CON-TEST IS IN TEN DAYS... THREE DAYS HAVE ALREADY PASSED AND I HAVEN'T COME UP WITH ANYTHING... THIS IS NO WAY TO BECOME A COMIC ARTIST!
I HATE COMICS.
BSC
RING RING RING RING R

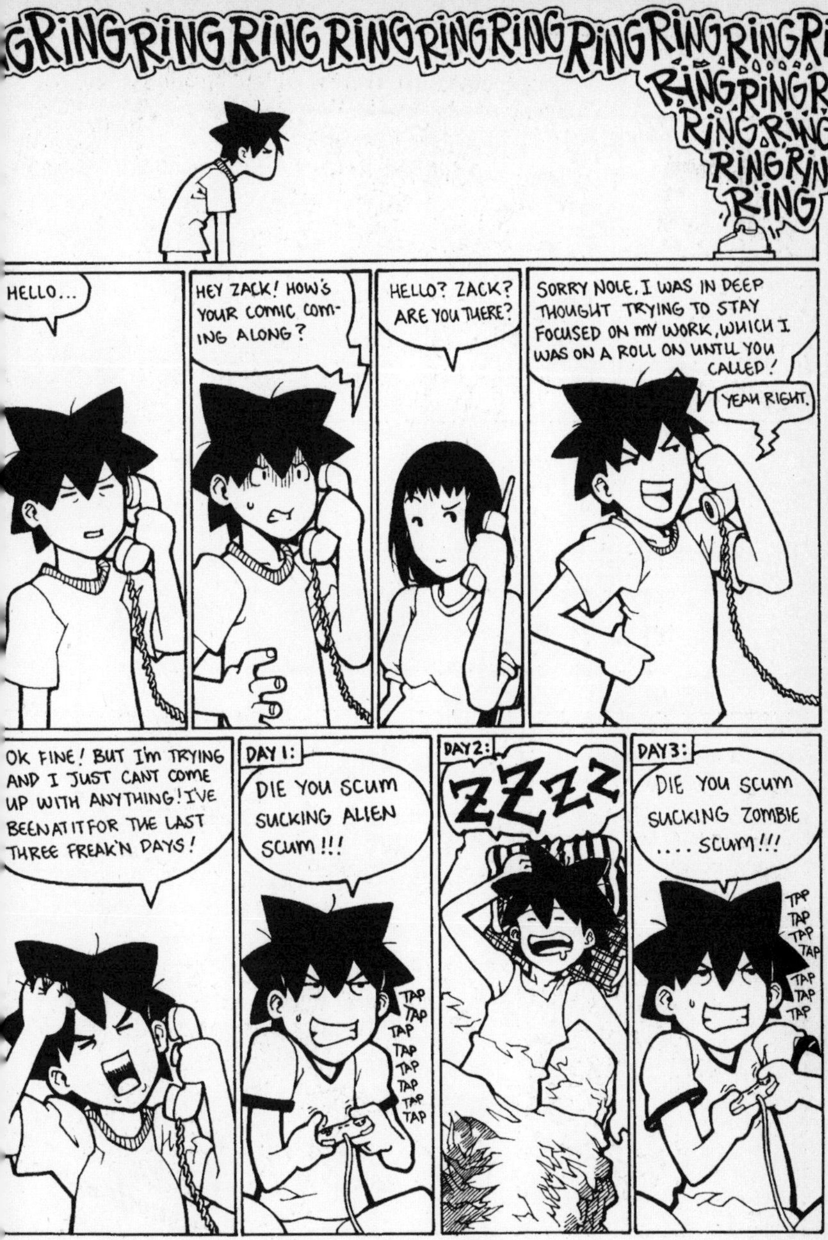
RINGRINGRINGRINGRINGRINGRINGRINGRINGRING
RINGRINGRING
RINGRING
RINGRING
RING
HELLO...
HEY ZACK! HOW'S YOUR COMIC COMING ALONG?
HELLO? ZACK? ARE YOU THERE?
SORRY NOLE, I WAS IN DEEP THOUGHT TRYING TO STAY FOCUSED ON MY WORK, WHICH I WAS ON A ROLL ON UNTIL YOU CALLED!
YEAH RIGHT.
OK FINE! BUT I'm TRYING AND I JUST CANT COME UP WITH ANYTHING! I'VE BEEN AT IT FOR THE LAST THREE FREAK'N DAYS!
DAY 1:
DIE YOU SCUM SUCKING ALIEN SCUM!!!
TAP TAP TAP TAP TAP TAP TAP TAP
DAY 2:
ZZZZ
DAY 3:
DIE YOU SCUM SUCKING ZOMBIE .... SCUM!!!
TAP TAP TAP TAP TAP TAP TAP

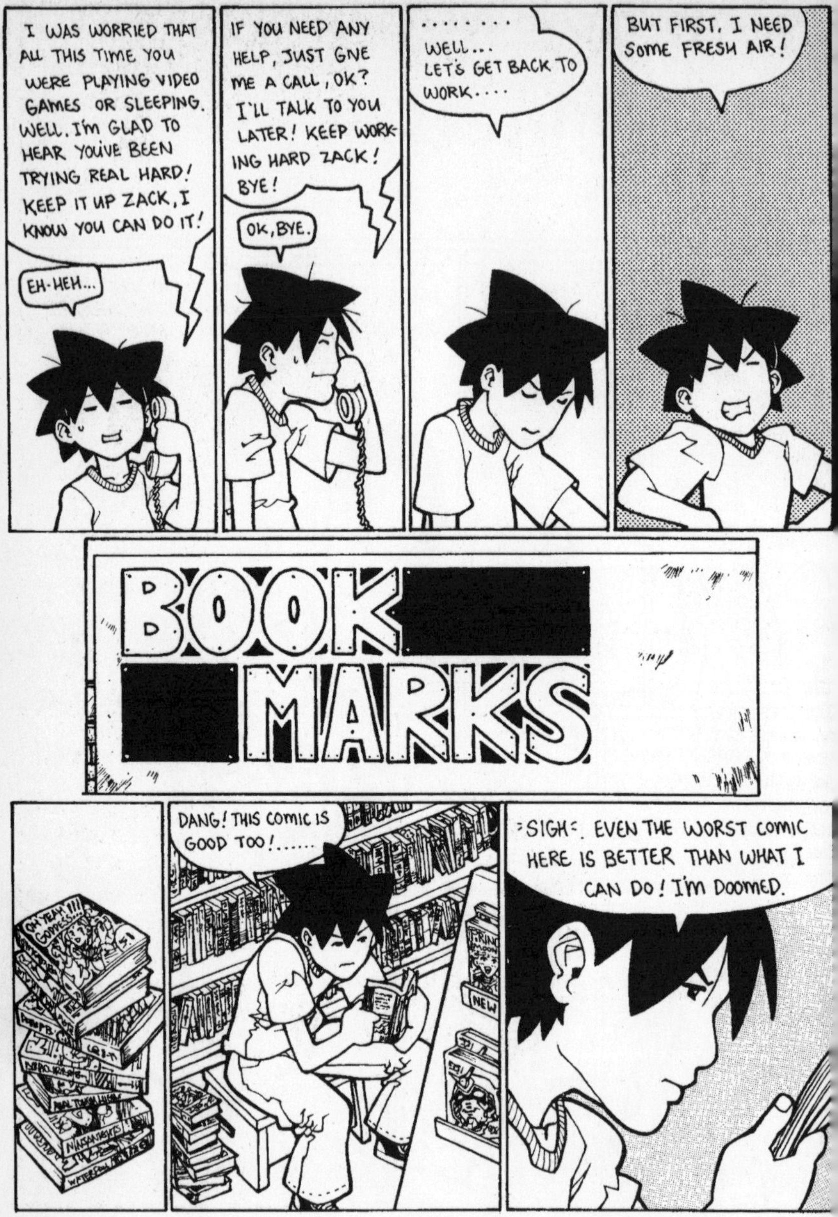
I WAS WORRIED THAT ALL THIS TIME YOU WERE PLAYING VIDEO GAMES OR SLEEPING. WELL, I'M GLAD TO HEAR YOU'VE BEEN TRYING REAL HARD! KEEP IT UP ZACK, I KNOW YOU CAN DO IT!
EH-HEH...
IF YOU NEED ANY HELP, JUST GIVE ME A CALL, OK? I'LL TALK TO YOU LATER! KEEP WORKING HARD ZACK! BYE!
OK, BYE.
....
WELL... LET'S GET BACK TO WORK....
BUT FIRST, I NEED SOME FRESH AIR!
BOOK MARKS
DANG! THIS COMIC IS GOOD TOO!......
NEW
=SIGH=. EVEN THE WORST COMIC HERE IS BETTER THAN WHAT I CAN DO! I'M DOOMED.

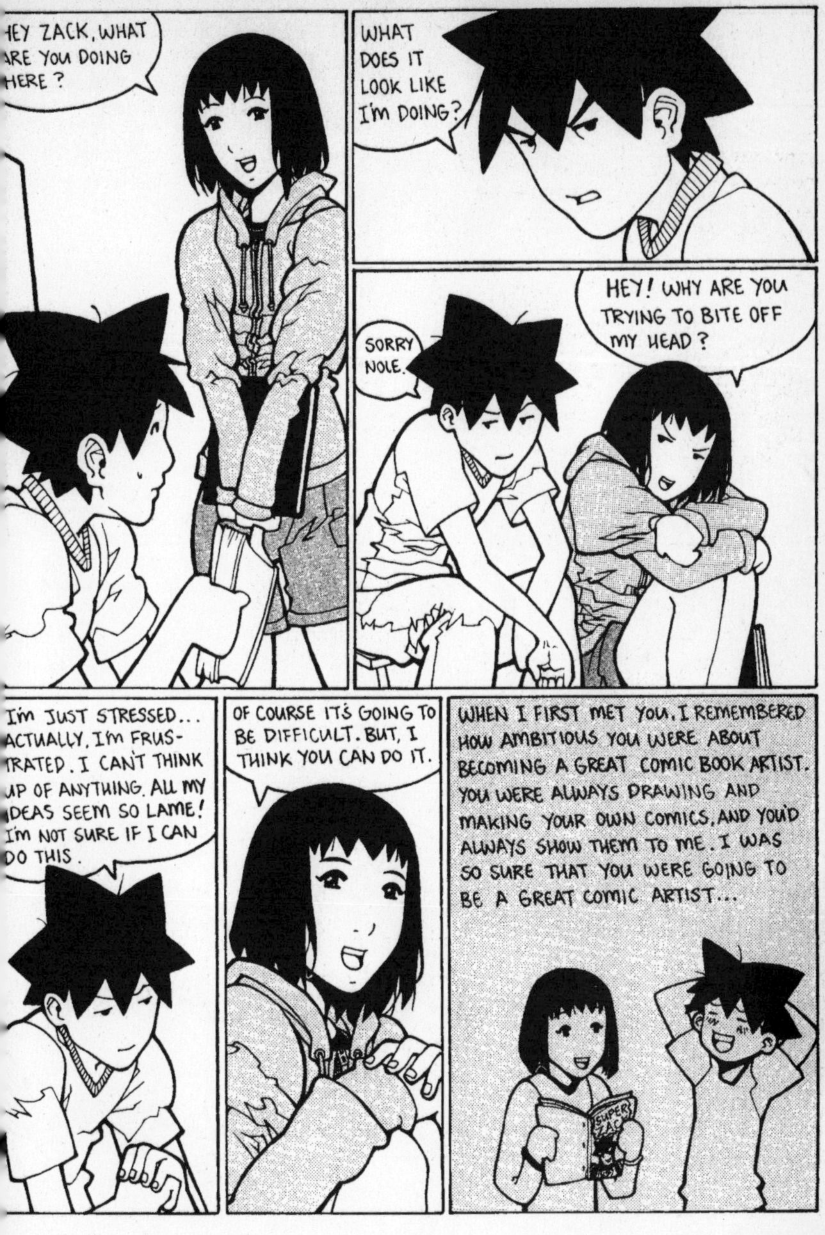
HEY ZACK, WHAT ARE YOU DOING HERE?
WHAT DOES IT LOOK LIKE I'M DOING?
SORRY NOLE.
HEY! WHY ARE YOU TRYING TO BITE OFF MY HEAD?
I'M JUST STRESSED... ACTUALLY, I'M FRUS-TRATED. I CAN'T THINK UP OF ANYTHING. ALL MY IDEAS SEEM SO LAME! I'M NOT SURE IF I CAN DO THIS.
OF COURSE IT'S GOING TO BE DIFFICULT. BUT, I THINK YOU CAN DO IT.
WHEN I FIRST MET YOU, I REMEMBERED HOW AMBITIOUS YOU WERE ABOUT BECOMING A GREAT COMIC BOOK ARTIST. YOU WERE ALWAYS DRAWING AND MAKING YOUR OWN COMICS, AND YOU'D ALWAYS SHOW THEM TO ME. I WAS SO SURE THAT YOU WERE GOING TO BE A GREAT COMIC ARTIST...
SUPER ZAC

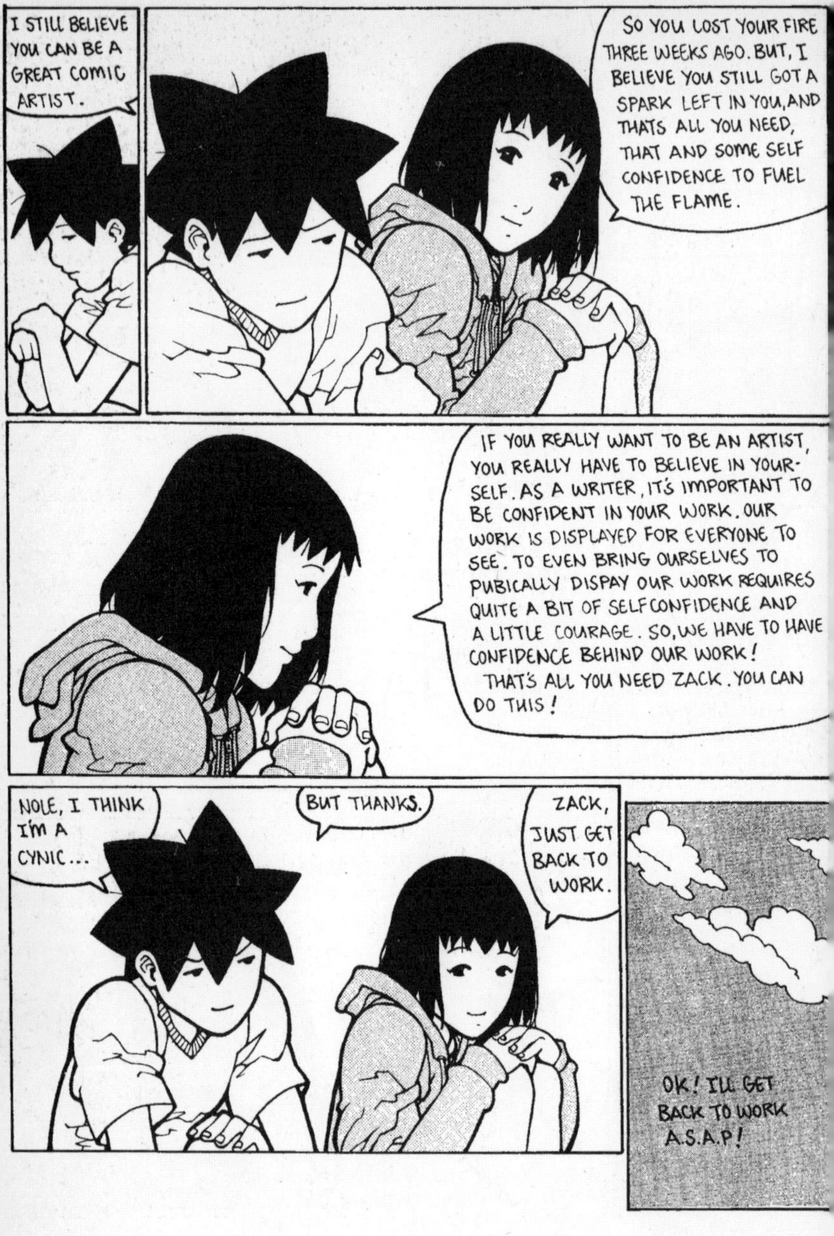
I STILL BELIEVE YOU CAN BE A GREAT COMIC ARTIST.
SO YOU LOST YOUR FIRE THREE WEEKS AGO. BUT, I BELIEVE YOU STILL GOT A SPARK LEFT IN YOU, AND THATS ALL YOU NEED, THAT AND SOME SELF CONFIDENCE TO FUEL THE FLAME.
IF YOU REALLY WANT TO BE AN ARTIST, YOU REALLY HAVE TO BELIEVE IN YOURSELF. AS A WRITER, IT'S IMPORTANT TO BE CONFIDENT IN YOUR WORK. OUR WORK IS DISPLAYED FOR EVERYONE TO SEE. TO EVEN BRING OURSELVES TO PUBICALLY DISPAY OUR WORK REQUIRES QUITE A BIT OF SELF CONFIDENCE AND A LITTLE COURAGE. SO, WE HAVE TO HAVE CONFIDENCE BEHIND OUR WORK! THAT'S ALL YOU NEED ZACK. YOU CAN DO THIS!
NOLE, I THINK I'M A CYNIC...
BUT THANKS.
ZACK, JUST GET BACK TO WORK.
OK! I'LL GET BACK TO WORK A.S.A.P!

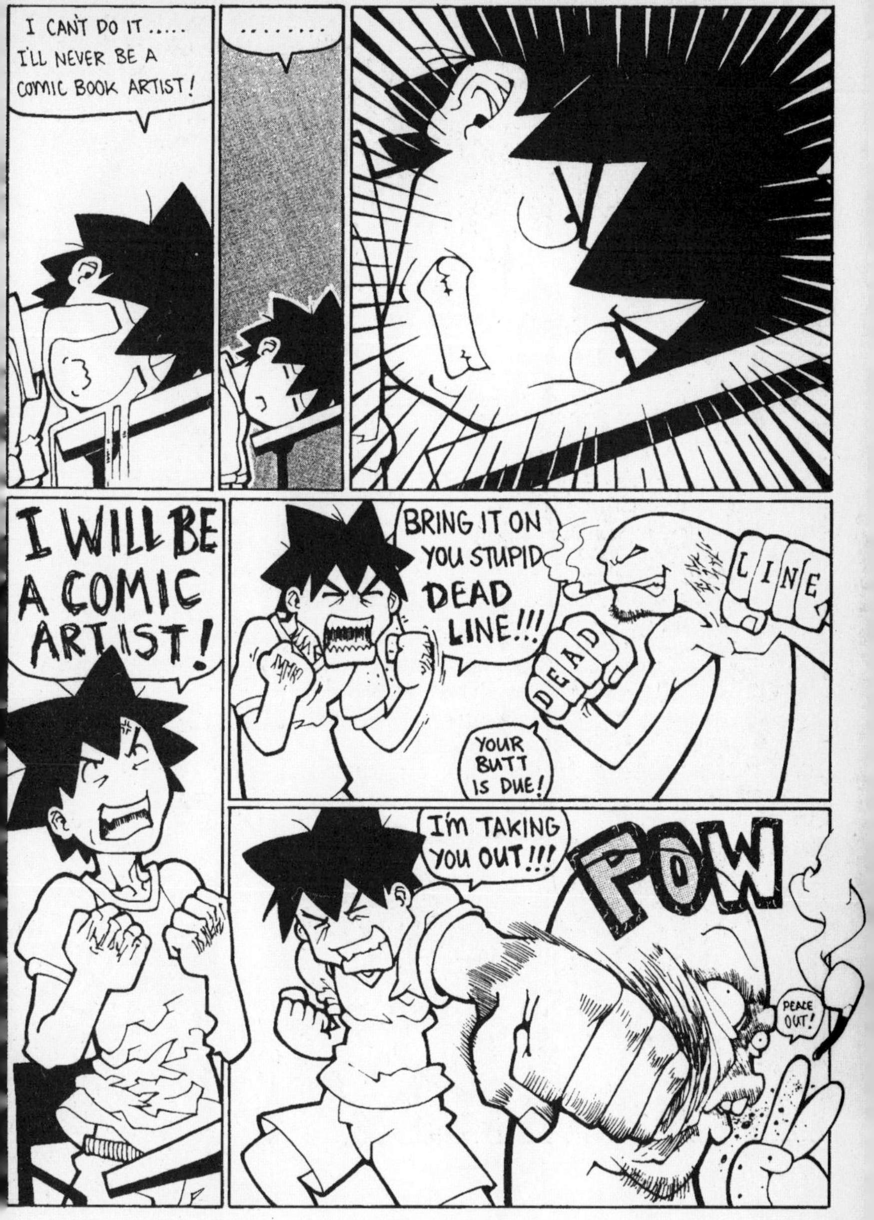
I CAN'T DO IT .....
I'LL NEVER BE A COMIC BOOK ARTIST!
....
I WILL BE A COMIC ARTIST!
BRING IT ON YOU STUPID DEAD LINE!!!
LINE
DEAD
YOUR BUTT IS DUE!
I'M TAKING YOU OUT!!!
POW
PEACE OUT!

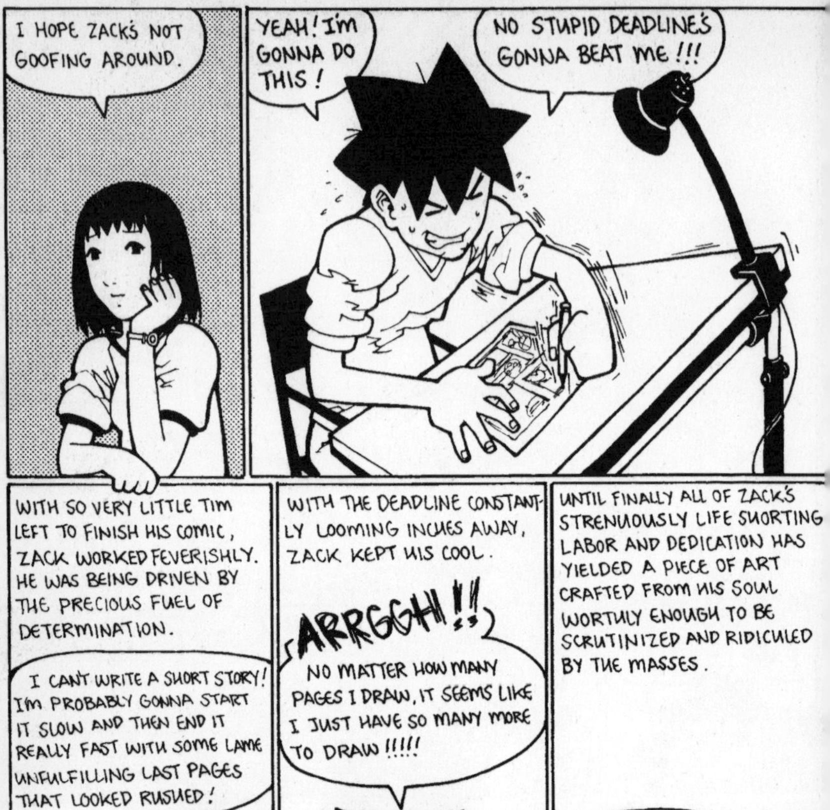
I HOPE ZACK'S NOT GOOFING AROUND.
YEAH! I'm GONNA DO THIS!
NO STUPID DEADLINE'S GONNA BEAT ME!!!
WITH SO VERY LITTLE TIM LEFT TO FINISH HIS COMIC, ZACK WORKED FEVERISHLY. HE WAS BEING DRIVEN BY THE PRECIOUS FUEL OF DETERMINATION.
I CAN'T WRITE A SHORT STORY! I'M PROBABLY GONNA START IT SLOW AND THEN END IT REALLY FAST WITH SOME LAME UNFULFILLING LAST PAGES THAT LOOKED RUSHED!
WITH THE DEADLINE CONSTANTLY LOOMING INCHES AWAY, ZACK KEPT HIS COOL.
ARRGGH!!
NO MATTER HOW MANY PAGES I DRAW, IT SEEMS LIKE I JUST HAVE SO MANY MORE TO DRAW!!!!!
UNTIL FINALLY ALL OF ZACK'S STRENUOUSLY LIFE SHORTING LABOR AND DEDICATION HAS YIELDED A PIECE OF ART CRAFTED FROM HIS SOUL WORTHLY ENOUGH TO BE SCRUTINIZED AND RIDICULED BY THE MASSES.
GOOD RIDDANCE!
SHOVE
MAIL BOX

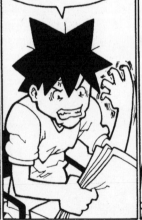

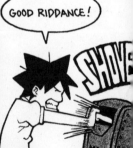

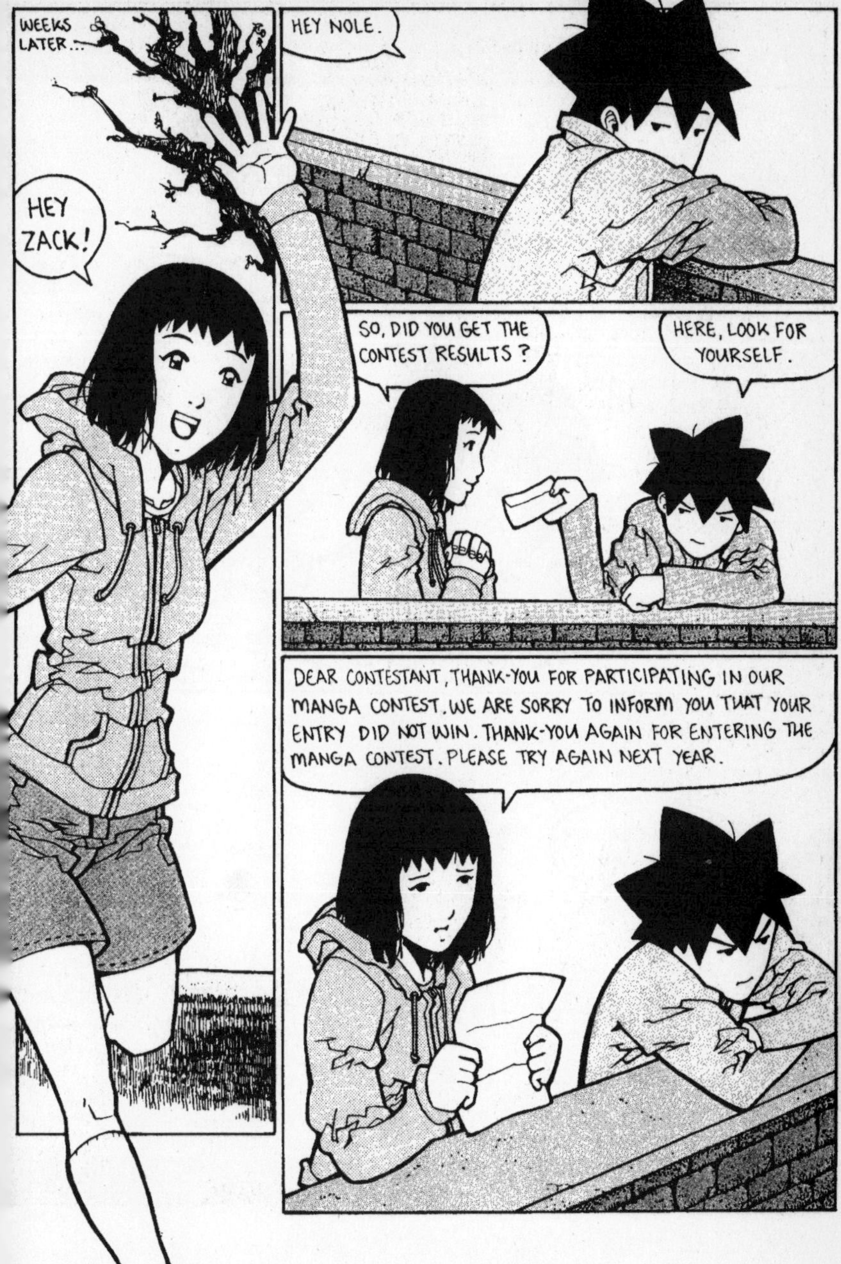
WEEKS LATER...
HEY ZACK!
HEY NOLE.
SO, DID YOU GET THE CONTEST RESULTS?
HERE, LOOK FOR YOURSELF.
DEAR CONTESTANT, THANK-YOU FOR PARTICIPATING IN OUR MANGA CONTEST. WE ARE SORRY TO INFORM YOU THAT YOUR ENTRY DID NOT WIN. THANK-YOU AGAIN FOR ENTERING THE MANGA CONTEST. PLEASE TRY AGAIN NEXT YEAR.

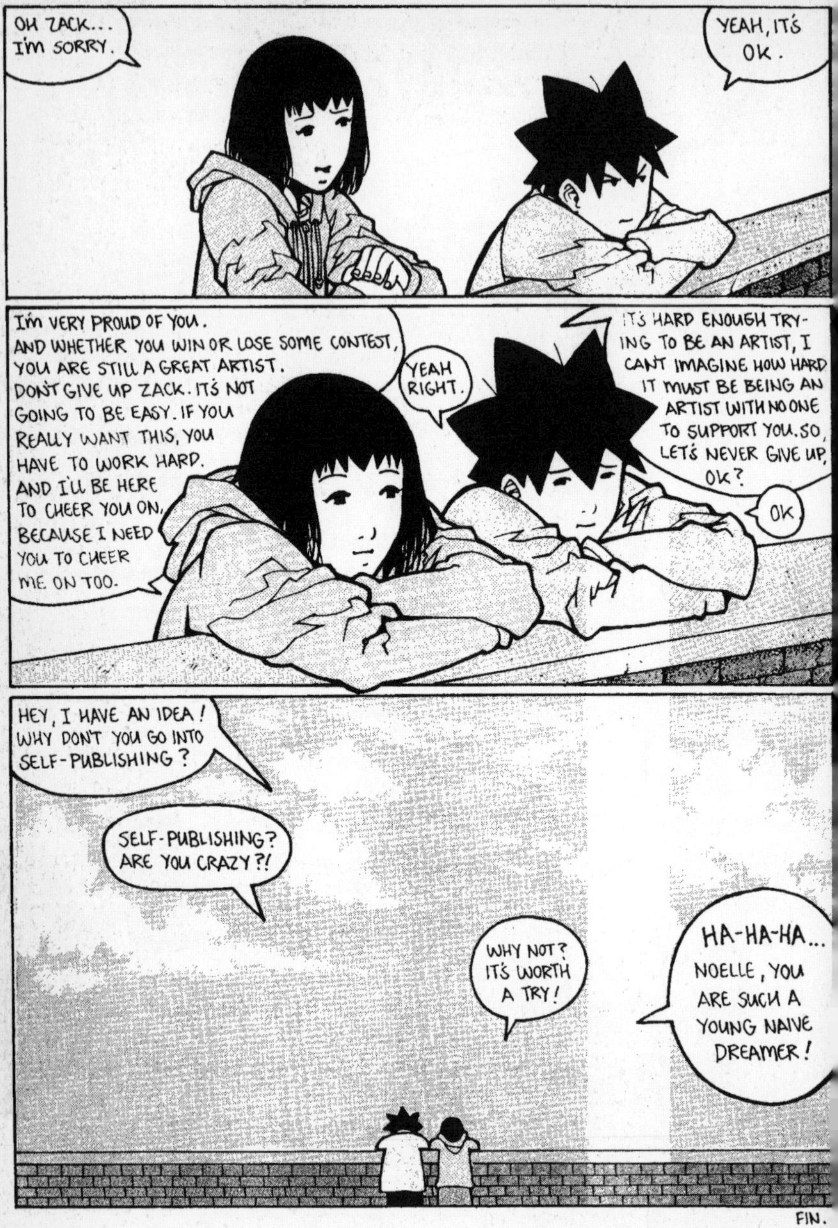
OH ZACK...
I'M SORRY.
YEAH, IT'S OK.
I'M VERY PROUD OF YOU. AND WHETHER YOU WIN OR LOSE SOME CONTEST, YOU ARE STILL A GREAT ARTIST. DON'T GIVE UP ZACK. IT'S NOT GOING TO BE EASY. IF YOU REALLY WANT THIS, YOU HAVE TO WORK HARD. AND I'LL BE HERE TO CHEER YOU ON, BECAUSE I NEED YOU TO CHEER ME ON TOO.
YEAH RIGHT.
IT'S HARD ENOUGH TRYING TO BE AN ARTIST, I CANT IMAGINE HOW HARD IT MUST BE BEING AN ARTIST WITH NO ONE TO SUPPORT YOU. SO, LET'S NEVER GIVE UP, OK?
OK
HEY, I HAVE AN IDEA! WHY DON'T YOU GO INTO SELF-PUBLISHING?
SELF-PUBLISHING? ARE YOU CRAZY?!
WHY NOT? IT'S WORTH A TRY!
HA-HA-HA... NOELLE, YOU ARE SUCH A YOUNG NAIVE DREAMER!

FIN.

::

OPHELIA'S ASSASSINATION: veritas :: RUNNER UP ::

Kelli Hoover was born in 1987 in Portsmouth, Virginia, and now lives in Sun Prairie, Wisconsin. The Japanese name given to her by her grandmother is Chika, and she sometimes goes by Masayume.

Inspiration for this story:
It's a side story that includes characters from a larger story.

Favorite Manga:
Angelique, Angel Sanctuary, Chobits, Mitchu Gumi (my friend Hoto's online manga)

Favorite Manga Artists:
I aspire to be like CLAMP, but I have to say my favorite is Kaori Yuki.

....

Judge's Comments:
The most striking aspect of "Ophelia's Assassination" is Kelli Hoover's commanding use of allegory to create a powerful metaphor for the concept of Justice. These semi-allegorical angels (with names such as Jury, Justice, Trial, Axiom and Penalty) are imbued with the flawed human condition, and therefore reflect how humanity, too, is quick to do away with the protections of justice—the trial, the jury—when filled with the darker human emotions such as jealousy, rage and—perhaps the most insidious and dangerous feeling of all—fear.

Lithe, seemingly androgynous angels are rendered here in simple line drawings that become richer as the story moves toward its chilling conclusion. But the author returns to line drawing in the last few panels, the very last panel done in black and white negative, distancing the character of Jury—the central protagonist in this story of angel infighting—from the reader. In the absence of Justice and with the corruption of Trial, Jury becomes an obsolete force in the Inner Circle of angels.

When we, as a people, eliminate Justice, we surrender to Axiom and Penalty, presuming guilt in a suspect who no longer has a trial through which to speak and a jury to hear his appeals.
-Luis Reyes

::

174

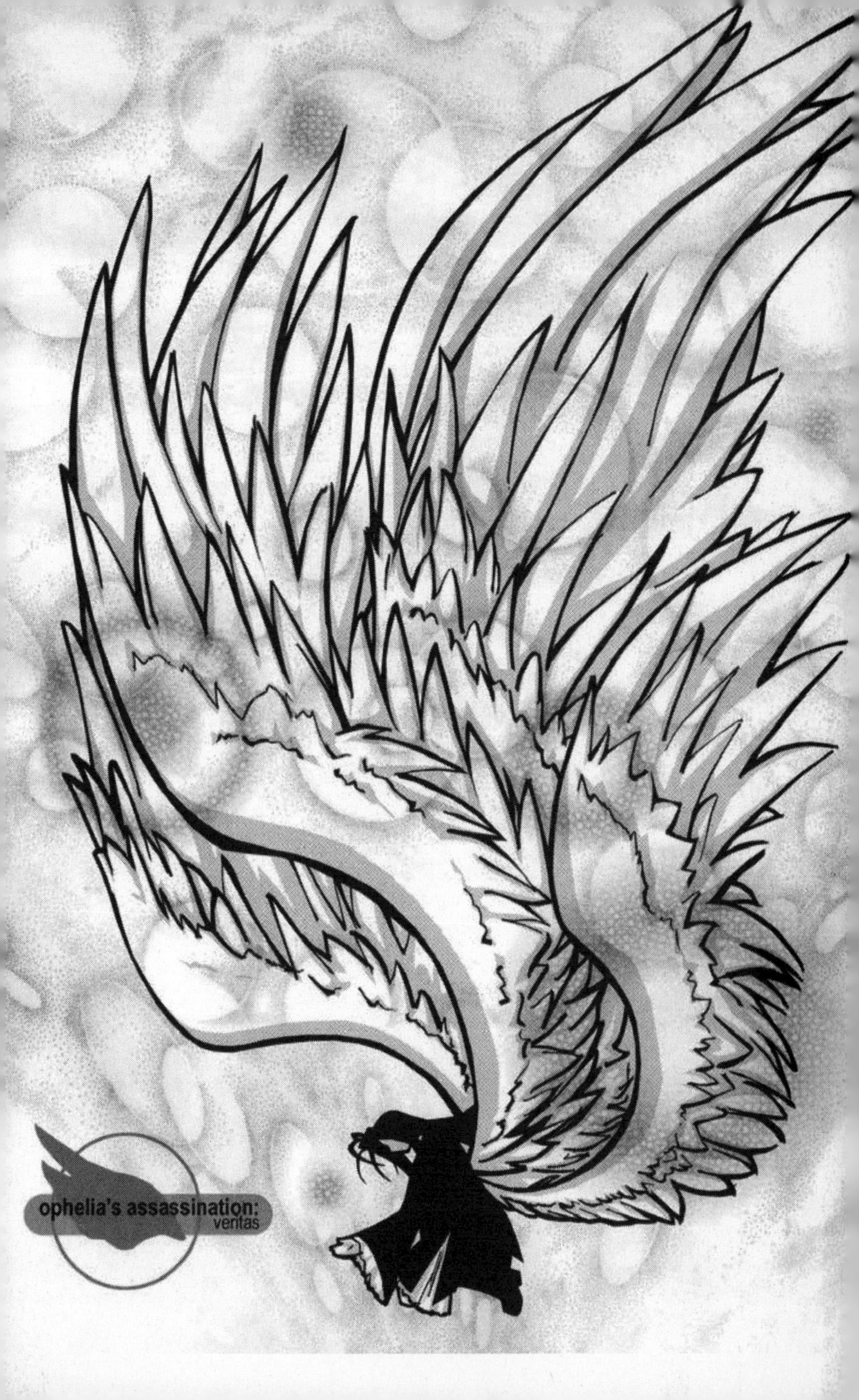
ophelia's assassination:
veritas

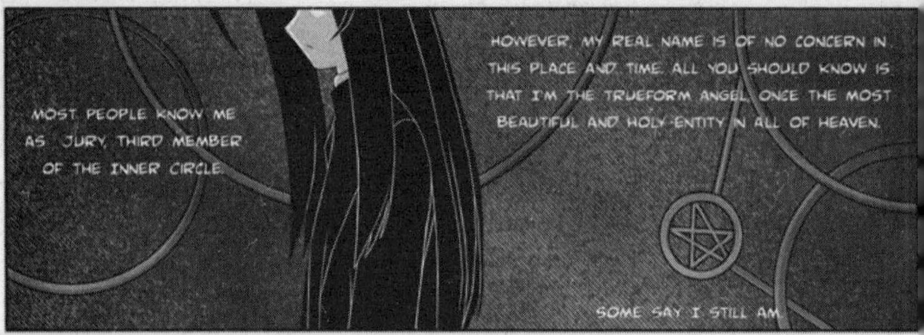
MOST PEOPLE KNOW ME AS JURY, THIRD MEMBER OF THE INNER CIRCLE.
HOWEVER, MY REAL NAME IS OF NO CONCERN IN THIS PLACE AND TIME. ALL YOU SHOULD KNOW IS THAT I'M THE TRUEFORM ANGEL, ONCE THE MOST BEAUTIFUL AND HOLY-ENTITY IN ALL OF HEAVEN.
SOME SAY I STILL AM.
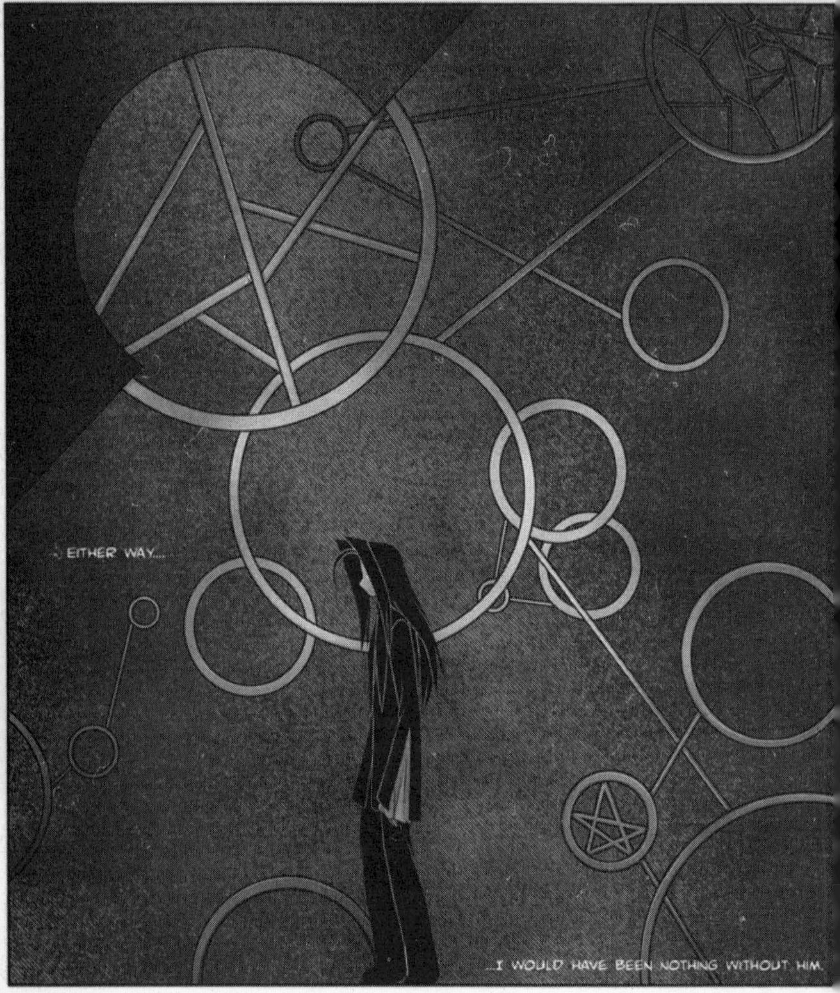
...EITHER WAY...
...I WOULD HAVE BEEN NOTHING WITHOUT HIM.

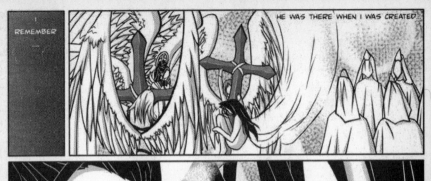

REMEMBER
1

HE WAS THERE WHEN I WAS CREATED.

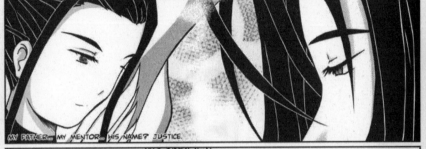

MY FATHER... MY MENTOR... HIS NAME? JUSTICE.

I WAS INTRODUCED TO THE INNER CIRCLE, THE MOST POWERFUL GROUP OF ANGELS IN ALL OF HEAVEN.

...THEY FOUND THOSE GUILTY OF CRIMES, AND PUNISHED THEM.

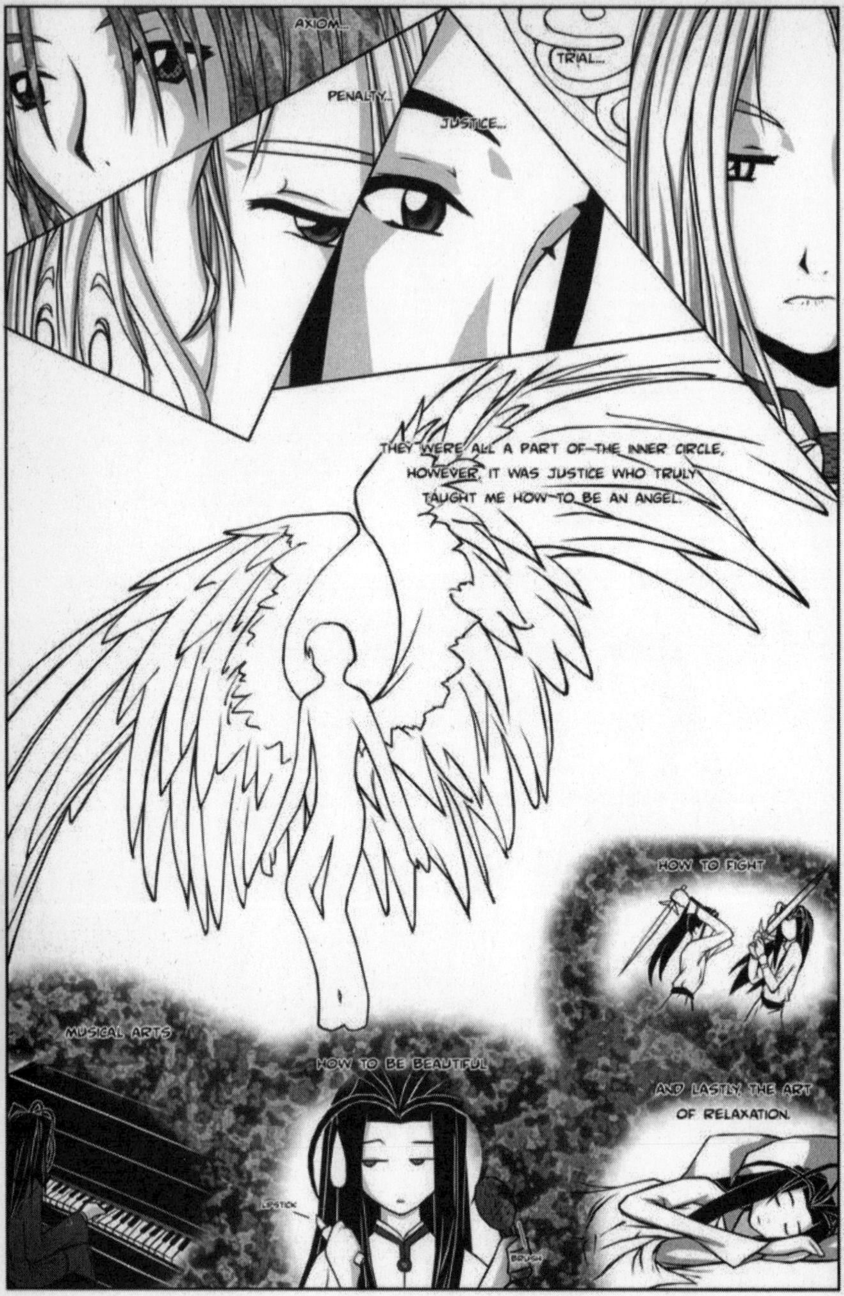
AXIOM...
PENALTY...
JUSTICE...
TRIAL...
THEY WERE ALL A PART OF THE INNER CIRCLE, HOWEVER, IT WAS JUSTICE WHO TRULY TAUGHT ME HOW TO BE AN ANGEL.
HOW TO FIGHT
MUSICAL ARTS
HOW TO BE BEAUTIFUL
LIPSTICK
BRUSH
AND LASTLY, THE ART OF RELAXATION.

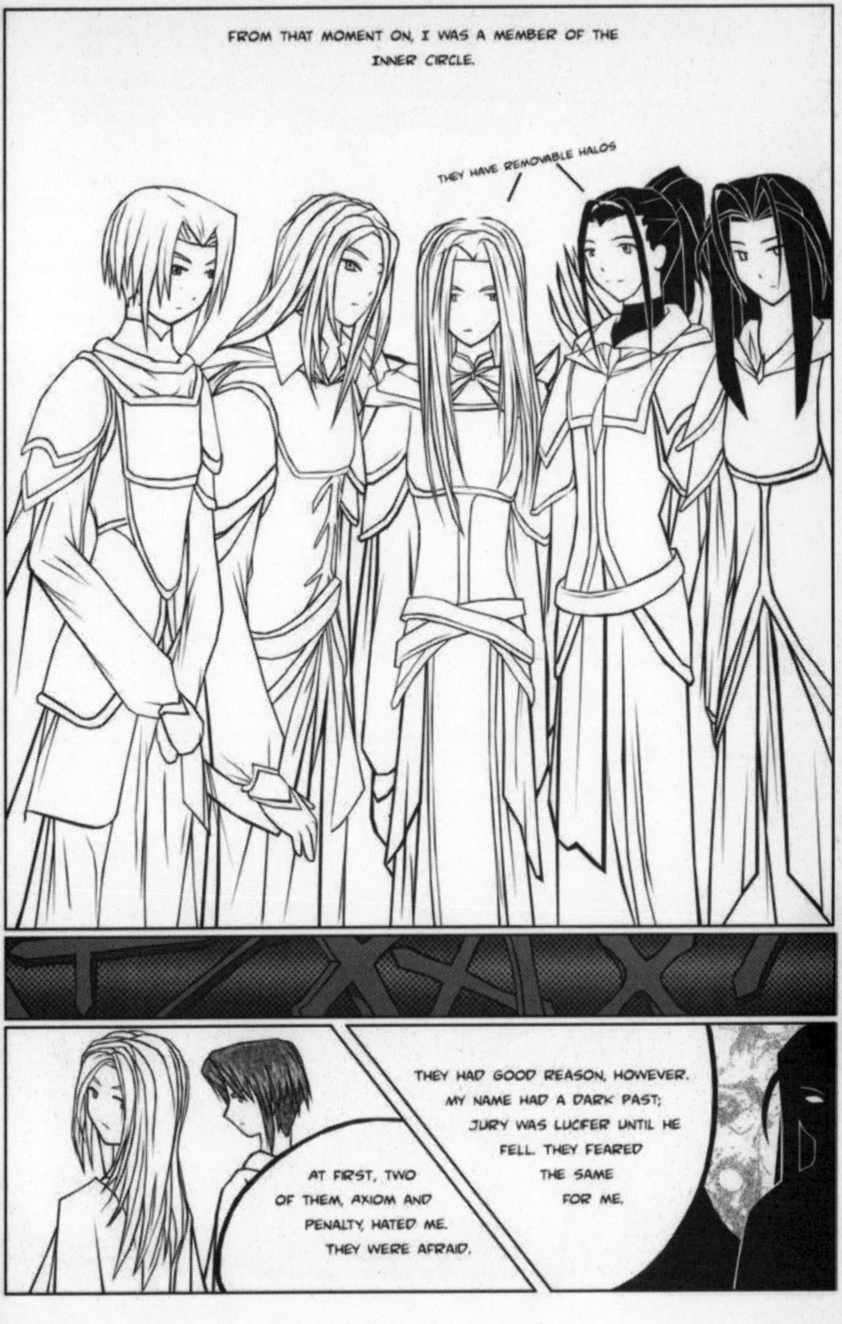
FROM THAT MOMENT ON, I WAS A MEMBER OF THE INNER CIRCLE.
THEY HAVE REMOVABLE HALOS
AT FIRST, TWO OF THEM, AXIOM AND PENALTY, HATED ME. THEY WERE AFRAID.
THEY HAD GOOD REASON, HOWEVER. MY NAME HAD A DARK PAST; JURY WAS LUCIFER UNTIL HE FELL. THEY FEARED THE SAME FOR ME.

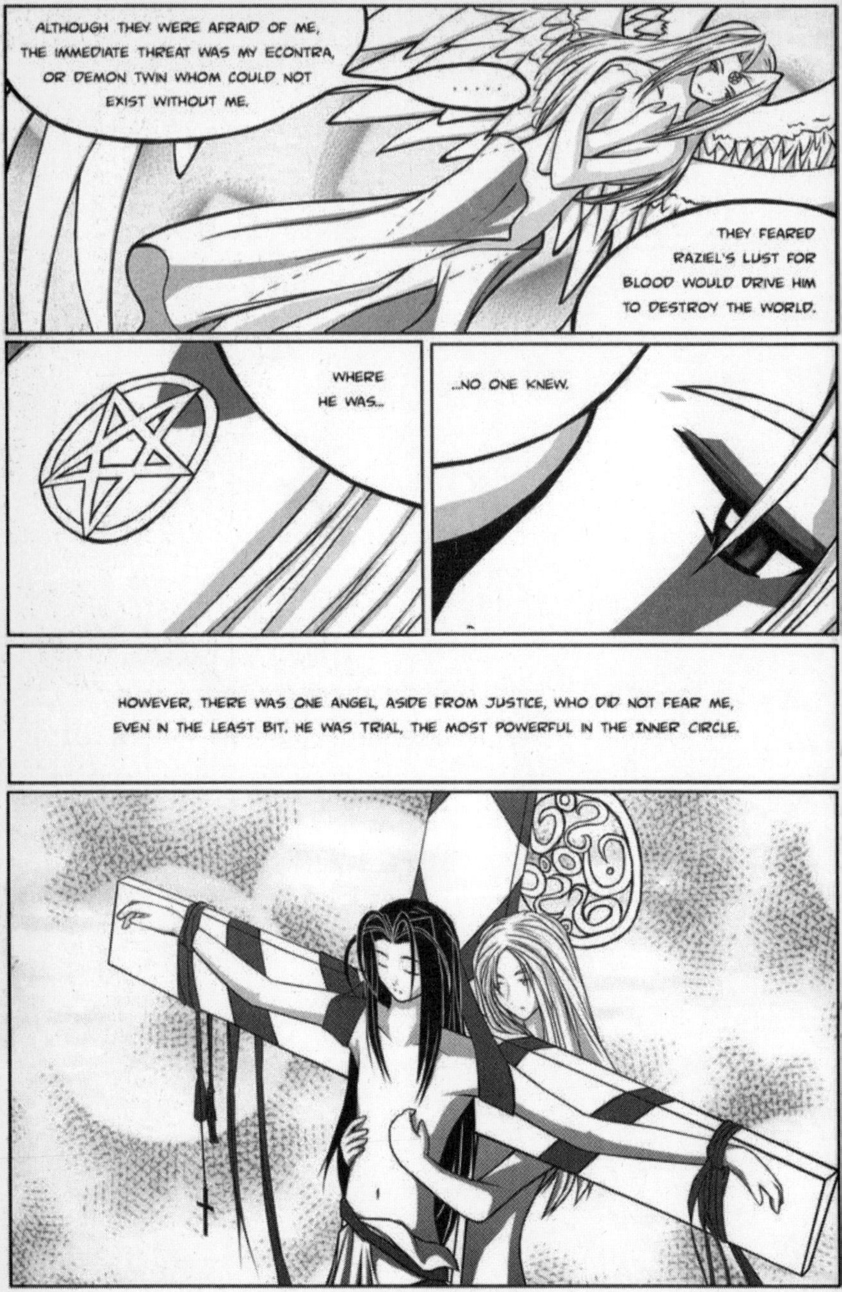
ALTHOUGH THEY WERE AFRAID OF ME, THE IMMEDIATE THREAT WAS MY ECONTRA, OR DEMON TWIN WHOM COULD NOT EXIST WITHOUT ME.
......
THEY FEARED RAZIEL'S LUST FOR BLOOD WOULD DRIVE HIM TO DESTROY THE WORLD.
WHERE HE WAS...
...NO ONE KNEW.
HOWEVER, THERE WAS ONE ANGEL, ASIDE FROM JUSTICE, WHO DID NOT FEAR ME, EVEN IN THE LEAST BIT. HE WAS TRIAL, THE MOST POWERFUL IN THE INNER CIRCLE.

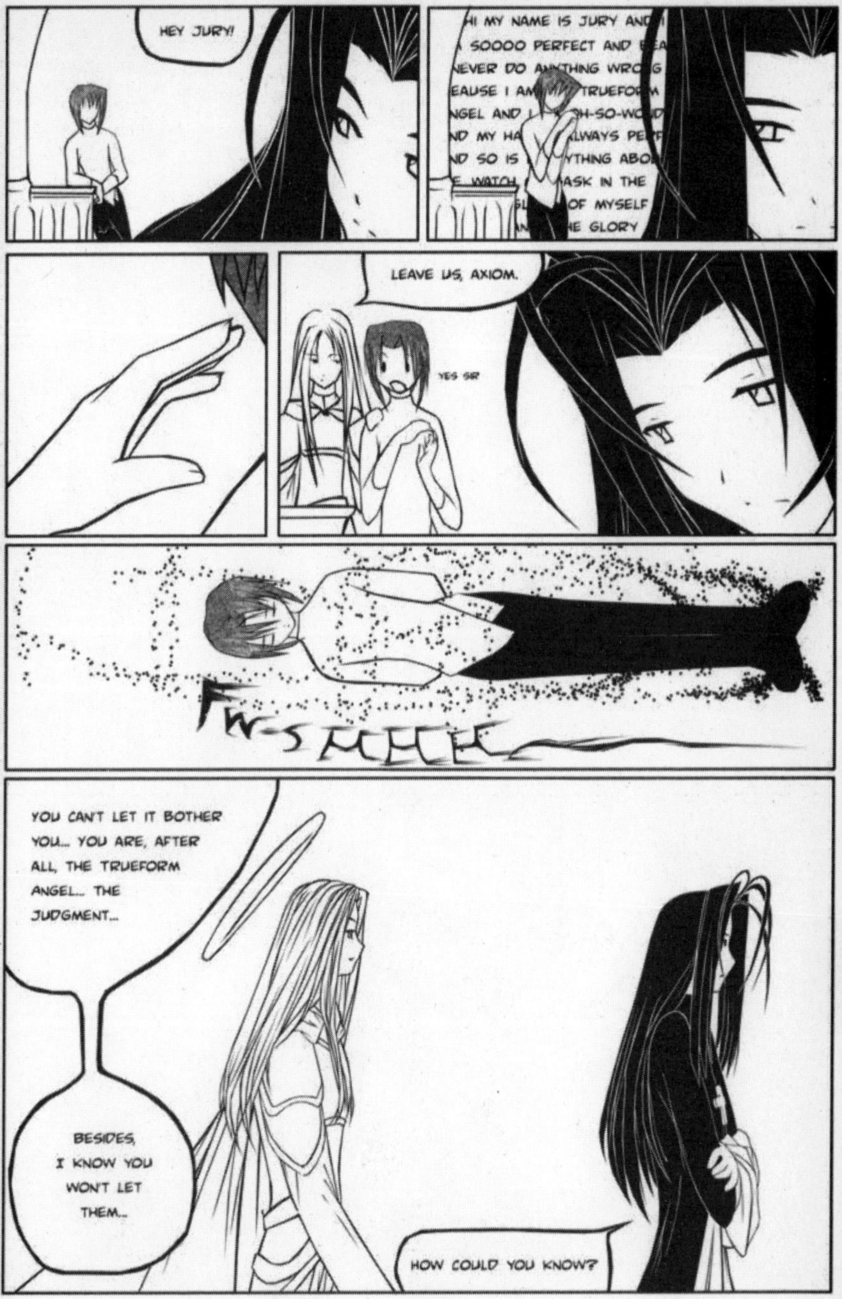
HEY JURY!
HI MY NAME IS JURY AND
SOOOO PERFECT AND
NEVER DO
I AM
TRUEFORM
AND
AND MY
ALWAYS
AND SO IS
IN THE
OF MYSELF
GLORY
LEAVE US, AXIOM.
YES SIR
FWSHHH
YOU CAN'T LET IT BOTHER YOU... YOU ARE, AFTER ALL, THE TRUEFORM ANGEL... THE JUDGMENT...
BESIDES, I KNOW YOU WON'T LET THEM...
HOW COULD YOU KNOW?

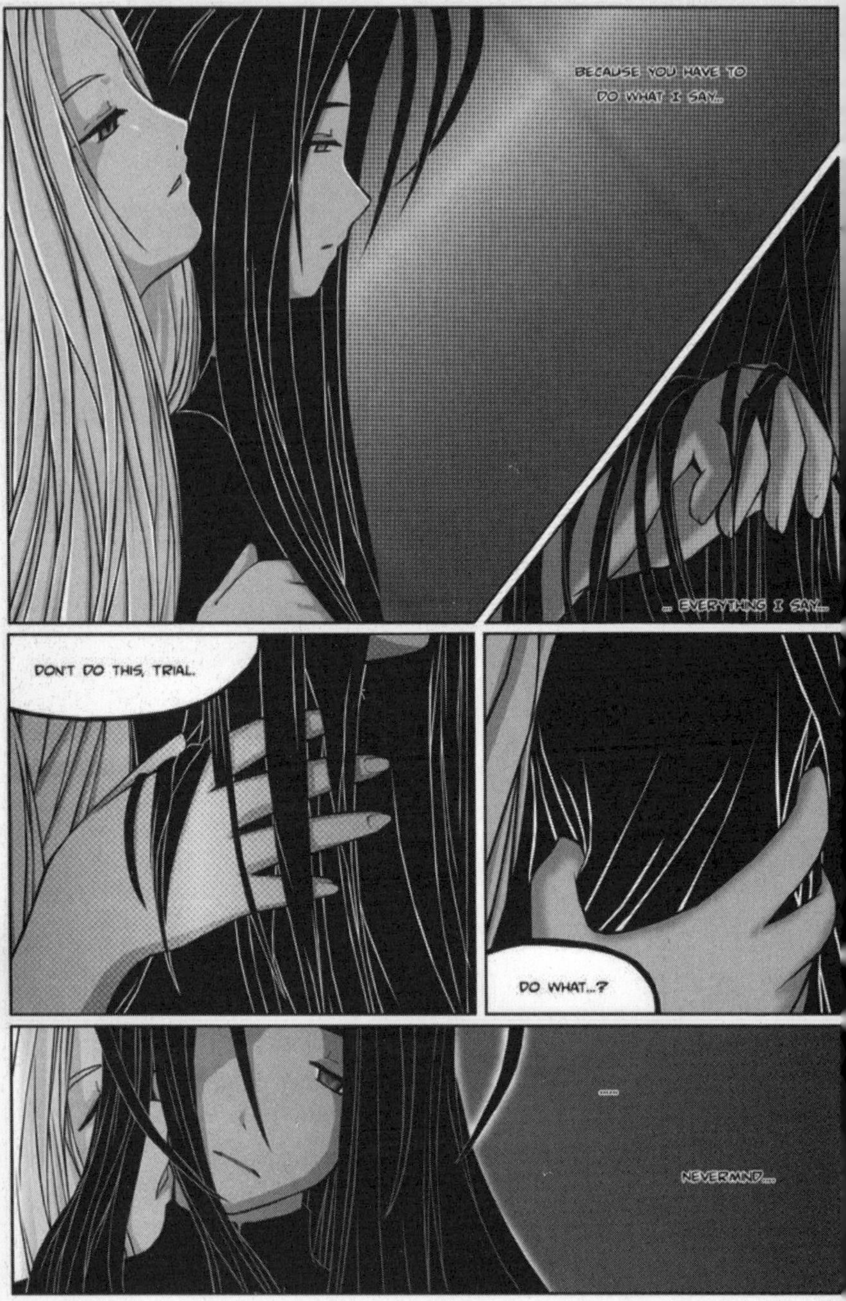
BECAUSE YOU HAVE TO DO WHAT I SAY...
... EVERYTHING I SAY...
DON'T DO THIS, TRIAL.
DO WHAT...?
.....
NEVERMIND....

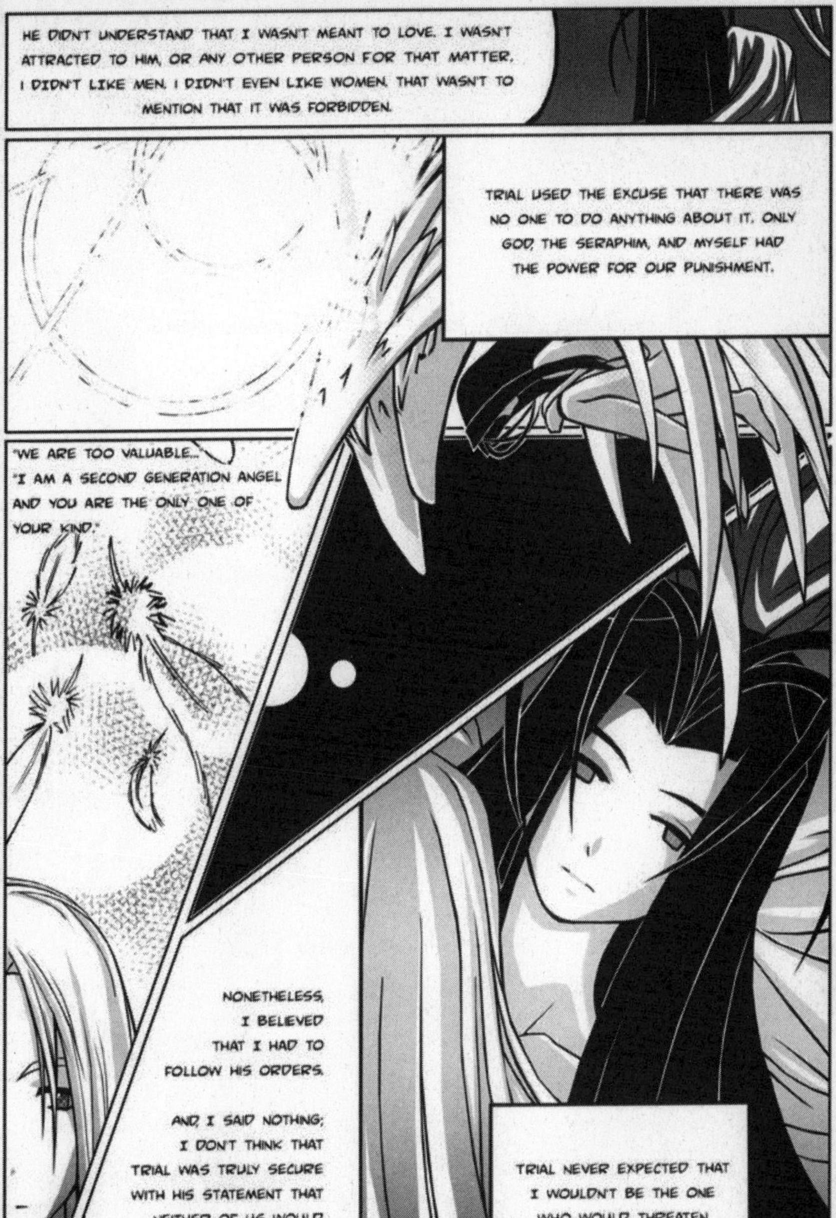
HE DIDN'T UNDERSTAND THAT I WASN'T MEANT TO LOVE. I WASN'T ATTRACTED TO HIM, OR ANY OTHER PERSON FOR THAT MATTER. I DIDN'T LIKE MEN. I DIDN'T EVEN LIKE WOMEN. THAT WASN'T TO MENTION THAT IT WAS FORBIDDEN.
TRIAL USED THE EXCUSE THAT THERE WAS NO ONE TO DO ANYTHING ABOUT IT. ONLY GOD, THE SERAPHIM, AND MYSELF HAD THE POWER FOR OUR PUNISHMENT.
"WE ARE TOO VALUABLE..." "I AM A SECOND GENERATION ANGEL AND YOU ARE THE ONLY ONE OF YOUR KIND."
NONETHELESS, I BELIEVED THAT I HAD TO FOLLOW HIS ORDERS.
AND, I SAID NOTHING; I DON'T THINK THAT TRIAL WAS TRULY SECURE WITH HIS STATEMENT THAT NEITHER OF US WOULD BE PUNISHED.
TRIAL NEVER EXPECTED THAT I WOULDN'T BE THE ONE WHO WOULD THREATEN TO TELL.

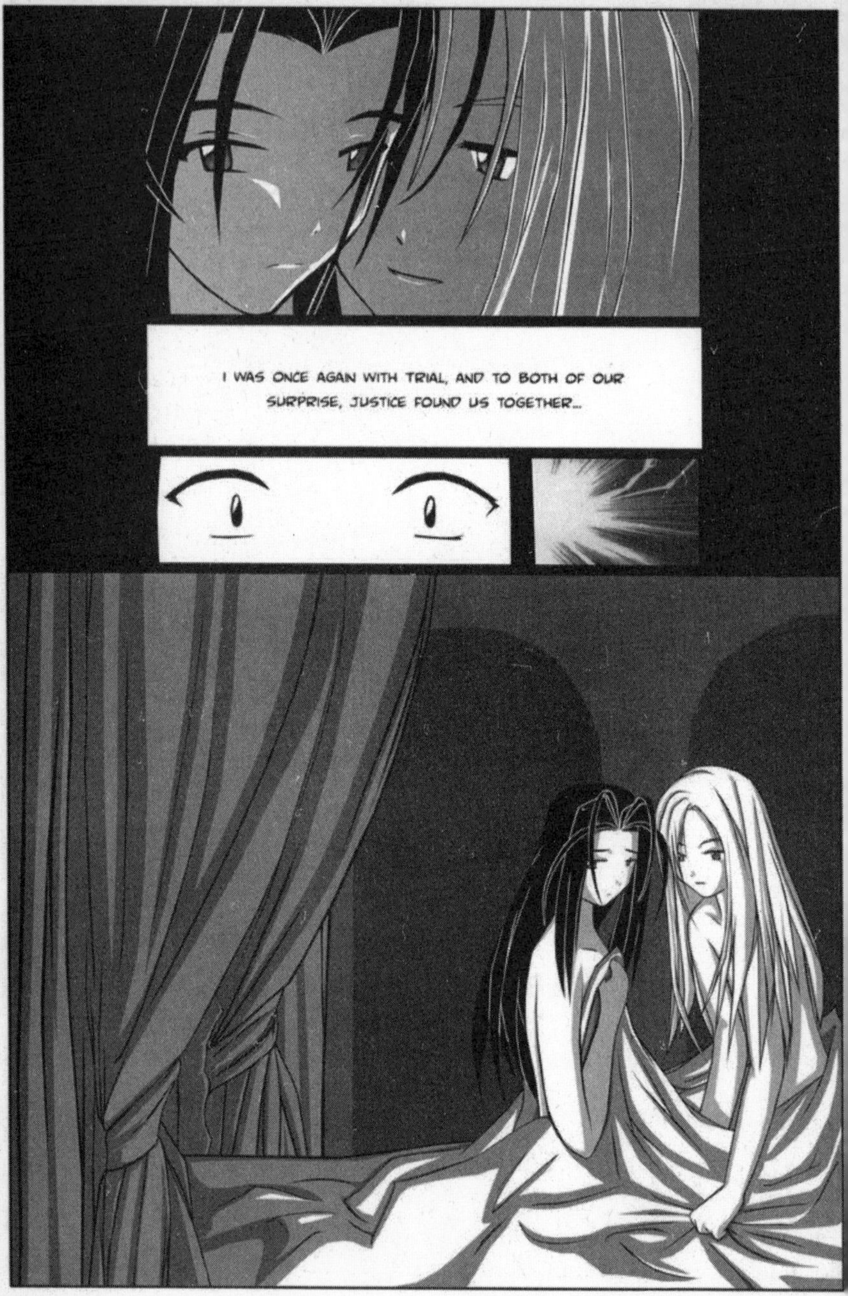
I WAS ONCE AGAIN WITH TRIAL, AND TO BOTH OF OUR SURPRISE, JUSTICE FOUND US TOGETHER...

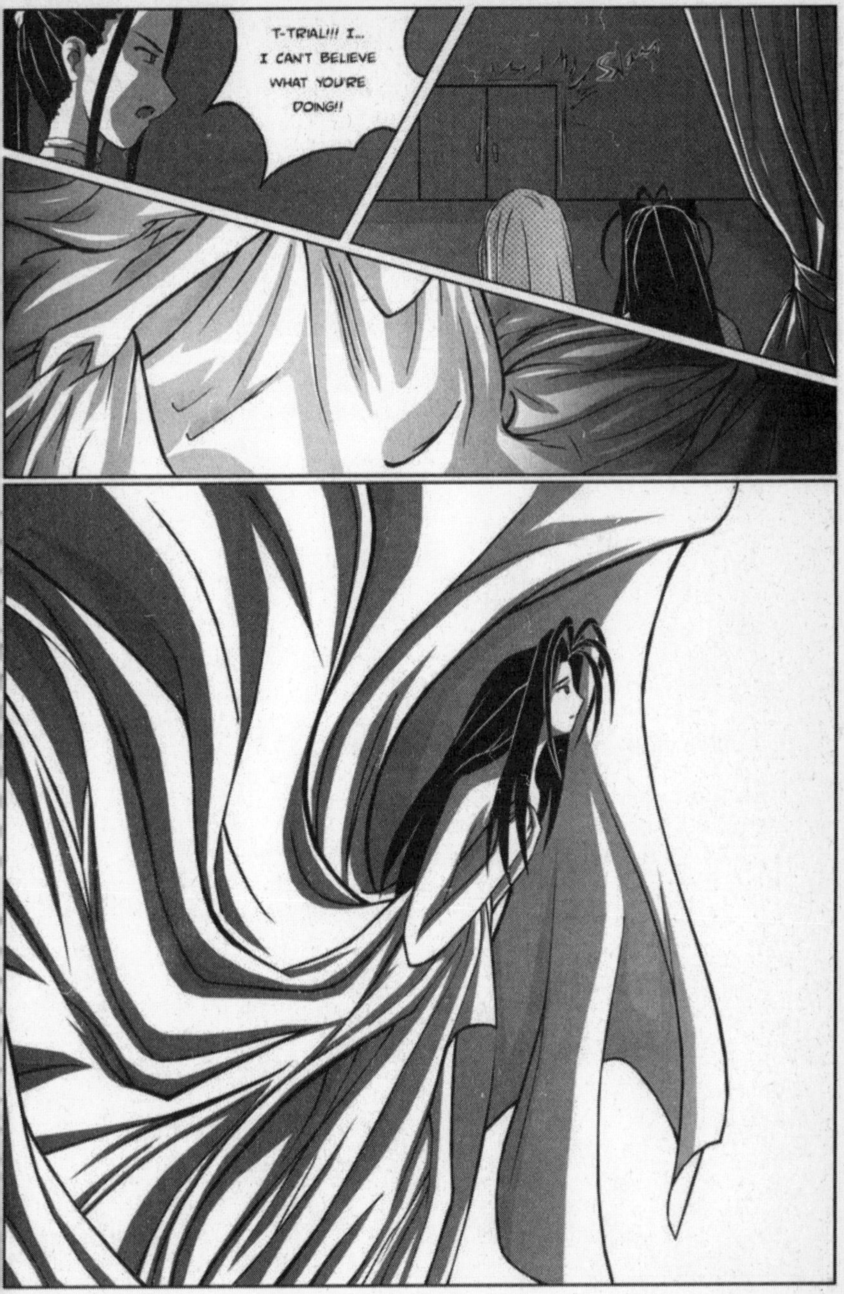
T-TRIAL!!! I...
I CAN'T BELIEVE
WHAT YOU'RE
DOING!!

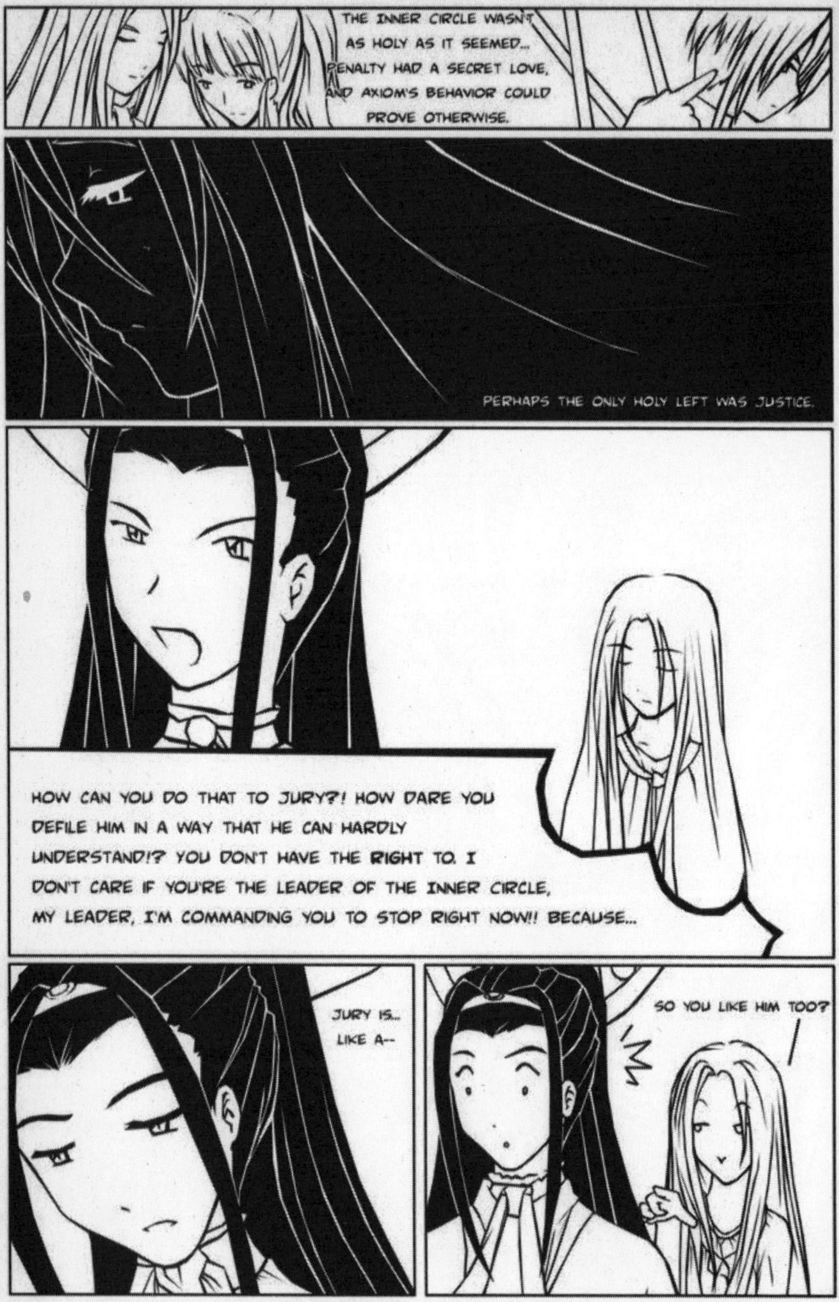
THE INNER CIRCLE WASN'T AS HOLY AS IT SEEMED... PENALTY HAD A SECRET LOVE, AND AXIOM'S BEHAVIOR COULD PROVE OTHERWISE.
PERHAPS THE ONLY HOLY LEFT WAS JUSTICE.
HOW CAN YOU DO THAT TO JURY?! HOW DARE YOU DEFILE HIM IN A WAY THAT HE CAN HARDLY UNDERSTAND!? YOU DON'T HAVE THE RIGHT TO. I DON'T CARE IF YOU'RE THE LEADER OF THE INNER CIRCLE, MY LEADER, I'M COMMANDING YOU TO STOP RIGHT NOW!! BECAUSE...
JURY IS... LIKE A--
SO YOU LIKE HIM TOO?

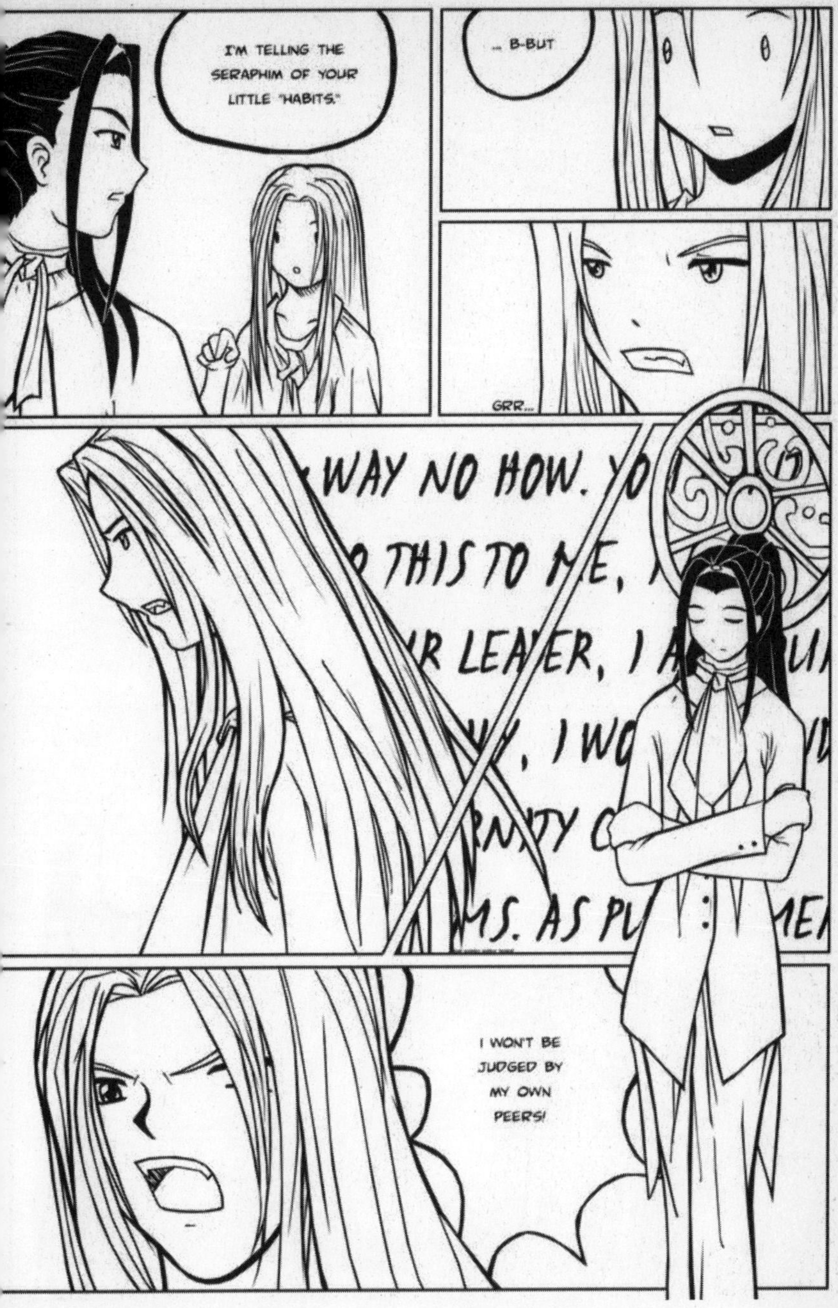
I'M TELLING THE SERAPHIM OF YOUR LITTLE "HABITS."
... B-BUT
GRR...
WAY NO HOW.
I WON'T BE JUDGED BY MY OWN PEERS!

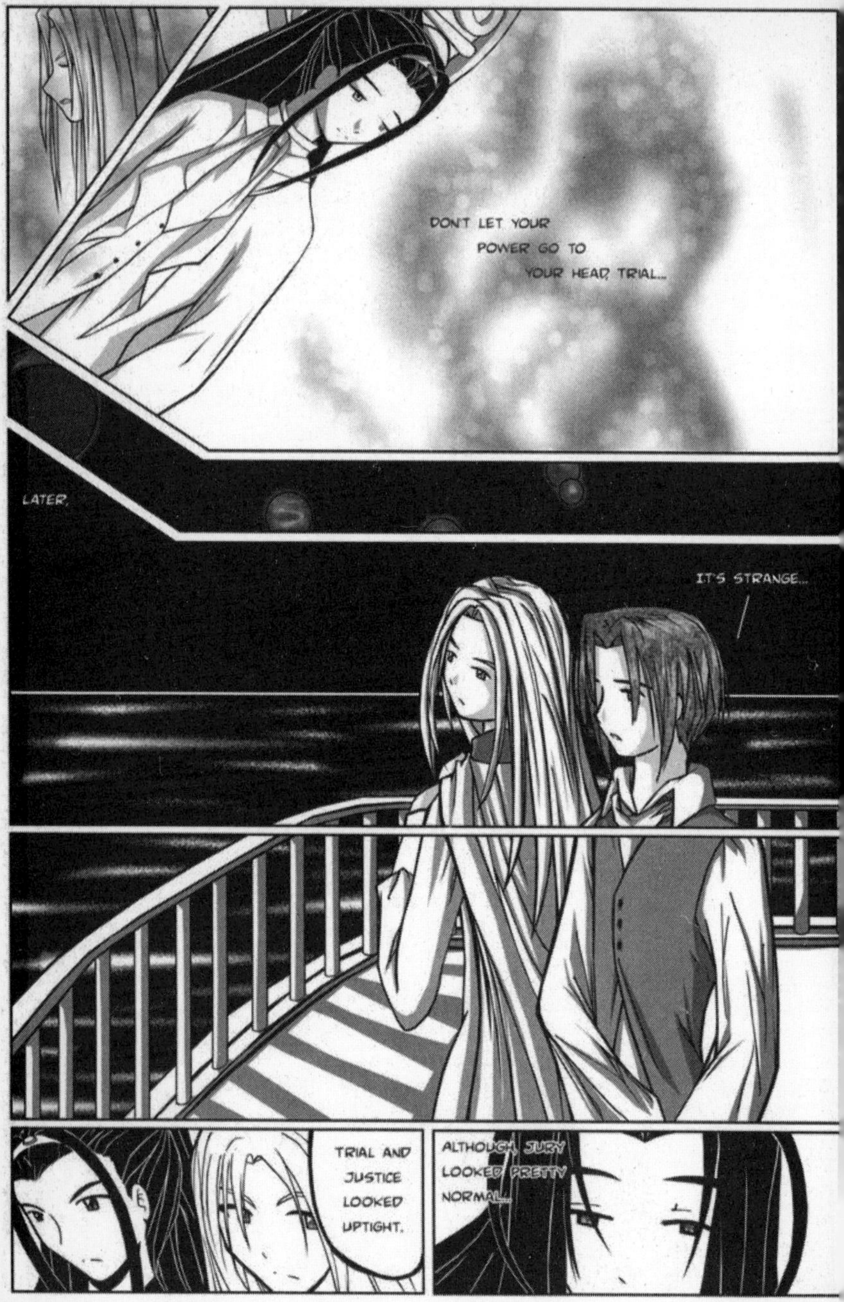
DON'T LET YOUR POWER GO TO YOUR HEAD, TRIAL...
LATER,
IT'S STRANGE...
TRIAL AND JUSTICE LOOKED UPTIGHT.
ALTHOUGH JURY LOOKED PRETTY NORMAL...

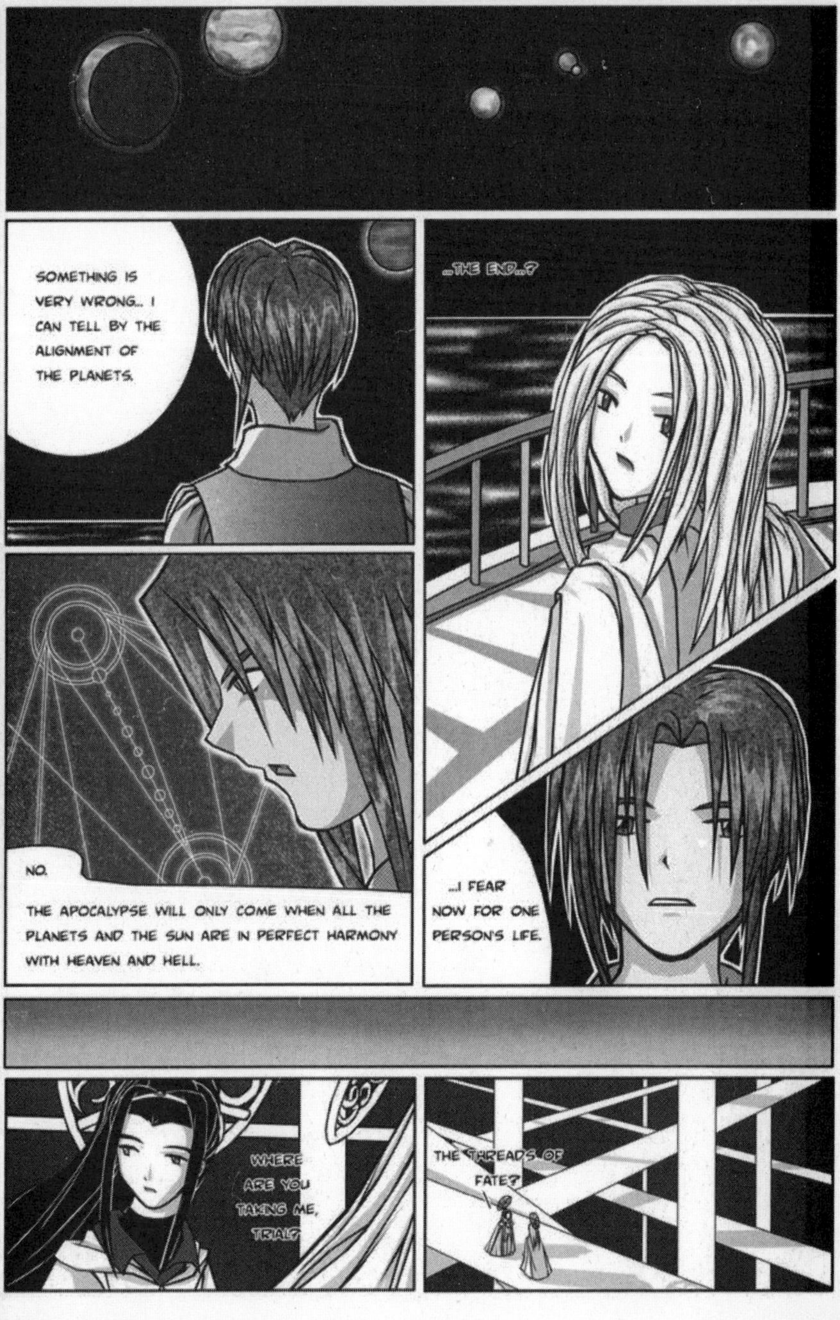
SOMETHING IS VERY WRONG... I CAN TELL BY THE ALIGNMENT OF THE PLANETS.
...THE END...?
NO.
THE APOCALYPSE WILL ONLY COME WHEN ALL THE PLANETS AND THE SUN ARE IN PERFECT HARMONY WITH HEAVEN AND HELL.
...I FEAR NOW FOR ONE PERSON'S LIFE.
WHERE ARE YOU TAKING ME, TRIAL?
THE THREADS OF FATE?

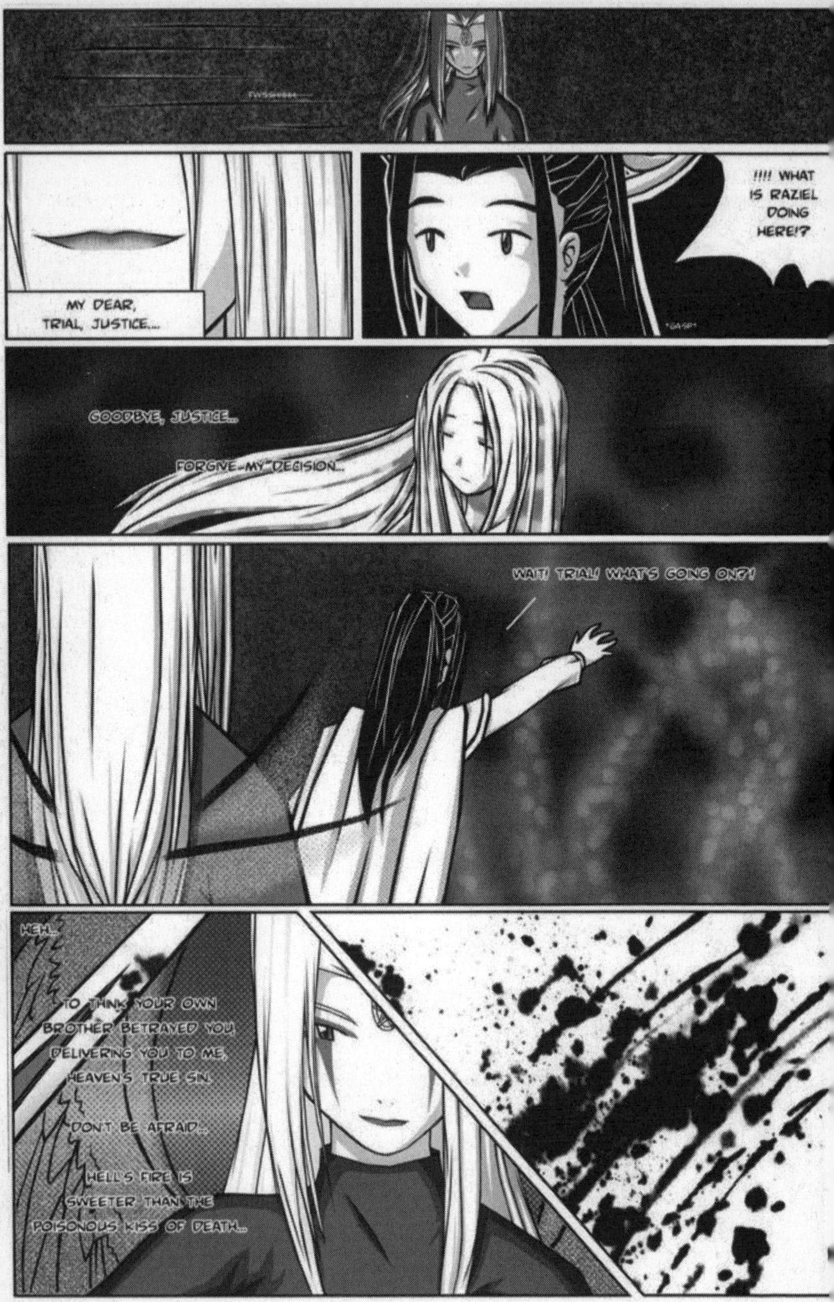
MY DEAR,
TRIAL, JUSTICE...
!!!! WHAT IS RAZIEL DOING HERE!?
GASP
GOODBYE, JUSTICE...
FORGIVE MY DECISION...
WAIT! TRIAL! WHAT'S GOING ON?!
HEH...
TO THINK YOUR OWN BROTHER BETRAYED YOU, DELIVERING YOU TO ME, HEAVEN'S TRUE SIN.
DON'T BE AFRAID...
HELL'S FIRE IS SWEETER THAN THE POISONOUS KISS OF DEATH...

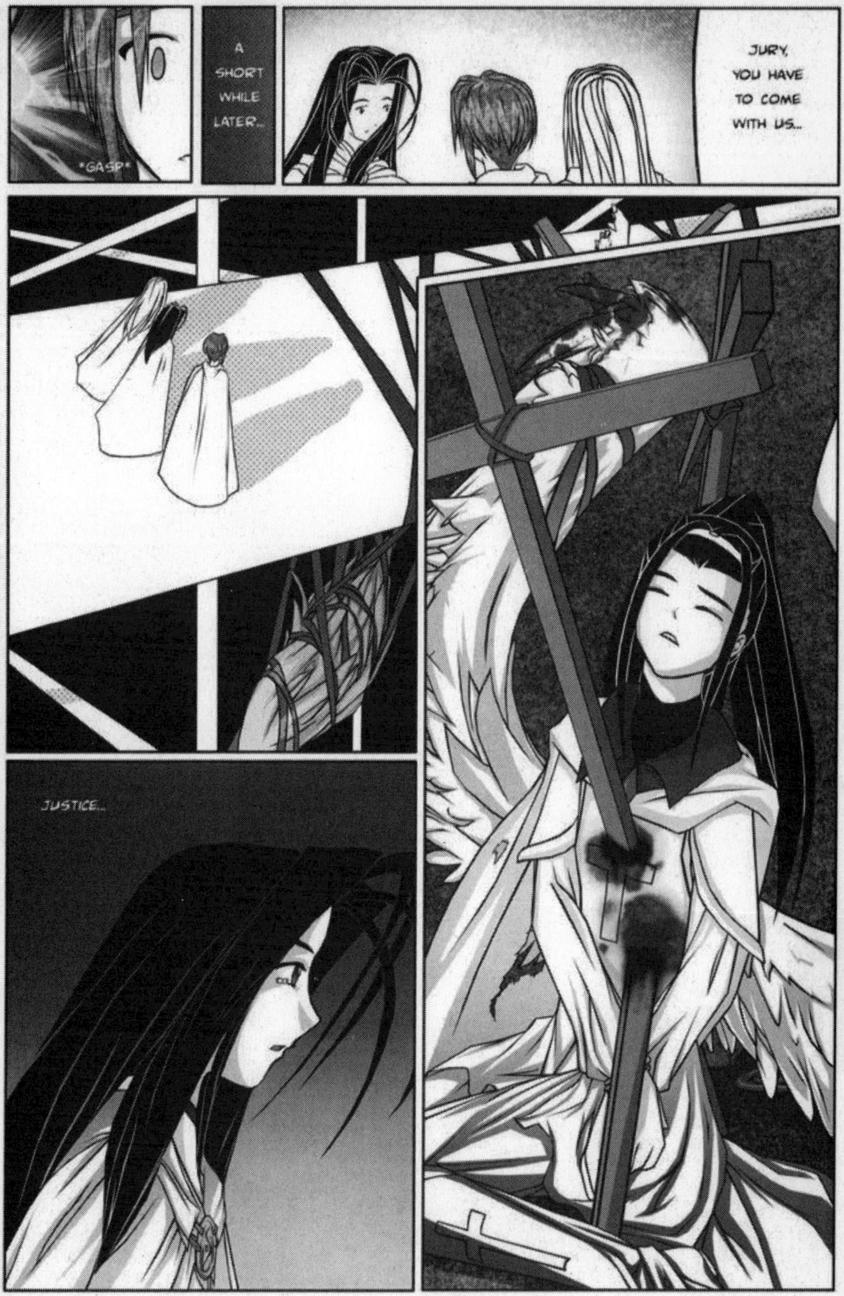
GASP
A SHORT WHILE LATER...
JURY, YOU HAVE TO COME WITH US...
JUSTICE...

DON'T, JURY...

A SERAPHIM IS COMING.

TRIAL WANTS NO REPLACEMENT FOR JUSTICE
AS HE WANTED ONE FOR JURY.

...

IT IS DECIDED FOR US TO ONLY PUNISH
EXTREME WRONGDOER'S.
THE INNER CIRCLE WILL
STILL CONTINUE WITHOUT JUSTICE.

I'M SORRY...

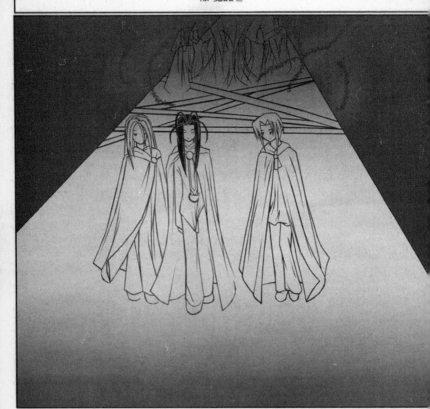

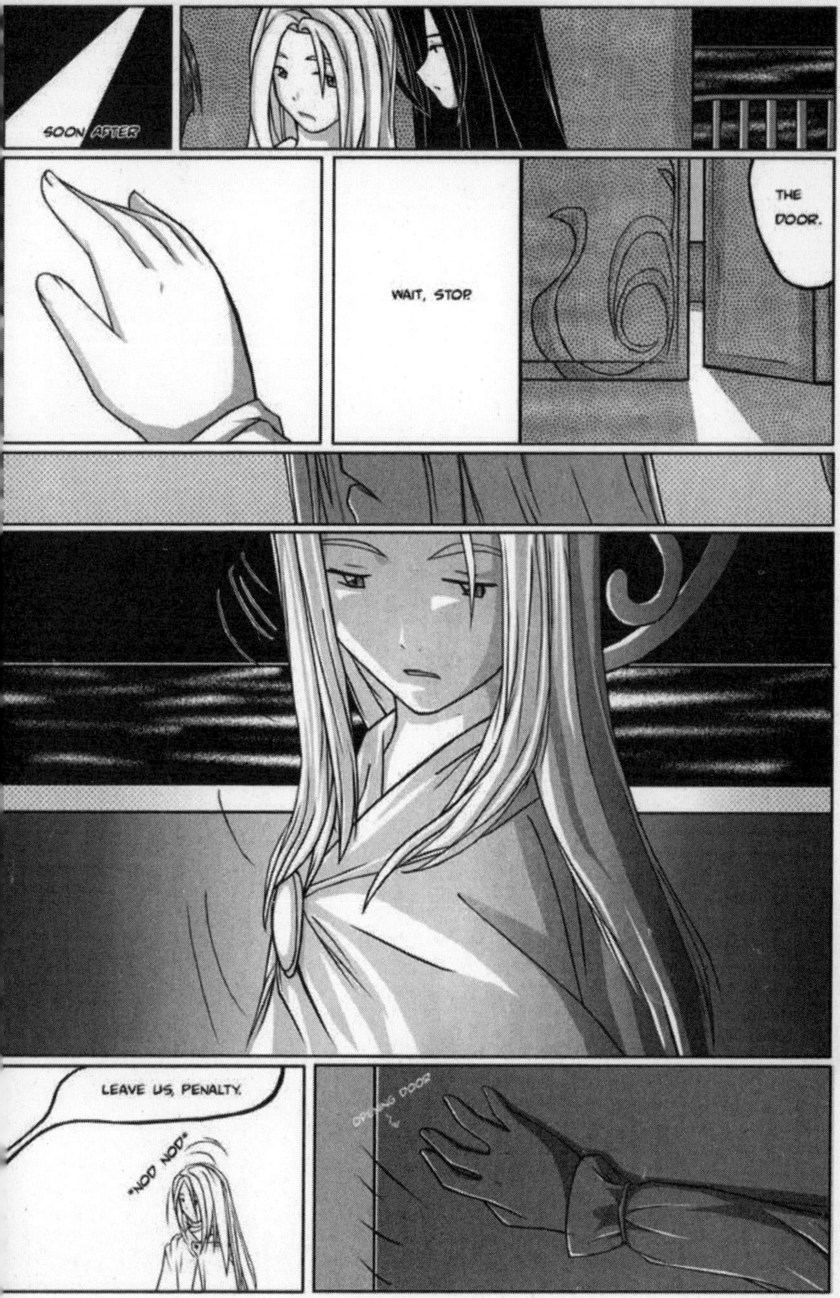
SOON AFTER
WAIT, STOP?
THE DOOR.
LEAVE US, PENALTY.
NOD NOD

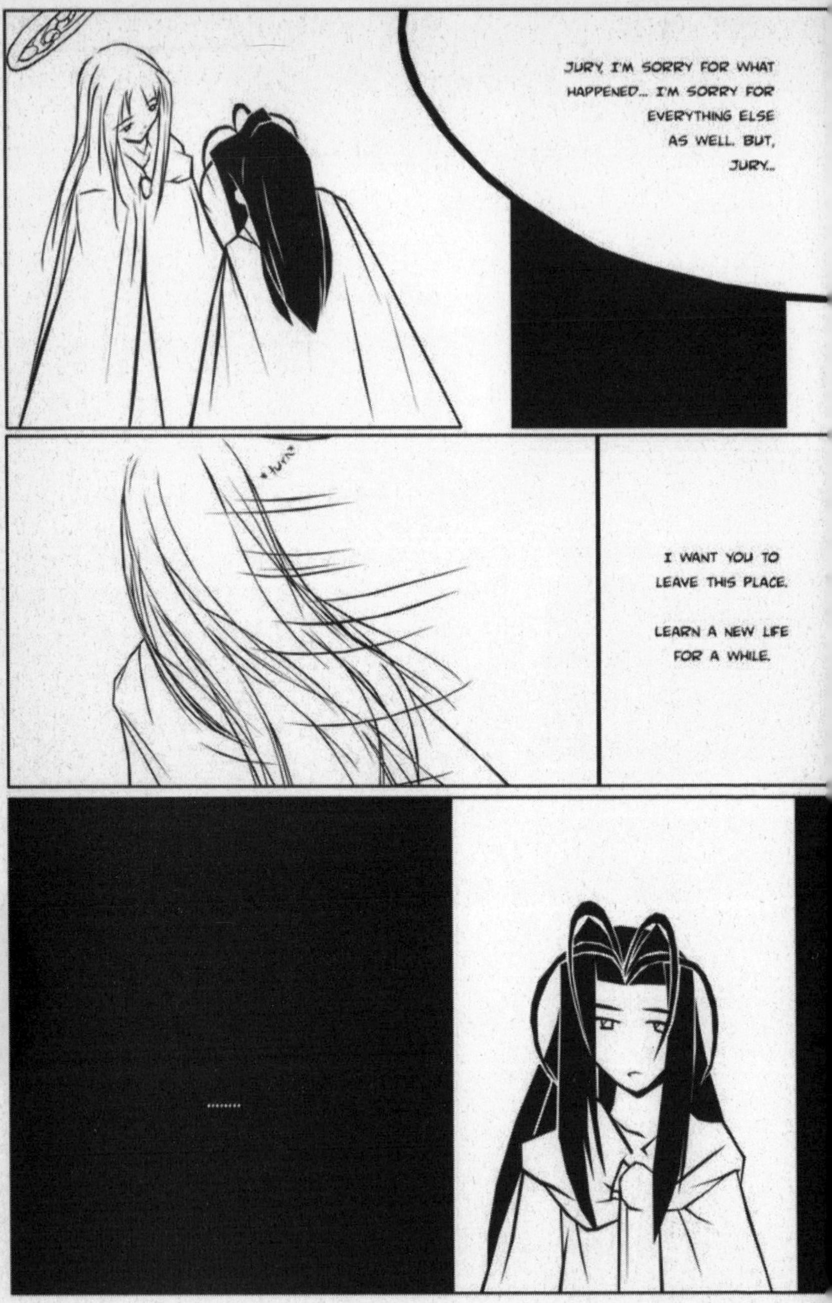
JURY, I'M SORRY FOR WHAT HAPPENED... I'M SORRY FOR EVERYTHING ELSE AS WELL. BUT, JURY...
turn
I WANT YOU TO LEAVE THIS PLACE.
LEARN A NEW LIFE FOR A WHILE.
....

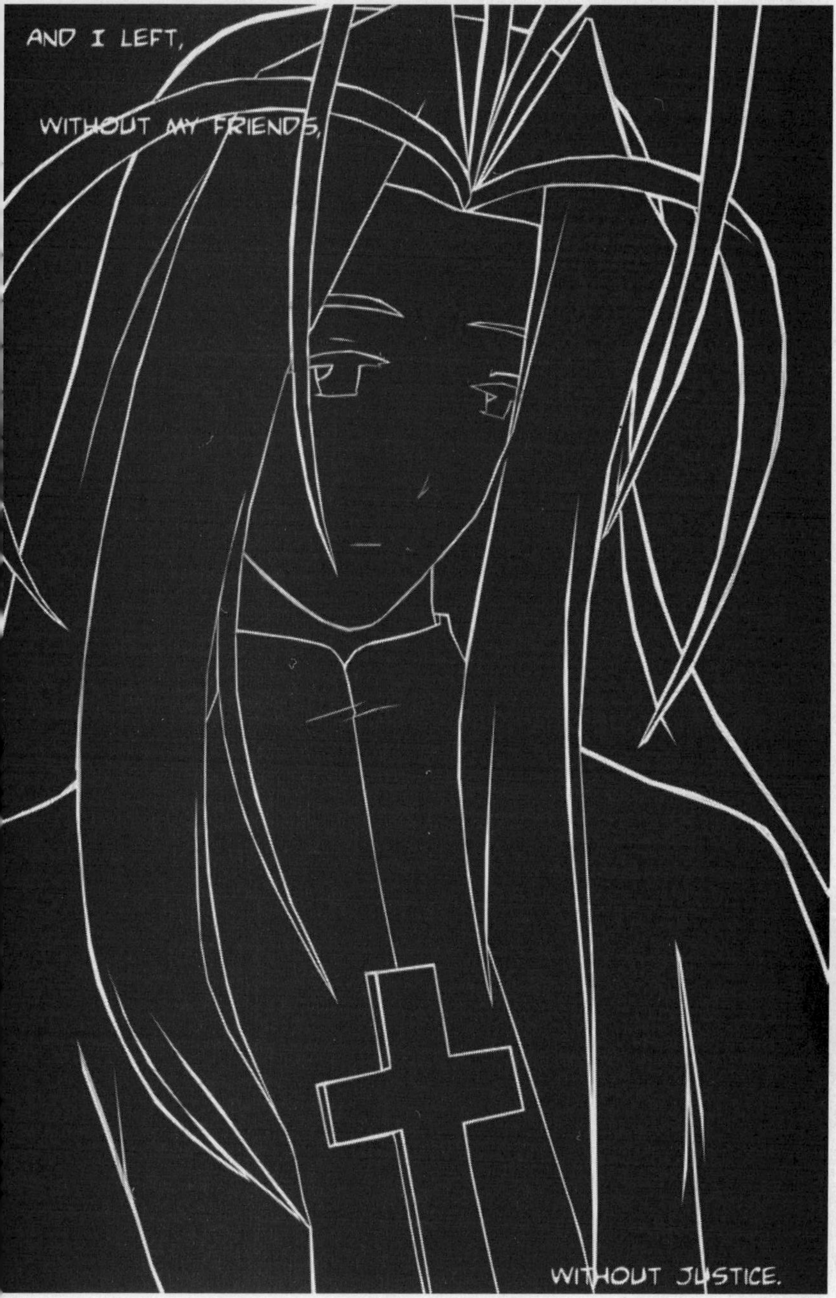
AND I LEFT,
WITHOUT MY FRIENDS,
WITHOUT JUSTICE.

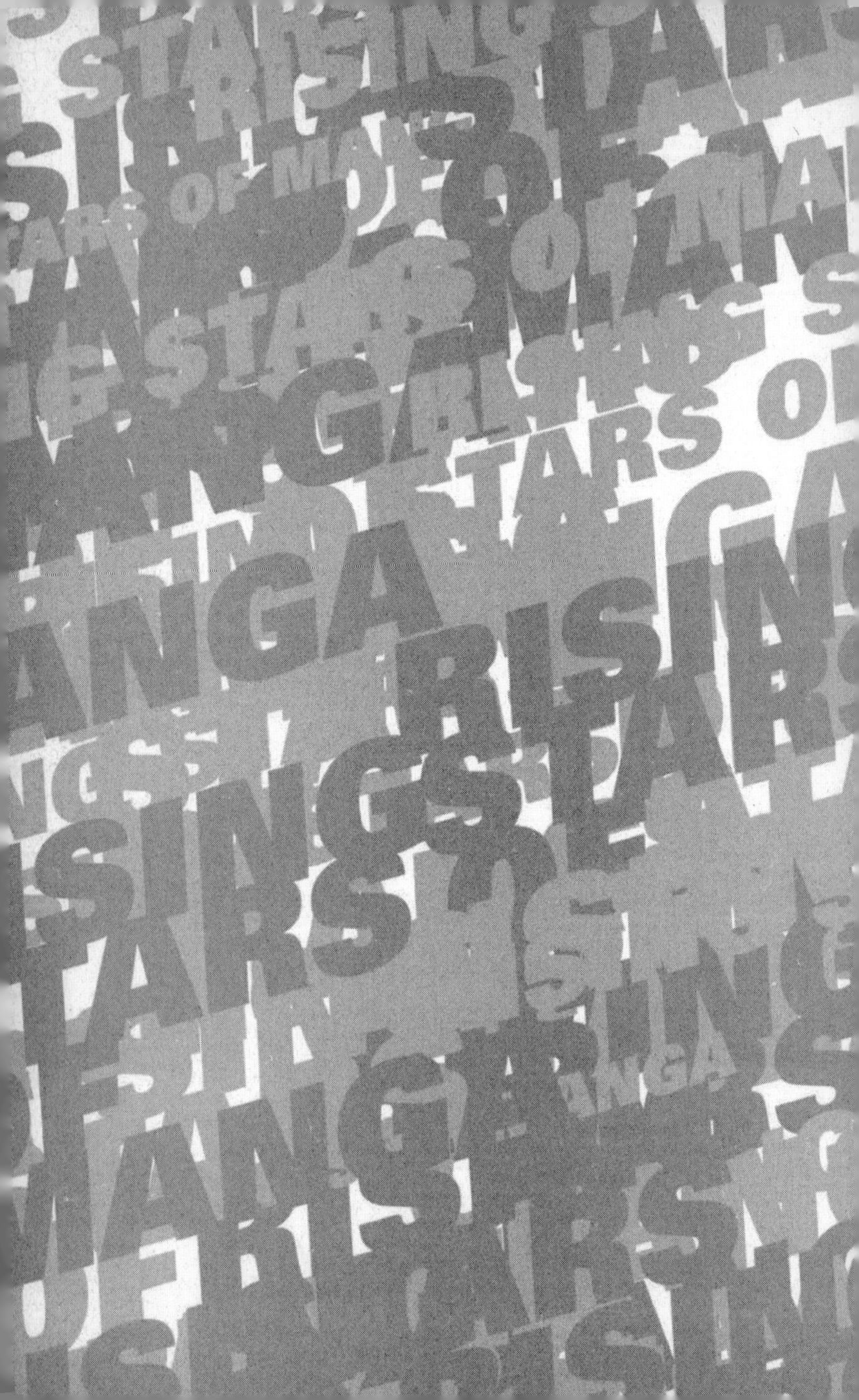

PRIEST
TOKYOPOP
HE QUICK & THE UNDEAD
N ONE MACABRE MANGA.
AVAILABLE NOW
www.TOKYOPOP.com
PRIEST © MIN-WOO HYUNG. TOKYOPOP is a registered trademark of Mixx Entertainment Inc.

::

ZERO :: RUNNER UP ::

Tracy Cox was born in 1965 in Detroit and currently works as a graphic designer and illustrator in San Francisco. She went to art school at The Center for Creative Studies, College of Art and Design in Detroit. A 13-page comic project she worked on with Dr. Madd Vibe (AKA Angelo Moore, former lead singer of *Fishbone*) will soon be published as a CD comic insert.

Inspiration for this story:
The main inspiration was a blues song I heard on the radio by Little Milton called "Eight Men, Four Women" from the album Little Milton Live at Westville Prison. The song was so passionate that I had to ask myself, "What would it take for someone to put this much of himself into a song?" And that's how ZERO started.

Favorite Manga:
Mai, The Psychic Girl; Domu; Thb; Benkei in New York; Akira; Lone Wolf and Cub

Favorite Manga Artists:
Katsuhiro Otomo, Pope, Ikegami

....

Judge's Comments:
In "Zero", creator Tracy Cox uses sharp contrast and a highly stylized design to tell the sobering tale of a pop singer impaled on the truth of his art. Cox employs inventiveness in piecing together the story, like a dream, one thought building upon the subtext of the previous.

Particularly impressive is the comic's ability to create physical manifestations of the character's emotional states of being, such as in the middle of the story when his inability to truly get close to anyone is represented by spikes protruding from his body. Surreal dreamscapes serve to illustrate his psychological malaise.

The story itself is a sophisticated short, spanning the rise and fall of a pop singer—registering the crests and troughs of his career as he stands on the divide between integrity and selling out to the music business—in loaded, syncopated images. Of course, love comes into play, but even that gets caught in the grinding cogs of his vocation, Z himself coming to the realization that he doesn't have the capacity to love.
-Luis Reyes

ZERO / **RUNNER UP** / RISING.STARS.OF.MANGA.2003

zero

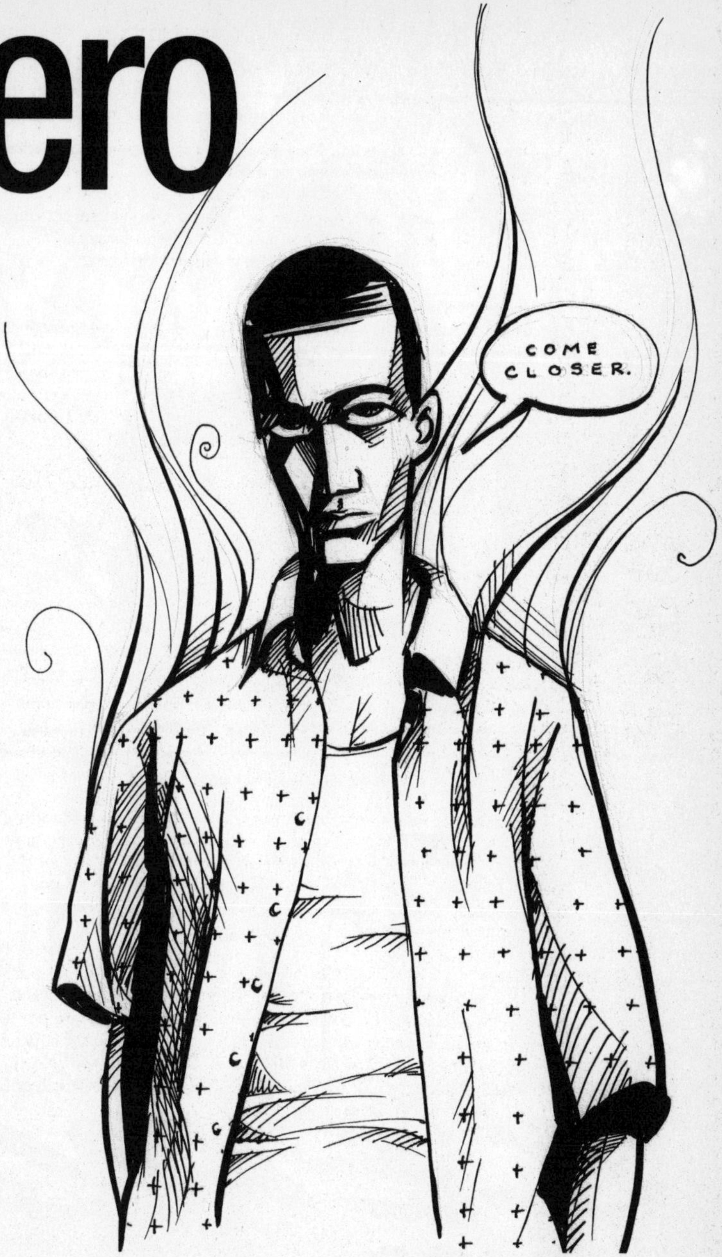
COME CLOSER.

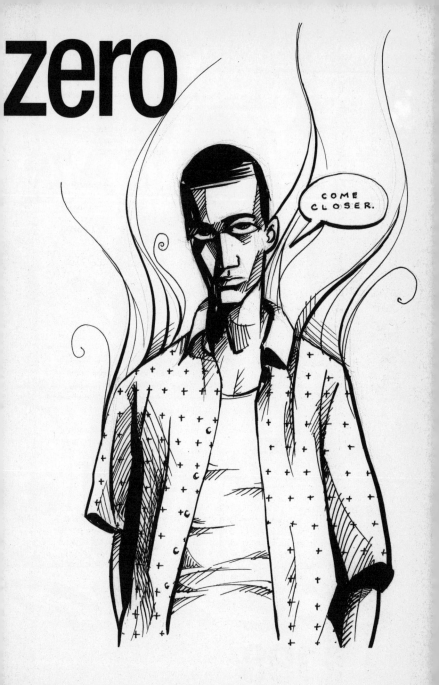

LET ME ASK YOU JUST THIS *ONE THING:*
WHAT WOULD *YOU* DO?
HOW WOULD *YOU* FEEL?
WHO WOULD *YOU* BE?

LETTERS BY BLAME

ZERO

BY TRACY COX

©2002

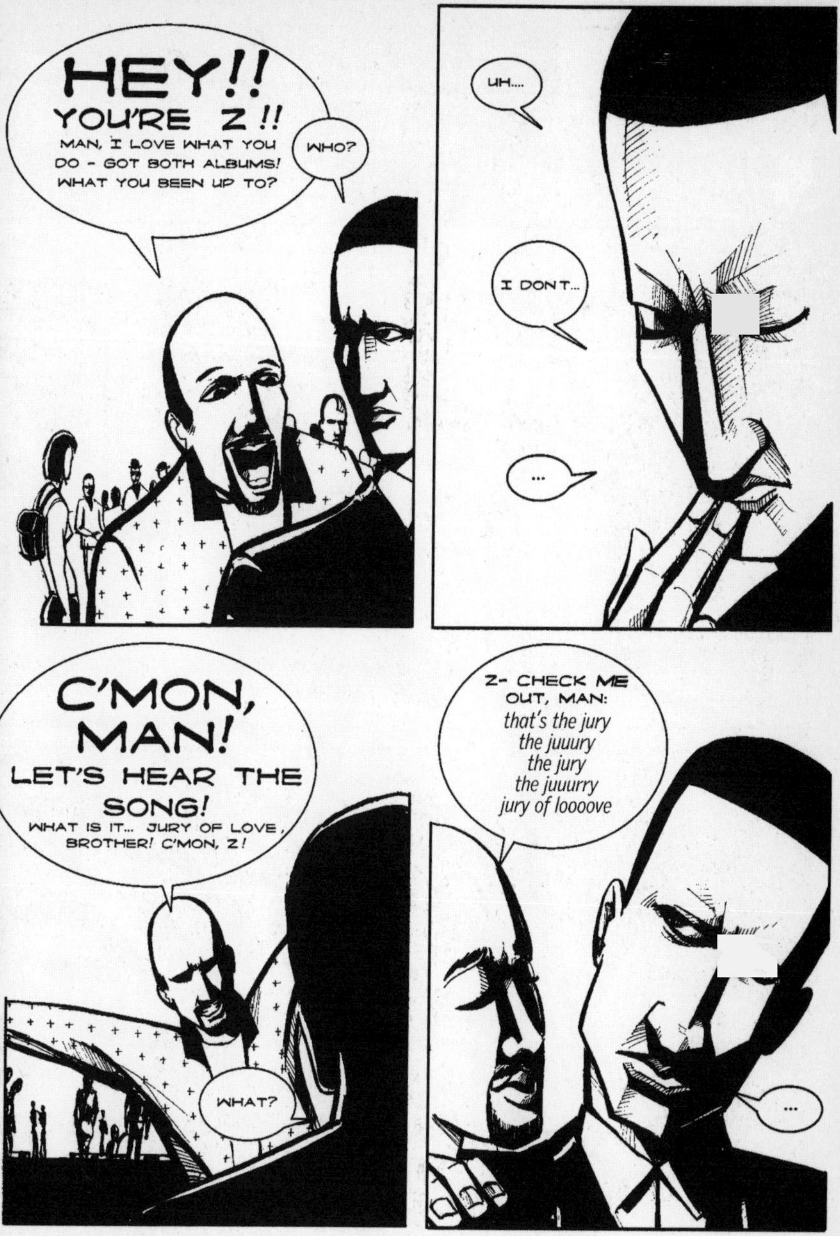
HEY!! YOU'RE Z!! MAN, I LOVE WHAT YOU DO - GOT BOTH ALBUMS! WHAT YOU BEEN UP TO?
WHO?
UH....
I DON'T...
...
C'MON, MAN! LET'S HEAR THE SONG! WHAT IS IT... JURY OF LOVE, BROTHER! C'MON, Z!
WHAT?
Z- CHECK ME OUT, MAN: that's the jury the juuury the jury the juuurry jury of loooove
...

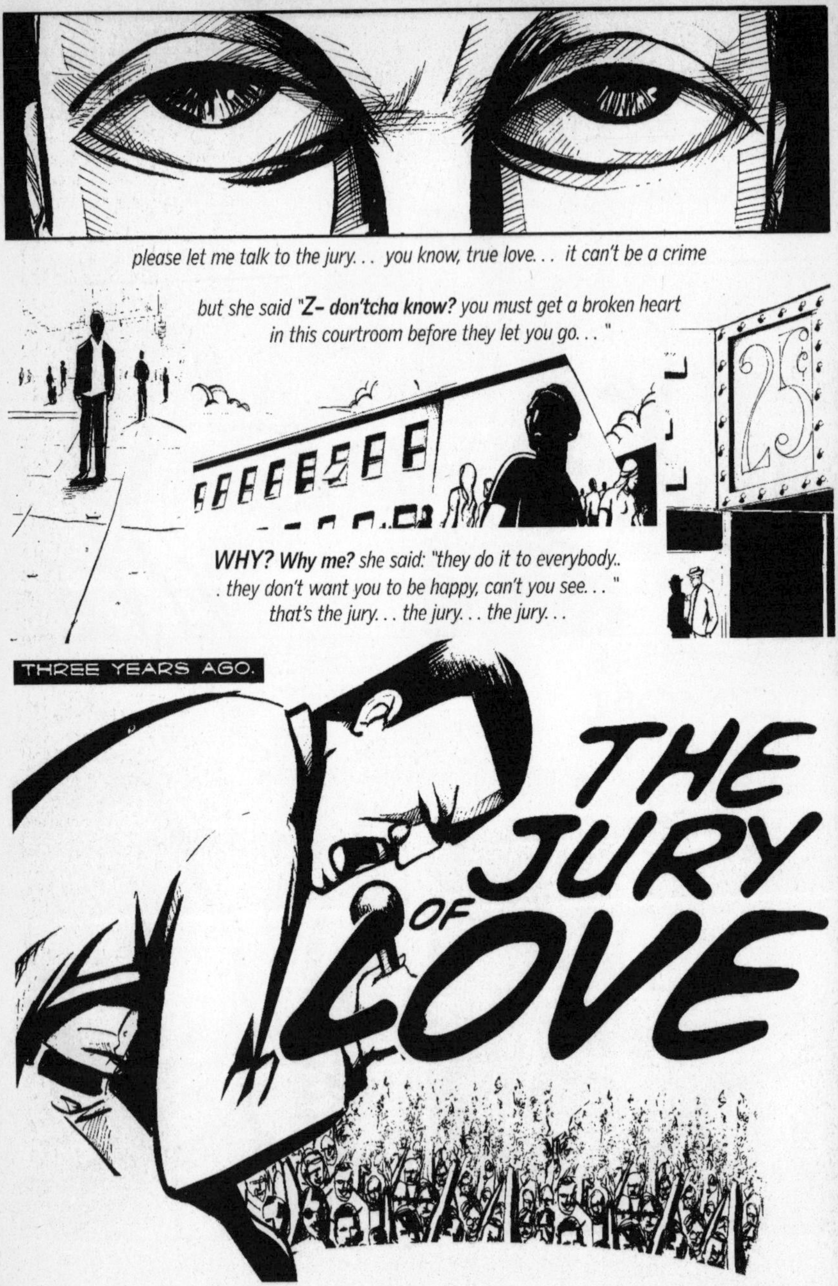
please let me talk to the jury... you know, true love... it can't be a crime
but she said "Z- don'tcha know? you must get a broken heart in this courtroom before they let you go..."
25¢
WHY? Why me? she said: "they do it to everybody.. . they don't want you to be happy, can't you see..."
that's the jury... the jury... the jury...
THREE YEARS AGO.
THE JURY OF LOVE

ON THE HEELS OF HIS UNDERGROUND HIT JURY OF LOVE, ZACHARY JONES, A.K.A **Z**, CATAPULTED TO THE UPPER ECHELON OF SOUL SINGERS IN THE UNITED STATES.

HIS EARLY PERFORMANCES QUICKLY BECAME LEGENDARY.

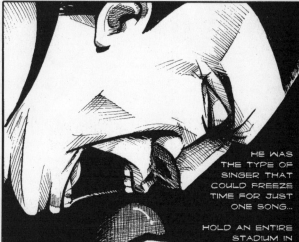

HE WAS THE TYPE OF SINGER THAT COULD FREEZE TIME FOR JUST ONE SONG...

HOLD AN ENTIRE STADIUM IN PERFECT SILENCE...

AND FINISH **STRONG.**

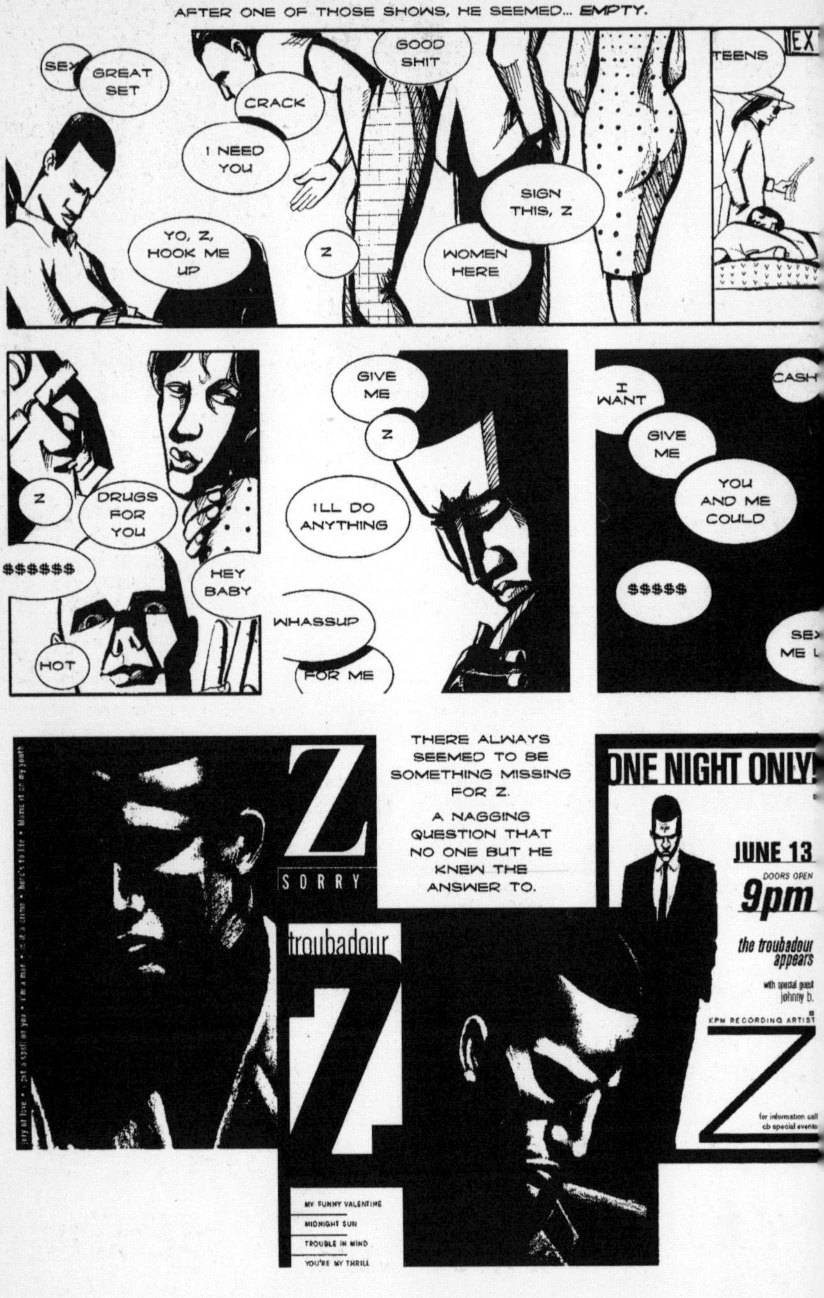
AFTER ONE OF THOSE SHOWS, HE SEEMED... *EMPTY.*
SEX
GREAT SET
CRACK
GOOD SHIT
I NEED YOU
YO, Z, HOOK ME UP
Z
SIGN THIS, Z
WOMEN HERE
TEENS
Z
DRUGS FOR YOU
$$$$$$
HEY BABY
HOT
GIVE ME
Z
ILL DO ANYTHING
WHASSUP
FOR ME
I WANT
CASH
GIVE ME
YOU AND ME COULD
$$$$$
jury of love • i put a spell on you • i'm a man • is it a crime • here's to life • blame it on my youth
Z
SORRY
THERE ALWAYS SEEMED TO BE SOMETHING MISSING FOR Z.
A NAGGING QUESTION THAT NO ONE BUT HE KNEW THE ANSWER TO.
ONE NIGHT ONLY!
JUNE 13
DOORS OPEN
9pm
the troubadour appears
with special guest johnny b.
KPM RECORDING ARTIST
Z
for information call
cb special events
troubadour
Z
MY FUNNY VALENTINE
MIDNIGHT SUN
TROUBLE IN MIND
YOU'RE MY THRILL

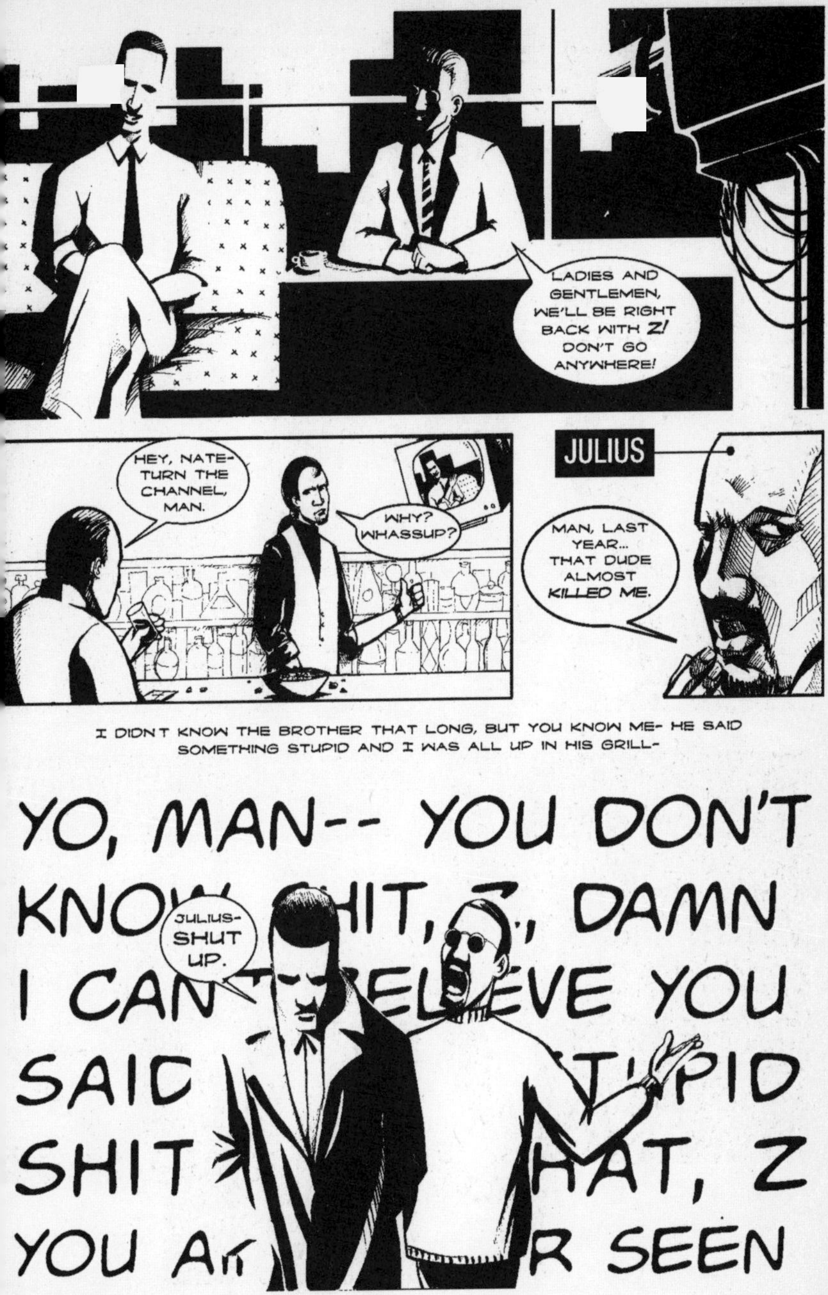
LADIES AND GENTLEMEN, WE'LL BE RIGHT BACK WITH Z! DON'T GO ANYWHERE!
HEY, NATE- TURN THE CHANNEL, MAN.
WHY? WHASSUP?
JULIUS
MAN, LAST YEAR... THAT DUDE ALMOST KILLED ME.
I DIDN'T KNOW THE BROTHER THAT LONG, BUT YOU KNOW ME- HE SAID SOMETHING STUPID AND I WAS ALL UP IN HIS GRILL-
YO, MAN-- YOU DON'T
KNO
HIT,
DAMN
JULIUS- SHUT UP.
I CAN
VE YOU
SAID
PID
SHIT
HAT, Z
YOU A
R SEEN

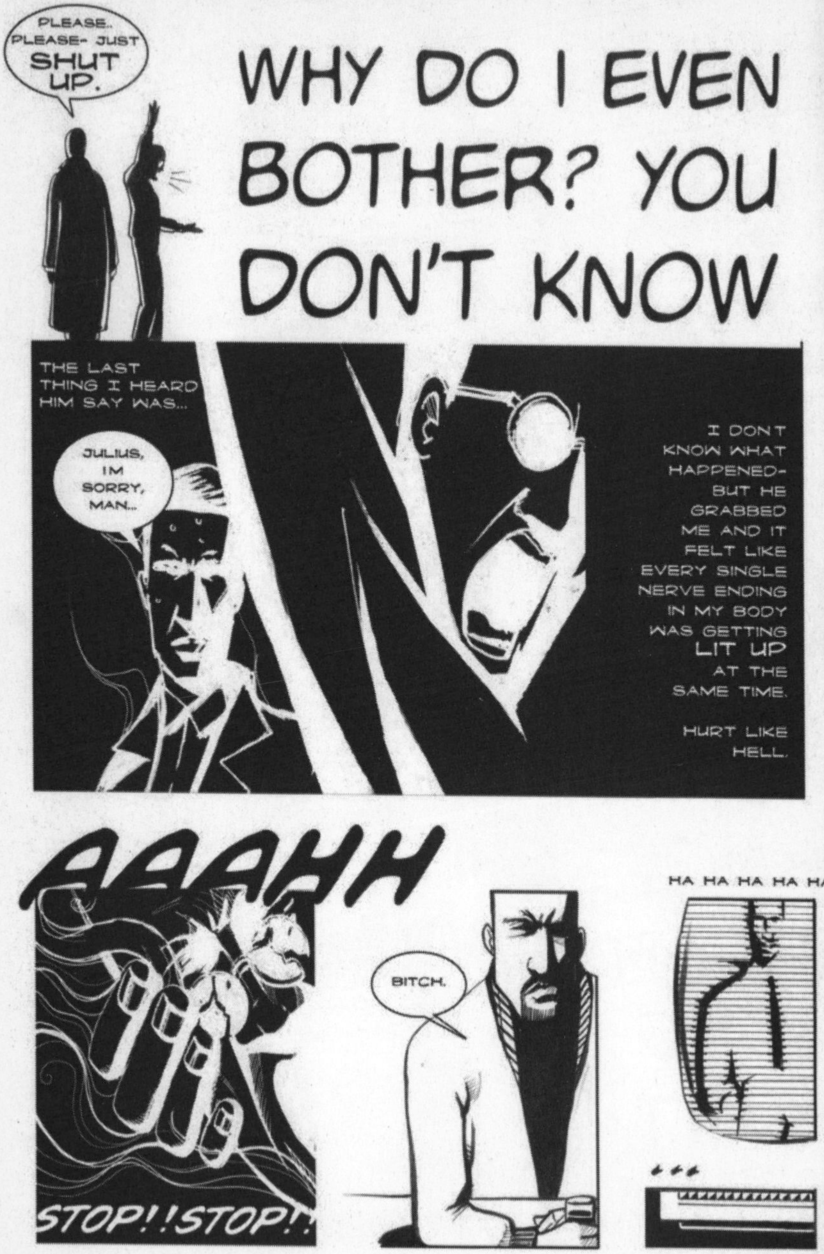
PLEASE.. PLEASE- JUST SHUT UP.
WHY DO I EVEN BOTHER? YOU DON'T KNOW
THE LAST THING I HEARD HIM SAY WAS...
JULIUS, IM SORRY, MAN...
I DONT KNOW WHAT HAPPENED- BUT HE GRABBED ME AND IT FELT LIKE EVERY SINGLE NERVE ENDING IN MY BODY WAS GETTING LIT UP AT THE SAME TIME.
HURT LIKE HELL.
AAAHH
STOP!!STOP!!
BITCH.
HA HA HA HA HA

JUST ABOUT EVERYONE WHO KNEW Z ENDED UP GETTING HURT...

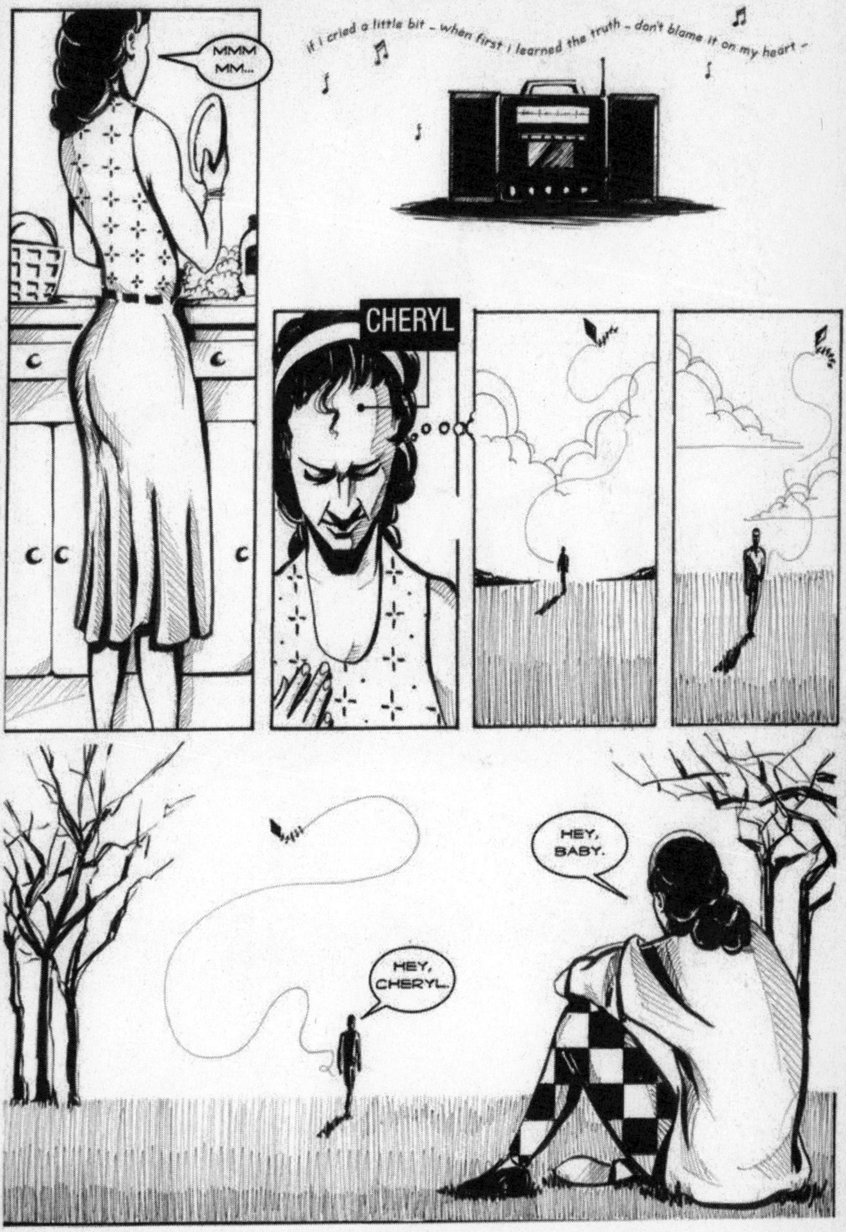
MMM
MM...
if i cried a little bit – when first i learned the truth – don't blame it on my heart –
CHERYL
HEY,
BABY.
HEY,
CHERYL.

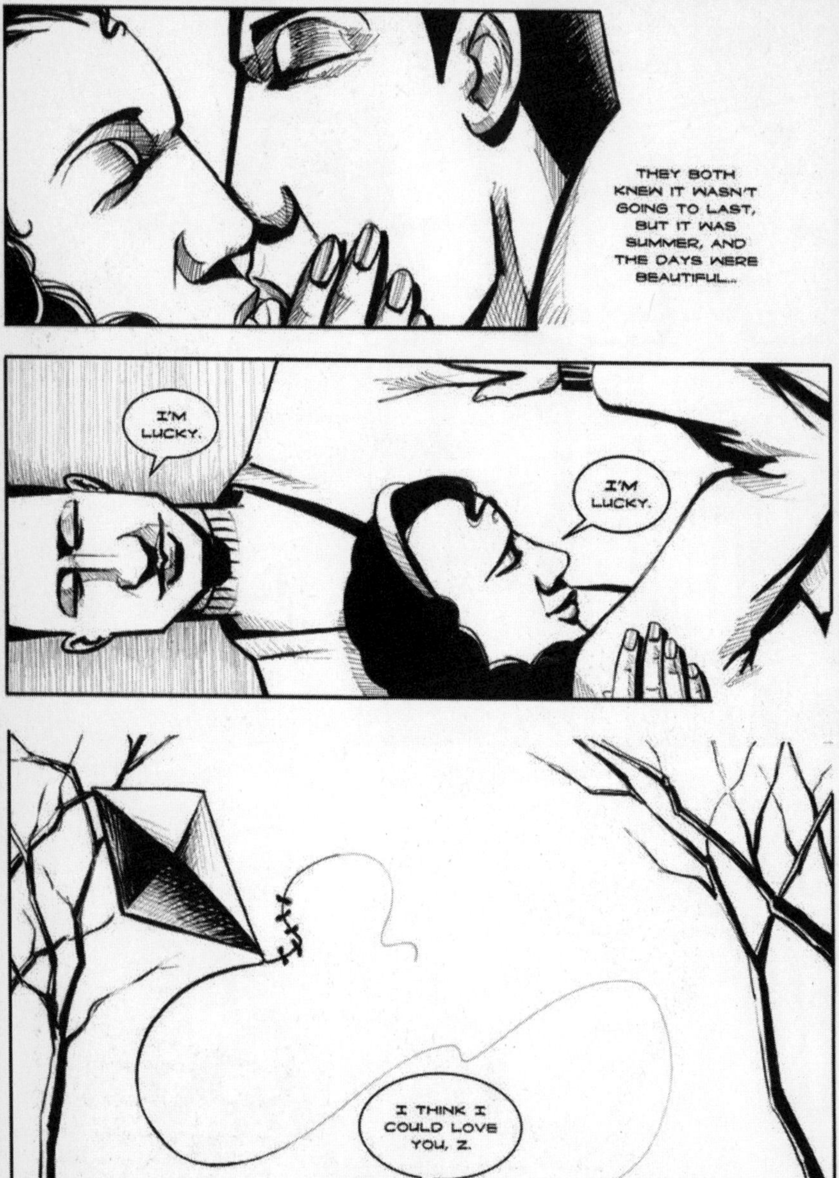
THEY BOTH KNEW IT WASN'T GOING TO LAST, BUT IT WAS SUMMER, AND THE DAYS WERE BEAUTIFUL...
I'M LUCKY.
I'M LUCKY.
I THINK I COULD LOVE YOU, Z.
...

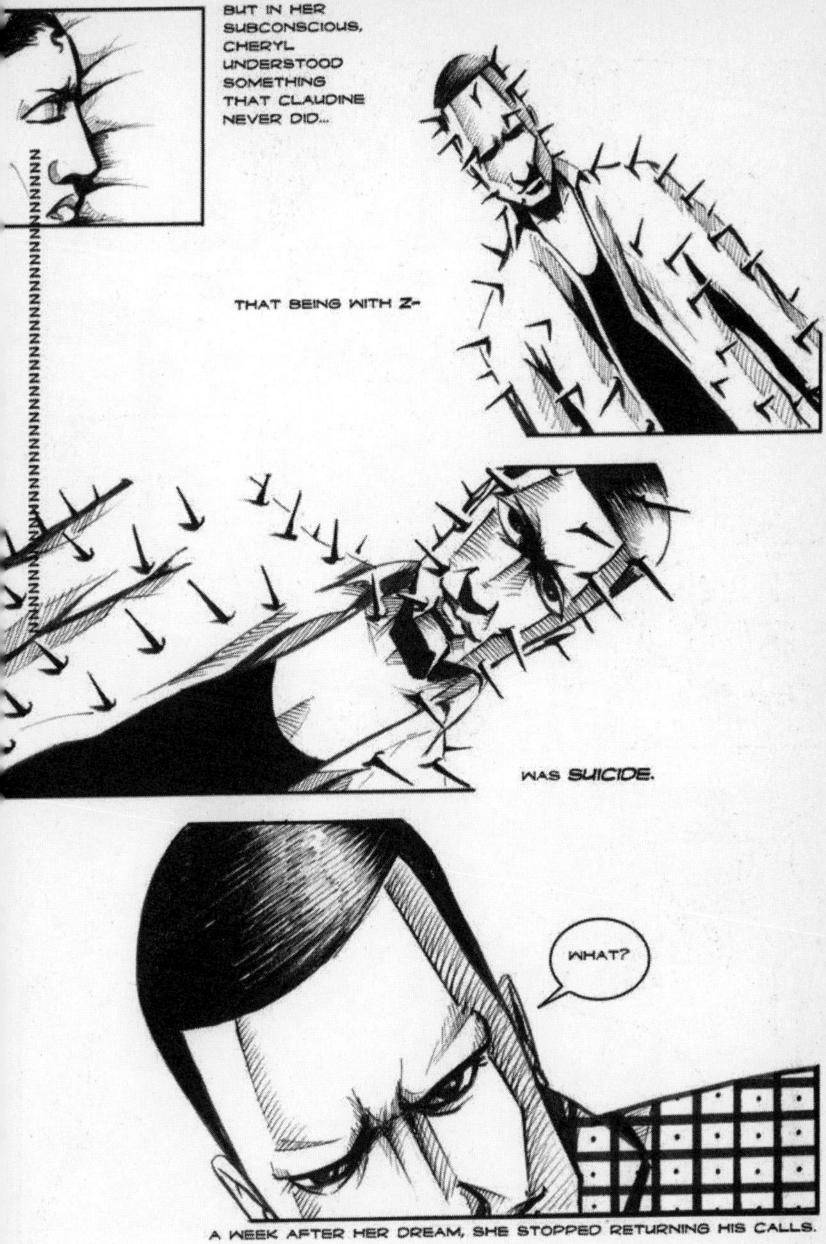
BUT IN HER SUBCONSCIOUS, CHERYL UNDERSTOOD SOMETHING THAT CLAUDINE NEVER DID...
NNNNNNNNNNNNNNNNNNNNNNNNNNNNNNNNNNN
THAT BEING WITH Z-
WAS *SUICIDE.*
WHAT?
A WEEK AFTER HER DREAM, SHE STOPPED RETURNING HIS CALLS.

THEN- FATE SEEMED TO SMILE ON Z...

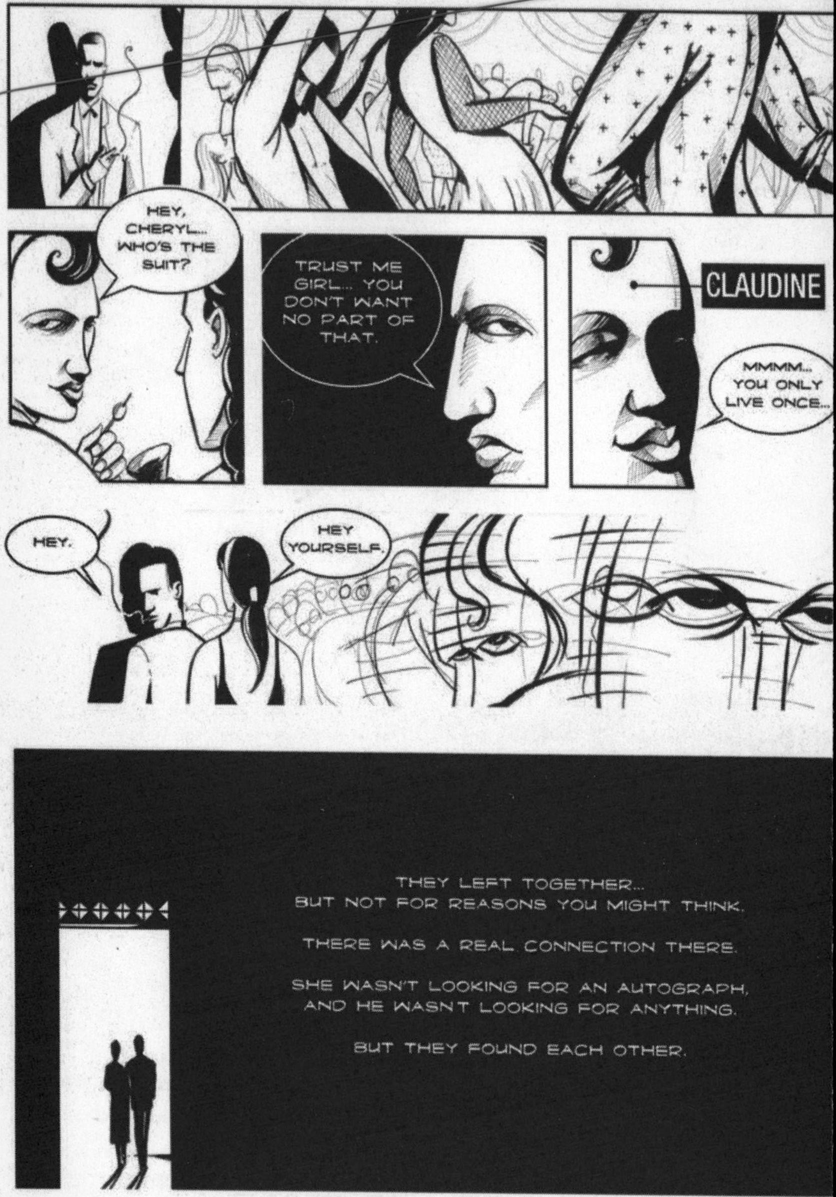
HEY, CHERYL... WHO'S THE SUIT?
TRUST ME GIRL... YOU DON'T WANT NO PART OF THAT.
CLAUDINE
MMMM... YOU ONLY LIVE ONCE...
HEY.
HEY YOURSELF.
THEY LEFT TOGETHER...
BUT NOT FOR REASONS YOU MIGHT THINK.
THERE WAS A REAL CONNECTION THERE.
SHE WASN'T LOOKING FOR AN AUTOGRAPH,
AND HE WASN'T LOOKING FOR ANYTHING.
BUT THEY FOUND EACH OTHER.

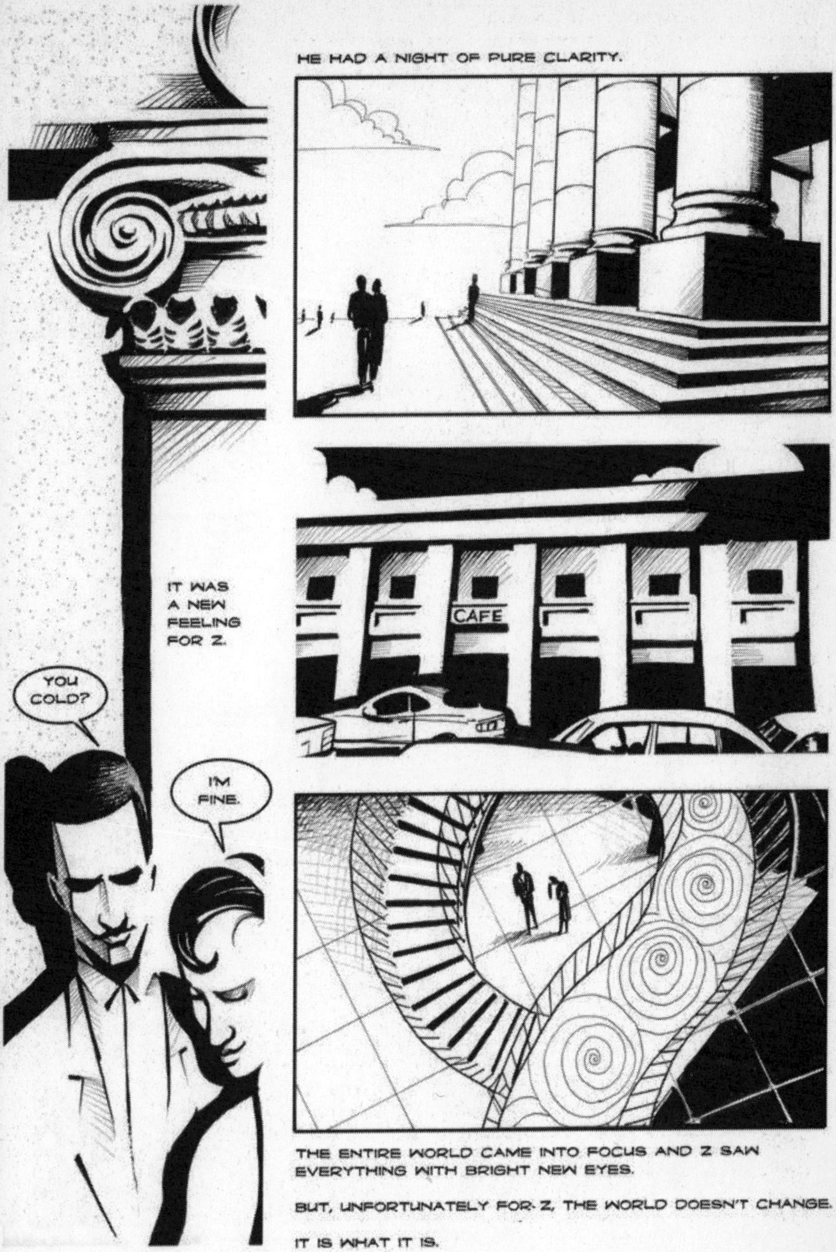
IT WAS A NEW FEELING FOR Z.
YOU COLD?
I'M FINE.
HE HAD A NIGHT OF PURE CLARITY.
CAFE
THE ENTIRE WORLD CAME INTO FOCUS AND Z SAW EVERYTHING WITH BRIGHT NEW EYES.
BUT, UNFORTUNATELY FOR Z, THE WORLD DOESN'T CHANGE.
IT IS WHAT IT IS.

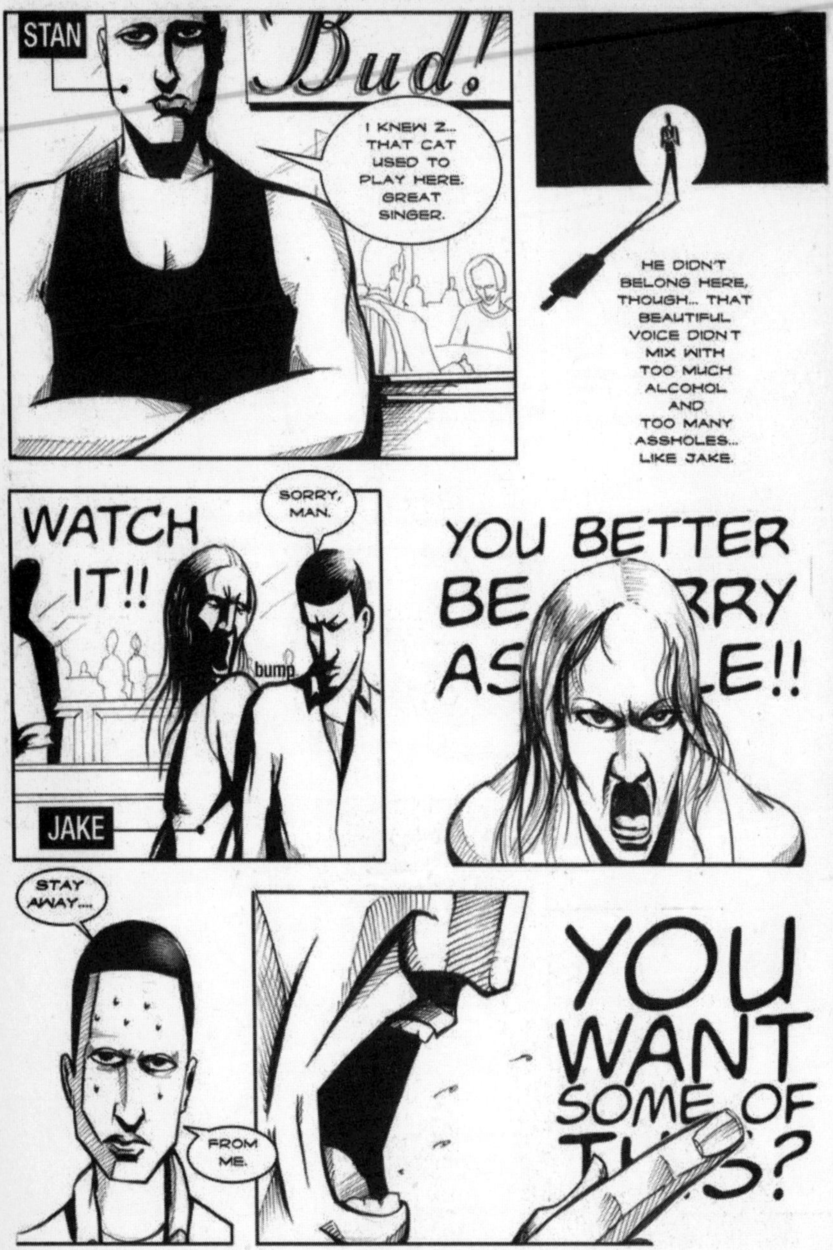
STAN
Bud!
I KNEW Z... THAT CAT USED TO PLAY HERE. GREAT SINGER.
HE DIDN'T BELONG HERE, THOUGH... THAT BEAUTIFUL VOICE DIDN'T MIX WITH TOO MUCH ALCOHOL AND TOO MANY ASSHOLES... LIKE JAKE.
WATCH IT!!
SORRY, MAN.
bump
JAKE
YOU BETTER BE SORRY ASSHOLE!!
STAY AWAY....
FROM ME.
YOU WANT SOME OF THIS?

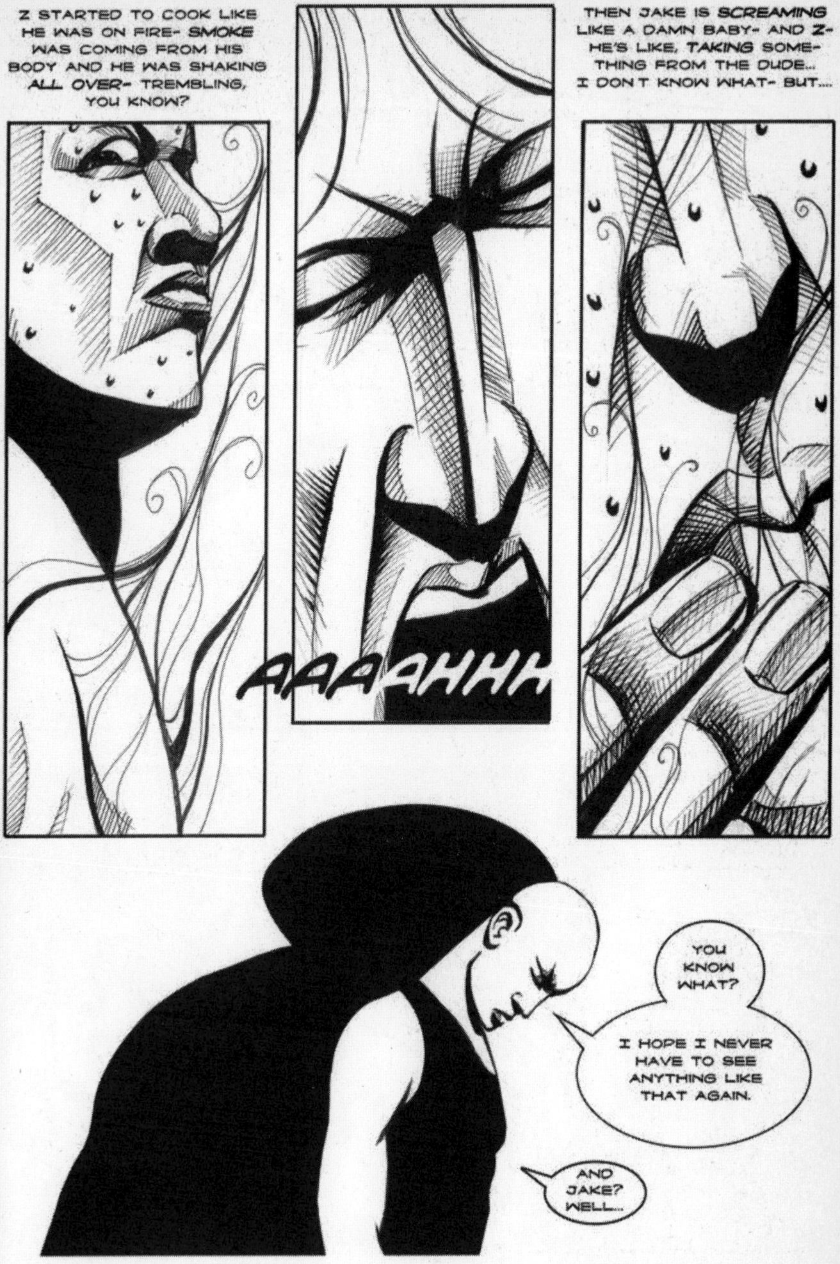
Z STARTED TO COOK LIKE HE WAS ON FIRE- SMOKE WAS COMING FROM HIS BODY AND HE WAS SHAKING ALL OVER- TREMBLING, YOU KNOW?
AAAAHHH
THEN JAKE IS SCREAMING LIKE A DAMN BABY- AND Z- HE'S LIKE, TAKING SOMETHING FROM THE DUDE... I DON'T KNOW WHAT- BUT....
YOU KNOW WHAT?
I HOPE I NEVER HAVE TO SEE ANYTHING LIKE THAT AGAIN.
AND JAKE? WELL...

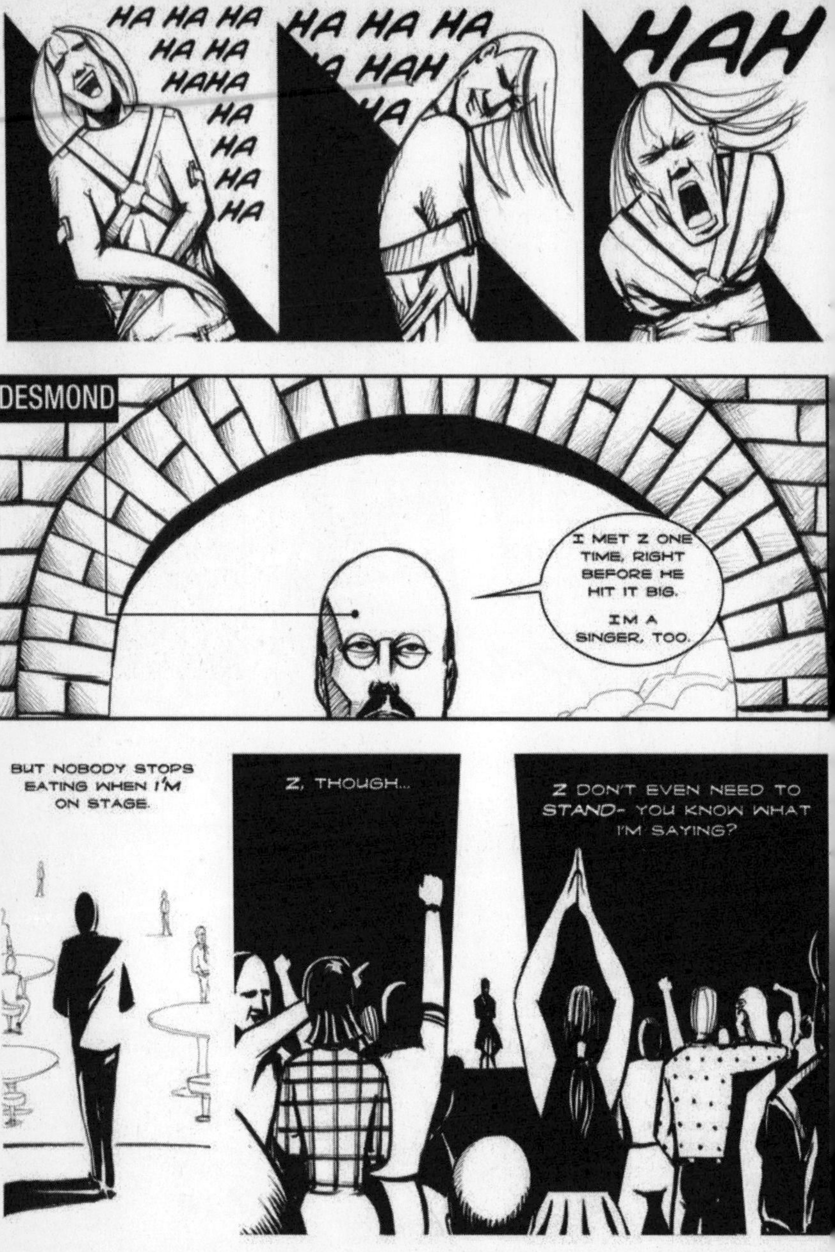
HA HA HA
HA HA
HAHA
HA
HA
HA
HA
HA HA HA
HAH
HA
HAH
DESMOND
I MET Z ONE TIME, RIGHT BEFORE HE HIT IT BIG.
I'M A SINGER, TOO.
BUT NOBODY STOPS EATING WHEN I'M ON STAGE.
Z, THOUGH...
Z DON'T EVEN NEED TO STAND- YOU KNOW WHAT I'M SAYING?

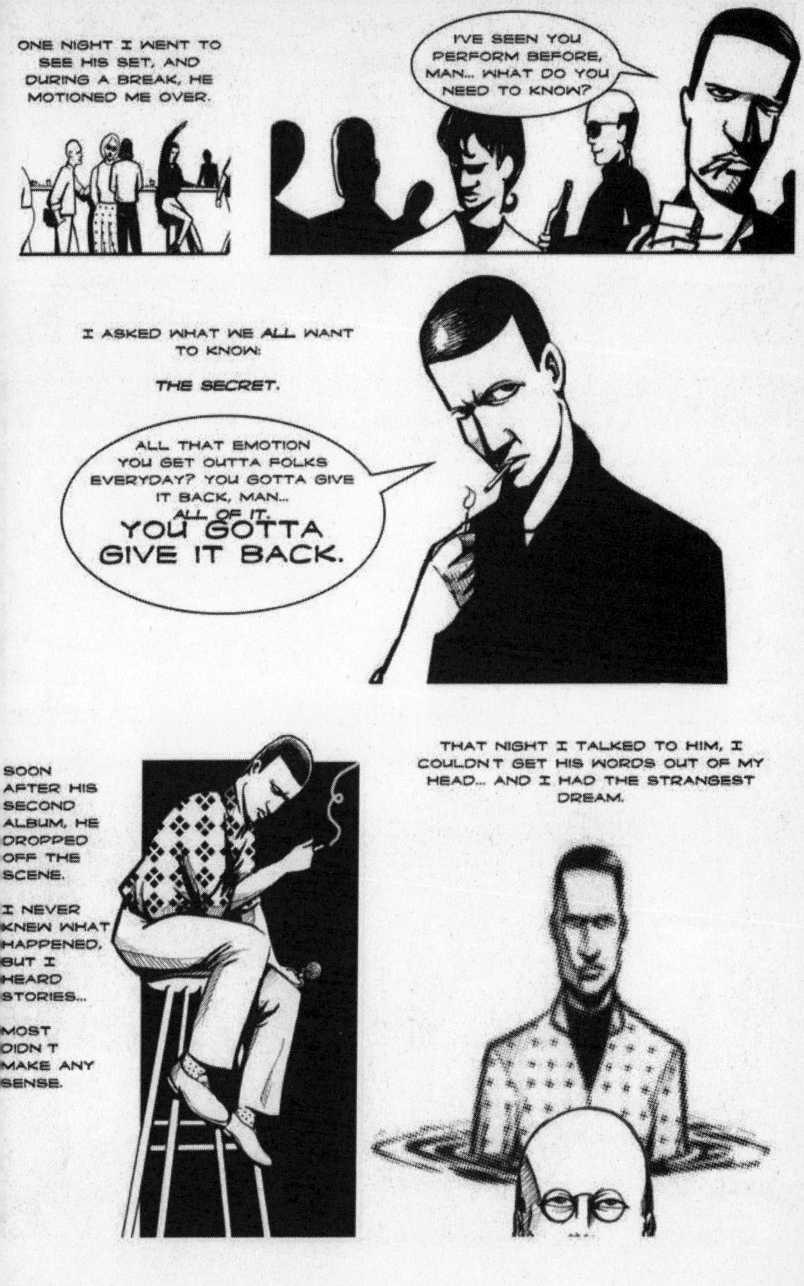
ONE NIGHT I WENT TO SEE HIS SET, AND DURING A BREAK, HE MOTIONED ME OVER.
I'VE SEEN YOU PERFORM BEFORE, MAN... WHAT DO YOU NEED TO KNOW?
I ASKED WHAT WE ALL WANT TO KNOW:
THE SECRET.
ALL THAT EMOTION YOU GET OUTTA FOLKS EVERYDAY? YOU GOTTA GIVE IT BACK, MAN... ALL OF IT... YOU GOTTA GIVE IT BACK.
SOON AFTER HIS SECOND ALBUM, HE DROPPED OFF THE SCENE.
I NEVER KNEW WHAT HAPPENED, BUT I HEARD STORIES...
MOST DIDN'T MAKE ANY SENSE.
THAT NIGHT I TALKED TO HIM, I COULDN'T GET HIS WORDS OUT OF MY HEAD... AND I HAD THE STRANGEST DREAM.

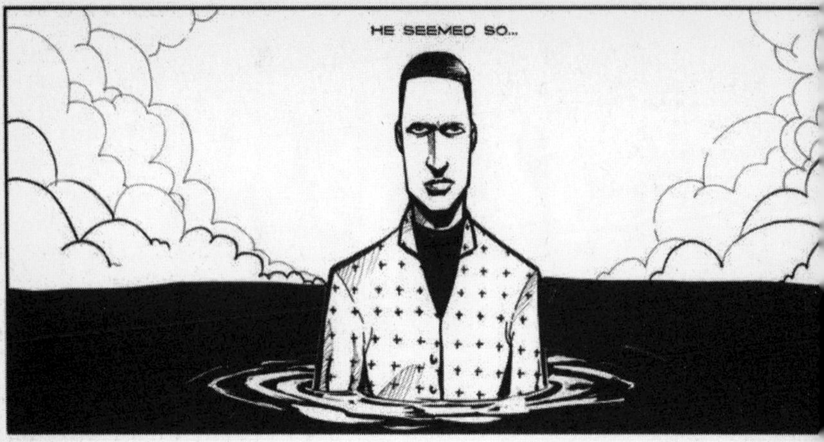
HE SEEMED SO...

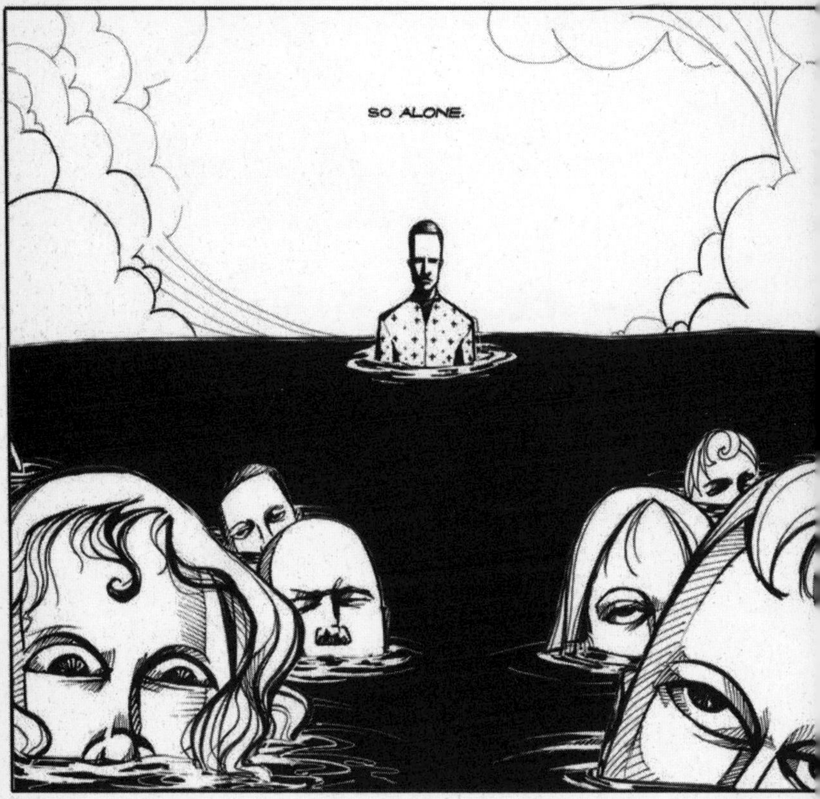
SO ALONE.

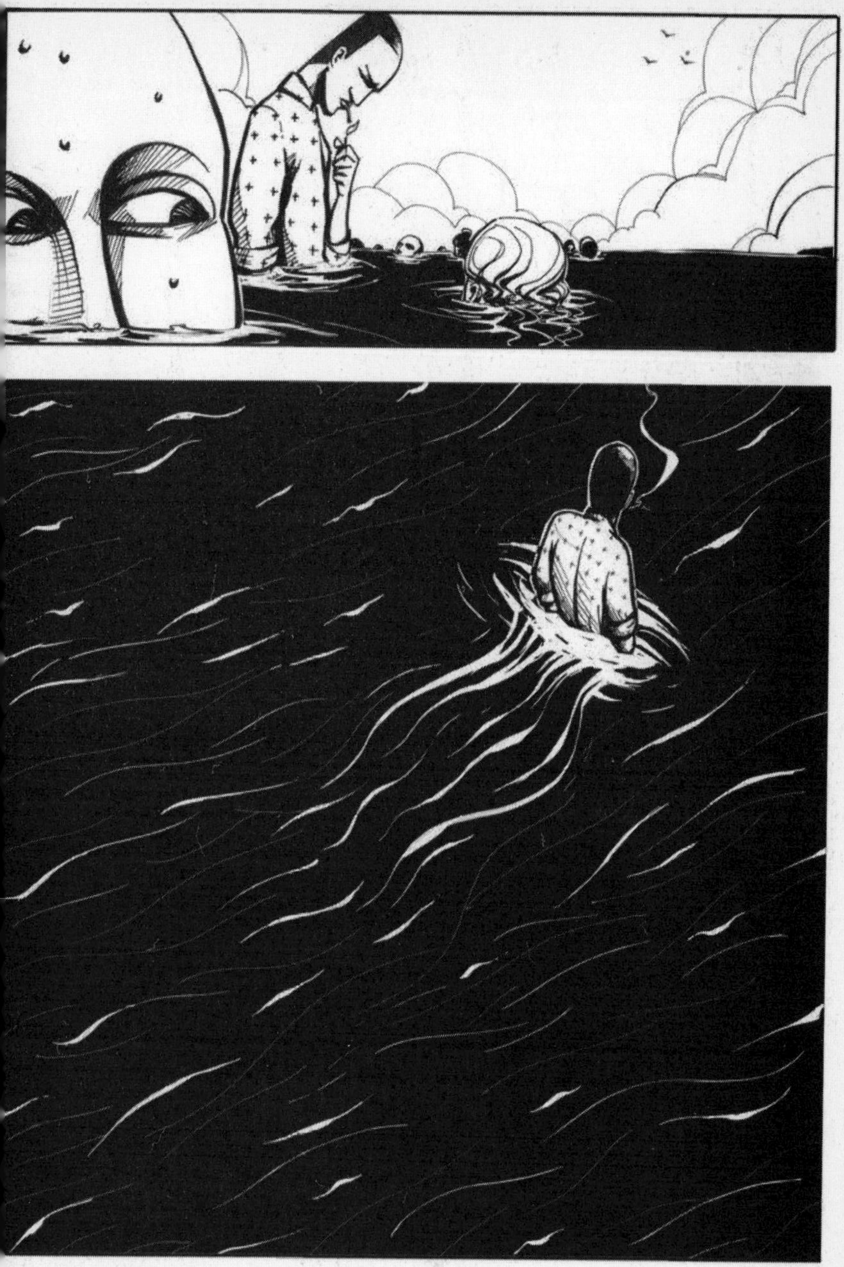

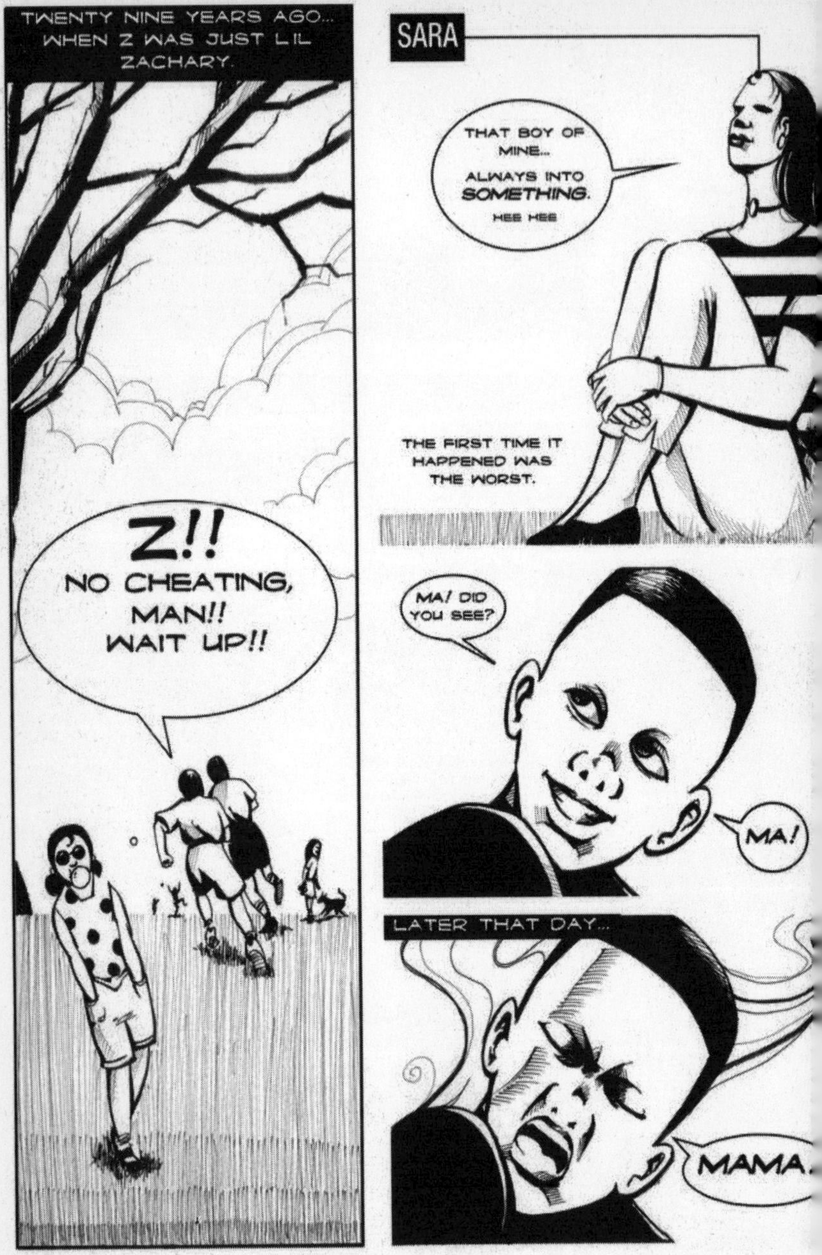
TWENTY NINE YEARS AGO... WHEN Z WAS JUST LIL ZACHARY.
Z!! NO CHEATING, MAN!! WAIT UP!!
SARA
THAT BOY OF MINE... ALWAYS INTO SOMETHING. HEE HEE
THE FIRST TIME IT HAPPENED WAS THE WORST.
MA! DID YOU SEE?
MA!
LATER THAT DAY...
MAMA.

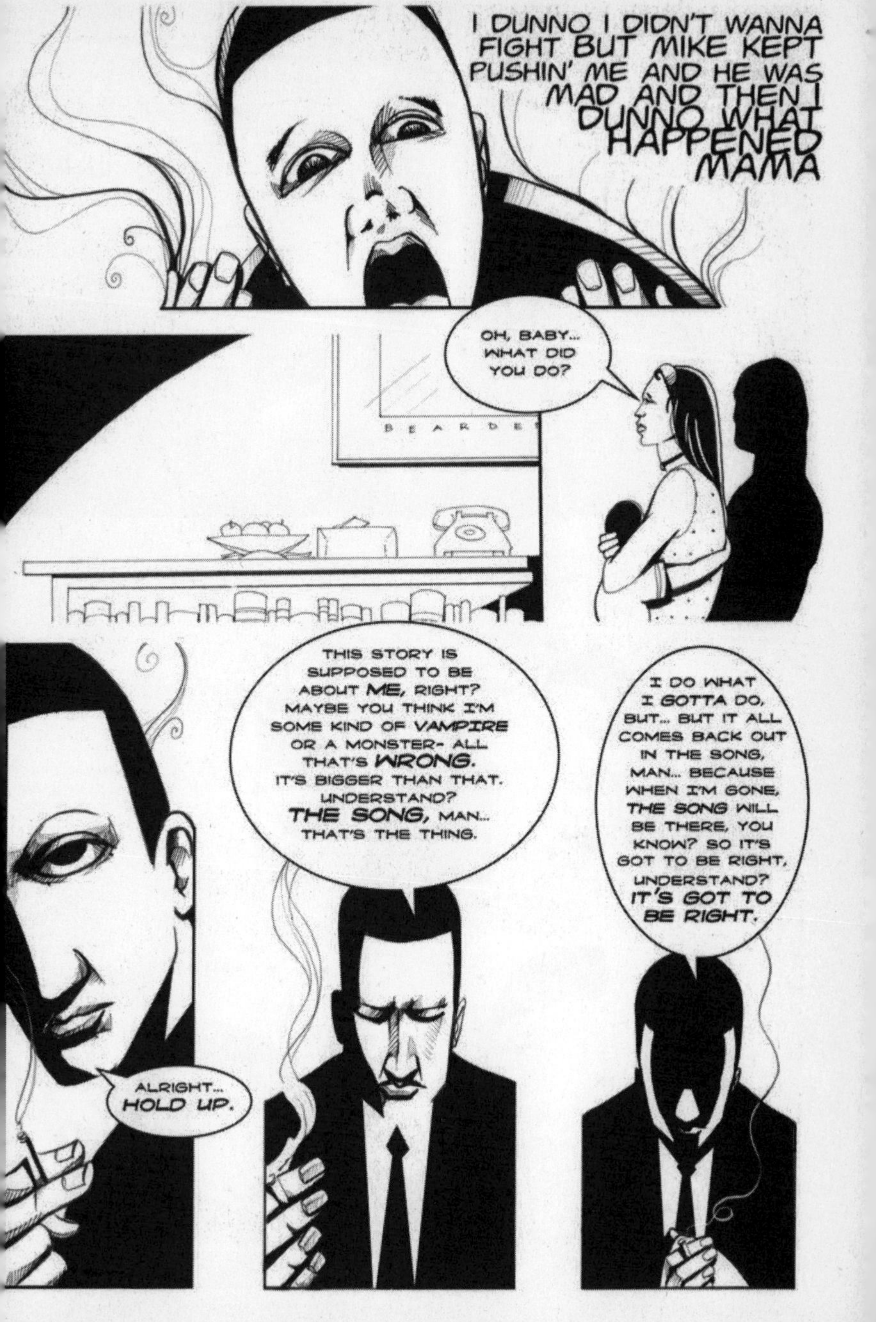
I DUNNO I DIDN'T WANNA FIGHT BUT MIKE KEPT PUSHIN' ME AND HE WAS MAD AND THEN I DUNNO WHAT HAPPENED MAMA
OH, BABY... WHAT DID YOU DO?
BEARDE
ALRIGHT... HOLD UP.
THIS STORY IS SUPPOSED TO BE ABOUT ME, RIGHT? MAYBE YOU THINK I'M SOME KIND OF VAMPIRE OR A MONSTER- ALL THAT'S WRONG. IT'S BIGGER THAN THAT. UNDERSTAND? THE SONG, MAN... THAT'S THE THING.
I DO WHAT I GOTTA DO, BUT... BUT IT ALL COMES BACK OUT IN THE SONG, MAN... BECAUSE WHEN I'M GONE, THE SONG WILL BE THERE, YOU KNOW? SO IT'S GOT TO BE RIGHT, UNDERSTAND? IT'S GOT TO BE RIGHT.

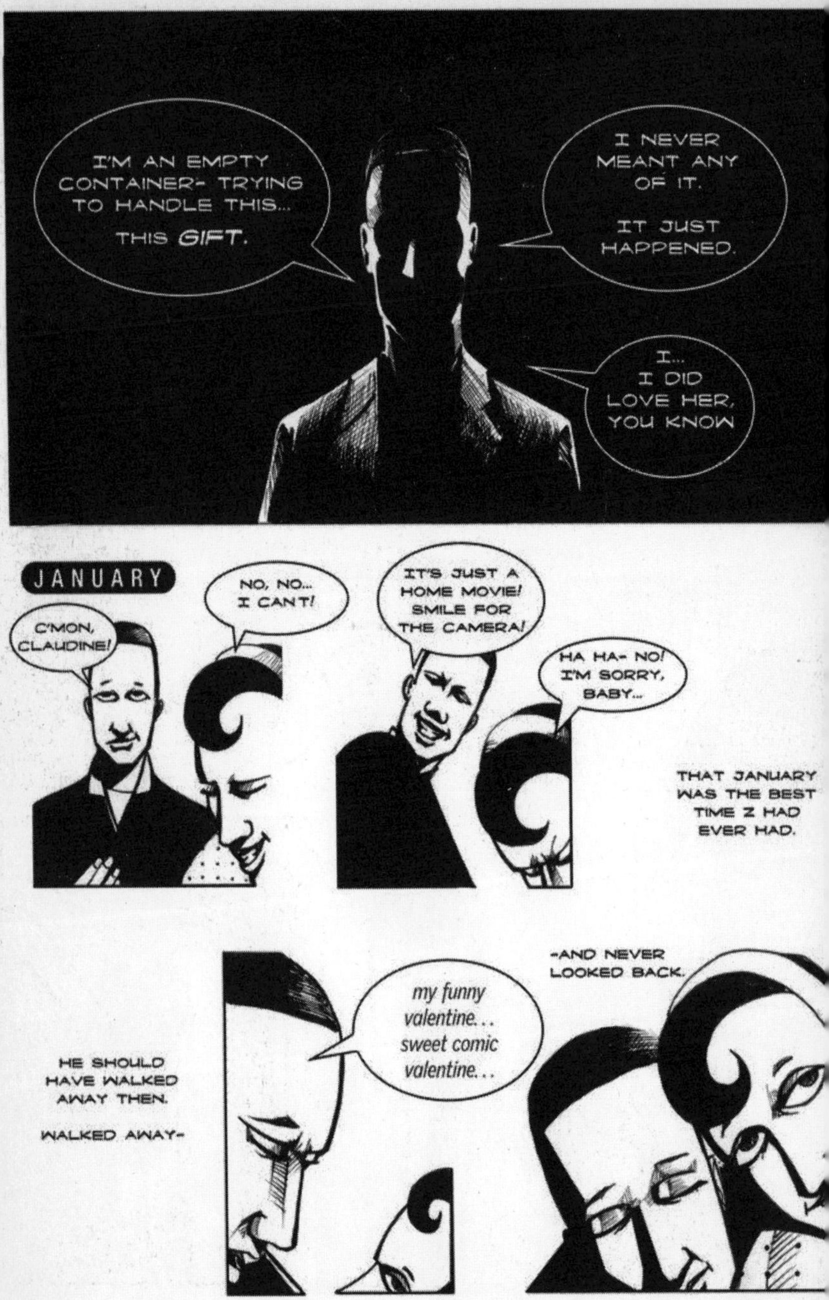
I'M AN EMPTY CONTAINER- TRYING TO HANDLE THIS... THIS *GIFT*.
I NEVER MEANT ANY OF IT.
IT JUST HAPPENED.
I... I DID LOVE HER, YOU KNOW
JANUARY
C'MON, CLAUDINE!
NO, NO... I CANT!
IT'S JUST A HOME MOVIE! SMILE FOR THE CAMERA!
HA HA- NO! I'M SORRY, BABY...
THAT JANUARY WAS THE BEST TIME Z HAD EVER HAD.
HE SHOULD HAVE WALKED AWAY THEN.
WALKED AWAY-
my funny valentine... sweet comic valentine...
-AND NEVER LOOKED BACK.

MARCH

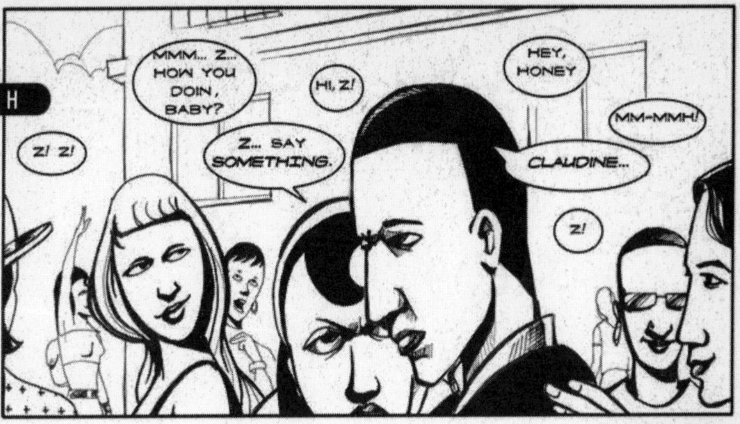
Z! Z!
MMM... Z... HOW YOU DOIN, BABY?
Z... SAY *SOMETHING.*
HI, Z!
HEY, HONEY
CLAUDINE...
MM-MMH!
Z!

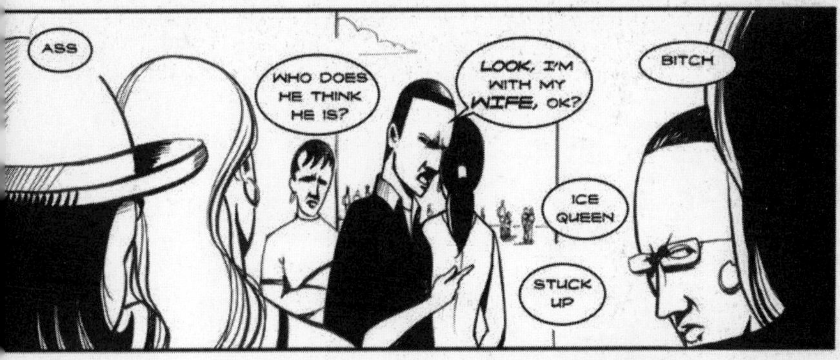
ASS
WHO DOES HE THINK HE IS?
LOOK, I'M WITH MY ***WIFE,*** OK?
BITCH
ICE QUEEN
STUCK UP

THAT WAS THE LAST TIME THEY WOULD TRULY BE HAPPY...

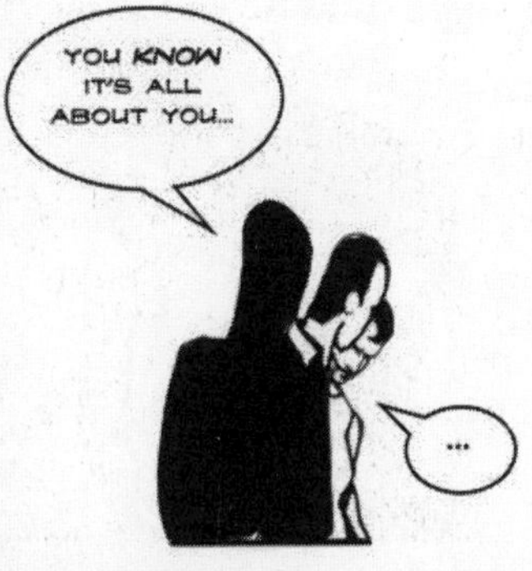
YOU *KNOW* IT'S ALL ABOUT YOU...
...

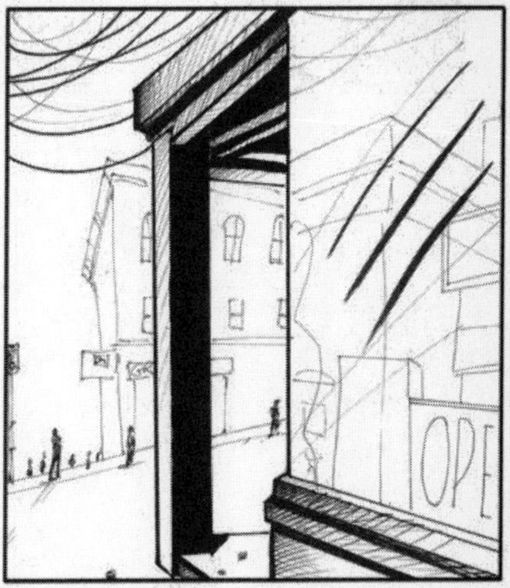
OPE

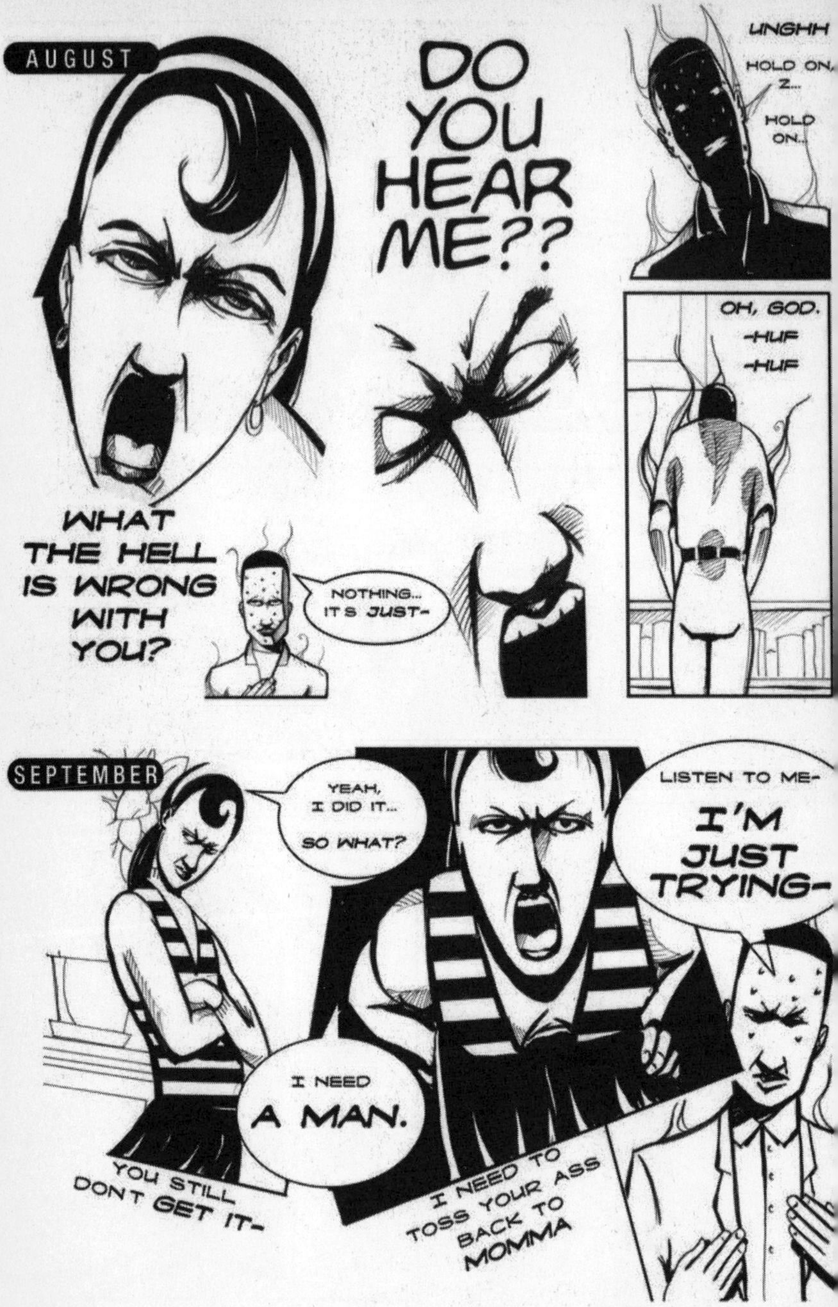
AUGUST
WHAT THE HELL IS WRONG WITH YOU?
NOTHING... IT'S JUST-
DO YOU HEAR ME??
UNGHH
HOLD ON, Z...
HOLD ON...
OH, GOD.
-HUF
-HUF
SEPTEMBER
YEAH, I DID IT... SO WHAT?
YOU STILL DON'T GET IT-
I NEED A MAN.
I NEED TO TOSS YOUR ASS BACK TO MOMMA
LISTEN TO ME-
I'M JUST TRYING-

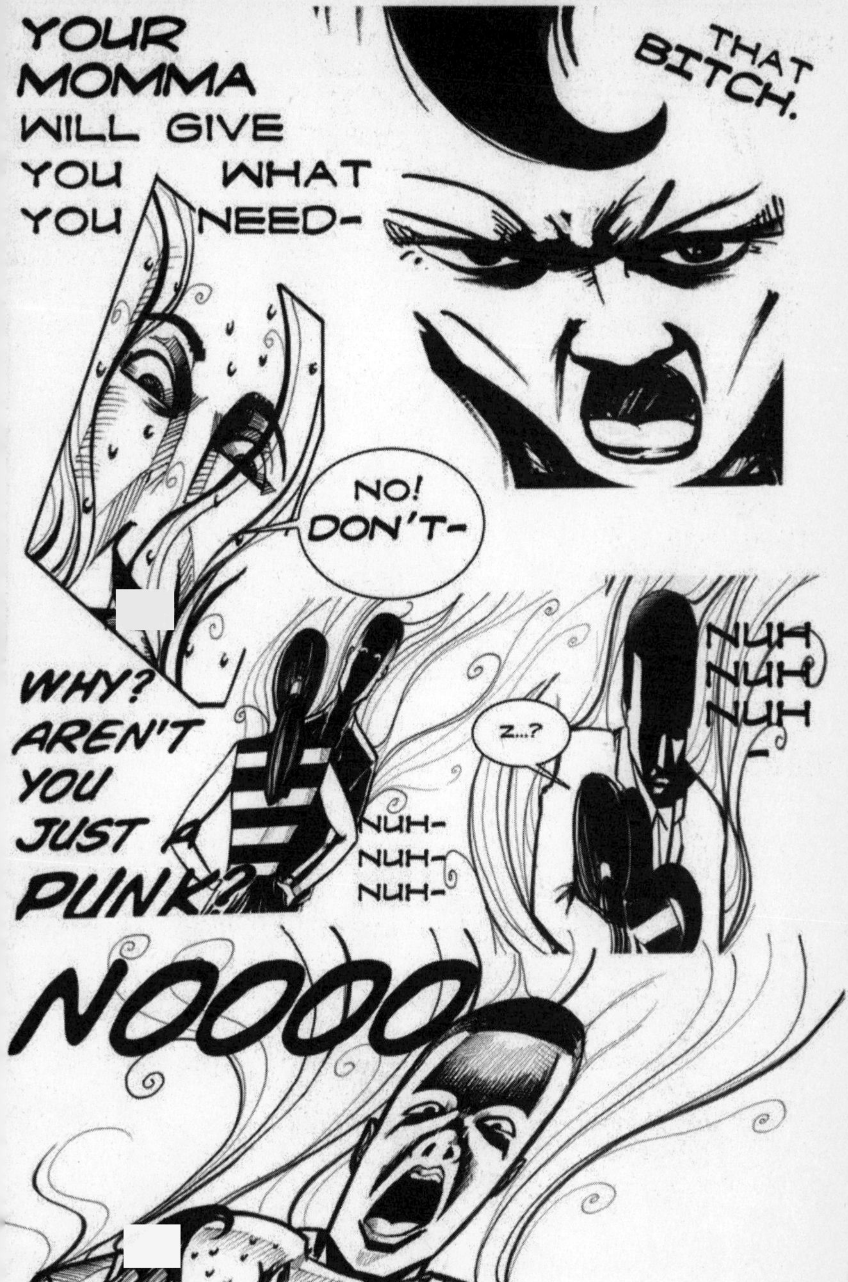
YOUR MOMMA WILL GIVE YOU WHAT YOU NEED-
THAT BITCH.
NO! DON'T-
WHY? AREN'T YOU JUST A PUNK?
NUH- NUH- NUH-
Z...?
NUH NUH NUH -
NOOOO

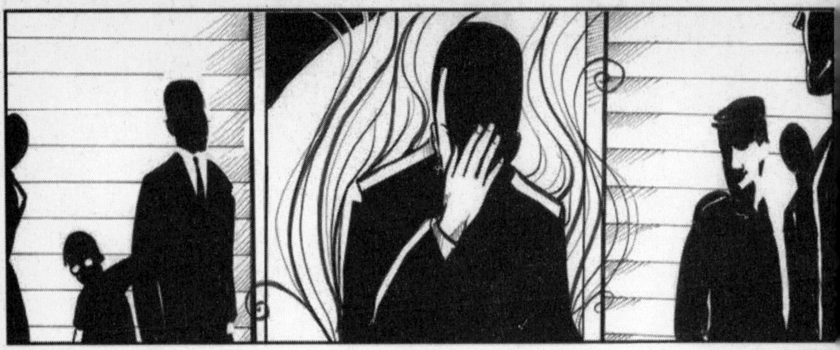

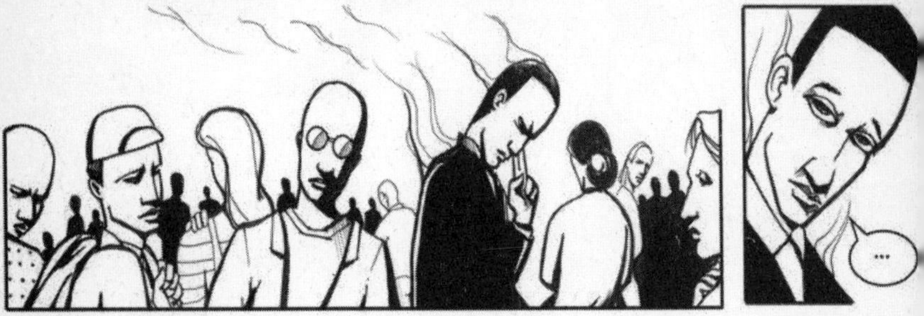
...

WELL... WHAT WOULD *YOU* DO?

HOW WOULD **YOU** FEEL?

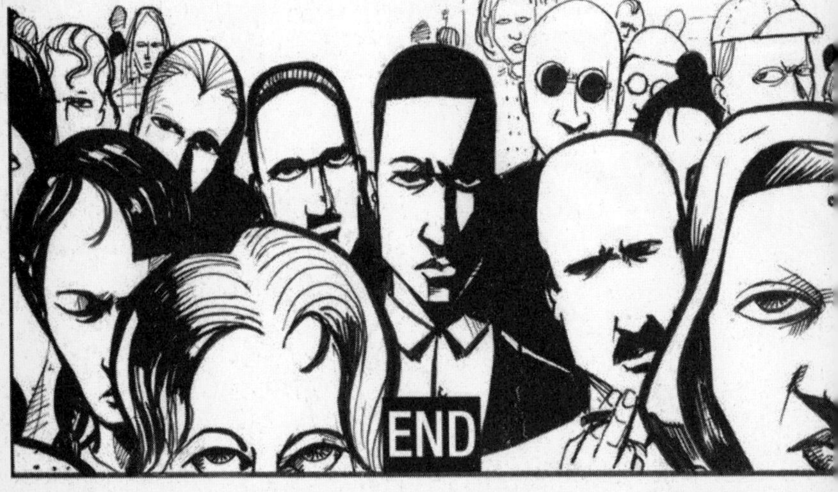
END

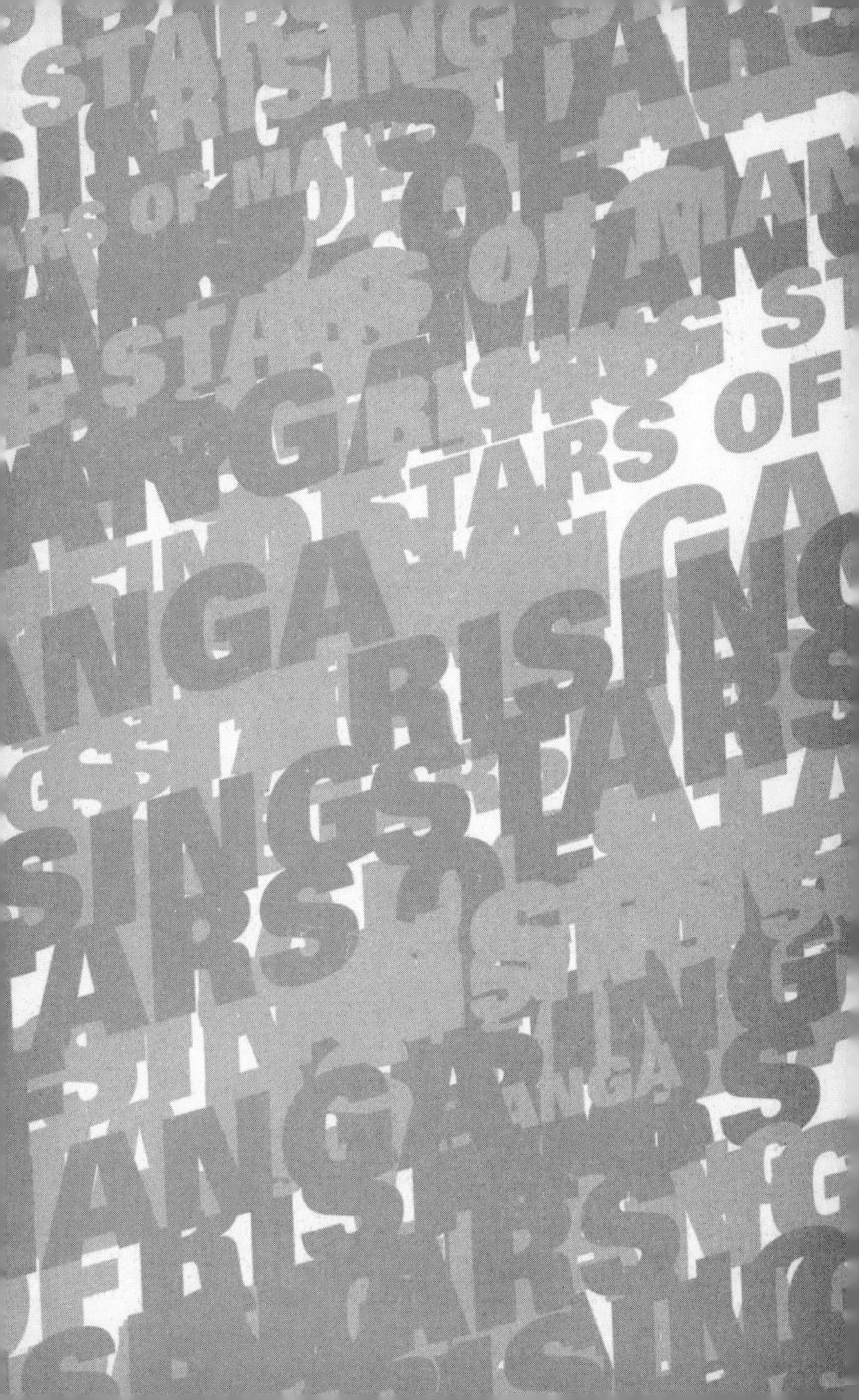

PROPER MAGIC

RUNNER UP

RISING.STARS.OF.MANGA.2003

::

THE PROPER MAGIC :: RUNNER UP ::

Jon Lyons was born in 1982 in St. Paul, Minnesota, and is now in college in Madison, Wisconsin.

Inspiration for this story:
It evolved out of an idea for a series I came up with on the way to math class Freshman year. When I heard about the contest, I just trimmed down the story, changed some of the characters, and compacted it to fit within the requisite number of pages. I wouldn't really say it was inspired by anything, since I was trying to come up with something original, but I can definitely pick out some similarities with other works I've seen.

Favorite Manga:
Definitely Urusei Yatsura, followed closely by the rest of Takahashi's works. I also like the work of Masamune Shirow and Katsuhiro Otomo.

Favorite Manga Artists:
Rumiko Takahashi, Satoshi Urushihara, Kennichi Sonoda

Judge's Comments:
In a post-apocalyptic desert world, there are only traders and buyers, bandits, monks and pacifists. The wisdom of the ancients has been lost and a primitive culture is all that remains. Yet things have been stable... until now. A reluctant hero is dragged into a conflict where he must wrestle with a mysterious device to save the world. And what a world it is!

Jonathan Lyons' story is supported by artwork ranging from simple to highly detailed, painting a picture of a desert land peopled by ragged survivors. His themes are drawn from the traditions of science fiction and feel firmly American. High points include the carefully-rendered spaceships and creative use of lettering that represents the languages of several cultures.
-Jeremy Ross

::

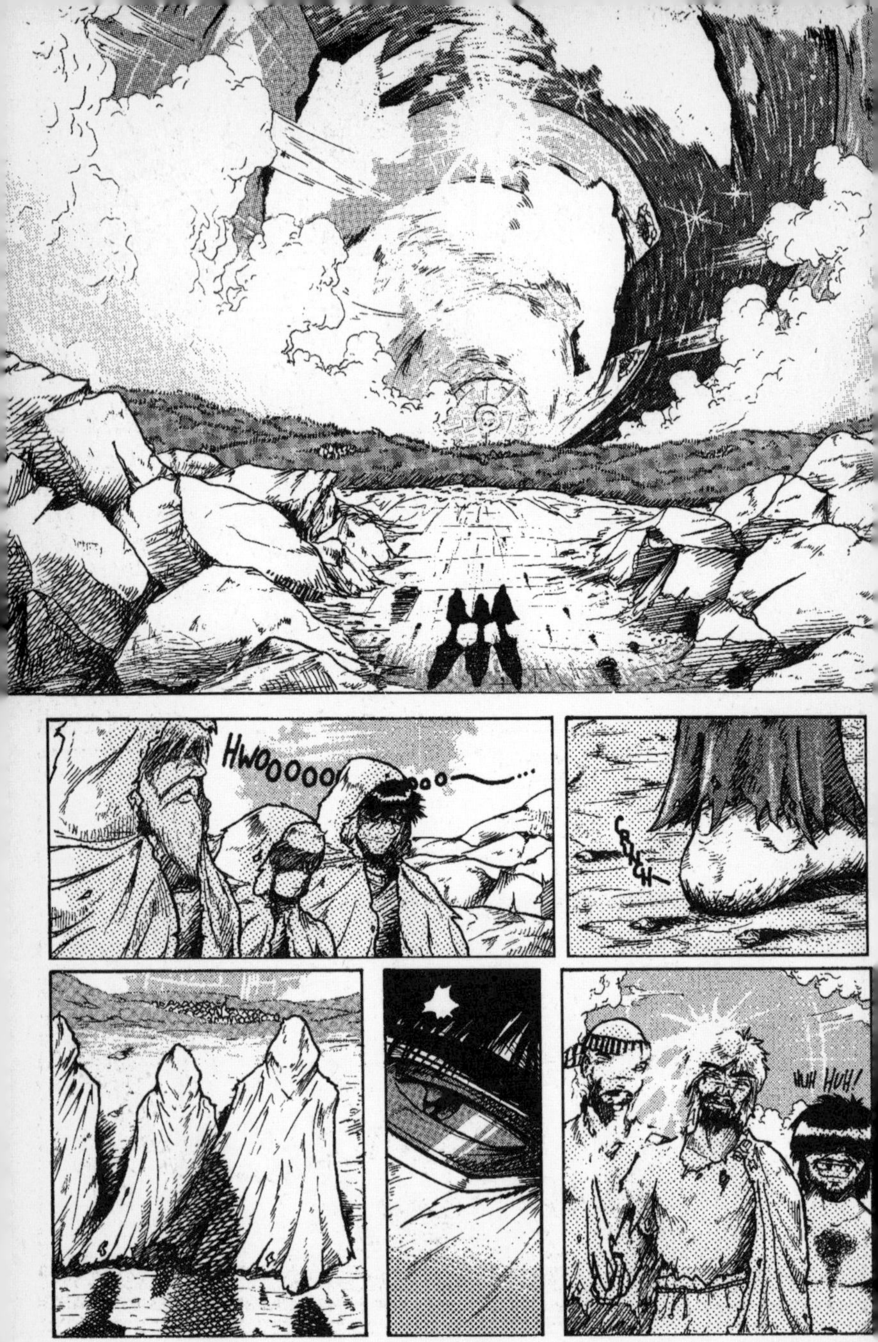
HWOOOOOOOOOO—...
CRUNCH
HUH HUH!

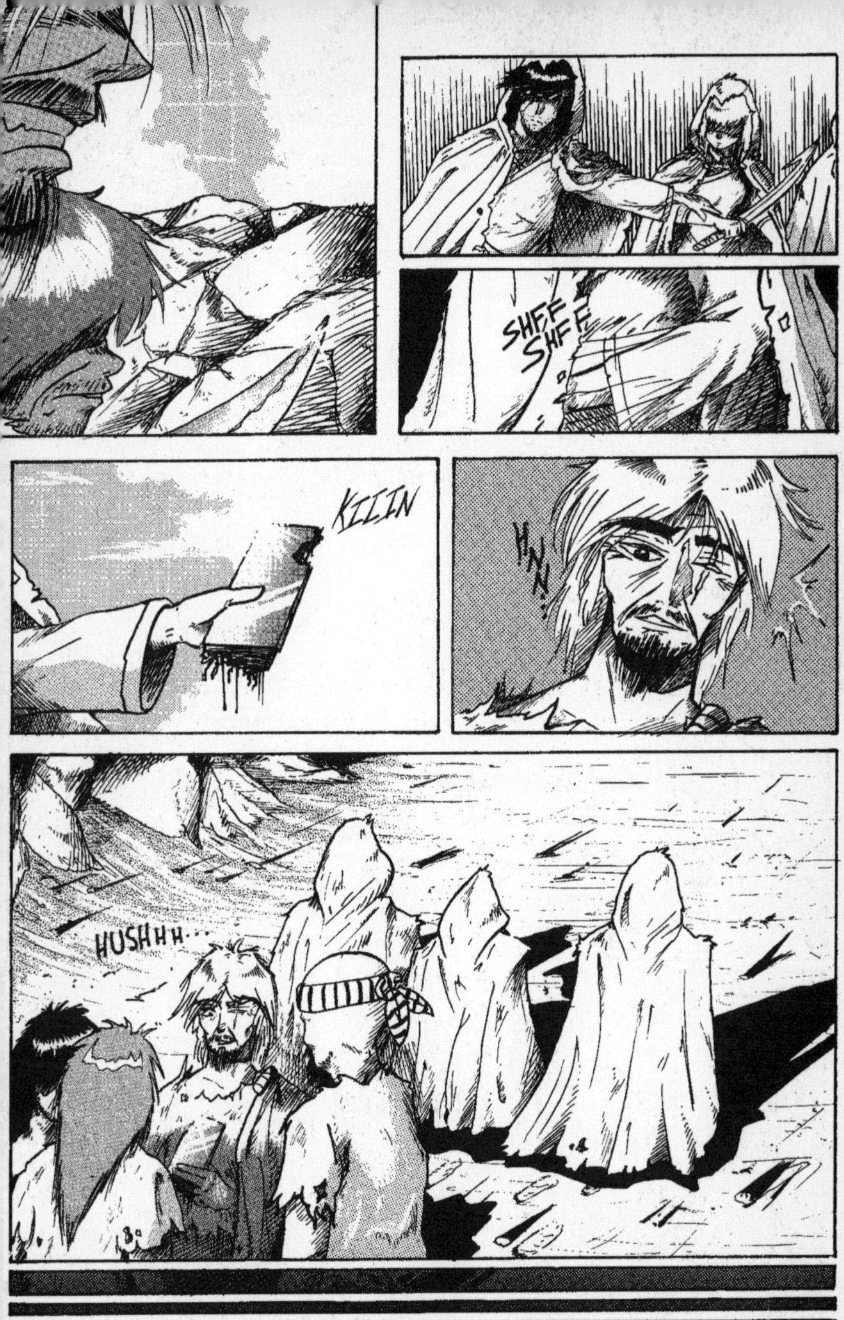
SHFF
SHFF
KIIIN
HNN..
HUSHHH...

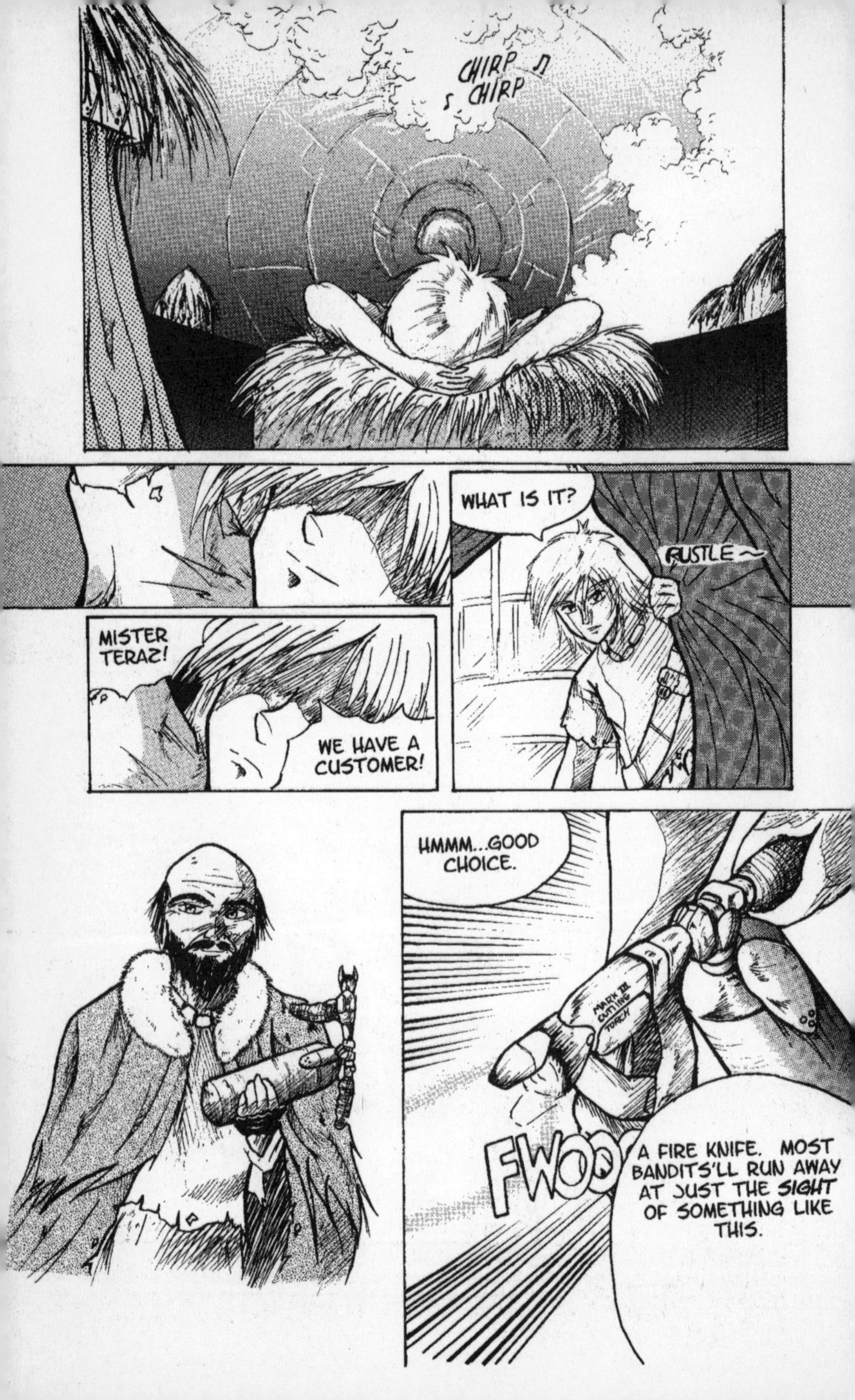
CHIRP CHIRP
WHAT IS IT?
RUSTLE~
MISTER TERAZ!
WE HAVE A CUSTOMER!
HMMM...GOOD CHOICE.
MARK III CUTTING TORCH
FWOO
A FIRE KNIFE. MOST BANDITS'LL RUN AWAY AT JUST THE SIGHT OF SOMETHING LIKE THIS.

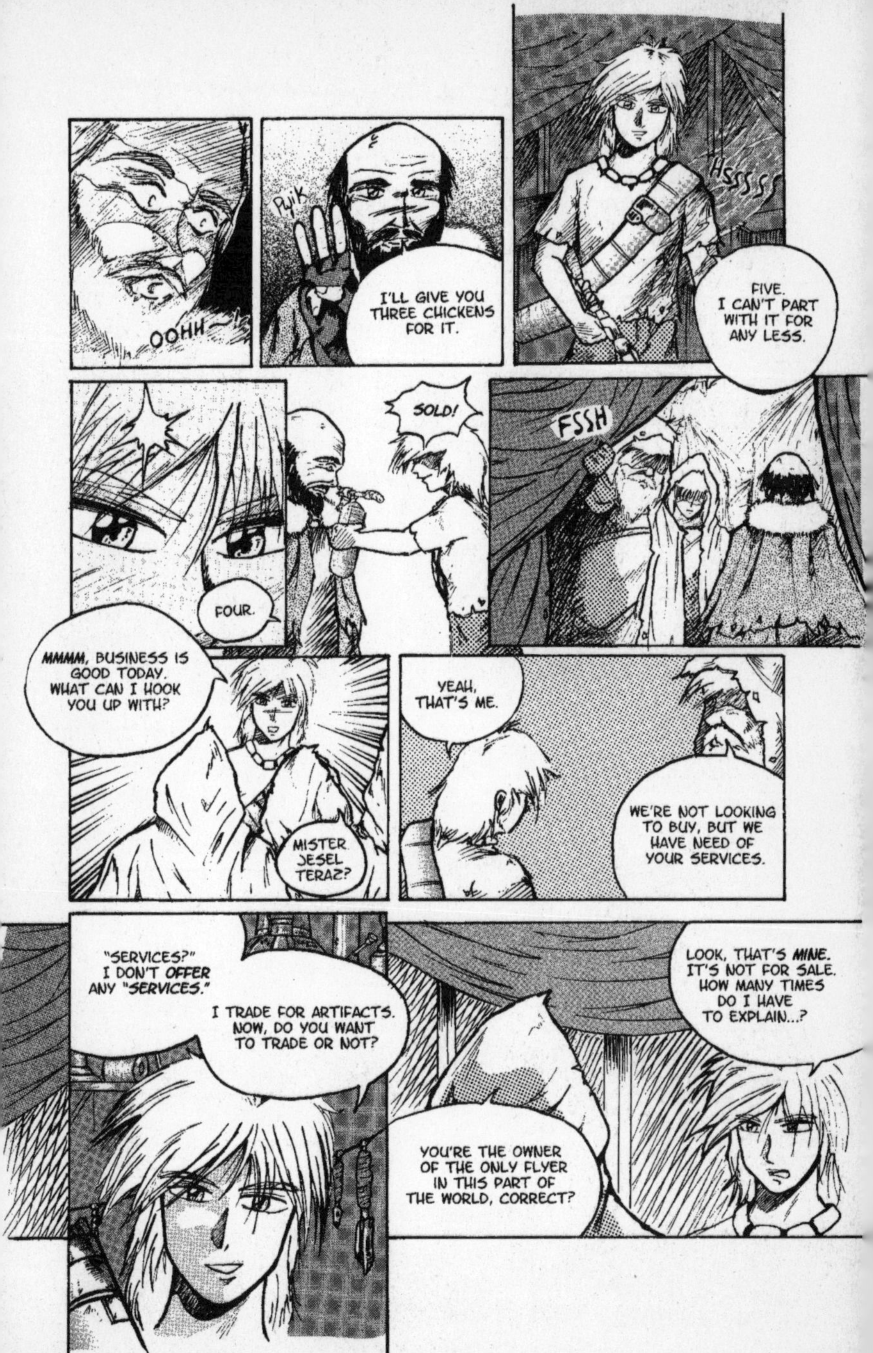
OOHH~
PWIK
I'LL GIVE YOU THREE CHICKENS FOR IT.
HSSSSS
FIVE. I CAN'T PART WITH IT FOR ANY LESS.
FOUR.
SOLD!
FSSH
MMMM, BUSINESS IS GOOD TODAY. WHAT CAN I HOOK YOU UP WITH?
MISTER JESEL TERAZ?
YEAH, THAT'S ME.
WE'RE NOT LOOKING TO BUY, BUT WE HAVE NEED OF YOUR SERVICES.
"SERVICES?" I DON'T OFFER ANY "SERVICES."
I TRADE FOR ARTIFACTS. NOW, DO YOU WANT TO TRADE OR NOT?
YOU'RE THE OWNER OF THE ONLY FLYER IN THIS PART OF THE WORLD, CORRECT?
LOOK, THAT'S MINE. IT'S NOT FOR SALE. HOW MANY TIMES DO I HAVE TO EXPLAIN...?

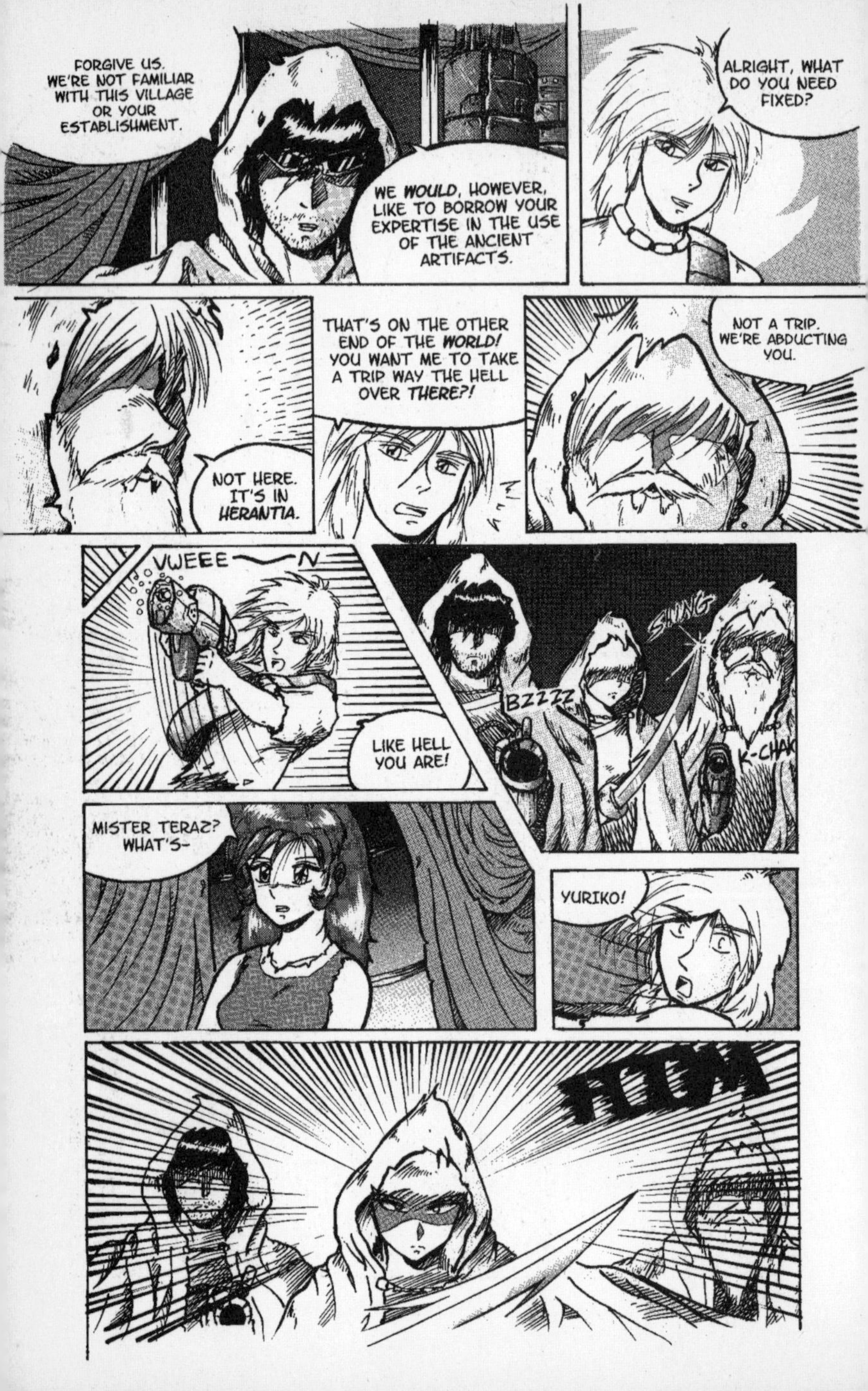
FORGIVE US. WE'RE NOT FAMILIAR WITH THIS VILLAGE OR YOUR ESTABLISHMENT.
WE WOULD, HOWEVER, LIKE TO BORROW YOUR EXPERTISE IN THE USE OF THE ANCIENT ARTIFACTS.
ALRIGHT, WHAT DO YOU NEED FIXED?
NOT HERE. IT'S IN HERANTIA.
THAT'S ON THE OTHER END OF THE WORLD! YOU WANT ME TO TAKE A TRIP WAY THE HELL OVER THERE?!
NOT A TRIP. WE'RE ABDUCTING YOU.
VWEEE—N
LIKE HELL YOU ARE!
SHING
BZZZZ
K-CHAK
MISTER TERAZ? WHAT'S-
YURIKO!

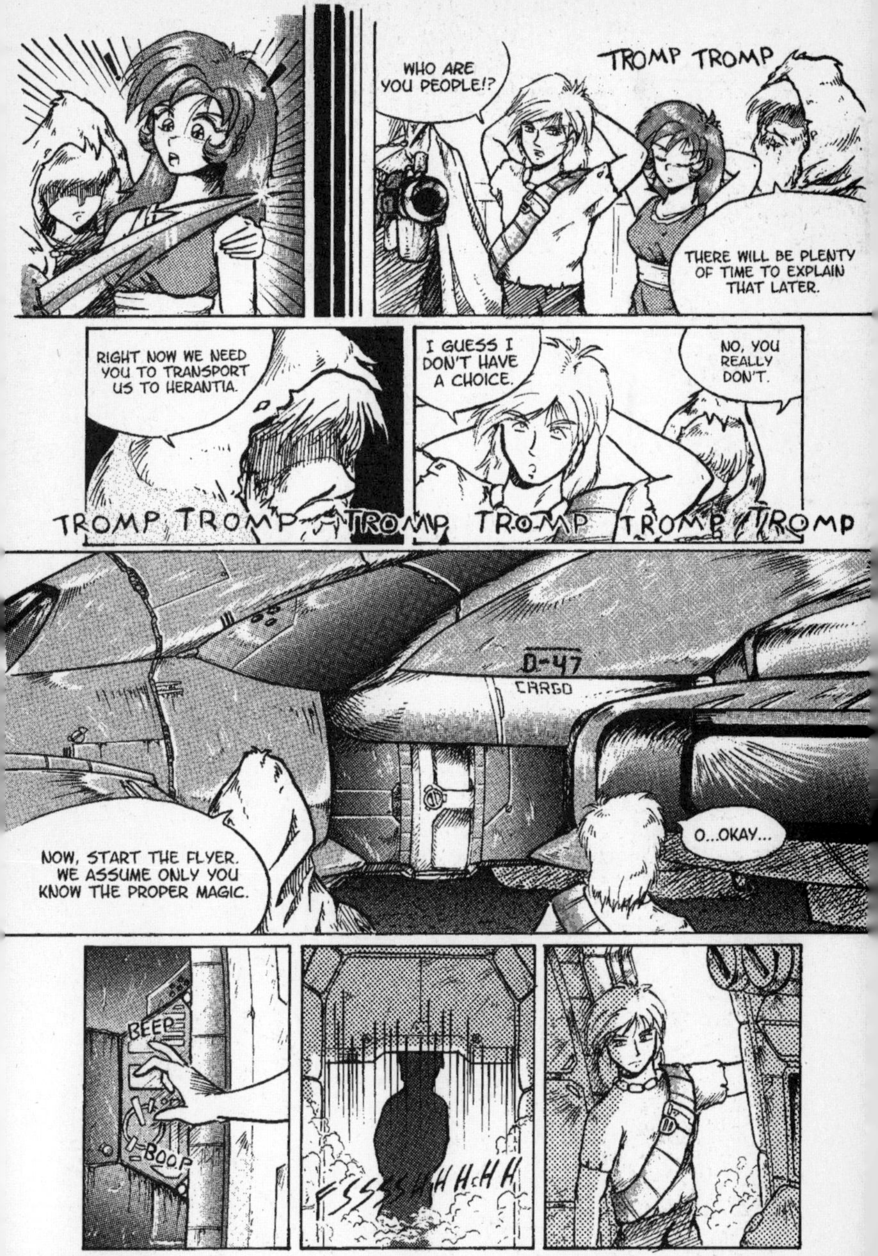
WHO ARE YOU PEOPLE!?
TROMP TROMP
THERE WILL BE PLENTY OF TIME TO EXPLAIN THAT LATER.
RIGHT NOW WE NEED YOU TO TRANSPORT US TO HERANTIA.
I GUESS I DON'T HAVE A CHOICE.
NO, YOU REALLY DON'T.
TROMP TROMP TROMP TROMP TROMP TROMP
D-47
CARGO
NOW, START THE FLYER. WE ASSUME ONLY YOU KNOW THE PROPER MAGIC.
O...OKAY...
BEEP
BOOP
FSSSSHHHHH

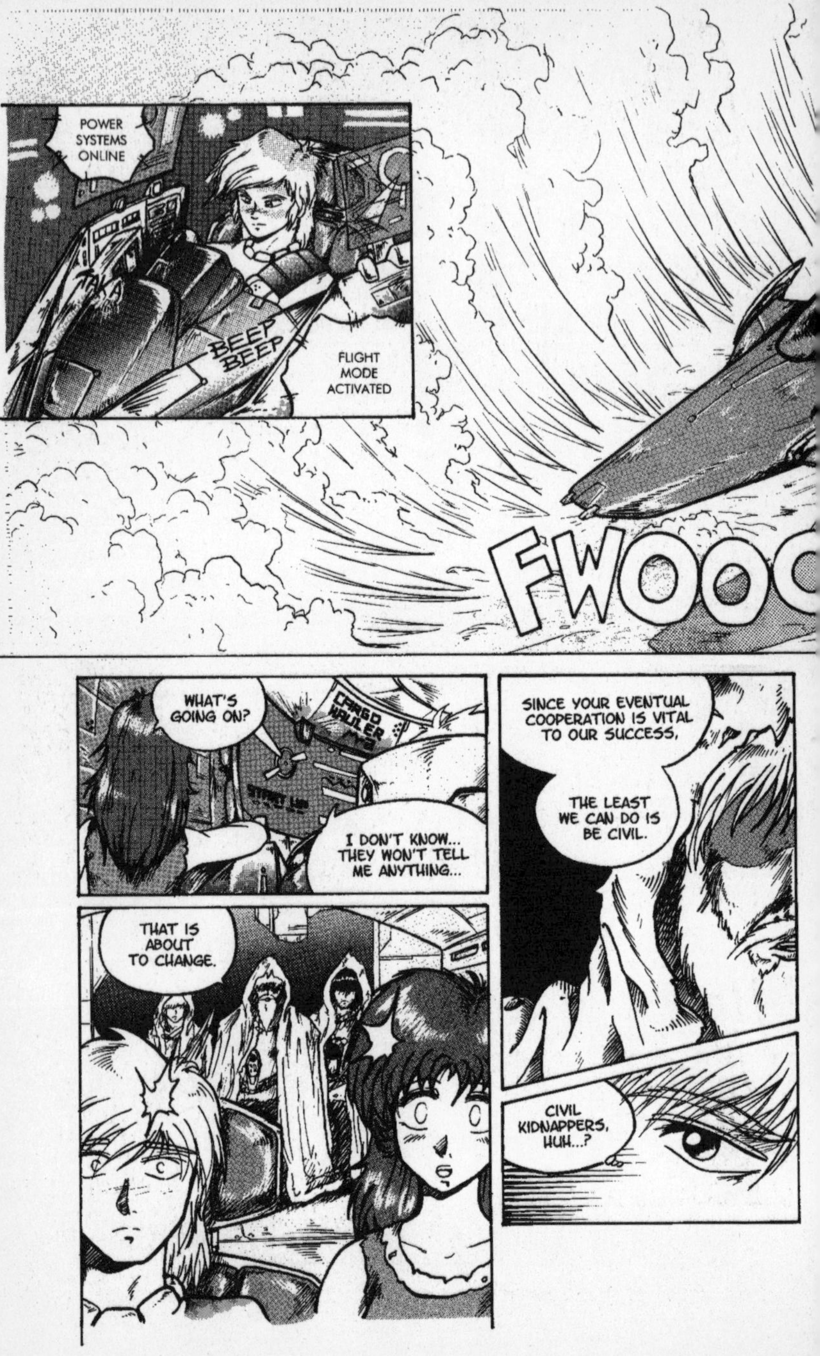
POWER SYSTEMS ONLINE
BEEP BEEP
FLIGHT MODE ACTIVATED
FWOO
WHAT'S GOING ON?
I DON'T KNOW... THEY WON'T TELL ME ANYTHING...
THAT IS ABOUT TO CHANGE.
SINCE YOUR EVENTUAL COOPERATION IS VITAL TO OUR SUCCESS,
THE LEAST WE CAN DO IS BE CIVIL.
CIVIL KIDNAPPERS, HUH...?

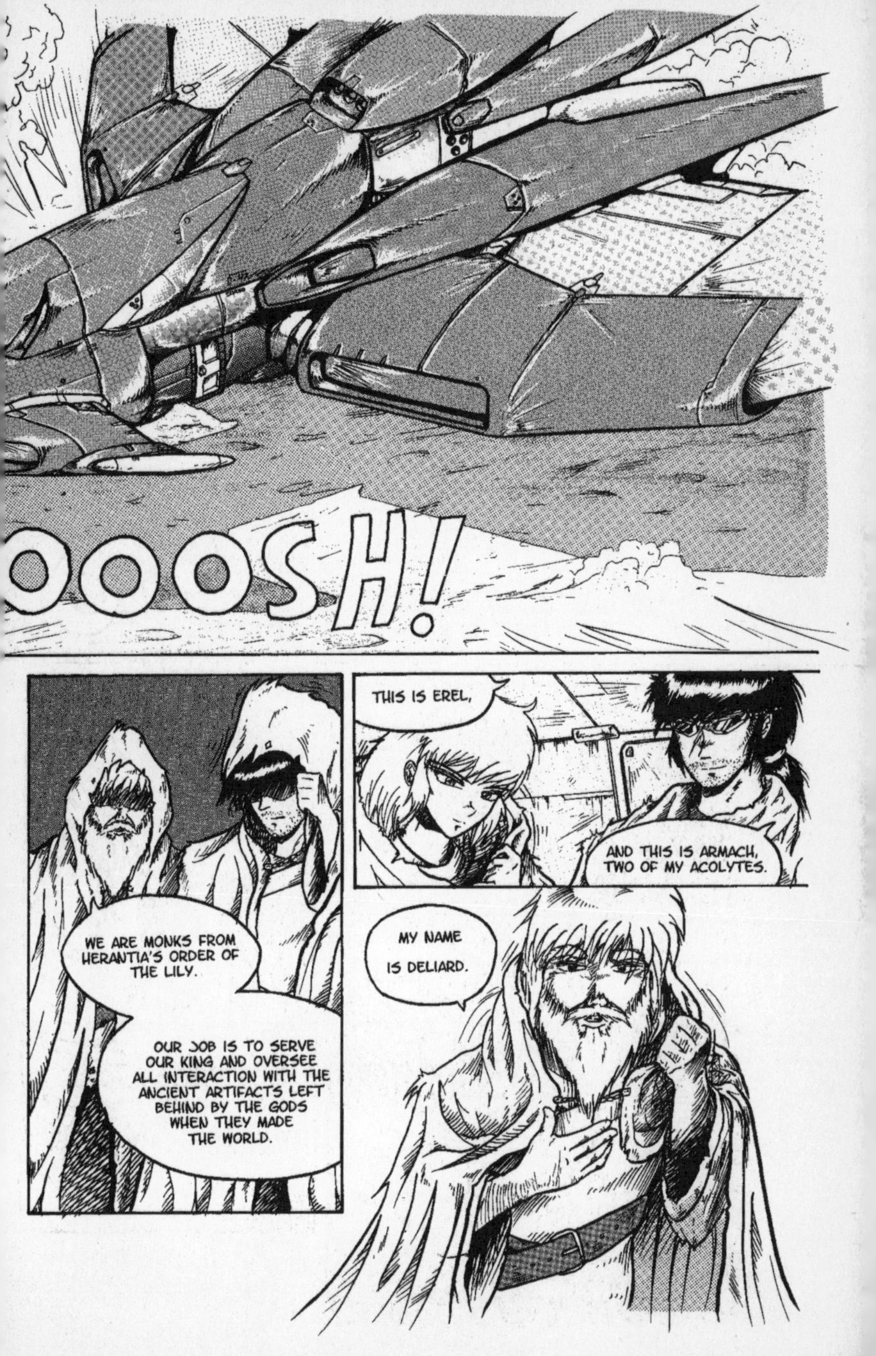
OOOSH!
WE ARE MONKS FROM HERANTIA'S ORDER OF THE LILY.
OUR JOB IS TO SERVE OUR KING AND OVERSEE ALL INTERACTION WITH THE ANCIENT ARTIFACTS LEFT BEHIND BY THE GODS WHEN THEY MADE THE WORLD.
THIS IS EREL,
AND THIS IS ARMACH, TWO OF MY ACOLYTES.
MY NAME IS DELIARD.

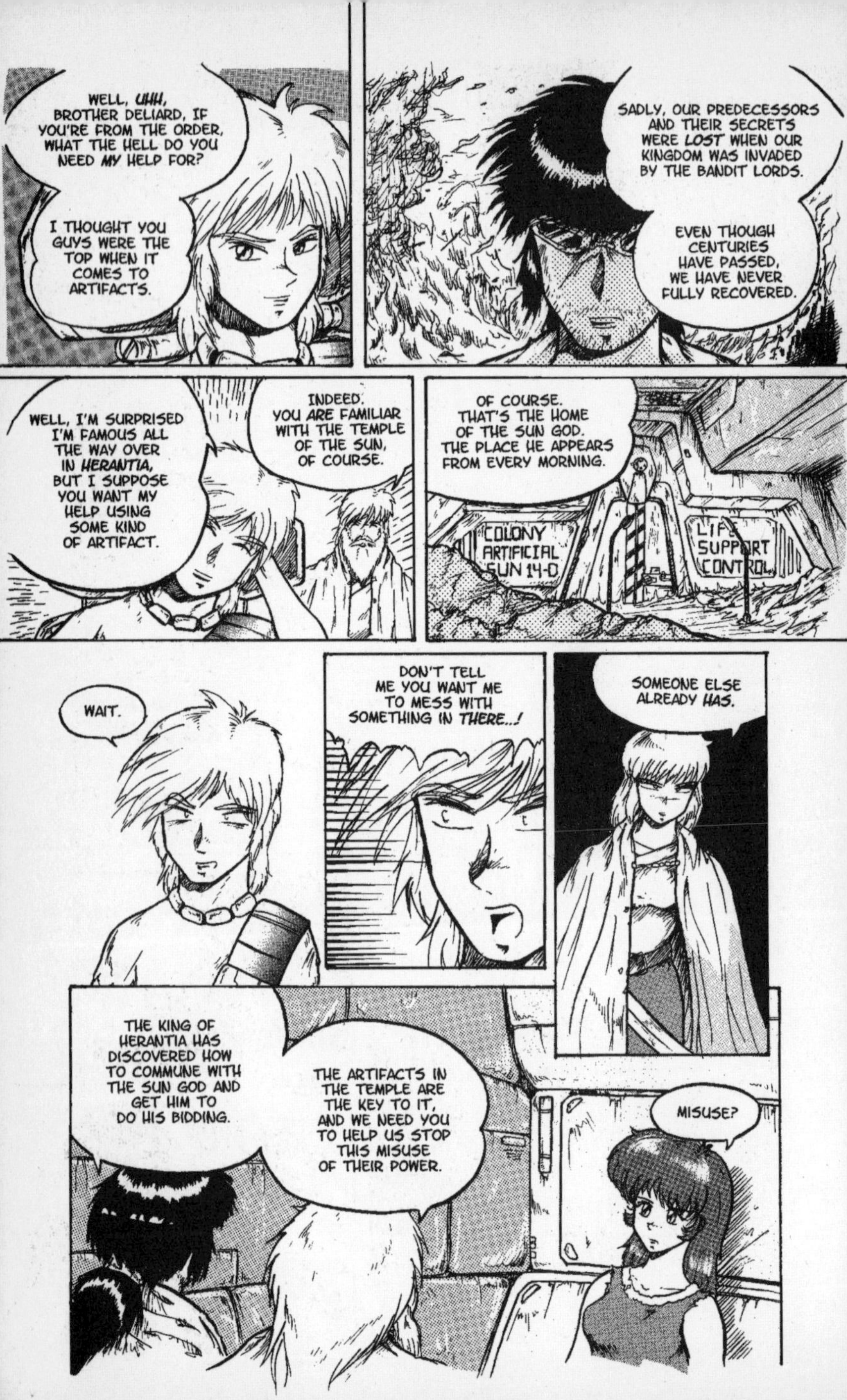
WELL, UHH, BROTHER DELIARD, IF YOU'RE FROM THE ORDER, WHAT THE HELL DO YOU NEED MY HELP FOR?
I THOUGHT YOU GUYS WERE THE TOP WHEN IT COMES TO ARTIFACTS.
SADLY, OUR PREDECESSORS AND THEIR SECRETS WERE LOST WHEN OUR KINGDOM WAS INVADED BY THE BANDIT LORDS.
EVEN THOUGH CENTURIES HAVE PASSED, WE HAVE NEVER FULLY RECOVERED.
WELL, I'M SURPRISED I'M FAMOUS ALL THE WAY OVER IN HERANTIA, BUT I SUPPOSE YOU WANT MY HELP USING SOME KIND OF ARTIFACT.
INDEED. YOU ARE FAMILIAR WITH THE TEMPLE OF THE SUN, OF COURSE.
OF COURSE. THAT'S THE HOME OF THE SUN GOD. THE PLACE HE APPEARS FROM EVERY MORNING.
COLONY ARTIFICIAL SUN 14-D
LIFE SUPPORT CONTROL
WAIT.
DON'T TELL ME YOU WANT ME TO MESS WITH SOMETHING IN THERE...!
SOMEONE ELSE ALREADY HAS.
THE KING OF HERANTIA HAS DISCOVERED HOW TO COMMUNE WITH THE SUN GOD AND GET HIM TO DO HIS BIDDING.
THE ARTIFACTS IN THE TEMPLE ARE THE KEY TO IT, AND WE NEED YOU TO HELP US STOP THIS MISUSE OF THEIR POWER.
MISUSE?

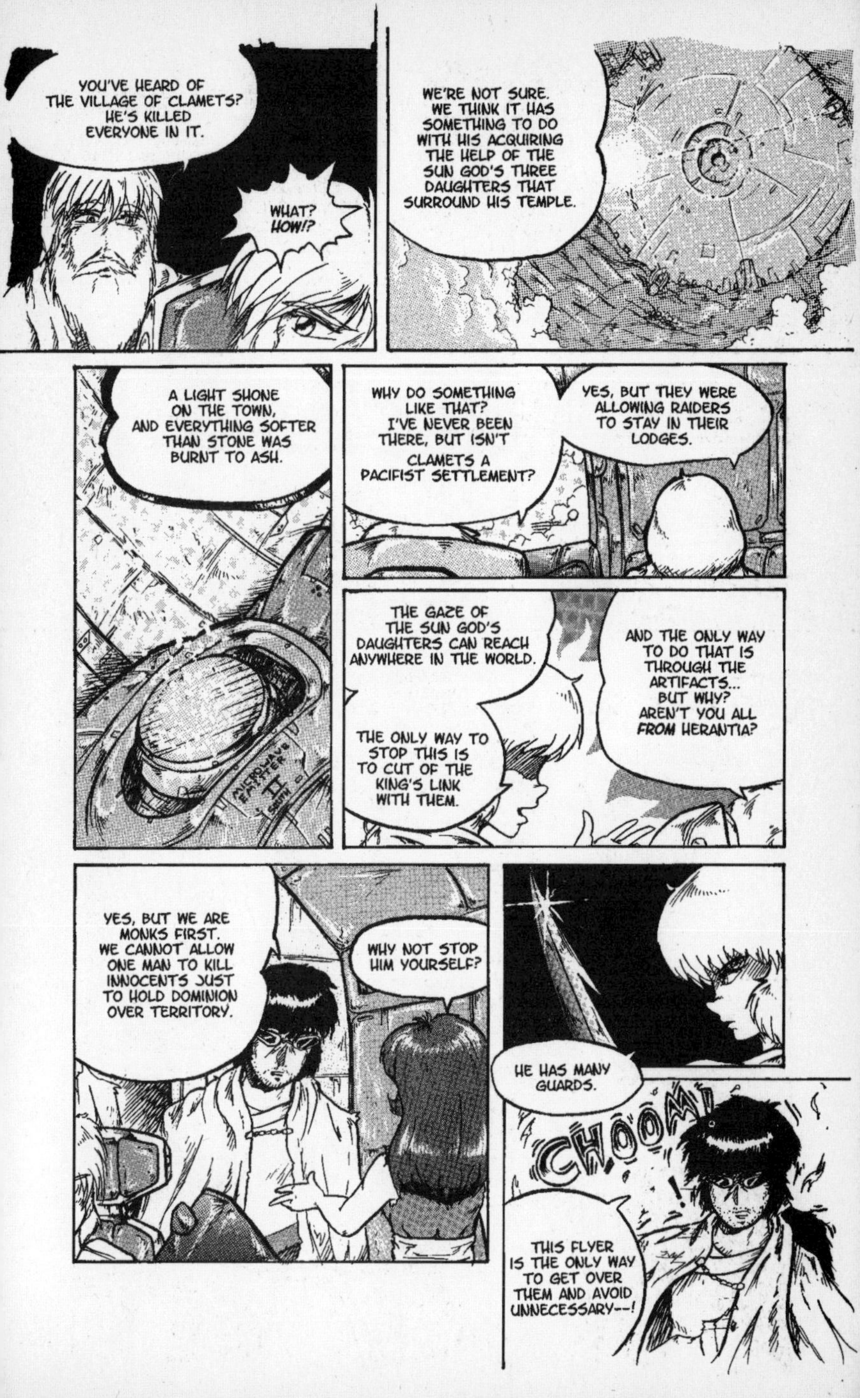
YOU'VE HEARD OF THE VILLAGE OF CLAMETS? HE'S KILLED EVERYONE IN IT.
WHAT? HOW!?
WE'RE NOT SURE. WE THINK IT HAS SOMETHING TO DO WITH HIS ACQUIRING THE HELP OF THE SUN GOD'S THREE DAUGHTERS THAT SURROUND HIS TEMPLE.
A LIGHT SHONE ON THE TOWN, AND EVERYTHING SOFTER THAN STONE WAS BURNT TO ASH.
MICROWAVE EMITTER II SOUTH
WHY DO SOMETHING LIKE THAT? I'VE NEVER BEEN THERE, BUT ISN'T CLAMETS A PACIFIST SETTLEMENT?
YES, BUT THEY WERE ALLOWING RAIDERS TO STAY IN THEIR LODGES.
THE GAZE OF THE SUN GOD'S DAUGHTERS CAN REACH ANYWHERE IN THE WORLD.
THE ONLY WAY TO STOP THIS IS TO CUT OF THE KING'S LINK WITH THEM.
AND THE ONLY WAY TO DO THAT IS THROUGH THE ARTIFACTS... BUT WHY? AREN'T YOU ALL FROM HERANTIA?
YES, BUT WE ARE MONKS FIRST. WE CANNOT ALLOW ONE MAN TO KILL INNOCENTS JUST TO HOLD DOMINION OVER TERRITORY.
WHY NOT STOP HIM YOURSELF?
HE HAS MANY GUARDS.
CHOOM!
!
THIS FLYER IS THE ONLY WAY TO GET OVER THEM AND AVOID UNNECESSARY--!

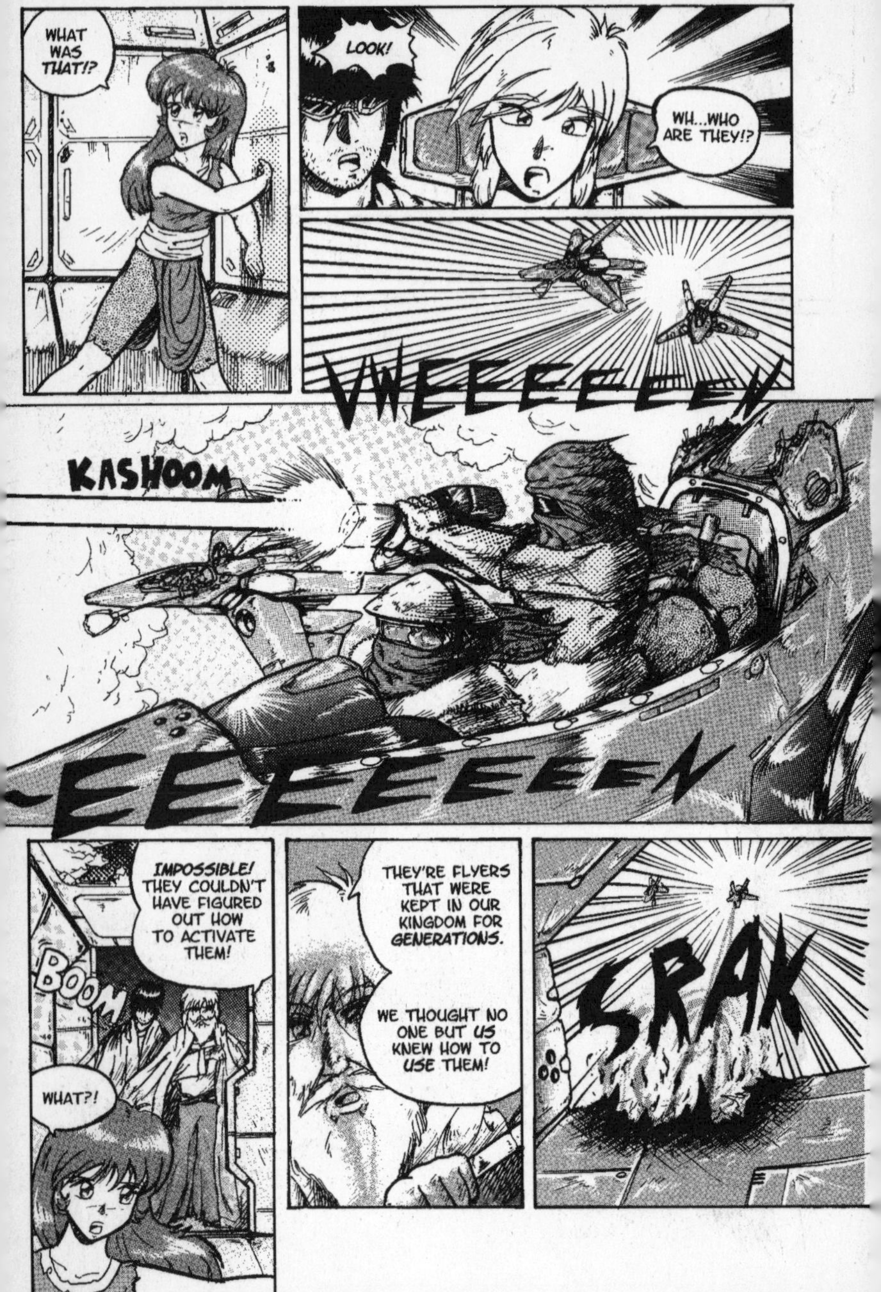
WHAT WAS THAT!?
LOOK!
WH...WHO ARE THEY!?
VWEEEEEEEN
KASHOOM
EEEEEEEEN
IMPOSSIBLE! THEY COULDN'T HAVE FIGURED OUT HOW TO ACTIVATE THEM!
BOOM
WHAT?!
THEY'RE FLYERS THAT WERE KEPT IN OUR KINGDOM FOR GENERATIONS.
WE THOUGHT NO ONE BUT US KNEW HOW TO USE THEM!
SRAK

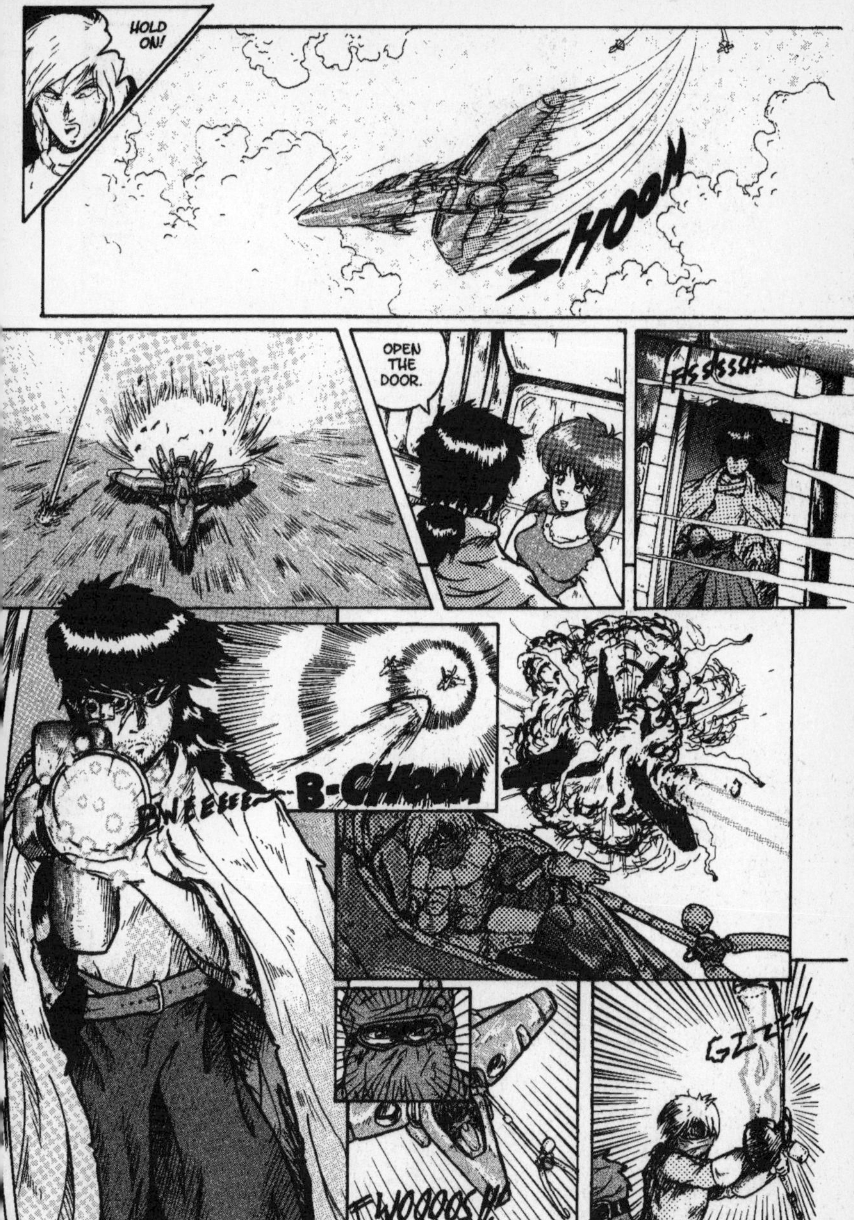
HOLD ON!
SHOOM
OPEN THE DOOR.
FSSSSSH
BWEEEEE
B-CHOOM
GZZZZ
FWOOOOSH!!

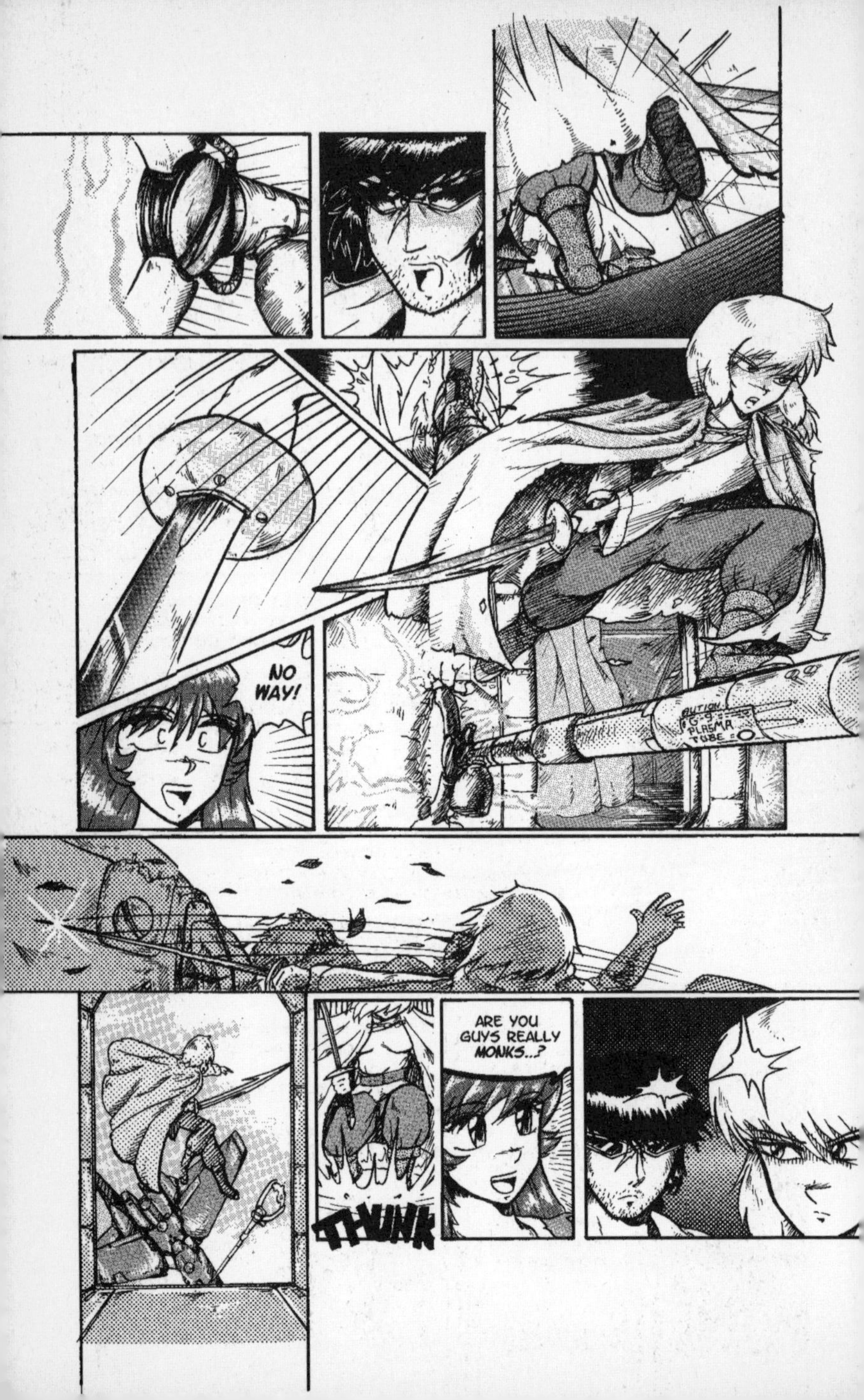
NO WAY!
AUTION G-9 PLASMA TUBE
THUNK
ARE YOU GUYS REALLY MONKS...?

WE'RE COMING UP ON THE TEMPLE. I'LL SET US DOWN OVER *THERE*.

FWOOOOON...

MMM...FEELS GOOD TO GET SOME FRESH AIR.

T.G.C. COLONY SHIP TRAVERSER
LIFE SUPPORT SYSTEM CONTROL STATION
ARTIFICIAL SUN

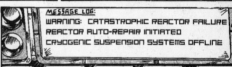

MESSAGE LOG:
WARNING: CATASTROPHIC REACTOR FAILURE
REACTOR AUTO-REPAIR INITIATED
CRYOGENIC SUSPENSION SYSTEMS OFFLINE

EMERGENCY: 3247 AD
ALL CRYO PODS:
REVIVAL PROCEDURE COMPLETE
IRREVERSIBLE NEUROLOGICAL DAMAGE DETECTED
MEMORY LOSS DETECTED
CYLINDER SECTION ENVIRONMENTAL
PREPARATIONS COMPLETE

MAN...MY DAD USED TO TELL ME ABOUT THIS PLACE.

HE'D USE THE FLYER TO TAKE PILGRIMS HERE...

MINE, TOO...IT'S AMAZING ALL THE TWO OF THEM WERE ABLE TO LEARN HOW TO USE TOGETHER...

CURRENT DATE:
5692 AD
[DATA LOST]
....

MAIN COMPUTER:
HIGHER FUNCTIONS OFFLINE
SHIP NAVIGATION SYSTEM:
OFFLINE
OVERHAUL RECCOMENDED

WHAT THE KING'S DOING HERE PROBABLY WOULDN'T BE *POSSIBLE* WITHOUT THEIR WORK.

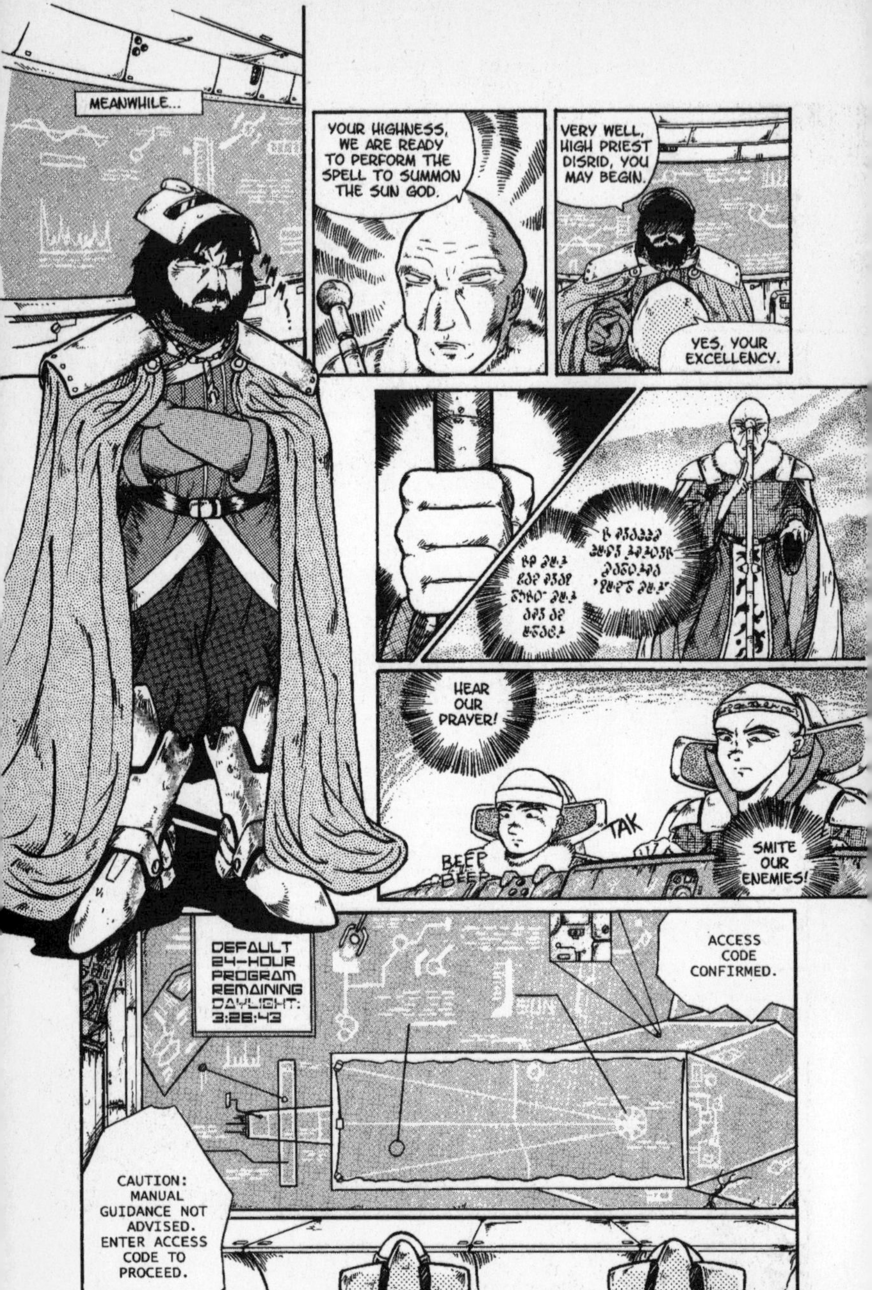
MEANWHILE...
YOUR HIGHNESS, WE ARE READY TO PERFORM THE SPELL TO SUMMON THE SUN GOD.
VERY WELL, HIGH PRIEST DISRID, YOU MAY BEGIN.
YES, YOUR EXCELLENCY.
HEAR OUR PRAYER!
TAK
BEEP BEEP
SMITE OUR ENEMIES!
DEFAULT 24-HOUR PROGRAM REMAINING DAYLIGHT: 3:28:43
SUN
ACCESS CODE CONFIRMED.
CAUTION: MANUAL GUIDANCE NOT ADVISED. ENTER ACCESS CODE TO PROCEED.

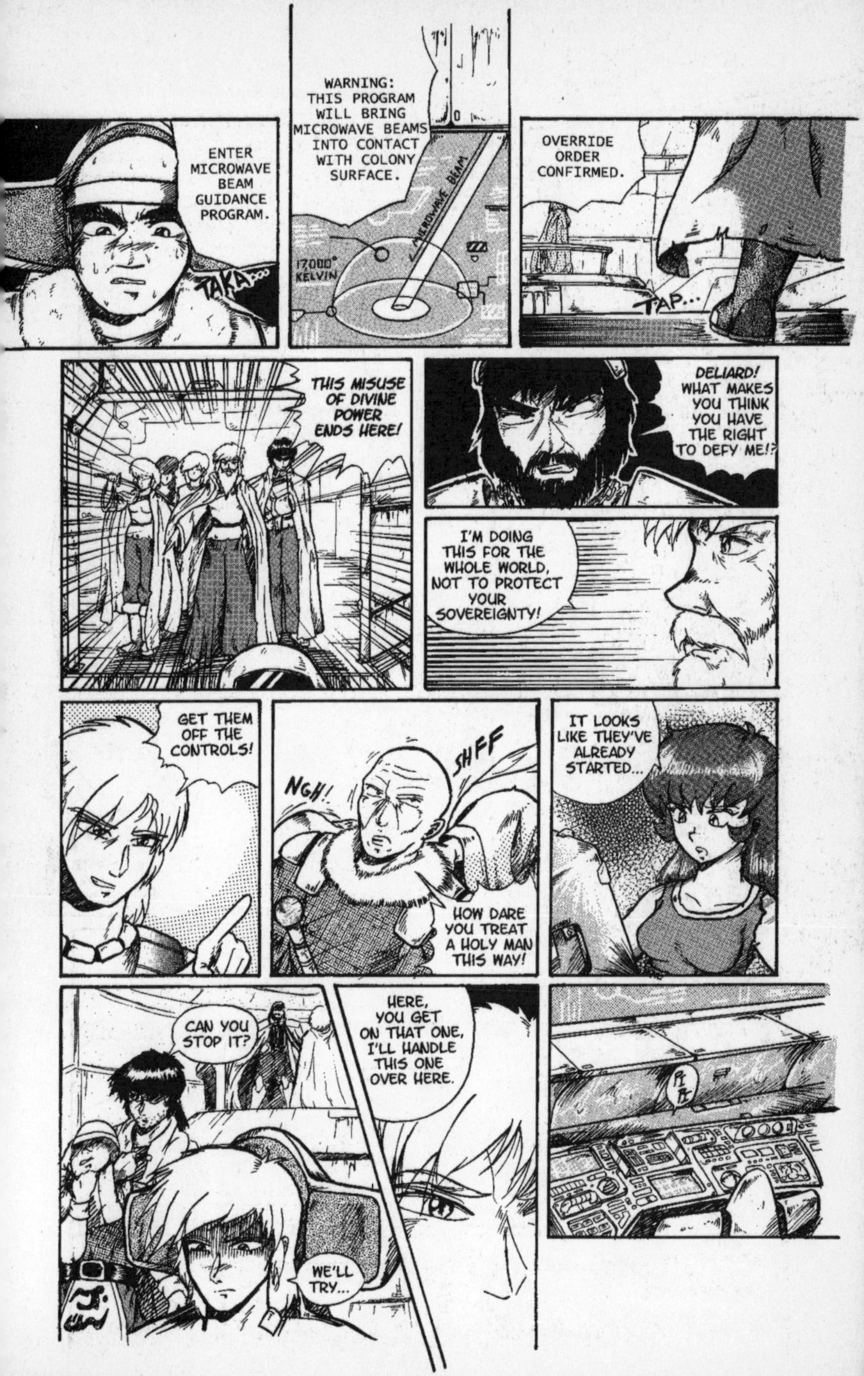
ENTER MICROWAVE BEAM GUIDANCE PROGRAM.
TAKA...
WARNING: THIS PROGRAM WILL BRING MICROWAVE BEAMS INTO CONTACT WITH COLONY SURFACE.
MICROWAVE BEAM
17,000° KELVIN
OVERRIDE ORDER CONFIRMED.
TAP...
THIS MISUSE OF DIVINE POWER ENDS HERE!
DELIARD! WHAT MAKES YOU THINK YOU HAVE THE RIGHT TO DEFY ME!?
I'M DOING THIS FOR THE WHOLE WORLD, NOT TO PROTECT YOUR SOVEREIGNTY!
GET THEM OFF THE CONTROLS!
NGH!
SHFF
HOW DARE YOU TREAT A HOLY MAN THIS WAY!
IT LOOKS LIKE THEY'VE ALREADY STARTED...
CAN YOU STOP IT?
WE'LL TRY...
HERE, YOU GET ON THAT ONE, I'LL HANDLE THIS ONE OVER HERE.

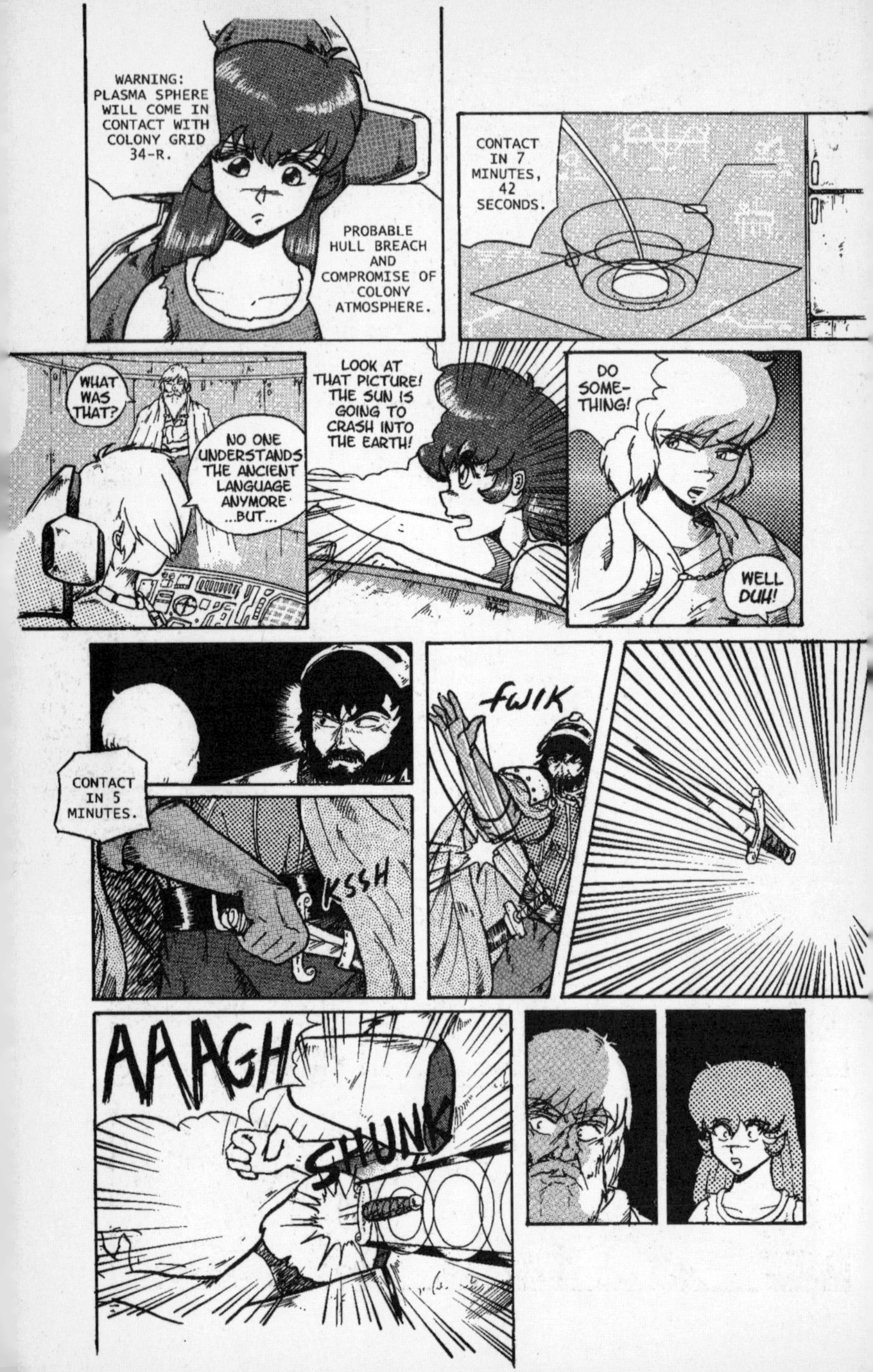
WARNING: PLASMA SPHERE WILL COME IN CONTACT WITH COLONY GRID 34-R.
PROBABLE HULL BREACH AND COMPROMISE OF COLONY ATMOSPHERE.
CONTACT IN 7 MINUTES, 42 SECONDS.
WHAT WAS THAT?
NO ONE UNDERSTANDS THE ANCIENT LANGUAGE ANYMORE ...BUT...
LOOK AT THAT PICTURE! THE SUN IS GOING TO CRASH INTO THE EARTH!
DO SOME-THING!
WELL DUH!
CONTACT IN 5 MINUTES.
KSSH
FWIK
AAAGH
SHUNK

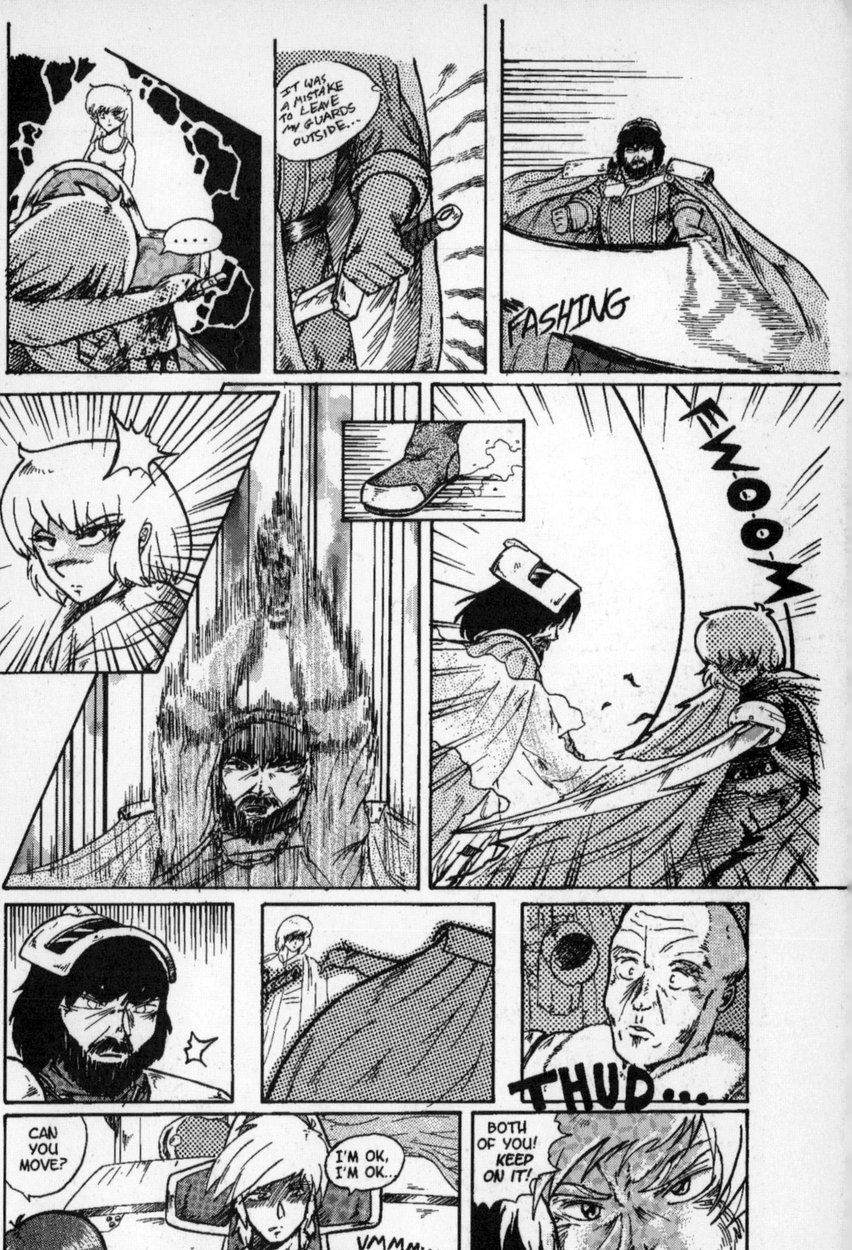
....
IT WAS A MISTAKE TO LEAVE MY GUARDS OUTSIDE...
FASHING
FWOOOM
THUD...
CAN YOU MOVE?
I'M OK, I'M OK..
VMMM...
BOTH OF YOU! KEEP ON IT!

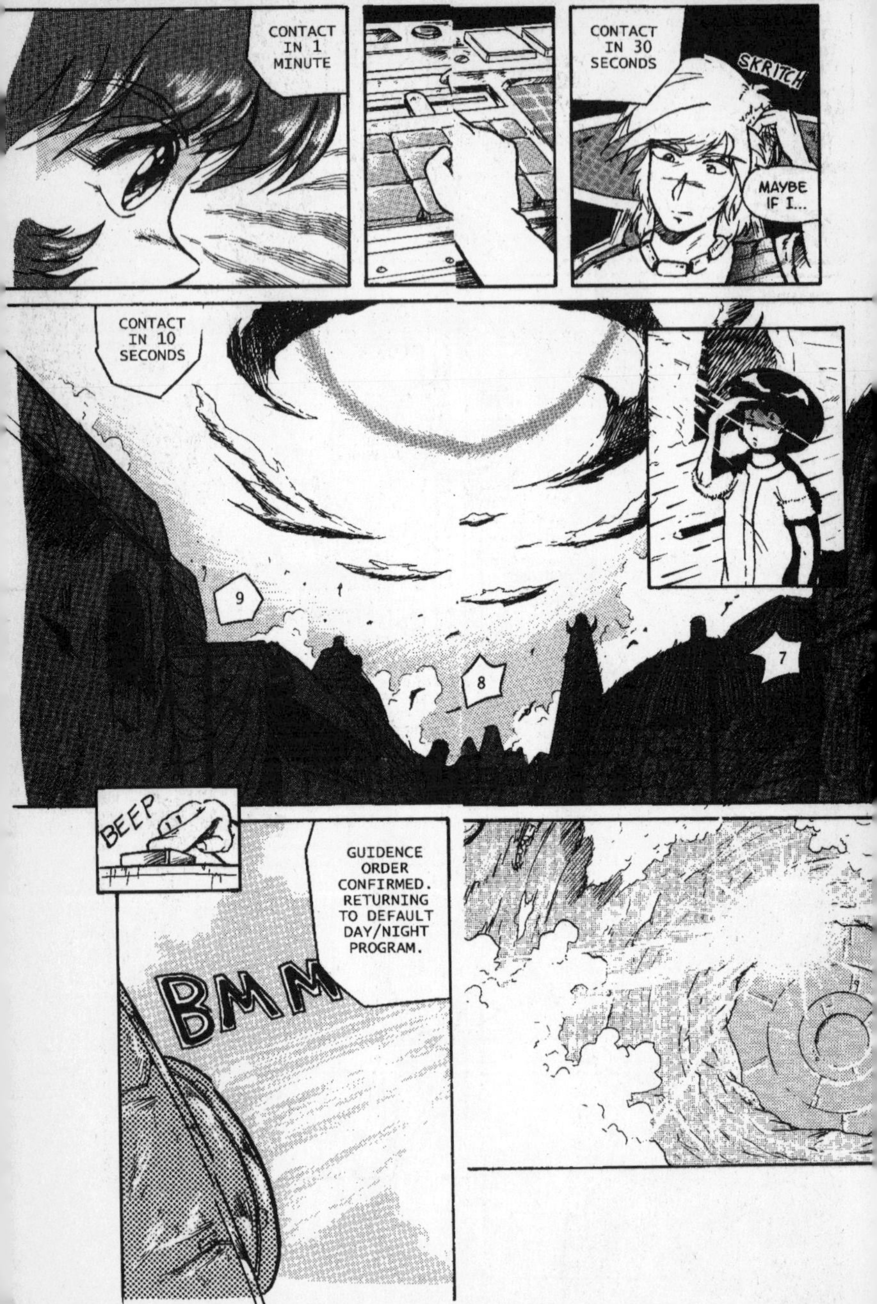
CONTACT IN 1 MINUTE
CONTACT IN 30 SECONDS
SKRITCH
MAYBE IF I...
CONTACT IN 10 SECONDS
9
8
7
BEEP
GUIDENCE ORDER CONFIRMED. RETURNING TO DEFAULT DAY/NIGHT PROGRAM.
BMM

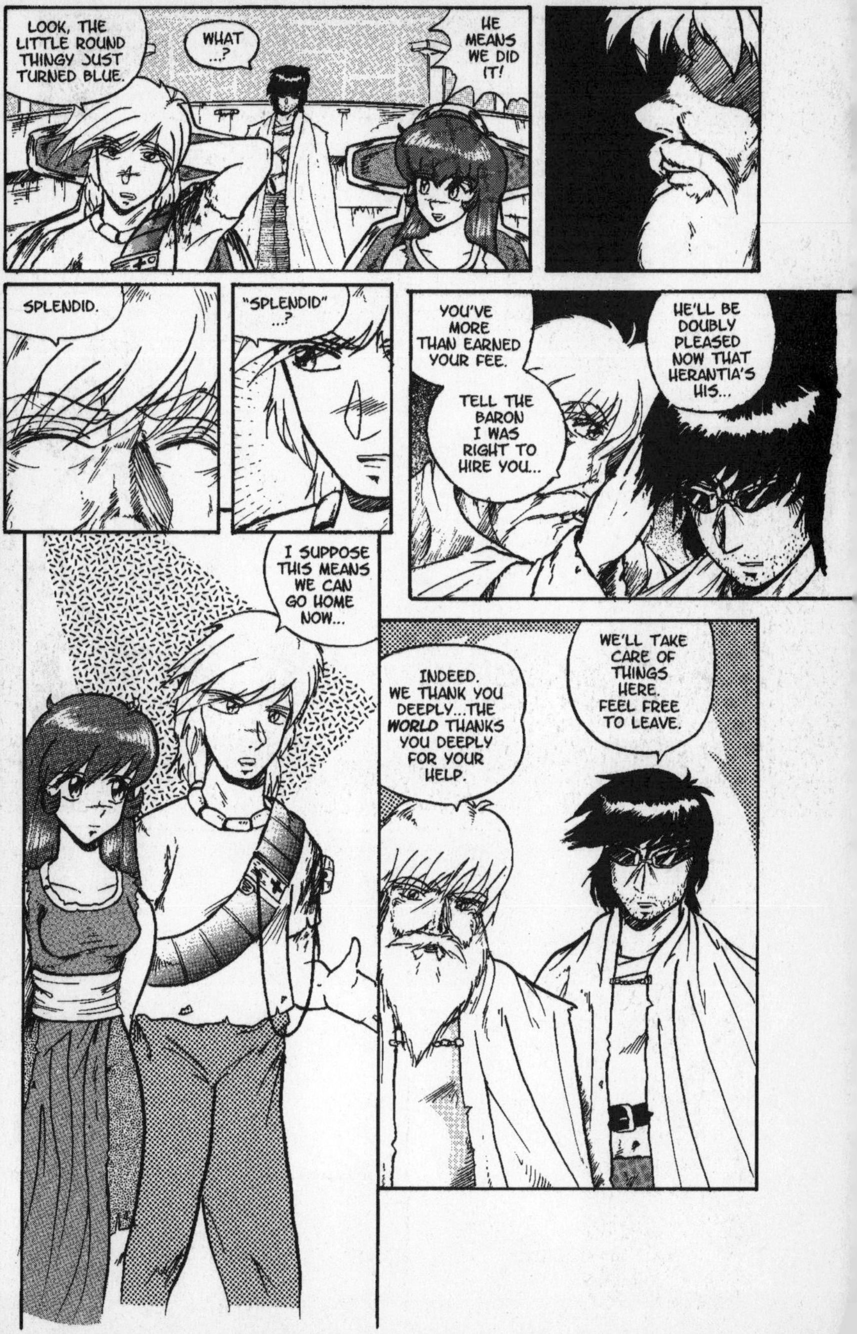
LOOK, THE LITTLE ROUND THINGY JUST TURNED BLUE.
WHAT ...?
HE MEANS WE DID IT!
SPLENDID.
"SPLENDID" ...?
YOU'VE MORE THAN EARNED YOUR FEE.
TELL THE BARON I WAS RIGHT TO HIRE YOU...
HE'LL BE DOUBLY PLEASED NOW THAT HERANTIA'S HIS...
I SUPPOSE THIS MEANS WE CAN GO HOME NOW...
INDEED. WE THANK YOU DEEPLY...THE *WORLD* THANKS YOU DEEPLY FOR YOUR HELP.
WE'LL TAKE CARE OF THINGS HERE. FEEL FREE TO LEAVE.

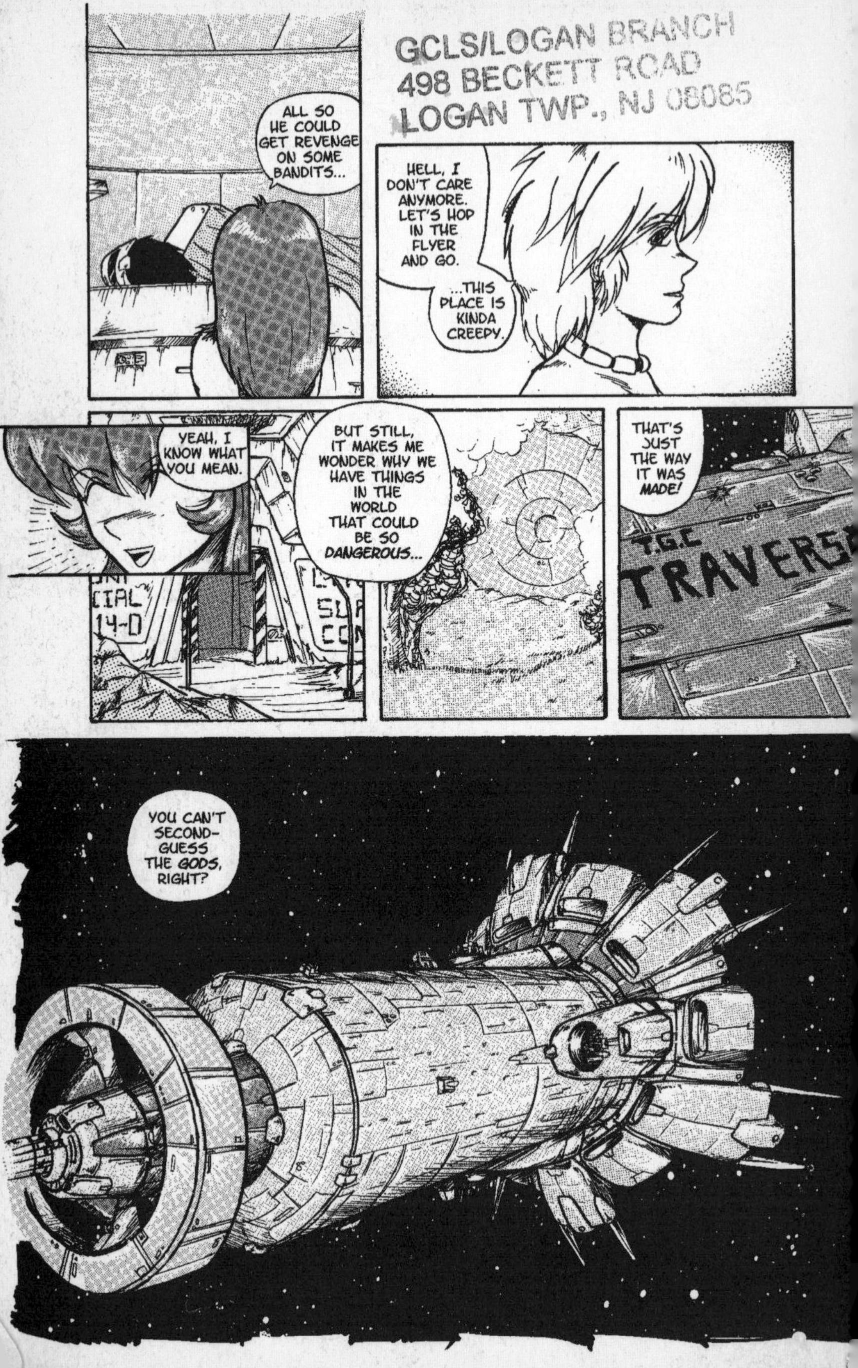
ALL SO HE COULD GET REVENGE ON SOME BANDITS...
HELL, I DON'T CARE ANYMORE. LET'S HOP IN THE FLYER AND GO.
...THIS PLACE IS KINDA CREEPY.
YEAH, I KNOW WHAT YOU MEAN.
BUT STILL, IT MAKES ME WONDER WHY WE HAVE THINGS IN THE WORLD THAT COULD BE SO *DANGEROUS*...
THAT'S JUST THE WAY IT WAS *MADE!*
T.G.C
TRAVERS
YOU CAN'T SECOND-GUESS THE *GODS*, RIGHT?